Advances in

THE STUDY OF BEHAVIOR

VOLUME 21

Advances in
THE STUDY OF
BEHAVIOR

Edited by

Peter J. B. Slater
Department of Biology and Preclinical Medicine
University of St. Andrews
Fife, Scotland

Jay S. Rosenblatt
Institute of Animal Behavior
Rutgers University
Newark, New Jersey

Colin Beer
Institute of Animal Behavior
Rutgers University
Newark, New Jersey

Manfred Milinski
Abteilung Verhaltensökologie
Zoologisches Institut
Universität Bern
Hinterkappelen, Switzerland

VOLUME 21

ACADEMIC PRESS, INC.
Harcourt Brace Jovanovich, Publishers

San Diego   New York   Boston
London   Sydney   Tokyo   Toronto

Academic Press, Inc.
1250 Sixth Avenue, San Diego, California 92101

United Kingdom Edition published by
Academic Press Limited
24–28 Oval Road, London NW1 7DX

Library of Congress Catalog Number: 64-8031

International Standard Book Number: 0-12-004521-4

PRINTED IN THE UNITED STATES OF AMERICA
92 93 94 95 96 97   BB   9 8 7 6 5 4 3 2 1

Contents

Contributors ix
Preface xi

Primate Social Relationships: Their Determinants and Consequences
ERIC B. KEVERNE

I. Introduction 1
II. Social Rank and Sexual Behavior among Males 4
III. Social Rank and Aggressive Behavior among Males 7
IV. Rank, Behavior, and the Stress Hormones 11
V. Concluding Remarks 28
VI. Summary 30
References 32

The Role of Parasites in Sexual Selection: Current Evidence and Future Directions
MARLENE ZUK

I. Introduction 39
II. Original Predictions of the Hamilton–Zuk Hypothesis 41
III. Interspecific Tests 42
IV. Why Parasites? 48
V. Intraspecific Tests Reconsidered 57
VI. Conclusions 61
VII. Summary 62
References 63

Conceptual Issues in Cognitive Ethology
COLIN BEER

I. Historical Introduction 69
II. Awareness, Consciousness, and Imagery 75
III. Awareness and Language 85
IV. Actions, Intentions, and Functions 89

V. Intentionality, Folk Psychology, and Cognitive Science   93
VI. Summary Conclusions.   104
    References   105

Responses to Warning Coloration in Avian Predators

W. SCHULER AND T. J. ROPER

I. The Problem of Warning Coloration.   111
II. Responses of Birds to Warningly Colored Prey.   118
III. Discussion   138
IV. Summary   141
    References   143

Analysis and Interpretation of Orb Spider Exploration and Web-building Behavior

FRITZ VOLLRATH

I. Introduction   147
II. The Web Spider's Orientation Skills.   152
III. Unravelling the *Araneus* Orb   163
IV. Manipulation of the Threads.   178
V. Orb Webs as a Dynamic Filter   182
VI. Webs and Life History.   188
VII. Conclusions   189
VIII. Summary   190
    References   191

Motor Aspects of Masculine Sexual Behavior in Rats and Rabbits

GABRIELA MORALÍ AND CARLOS BEYER

I. Introduction   201
II. Polygraphic Techniques for the Analysis of the Motor and
    Genital Components of the Male Copulatory Pattern   202
III. Morphology of the Masculine Copulatory Motor Pattern
    in the Rat.   206
IV. Morphology of the Masculine Copulatory Motor Pattern
    in the Rabbit   215
V. Central Mediation of the Male Copulatory Motor Pattern   219
VI. Hormonal Factors in the Regulation of the Morphology
    of Copulatory Behavior.   224
VII. Concluding Remarks.   231

VIII. Summary   234
      References   234

On the Nature and Evolution of Imitation in the Animal Kingdom:
Reappraisal of a Century of Research

A. WHITEN AND R. HAM

  I. Introduction   239
 II. Four Influential Legacies of Nineteenth-Century
     Comparative Psychology.   240
III. Defining and Distinguishing Imitative Phenomena Today   244
 IV. New Methodologies   253
  V. The Distribution of Imitation in the Animal Kingdom   256
 VI. Explaining the Distribution of Imitation: Computational
     Requirements of Imitating the Seen versus the Heard.   270
VII. Conclusion   275
VIII. Summary   276
      References   277

      Index   285

Contributors

Numbers in parentheses indicate the pages on which the authors' contributions begin.

COLIN BEER (69), *Institute of Animal Behavior, Rutgers University, Newark, New Jersey 07102*

CARLOS BEYER (201), *Centro de Investigación en Reproducción Animal, CINVESTAV-UAT, Tlaxcala 90000, Mexico*

R. HAM (239), *Scottish Primate Research Group, Psychological Laboratory, University of St. Andrews, St. Andrews, Fife KY16 9JU, Scotland*

ERIC B. KEVERNE (1), *Sub-Department of Animal Behaviour, University of Cambridge, Madingley, Cambridge CB3 8AA, England*

GABRIELA MORALÍ (201), *División de Neurociencias, Unidad de Investigación Biomédica del CMN, Instituto Mexicano del Serguro Social, México DF 03020, Mexico*

T. J. ROPER (111), *School of Biological Sciences, University of Sussex, Brighton BN1 9QG, England*

W. SCHULER (111), *Zoologisches Institut und Museum der Universität, D-3400 Göttingen, Germany*

FRITZ VOLLRATH (147), *Department of Zoology, University of Oxford, Oxford, England and Zoologisches Institut, Basel, Switzerland*

A. WHITEN (239), *Scottish Primate Research Group, Psychological Laboratory, University of St. Andrews, St. Andrews, Fife KY16 9JU, Scotland*

MARLENE ZUK (39), *Department of Biology, University of California, Riverside, Riverside, California 92521*

Preface

As it has for 25 years, *Advances in the Study of Behavior* continues to serve the increasing number of scientists who are engaged in the study of animal behavior by presenting their theoretical ideas and research to their colleagues and to those in neighboring fields. We hope that the series will continue to serve ". . . as a contribution to the development of cooperation and communication among scientists in our field." Traditional areas of animal behavior research have achieved new vigor by the links they have formed with related fields and by the closer relationship that now exists between those studying animal and human subjects. Though lately behavioral ecology and sociobiology have tended to overshadow other areas, the range of scientists studying behavior today is greater than ever before: from ecologists and evolutionary biologists, to geneticists, endocrinologists, pharmacologists, neurobiologists and developmental psychobiologists, as well as ethologists and comparative psychologists.

It is our intention, not to focus narrowly on one or a few of these fields, but to publish articles covering the best behavioral work from a broad spectrum, as the range of articles in the present volume shows. The skills and concepts of scientists in such diverse fields necessarily differ, making the task of developing cooperation and communication among them a difficult one. But it is one that is of great importance, and one to which the Editors and publisher of *Advances in the Study of Behavior* are committed. We will continue to provide the means to this end by publishing critical reviews, by inviting extended presentations of significant research programs, by encouraging the writing of theoretical syntheses and reformulations of persistent problems, and by highlighting especially penetrating research that introduces important new concepts.

With this volume Dr. Colin Beer retires as an Associate Editor, a position he has occupied for 15 years. Readers and authors have good reason to be grateful for his meticulous attention to editorial detail. His fellow editors are pleased that he has himself contributed a stimulating chapter to this volume. In his place we look forward to welcoming Dr. Charles T. Snowdon, of the University of Wisconsin at Madison, as an editor for the next volume, so maintaining both our breadth of editorial expertise and our balance between the two sides of the Atlantic.

Primate Social Relationships: Their Determinants and Consequences

Eric B. Keverne

SUB-DEPARTMENT OF ANIMAL BEHAVIOUR
UNIVERSITY OF CAMBRIDGE
MADINGLEY, CAMBRIDGE CB3 8AA, ENGLAND

I. Introduction

Some 15 years ago, in a review written for this series, I focused attention on hormonal mechanisms of primate behavior. That article was somewhat restricted in outlook, being exclusively concerned with primate dyads and the way in which gonadal hormones act both centrally and peripherally to influence sexual behavior (Keverne, 1976). In the concluding comments, I stated that "we are a long way from understanding how neuroendocrine mechanisms operate in the social group, where structure and organization modify or impair the effects of a given hormone on behaviour, and even modify the levels of hormones in individual animals themselves." Today we are at a stage where that understanding is clearer and, although these social–endocrine mechanisms have been studied in relatively few species, we are nevertheless able to derive some conclusions about the underlying principles.

Primates are by no means unique in having their behavior shaped by their social environment. In male mice, hamsters, rats, cats, rabbits, the ram, and the bull, to name a few, the presentation of an estrus female may increase plasma levels of testosterone and thereby enhance the expression of sexual behavior (Keverne *et al.*, 1985). Conversely, overcrowding and social stress in rodents may suppress gonadotrophin secretion and, in turn, reproductive behavior (Bronson, 1989). However, it is only among group-living primates that the social condition becomes all important, not only for the constraints this imposes on their behavior, but also for the way it enriches their behavioral development. In contrast to other mammals that are social for only part of the year, many primates live throughout the year, and indeed throughout life, in social groups. Even from the very early stages of development, when most infant monkeys relate to a very small part of the group, the dynamics of group interaction are brought to bear on

1

each young member through its mother, siblings, and peers (Simpson and Howe, 1986; Suomi, 1987).

In the adult, the sexual behavior of monkeys and apes is not so strictly regulated by gonadal hormones as appears to be the case in most other mammalian species. Captive and field studies of several monkey species have shown females to be receptive at all times of their cycle (Rowell, 1972; Dixson, 1983; Loy, 1987), and in the chimpanzee, mating has been observed during a substantial part of the menstrual cycle despite the handicap imposed on the male by the incompatibility of the female's sexual skin swelling (Lemmon and Allen, 1978). Other apes, such as the orangutan (Nadler, 1977; Maple *et al.,* 1979) and gorilla (Nadler *et al.,* 1983), have been observed to mate on most days of the menstrual cycle. For the most part, these observations have come from captive studies, and although they may not reflect real life events (Schurmann, 1982; Fossey, 1982), they nevertheless reveal the extended potential for sexual interactions. In marked contrast, captive studies on a wide range of nonprimate mammals have never revealed such a potential, and sexual activity is so closely tied to ovulation and reproduction that mating invariably leads to conception (Bronson, 1989). These findings support the view put forward long ago by Frank Beach (1951) that the primate brain has become largely "emancipated" from the fluctuations in gonadal hormone secretions. Of course, this does not mean that female monkeys are permanently receptive any more than women are permanently receptive. But it does mean that receptivity is not determined simply by hormonal (estrus) condition, but is amenable also to social influences and to higher order processing, integrating past experiences and partner preferences. It does not support Zuckerman's view that monkeys and apes have an "uninterrupted sexual and reproductive life," but it does lend support to his conclusion that there is "no implication that the sexual stimulus holding individuals together was ever totally absent" (Zuckerman, 1932). That is not to say that sexual behavior is the only or, indeed, the main proximal stimulus for maintaining troop cohesion, but the underlying potential for sexual behavior presents a very different picture from that which we observe in other female mammals, where sexual receptivity is primarily governed by the hormonal secretions of the gonads.

Emancipation of the neural mechanisms for behavior from endocrine control has not, however, been paralleled by somatic mechanisms, and in monkeys, as in women, ovarian hormones influence the attractiveness of females (Keverne, 1976). In monkeys, the coloration of the perineal area and vaginal odors serve as powerful cues to attract males. Such cues are entirely determined by ovarian hormones and are not under behavioral control. Likewise, the receptivity of females is indirectly influenced by the action of ovarian hormones on sexual-skin swellings. Although the female may actively invite sexual interactions, she cannot successfully receive the male unless her perineal swelling is turgid. Interestingly, a large perineal swelling also serves as a nonbehavioral means of selecting for high-ranking males. Because intromission is only possible with a rigidly sustained erection, low-ranking males that are anxious about interruptions are not going to perform effectively.

Neural mechanisms for behavior still respond to some endocrine secretions, as adrenal androgens are required to maintain both human and nonhuman primate sexual receptivity (Everitt *et al.,* 1972; Everitt and Herbert, 1975). These androgens are produced mainly by the adrenals in the female, and unlike the ovarian hormones, their secretion remains stable. However, recent studies have shown that even adrenal steroids are not necessary for the expression of sexual behavior in group-living rhesus monkeys (Lovejoy and Wallen, 1990). Although the social group situation is overly complex for addressing specific questions about endocrine variables, these studies lend further support to the view that endocrine determinants are secondary to social determinants of behavior.

For group-living primates, the organization of social structure has profound effects on the behavior of the individual (Hausfater, 1975; Dunbar, 1988). In many species, dominant males demand sexual prerogative so that the subordinate males have limited access to attractive females and thus produce fewer offspring (Berenstain and Wade, 1983; Chapais, 1983). Likewise, females of high rank engage more frequently in sexual interactions and produce more female offspring, which in turn are more likely to become dominant (Simpson and Simpson, 1982; Datta, 1983). It is therefore important to understand how the monkey's neuroendocrine system responds to the factors that shape and organize its society and determine its individual role within that society.

We have addressed this issue through long-term studies on the talapoin monkey (*Miopithecus talapoin*), which is the smallest cercopithecine primate, having a weight range of 800–1500 g for adult females and 1200–2500 g for males. The talapoin's natural habitat is the rain forest of West Africa, where animals normally live in both single- and mixed-sex groups consisting of up to 80 animals. Social groups of talapoins are very cohesive, with no permanently solitary individuals observed (Gautier-Hion, 1966, 1973); at night animals huddle in small subgroups, and during the day specific calls appear to maintain group cohesion. The home ranges of talapoin groups are large, population density is low, and no encounters between conspecific groups have been observed (Gautier-Hion, 1970, 1973, 1978). Networks of lianas overhanging rivers are preferred sleeping sites, and their distribution may regulate group spacing and population density. The small size of talapoins, the marked cohesiveness of their groups, their choice of sleeping sites, and other observations (see Gautier-Hion, 1973) suggest that predation may be an important influence on their social organization.

Our studies have taken place over 12 years on several experimental groups, each consisting of 3–5 adult males (intact and castrated) and a similar number of females (intact and ovariectomized). The monkeys were observed for 50 min

twice daily, with all animals being monitored continuously for sexual, aggressive, and social interactions (see Dixson *et al.*, 1975, for details of behavioral scoring). Each cage was divided into three parts by removable partitions;
the sexes were kept apart, the males occupying two thirds of the cage and the
females the remaining one third (isosexual condition). During treatment periods
when observations were made, access through the partitions separating males
from females was provided (heterosexual condition). A minimum of 1000 min of
observations was obtained for each treatment condition over a 3-week period.
Plasma levels of testosterone, cortisol, prolactin, LH, and progesterone were
measured in blood samples taken twice weekly by femoral venipuncture under
ketamine anesthesia using radioimmunoassay (RIA) techniques described elsewhere (Yodyingyuad *et al.*, 1982). Cerebrospinal fluid (CSF) levels of cortisol
(Herbert *et al.*, 1986), amine metabolites (Yodyingyuad *et al.*, 1985), and β-
endorphin (Martensz *et al.*, 1986) were measured following high-performance
liquid chromatography (HPLC) separation and RIA or electrochemical detection.
The social status of each monkey was assessed from its interactions with others
in the group, dominance being defined in terms of the direction of "spontaneous"
aggression among them.

II. Social Rank and Sexual Behavior among Males

The distribution of sexual behavior among male and female talapoin monkeys
is strongly influenced by each of their hierarchies. Figure 1 shows that for males
in the group, mounting of females is the exclusive prerogative of the high-
ranking males. This uneven distribution of sexual behavior applies equally to
other behaviors that are related to reproduction, with significant differences for
proceptive behavior, inspects, looks, and approaches to females, which all vary
according to rank (Fig. 2) (Keverne *et al.*, 1978a; Eberhart *et al.*, 1980). With
intact females, male competition is enhanced, because not all females are synchronized in their cycle of attractiveness. Nevertheless, the distribution of male
sexual behavior remains the same as that seen with ovariectomized estrogen-
primed females (closed circles, Fig. 1), even though a few, rather than several,
females are simultaneously attractive (open circles, Fig. 1).

Moving into the social group entails changes in gonadal status with respect to
rank, and it is conceivable that such testosterone changes might in themselves
account for the skewed distribution of sexual behaviors. A number of studies
have shown that social variables can modify the effects of a given hormone on
behavior (Dixson and Herbert, 1977) or the hormone levels in individual
monkeys (Rose *et al.*, 1971, 1975). Our own studies on talapoin monkeys have
shown that the dominant males tend to have higher levels of testosterone than
subordinates (Eberhart *et al.*, 1980), increasing by as much as 200–300% when

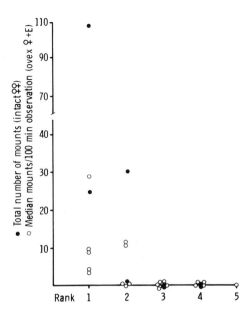

FIG. 1. Distribution of sexual behavior by males according to rank (7 groups). Open circles: all females in group ovariectomized and estrogen treated. Closed circles: all females in group intact and cycling.

dominant males interact with females in the heterosexual group. The circadian rhythm in plasma testosterone shows no overall differences according to rank in the isosexual condition, but as soon as physical interaction with the females is permitted, the levels of testosterone increase in dominant males and decrease in subordinates (Fig. 3). Although nocturnal increases occur in the testosterone levels of subordinate males, these only reach the lowest levels measured in dominants, and during the daylight hours, testosterone secretion decreases rapidly in subordinates compared with the isosexual condition (Martensz *et al.*, 1987).

Bearing in mind the relevance of testosterone to male sexual behavior, the question arises as to whether these differential changes in testosterone according to rank may also account for the differences in sexual behavior according to rank. To address this issue, males were castrated in their respective groups and given hormone replacement therapy. In this way, gonadal hormone levels could be either maintained at similar levels in all animals or selectively manipulated in specific individuals. Among dominant males, castration never completely eliminated their sexual interest in females and, although testosterone replacement "therapy" increased their sexual behavior, subordinates never copulated even after high doses of testosterone (Fig. 4). Moreover, the administration of suffi-

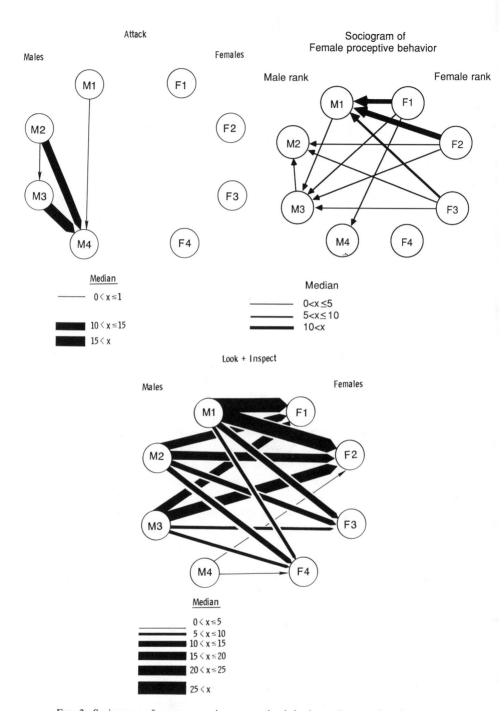

FIG. 2. Sociograms of overt aggression, proceptive behavior, and approach to inspect among males and females in their social group. M, males; F, females; 1–4, social ranks. Thickness of arrow represents relative level of behavior and to whom it is directed.

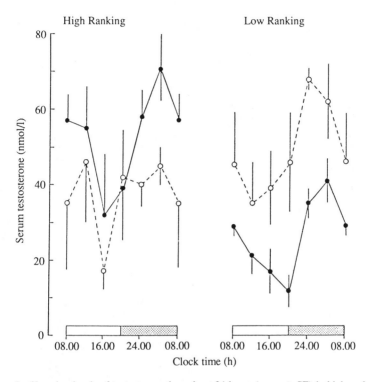

FIG. 3. Changing levels of testosterone throughout 24 hours (mean + SE) in high ranking and low ranking male talapoin monkeys. Open circles, isosexual groups; Closed circles, heterosexual groups (same males). (From Martensz *et al.*, 1987.)

cient testosterone to produce supranormal "physiological" levels in subordinate animals did not improve their status in the hierarchy (Dixson and Herbert, 1977). Gonadal hormones appear, therefore, to be without effect in determining the hierarchical distribution of sexual behavior within the group, and any influence they may have on male primate sexual behavior (Michael and Wilson, 1973) is secondary to social structure. Other aspects of behavior, especially the aggression they receive, are probably of greater significance because aggressive behavior is increased when the subordinates receive exogenous testosterone (Fig. 4).

III. SOCIAL RANK AND AGGRESSIVE BEHAVIOR AMONG MALES

Aggressive behavior, or at least the threat of potential aggression, may be of some importance for restricting the sexual behavior of subordinates. As a consequence of their low status they show increased withdrawals, increased visual

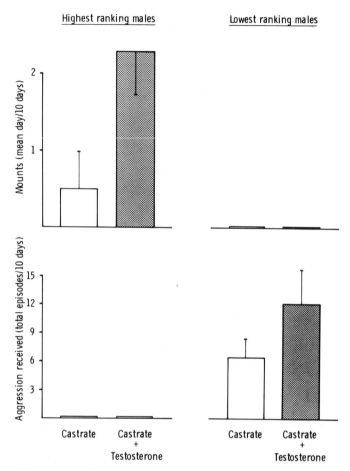

FIG. 4. Effects of castration on sexual and aggressive behavior in male talapoin monkeys. Testosterone replacement does not increase the sexual behavior of subordinates, but it does increase the aggression they receive.

monitoring and have restricted use of cage space. The ranks of individual monkeys according to the amount of visual monitoring they perform correlate significantly with the amount of aggression they receive (Fig. 5). However, the individuals that receive most visual monitoring are not necessarily the most aggressive (Keverne *et al.*, 1978b). The dominant male is always monitored highest by all other males in the group, even though he is rarely the most aggressive. Subordinates are controlled through intermediaries (see Fig. 2). Such a strategy frees the dominant male from continuous monitoring of all males in the group, and by keeping the intermediary males under control, aggression can be indirectly exerted on subordinates through the hierarchical chain of command.

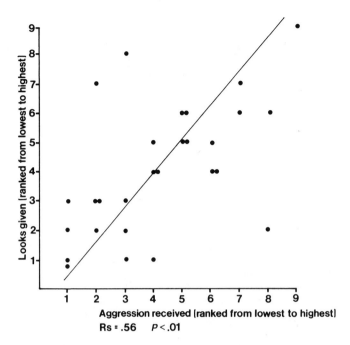

FIG. 5. Visual monitoring and aggressive behavior among talapoin monkeys. Animals are ranked in each group according to looks given and compared with aggression received (4 groups, 28 monkeys).

Such intimidation of subordinates, as witnessed from their high levels of monitoring and withdrawals from other males, undoubtedly places them under considerable stress. Whereas the stress hormone levels decrease in dominants once the group is established, they continue to rise in subordinate males. Thus, not only is sexual and aggressive behavior different among dominant and subordinate males, but the endocrine concomitants likewise differ.

Although altered endocrine activity forms an important part of the adaptive response to an animal's position in the social hierarchy, care is required in the interpretation of those findings. Differences in stress hormone levels between individual monkeys can be related both to rank and to the ongoing behavior, particularly aggressive behavior. The fact that there are these kinds of interaction between status and cortisol and between behavior and cortisol makes the contribution of each difficult to separate. Hence, the endocrine condition of animals at the time of sampling is going to be especially influenced by ongoing behavior during group formation (Scallet et al., 1981; McGuire et al., 1986) and more so by antecedent experiences (rank) when subjected to challenges in the established social group (Sapolsky, 1982; Stanton et al., 1985).

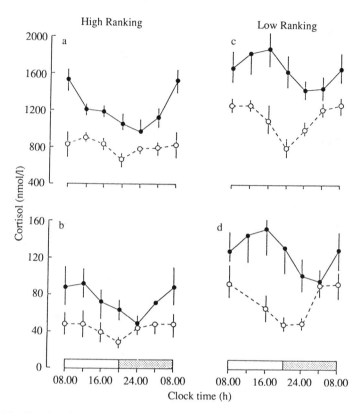

FIG. 6. Circadian rhythm of cortisol in plasma (a,c) and CSF (b,d) in high- and low-ranking males. Open circles show isosexual condition and closed circles show the same males in heterosexual condition. Low-ranking males receiving high aggression have high cortisol throughout the daylight hours. The proportion in CSF increases by 130% from isosexual to heterosexual condition compared with 75% in high-ranking males.

During group formation, cortisol and prolactin levels increase in all male talapoins, but with the establishment of the hierarchy, cortisol and prolactin decrease in dominant males while cortisol continues to increase in subordinates (Eberhart et al., 1983). As a consequence, the carrying capacity of cortisol-binding protein in plasma is exceeded and disproportionately high levels of cortisol are found in the extracellular fluid compartment of the brain (CSF) of subordinate males (Herbert et al., 1986). Moreover, the circadian rhythm of cortisol levels differs between dominant and subordinate males in heterosexual groups. Cortisol levels show the normal circadian rhythm of decreasing during the daylight hours and increasing at night in dominant males. In subordinate males that receive high levels of aggression, cortisol levels continue their increase into the daylight hours until late afternoon (Fig. 6). The behavioral consequences of chronically high cortisol levels have only been investigated through correlations, but disturbances of cortisol secretion are well recognized correlates of depressed mood states in people suffering from Cushing's disease, a syndrome produced by excessive quantities of glucocorticoids, (Rubin *et al.*, 1987; Halbreich *et al.*, 1985). There is also an extensive literature pointing to the particular significance of unpredictable stress, particularly if associated with loss of social support or an unfamiliar environment, as a major determinant in cortisol release (Levine *et al.*, 1989).

IV. RANK, BEHAVIOR, AND THE STRESS HORMONES

In talapoin monkeys that have experienced chronic social stress, removal from the group does not immediately result in reduced levels of plasma cortisol, and high levels may persist for some weeks after they are removed. Hence, the chronic effects of social subordination appear to carry over into other nonsocial situations. This not only applies to the so-called "stress" hormones, but also to sexual behavior itself. Subordinate males that have been sexually quiescent in their groups fail to interact sexually with females, at least in the short term (over 3 weeks), when given the opportunity in the absence of dominant males (Eberhart *et al.*, 1985) (Fig. 7). Out of six social groups, only one subordinate male was observed to be sexually active, and even here, all his interactions were initiated by females. Not all males had previously been pair-tested for sexual behavior prior to group formation, but of those that were, sexual behavior was observed to be high among males that subsequently became subordinate. This would suggest that high sexual activity is not a predictor of rank and there is no obvious predisposition for subordinance to be correlated with sexual inactivity. Males that became dominant showed enhancement of their sexual behavior in the group and continued to be sexually active even in the absence of other males.

Although testosterone levels increased in subordinates when they were with females in the absence of other males, so too did their stress hormones, cortisol and prolactin (Fig. 8) (Keverne *et al.*, 1982). These hormones increased when males that had experienced social subordination were housed with females, despite the fact that the aggression they received was substantially and significantly reduced, and was no different from that of males that had experienced social dominance in the same situation (Eberhart *et al.*, 1985).

Clearly then, learning and the behavioral experiences associated with social subordination play a large part, at least in the short term, in sustaining male sexual quiescence. Because of mortality and the greater incidence of mobility among dominant males, subordination may only be a transient phase in the life of these monkeys in their natural habitat. Nevertheless, the restrictions on sexual activity in the subordinates seen in these captive studies would, by reducing their

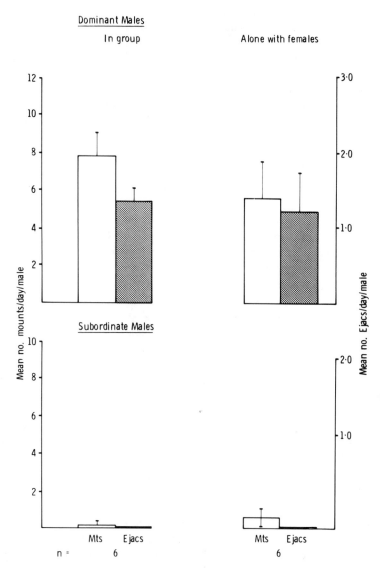

FIG. 7. Comparison of dominant (upper section) and subordinate (lower section) male sexual behavior with the females present in the group and other males absent from the group. Males experiencing long-term dominance (12–15 months) continue to show sexual behavior, but males that have been subordinate do not have their sexual behavior restored in the 3-week period they were tested.

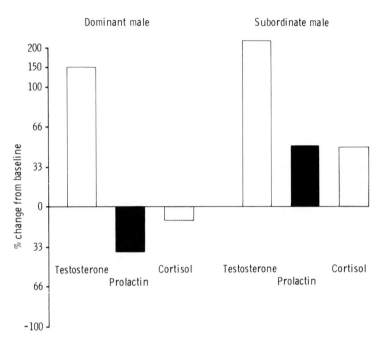

% Change in plasma testosterone, prolactin and cortisol on moving from isolation into the social group of females.

FIG. 8. Subordinate males show increases in stress hormones (cortisol and prolactin) on moving into a group of females in absence of other males, whereas dominant males do not. Testosterone increases in dominant and subordinate males.

competition with dominant males, decrease the constant need for overt violence and aggression. Subordinates themselves would, by remaining in the social group, gain the benefits of food and protection against predators, but only at a cost in the short term to their reproductive behavior.

A. SOCIAL RANK AND THE BEHAVIOR OF FEMALES

Like the males, female talapoin monkeys also form a social hierarchy that can be assessed by the direction of aggressive encounters. Although aggressive behavior among females is significantly less frequent than among males, social status has important consequences for many behaviors, including sexual activity (Fig. 9) and affiliative behavior (Fig. 10). Highest ranking females not only receive the most sexual attention, but they also solicit and approach males significantly more often than do the subordinate females (see Fig. 2) (Keverne, 1985). Although low-ranking females may not engage in as much sexual activity

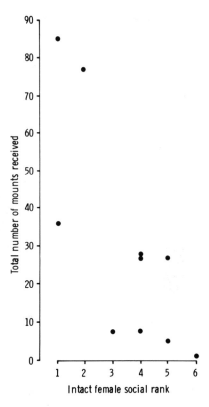

FIG. 9. Distribution of sexual interactions among intact females according to rank. Lower rank-ing females receive some sexual behavior unlike low-ranking males.

as dominant females, they are not totally excluded and, therefore, have the potential to conceive. This low aggression, with socially subordinate females maintaining sexual behavior, is in marked contrast to the high aggression re-ceived and absence of sexual behavior in subordinate males (Keverne *et al.*, 1985). Low-ranking females do not show the phase shift in their diurnal pattern of cortisol secretion, and levels of cortisol are no higher in subordinate females than in dominants (Martensz *et al.*, 1987). Moreover, the sexual behavior of low-ranking females is restored to high levels immediately on removal of other females from their social group, there being no evidence for the kind of condi-tioned suppression of sexual behavior seen in subordinate males (Keverne *et al.*, 1985).

An explanation for these differences in social stress and behavior seen between male and female talapoin monkeys is revealed when we examine the kind of behavioral strategies each sex uses. In the isosexual group, males score considerably higher than females on overt aggression (Figs. 2 and 11), but are not different from females with respect to displacements, a behavior that involves a mild form of noncontact aggression to occupy the position held by another monkey (Fig. 11). Females in the isosexual group show a high incidence of affiliative behavior (huddling and grooming), whereas males are low on affiliative interactions. As a result of interactions in the heterosexual group, males increase their overt aggression and reduce affiliation, whereas these aggressive behaviors decrease in females and their affiliative behaviors do not change (Fig. 12). Interestingly, the social hierarchy of females is easier to assess in terms of affiliative interactions than in terms of aggression, with high-ranking females receiving higher levels of grooming than others in their group. A sequence analysis of behavioral interactions reveals further differences between males and females during heterosexual interactions. For the males, the most likely behavior to follow within 30 sec of the approach of a female is mounting by the dominant male or either aggression or withdrawal, if the male is subordinate. High-ranking females solicit males more than low-ranking females, but the incidence of aggression that follows male contact is low and is not different according to female status. However, when low-ranking females solicit males, the most likely behavior to follow is solicitations from higher ranking females (Keverne *et al.*, 1985). In other words, high-ranking females compete for male attention, whereas high-ranking males show an overt suppression of the behavior of other males by aggressively attacking them. Hence, when low-ranking females are given access

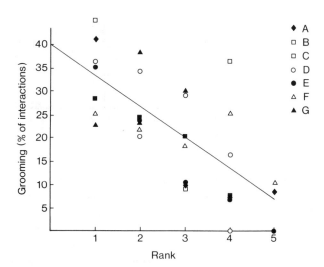

Fig. 10. Grooming behavior of females (A–G designates different groups) according to rank illustrates the higher proportion of grooming interactions that occur with higher ranking females.

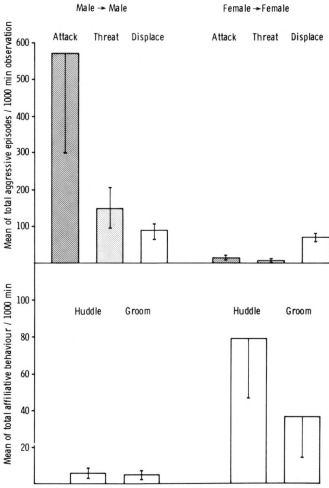

FIG. 11. Intrasexual aggressive behavior and affiliative behavior among males and among females living in the isosexual condition. (Six groups of monkeys.)

to males in the absence of other females, there is an immediate restoration of sexual behavior to high levels without concomitant increases in cortisol.

Not all females are immune from aggressive behavior, and in some heterosexual groups, mobbing attacks may occur on low-ranking females. The consequence of such behavior is high levels of prolactin, and reproductive suppression as revealed by a disruption of cyclicity in these females, or a failure to show LH surges in response to positive estrogen feedback when ovariectomized (Fig. 13)

(Bowman *et al.*, 1978). However, ovarian failure does not occur in all subordinate, intact female talapoin monkeys, although there is no doubting their relatively lower reproductive success (Abbott *et al.*, 1987). A comparison of reproductive suppression with free-living groups is made difficult by field conditions, but observations suggest that a 70% maximum of adult females show sex-skin swellings, implying cyclic disruption among the remaining 30% (Rowell and Dixon, 1975).

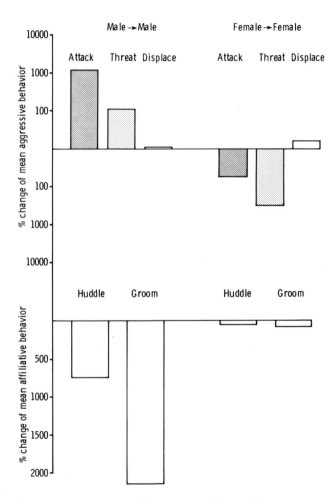

FIG. 12. Changes in aggressive and affiliative behavior (intrasexual) on moving from the isosexual to heterosexual condition.

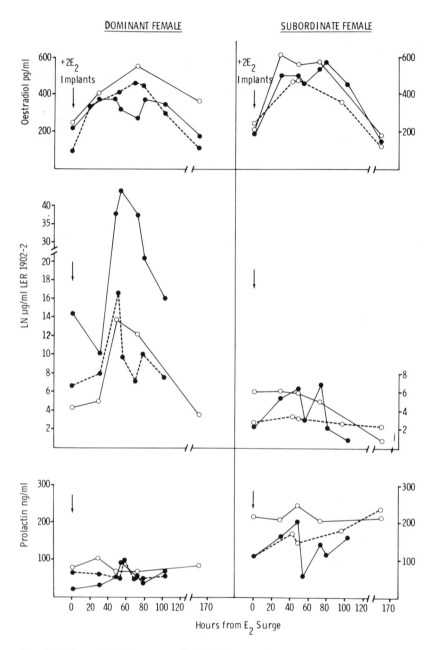

FIG. 13. Effects of positive estrogen feedback (upper section, estrogen-treated females receive a further 2 estrogen implants—arrow indicates time point) on LH release in high- and low-ranking females (receiving high aggression). Females in receipt of high aggression (subordinate) fail to show the LH surge necessary for ovulation and reproductive success and have high levels of plasma prolactin compared with dominant females (Bowman et al., 1978).

B. NEUROENDOCRINE MECHANISMS OF BEHAVIORAL INHIBITION

A question that remains unanswered by these studies is the neuroendocrine mechanism by which subordinate males become sexually inhibited. The changes in testosterone associated with social status in males are not in themselves causally related to these events, nor are the elevated levels of prolactin, as reducing these levels of prolactin by treatment with bromocriptine is without effect on the sexual behavior of subordinates. High levels of cortisol may, however, make some contribution to the behavioral profile of subordinates. Cortisol acts on the central nervous system to promote or inhibit the release of certain peptidergic systems (β-endorphin, CRF) that are themselves implicated in affiliative and anxiety states (Kalin and Shelton, 1989). Although the emphasis has been placed on sexual and aggressive behavior, subordinates are also low on affiliative scores (huddling and grooming) and high on anxiety scores (visual monitoring). Hence, changed activity in these peptidergic systems may represent the neural mechanisms responsible for the coordinated behavioral and endocrine responses of subordinates. Recent findings suggest that alterations in hypothalamic β-endorphin activity might underlie reproductive neuroendocrine function. Neurons synthesizing β-endorphin lie in and around the hypothalamic arcuate nucleus (de Kloet et al., 1981; Wilkes et al., 1980), an area of the brain known to be concerned with reproductive function. Infusions of β-endorphin into the brain of rodents inhibits both reproductive behavior and testosterone synthesis (Sirinathsinghji, 1984; Grossman and Rees, 1983). Increased levels of β-endorphin have been reported in the brain during periods of natural reproductive suppression, such as the nonbreeding season and pregnancy (Roberts et al., 1985; Wardlaw and Frantz, 1983). Although it would be inappropriate to extract and measure β-endorphin levels from the brains of talapoin monkeys, levels in CSF are good indicators of activity in intracerebral β-endorphin-containing neurons. Furthermore, measuring CSF levels allows repeated estimates to be made on the same animal under different conditions.

Subordinate male talapoins have approximately three times higher intracerebral extracellular levels of β-endorphin than do dominant animals (Martensz et al., 1986) (Fig. 14). Both this and the behavioral and neuroendocrine profile of such monkeys lead to the conclusion that this represents heightened activity in the β-endorphin neurones. This would be consistent with the low level of sexual behavior shown by subordinates and their depressed gonadal function compared with dominant males. This is also consistent with the observation that acute treatment of dominant males with the μ-receptor agonist (morphine) in low doses ($2 \mu g/kg^{-1}$) inhibits their sexual behavior, decreases testosterone secretion, and increases cortisol and prolactin, giving them an endocrine as well as behavioral profile similar to that of subordinates.

Monkeys of different rank can also be distinguished by the reactivity to opiate

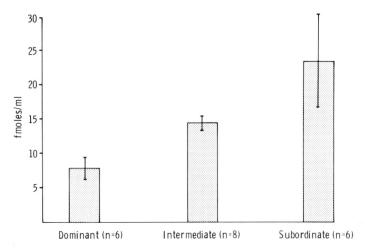

FIG. 14. Cerebrospinal fluid collected from cisterna magna has levels of β-endorphin approximately three times higher in subordinate than in dominant males.

blockade of the neuroendocrine system controlling LH secretion. Dominant males release significant amounts of LH in response to doses of naloxone as low as .25 mg/kg, whereas doses 20 times this concentration (5 mg/kg) are ineffective in subordinate monkeys (Martensz *et al.*, 1986). This represents an apparent inconsistency between the differential effects of opiate blockade with naloxone and postulated levels of activity or cerebral β-endorphin in these monkeys. However, chronically high levels of β-endorphin in subordinates may have down-regulated receptors to such an extent that they no longer respond to the acute administration of the antagonist. Though the exact interpretation of these results is not yet clear, they reinforce the conclusion that chronic subordination is associated with altered opiate activity, and this may be part of the neuroendocrine machinery of reproductive suppression characteristic of this condition.

A further paradox stems from the way in which opiate antagonists influence behavior in the social group. High-ranking males treated chronically with the opiate antagonist naltrexone show a significant reduction in sexual behavior, a deficit that does not recover rapidly after withdrawal of the drug (Meller *et al.*, 1980). Opiate receptor blockade does not alter aggression, but a consistent effect of the drug is to cause a marked increase in grooming invitations and, hence, grooming behavior, irrespective of rank and in both males and females (Fabre-Nys *et al.*, 1982).

In addition to its behavioral effects, naltrexone administration has consequences for hormone levels, which occur independently of social rank and are consistent even among animals living in social isolation. In most males, cortisol, LH, testosterone, and prolactin increase on administration of opiate receptor blockers (Fig. 15). This happens independently of the behavioral effects of opiate blockade, which require a higher drug dosage (Meller *et al.*, 1980). Such a separation of endocrine, social, and behavioral effects of opiate receptor blockade is essential to our interpretation of how the endogenous opiates may influence or be influenced by behavior. Clearly, the behavioral effects are not secondary to endocrine changes, as sex behavior declines when testosterone increases, and many endocrine effects are independent of status. Hence, any changes

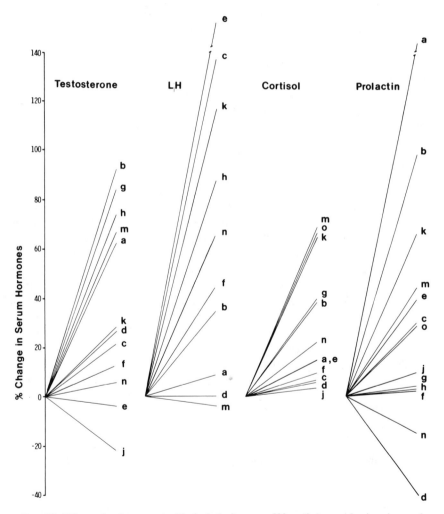

FIG. 15. Effects of opiate receptor blockade (naltrexone: 500 μg/kg) on endocrine changes in males. Testosterone, LH, cortisol, and prolactin all increase, whereas sexual behavior decreases (see Meller *et al.*, 1980); a–o designates individual males.

brought about in central opiate release are probably downstream from higher order processing, but at the brain's interface for endocrine consequences.

The data we have so far collected from monkeys living socially suggest that subordinate monkeys have much in common at the behavioral, neuroendocrine, and neural levels with nonsubordinate monkeys treated with the opiate receptor blockers naloxone or naltrexone. In other words, chronic subordination would seem to result in a failure of the monkey's brain to respond to its own endogenous opiates. I say a failure to respond, because the levels of these peptides are extraordinarily high and at least threefold higher than in dominants. Interestingly, increasing the levels of central opiates in the brains of dominant males also increases prolactin and decreases sexual behavior. Hence, chronically increasing or decreasing central opiates paradoxically have similar effects that can only be interpreted by invoking changes in the receptors. Because the behavioral effects are so widespread (on sexual, feeding, and maternal behavior), these may be explained by hypothesizing that endogenous opiates are involved in behavioral reward.

C. OPIATES AND REWARD

The role of opiates in the control of pain is well established, especially with respect to their analgesic actions in the spinal cord (Clement-Jones et al., 1980; Zieglgansberger, 1984). However, it would be misleading to imply that this is the only context in which the opiate system functions. The β-endorphin system in particular has a pronounced distribution of receptors to the limbic brain and associated areas (amygdala, hypothalamus, preoptic area, hippocampus, nucleus accumbens, and locus coeruleus) (Mansour et al., 1988). Through its interactions with steroid hormones and amines, particularly noradrenaline, β-endorphin influences neuroendocrine function (CRF-ACTH: Buckingham and Cooper, 1987; LHRH-LH: Yen and Jaffe, 1986; prolactin: Grossman and Rees, 1983) and sexual behavior (Sirinathsinghji, 1984). Feeding behavior has been reported to increase during acute infusions of morphine or β-endorphin into the amygdala (central nucleus), hypothalamus (ventromedial nucleus) or the accumbens (Shor-Posner et al., 1986), whereas naloxone decreases feeding when given centrally (Tim and Lowry, 1984).

Furthermore, β-endorphin has been implicated in autonomic responses including increases in heart rate and blood pressure. Although there is general agreement on the importance of β-endorphin for cardiovascular responses, it has proved difficult to identify the precise mechanism because the effects of intracerebral administration depend on the site of infusion, the state of the animal, and whether or not it was stressed (Pannen and Sapru, 1986). Much evidence suggests that endogenous opioid peptides participate in the regulation of several consummatory behaviors. Such a contribution is well documented for the ingestion of sweet substances (Siviy et al., 1982), and the control of masculine sexual behavior (Gessa and Paglietti, 1979) with particular respect to the male's assessment of the incentive motivational properties of an estrous female (Miller and Baum, 1987). Finally, there is an increasing amount of data to implicate β-endorphin in the early social bonding of mother and infant in a wide variety of mammals (cat, dog, guinea pig: Panksepp, 1986). Parturition, an event of importance to the immediate onset of maternal behavior in rodents (Gruber and Kristal, 1977; Mayer and Rosenblatt, 1984; Yeo and Keverne, 1986), and mother/infant selective bonding in sheep (Keverne et al., 1983; Poindron et al., 1984), has been shown to increase β-endorphin levels in the limbic brain (Wardlaw and Frantz, 1983).

In rodents, blocking the action of β-endorphin at parturition inhibits pup-licking and nest building (Mayer et al., 1985). In sheep, acute treatment with either opiate antagonists or agonists has no effect on ongoing maternal behavior, but the onset of maternal behavior is impaired by the antagonist naloxone (Kendrick and Keverne, 1989) and facilitated by the agonist morphine (Keverne and Kendrick, 1990).

Hence, a wide range of neuroendocrine and autonomic responses as well as motivated behaviors are influenced by this peptide. In fact, so wide is this range of central effects of β-endorphin that it is difficult to comprehend how so few neurones have the carrying capacity to code for all these functions, unless it is through their interaction with other neural systems such as dopamine (Wise and Raptis, 1986). It is surely no coincidence that the distributions of μ-receptors, for which β-endorphin is the endogenous ligand, overlap with those areas of the limbic brain that have been found to sustain electrical self-stimulation in the brain (Olds and Forbes, 1981). Endorphins have been described as critical factors in self-stimulation because the endorphin receptor blocker naloxone was found to depress self-stimulation at various sites in the limbic brain, whereas the endorphin agonist morphine supports self-administration and self-stimulation when injected at these sites (Stein, 1978). Likewise, drugs that enhance dopamine transmission are also self-administered and sustain self-stimulation, and at least some of the rewarding effects of endorphin agonists depend on interactions with the midbrain mesolimbic dopamine system. However, in some areas of the brain, notably the ventral striatum, drug studies have revealed that dopamine- and opioid-mediated effects are independent. In this area of the brain, it would seem that dopamine is concerned with the appetitive components of motivated behavior while opiates are more concerned with the consummatory components. Hence, both dopamine and β-endorphin are transmitters that participate in the neural mechanisms for reward. Whether or not they interact or are separable depends on the areas of the brain under consideration.

Both dopamine and opiate neural networks are also implicated in drug dependence. Opiates have been described as "alleviating the pain of loneliness and social withdrawal" (Hakan and Henrikson, 1987). If β-endorphin is indeed concerned with reward and the parts of the brain controlling social behavior provide a significant input to this "reward network," then it is hardly surprising that a breakdown in social attachments (e.g., through death, divorce, mother/infant separation) may result in a wide range of neuroendocrine, autonomic, psychiatric, and other dysfunctions (e.g., Rutter, 1985; House et al., 1988). Again, the most notable feature of opiate drug abuse is that it produces an initial positive affective state (Bardo and Risner, 1985) that is preferred to the state that existed prior to use. It is thought that the most consistent findings among heroin addicts are a history of antisocial behavior, high levels of depression, and low self-esteem (Marlatt and Baer, 1988). Moreover, the perceived level of reinforcement associated with the first drug experience has been found to be directly related to the magnitude of the subsequent drug habit (Haertzen et al., 1983). Clearly, the brain did not evolve to sustain drug administration or electrical stimulation, and the question arises as to what the functional significance of these neural systems might be in the context of the rewards accruing from natural behavior.

D. β-ENDORPHIN AND PRIMATE SOCIAL RELATIONSHIPS

Considerable attention has been given by sociobiologists to the advantages that have accrued among primates from living socially. These include finding food more efficiently (Clutton-Brock and Harvey, 1977), reducing the costs of predation (Bertram, 1978; van Schaik, 1983), and forming alliances to compete for access to feeding and sleeping sites (Wrangham, 1983). The advantages of social grouping may be different for each sex (Wrangham and Smuts, 1980); females rarely lack mates, whereas males often do, and food getting is an important social strategy for females, which means they often form more permanent alliances than males. Many primate societies are therefore referred to as being "female-bonded" (Wrangham, 1980).

Advantages such as these have formed the ultimate factors in the evolution of sociality. Although attempts have been made to describe proximate factors (Hinde, 1983), with particular emphasis on grooming (Seyfarth, 1983), little has been published on the underlying physiological mechanisms of social reward in primates. Although the consequences of social isolation in infant monkeys have been examined at the psychological (Suomi and Harlow, 1978) and physiological levels (Kraemer and McKinney, 1979; Suomi et al., 1978), little has been established on the neural or neurochemical substrates of social reward in primates. Several studies have pointed to the involvement of endogenous opioids as underlying social emotion and social attachment (Panksepp, 1986), and it has been suggested that the positive affect arising from the mother–infant relationship is mediated by cerebral endorphin-containing systems (Panksepp et al., 1978). This hypothesis was based on findings of opiate alleviation of the stress arising from mother/infant separation in guinea pigs and puppies. Other studies have reported that opiate receptor blockade interferes with maternal behavior and disrupts pup-retrieval in dogs (Panksepp, 1986). Paradoxically, the opiate agonist, morphine, has also been shown to disrupt maternal behavior in the rat, but this was thought to be due to interference with decreases in the endogenous ligand, β-endorphin, in mediating the expression of maternal behavior at parturition (Bridges and Grimm, 1982). Among primates, the β-endorphin system is activated by social grooming and opiate receptor blockade increases the motivation to be groomed and to groom, whereas morphine administration decreases it (Fig. 16) (Keverne et al., 1989). Blockade of opiate receptors with either naloxone or naltrexone results in monkeys increasing their need to be groomed (invitations) and their grooming of others, which is a behavioral strategy to initiate reciprocal grooming (Fabre-Nys et al., 1982). There are no effects on self-grooming or scratching. Because grooming is known to release central β-endorphin (Fig. 17), it seems likely that the increased grooming that a monkey requests is an attempt to compensate for loss of endogenous opiates induced by receptor blockade. Interestingly, dopamine blockade (sulpiride treatment; see Fig. 16) has no such effect on grooming interactions, which would suggest that dopamine, unlike the opiates, is not a part of the reward mechanism for this particular behavior.

Increased grooming and grooming invitations normally occur in pair bonding of primates during and following copulation (Michael et al., 1966), in cementing social relationships (Seyfarth et al., 1978), particularly between mothers and infants (Lee, 1983), in maintaining peace and cohesion in primate societies (Simpson, 1973), and following aggressive outbursts (Kummer, 1981). Grooming interactions form part of the normal behavioral repertoire of primates, occurring in different social situations and having in common the provision of bonding and comfort to the participants rather than being purely hygienic (Dunbar, 1989). It therefore appears that grooming is a significant proximate factor in social bonding and for activating the brain's opioid system as can be seen from the rapid increase in CSF β-endorphin contingent on receiving grooming. Hence, at the neural level the brain's endorphin system may provide the basis for a common bonding mechanism, but the nature of the relationships bonded clearly differ (Mother/infant; consortships; peers). Nevertheless, it is surely no coincidence that in primates all of these relationships share a strong mutual grooming component.

The question arises as to how this mechanism for socialization may have evolved and what, if anything, is special about the nature of primate societies. The social bonding of mother and infant is phylogenetically old, and endogenous opiates have been shown to be an important part of the neural mechanism in a number of mammalian species (dogs, guinea pigs, sheep, monkeys). In all these species there is also an element of broader social organization, but in none of them is it so complex as the social organization found in the catarrhine primates.

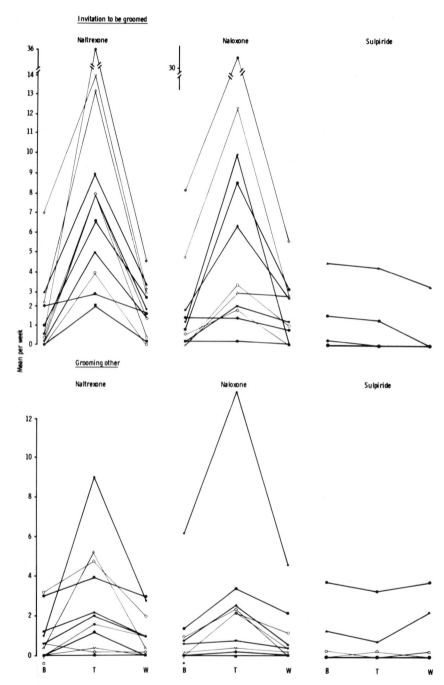

FIG. 16. Effects of opiate and dopamine antagonists (naltrexone, naloxone, and sulpiride) on requests to be groomed and grooming of talapoin monkeys. Only one monkey of the pair received treatment immediately prior to observation (within 3 minutes).

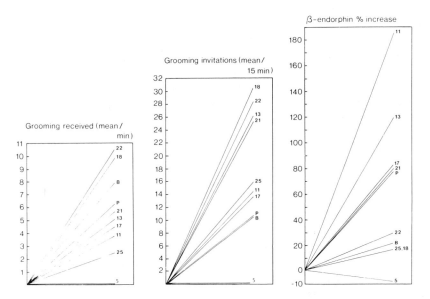

FIG. 17. Effects of grooming on increases in CSF β-endorphin in talapoin monkeys. (Keverne *et al.*, 1989). Numbers and letters designate individual identities of monkeys.

The extensive social organization of monkeys has depended both on the capacity for the kind of higher order neural processing that is essential to coding for complex relationships and on the way that these cognitive events can become part of the causal chain linking into the "emotional" limbic brain. Two major neural developments have made this possible.

First, there has been a shift in emphasis for the kind of neural systems that are called into action when the social environment influences behavior. In most mammals, olfaction plays an important role in behavioral processes (territorial marking, sexual attraction, kin recognition), and this information gains access to the "emotional" limbic brain via the amygdala (cortical and medial nuclei). The brain of mammals that live in complex social groups has undergone a progressive development of the neocortex, which in turn has gained access to limbic areas via the amygdala, namely the baso-lateral part, and this has also undergone a corresponding enlargement. This pathway to the limbic brain permits access of higher order sensory information, but only after prior processing in association cortex and cross-referencing to stored information on past experiences. Hence, the amygdala may be viewed as a sensory gateway to the limbic brain (Gaffan and Harrison, 1987) with both routes influencing primary motivated behaviors (feeding, sexual, and maternal). However, while the baso-lateral access to motivated behavioral control mechanisms is dominated by neocortical influences, the olfactory corticomedial access is subject to autonomic and endocrine influences. The changes in emphasis from principally olfactory, to olfactory and social, to principally social factors influencing primary motivated behaviors may be viewed as an evolutionary progression for the way in which the amygdala handles cortical input to the limbic brain. The differences among social mammals are matters of degree, but it is the brains of primates more than any other mammals that have undergone massive development of the association cortex. This permits a meaningful integration of complex social events that, together with other environmental events common to all mammals, become influential for motivated behavior (Appleton and Mishkin, 1986).

Second, for this higher order cortical processing relayed via the amygdala to have a major determining influence on motivated behavior, it has been important for the motivated behavior to become emancipated from strict endocrine and autonomic control mechanisms. It is only in the higher primates that this behavioral flexibility has been achieved to any considerable extent (Keverne, 1985). In monkeys, sexual behavior is not strictly related to estrus (Keverne, 1987) and maternal behavior does not cease at weaning, nor does it depend entirely on the endocrine secretions of pregnancy (Keverne, 1988). In lower mammals, motivation and cognitive processes are separable functions, but it is frequently the case that the former directs the latter. Hunger leads to feeding behavior, estrus to sexual behavior, and the endocrine priming of pregnancy directs maternal behavior. In primates such as ourselves, foraging in the supermarket begins long before we are hungry, and the preparation of food often promotes hunger. Mothers of adopted children are perfectly maternal without undergoing pregnancy and parturition, whereas the latter is no guarantee against infant neglect. Sexual behavior can and does occur at all stages of the life cycle and is intricately constrained and, indeed, shaped by the laws and dictates of society. Hence, this ability of higher order cognitive processing to have a determining influence on motivated and emotional behaviors has required a large degree of emancipation from the autonomic and endocrine control mechanisms.

With the evolutionary development of the cortex, cognitive as well as sensory events concerning information from the complex social environment can provide a functionally significant input into the limbic brain. Thus, social behavior acquires the status of a "second order" rewarding behavior, but in doing so, carries the costs that disruption to the social system may entail. Hence, the consequences of social exclusion are manifest in a cascade of malfunctions to all motivated behaviors (sexual, feeding, maternal) paralleled by endocrine and autonomic changes influencing well-being.

V.   Concluding Remarks

Behavior is a function of the brain's ability to compute the affective significance of information originating from the external environment, from within the body, and from within the brain itself, its memories and beliefs. An understanding of behavior benefits from a knowledge of all these functions and underlies the approach adopted in this chapter with respect to the social environment, endocrine status, and the brain's opiate system. One important conclusion to emerge is the relative independence of monkey behavior from gonadal influences. Although hormones may still effect odors (pheromones), sex-skin coloration, and swelling, these peripheral changes in attractiveness can be viewed as nature's insurance policy for optimizing reproductive success. However, emancipation of the brain has released behavior from the kind of motivational boundaries that constrain its expression in nonprimate mammals. The brain is thereby a blank disc in which to write the software for computing the outcome of interactions concerning the environment (social and natural) and stored memories. Motivated behavior may now be triggered by events that are several orders removed from stimuli that are effective for promoting such behavior in nonprimate mammals. Equally important for behavior has been the extension of the brain's endorphin mechanism, used principally in the bonding of mother and infant, to incorporate other relationships and thereby extend the social network.

Although it is unrealistic to consider any one peptidergic system to be chemically coded for a specific category of behavior, there is good reason to assume that β-endorphin is of importance in adult primate social interactions. The following summarizes evidence for such an assumption.

1. Social interactions of monkeys have been shown to have significant consequences for CSF β-endorphin, dependent on status. Chronic social subordination produces high levels of CSF β-endorphin that, because of the chronic status, produce a "down-regulation" of opiate receptors. This is probably why, in subordinate talapoin monkeys, unlike dominants, there is no dose response of LH release to receptor blockade by naloxone challenge (Martensz et al., 1986).

2. Sociosexual behaviors are impaired in dominant males following blockade of opiate receptors, despite the fact that such treatment elevates plasma testosterone (Meller et al., 1980).

3. Opiate receptor blockade enhances other behaviors, especially the affiliative behaviors of huddling and grooming (Fabre-Nys et al., 1982). In adult talapoin monkeys that have been socially isolated for 24 hours, such affiliative behaviors are high when reunited with peers, but not if the monkeys are pretreated with morphine that, like β-endorphin, acts preferentially on the μ-receptor (Keverne et al., 1989). Moreover, monkeys that have been socially isolated and allowed to interact without morphine treatment show a significant increase in their endogenous CSF β-endorphin (Keverne et al., 1989).

These acute separation studies reveal a significant reciprocal interaction between CSF opiates and affiliative social behavior. They can be interpreted in terms of opiates acting as part of a neural reward for social interactions, whereas social interactions in turn maintain "opiate tone." In the circumstances of chronic social subordination (low sexual and affiliative interactions, low status, high

cortisol, high anxiety) although CSF β-endorphin is high, it appears to be paradoxically ineffective owing to "down regulation" of receptors. This may in turn
have consequences for reproduction, as females become anovulatory (Bowman
et al., 1978) and subordinate males fail to show sexual activity even in the
temporary absence of dominants (Eberhart *et al.,* 1985).

Because dominance depends on the ability of monkeys to develop the social
skills necessary for manipulating complex relationships, evolution has tended to
select for a neural system providing cognitive control over the limbic brain.
Hence, a progressive enlargement of the neocortex with social reward as a
reinforcing mechanism has resulted in a brain with a striking capacity to learn
and remember the emotional significance of social stimuli and events. Such a
development may also have been significant for the more universal patterns of
relationships shown in human societies. Personal identity is profoundly influenced by emotional evaluations by the self of the self (Crook, 1989). Promotion
of self-esteem is often rooted in the credit attributed by others (kin, friends, or
society as a whole) to individuals as a result of their positive social actions.
Fulfillment of basic social commitments can lead to a feeling of well-being and
pleasure, whereas a loss of self-esteem can produce highly depressive states
leading to social withdrawal. It should therefore come as no surprise that individuals resort to the substitute reinforcers of heroin (opiate activation) or "crack"
(dopamine activation) when their social relationships fail and self-esteem declines.

VI. Summary

The sociosexual behavior of monkeys is best characterized by the high level of
dependence on social influences and the low level of dependence on endocrine
influences. In males, social status affects sexual behavior, social monitoring and
grooming, priority over access to food and cage space, and aggressive or avoidance interactions. Although largely independent of hormonal secretions from the
gonads, behavioral interactions within the social group have major consequences
for these and other endocrine systems. The levels of cortisol and prolactin are
higher in subordinate males and testosterone is lower, and the circadian rhythm
of these hormones may be phase-shifted relative to the social interactions that
occur in the daylight hours. The chronically high levels, and hence functional
uncoupling, of the cerebral β-endorphin system in subordinates is correlated with
the high levels of aggression they receive.

The behavioral interactions of females also relate to their hierarchy, but in a
way that is very different from males. Females show little overt aggression and
high levels of affiliative behavior, and while overt aggression increases among
males during heterosexual interactions, it decreases among females. The amount

of sexual activity males exhibit is largely determined from the outcome of their aggressive behavior, with high levels of intimidation and sexual suppression in subordinates. High-ranking females are not suppressive, but are more successful than their subordinates in soliciting male attention. The virtual absence of overt aggression among females results in cortisol levels that are indistinguishable across rank. The aggressive suppression of sexual activity in subordinate males has consequences for the interest they show in females, or rather the lack of it, even when the dominant males are absent. This "learned helplessness" is not seen in subordinate females, and they remain sexually active even in the presence of high-ranking females. However, the biological consequences of rank is similar for both males and females in that reproduction is less successful in subordinates. In the case of males, this results from behavioral suppression, whereas low-ranking females are less likely to ovulate and conceive.

Monkey groups are often referred to as being female-bonded on the basis of high levels of affiliative behavior and the social stability seen among females. In contrast, males are less affiliative, more aggressive, and often leave their natal social group, living a transient solitary existence. Hence, whatever the neural mechanism might be for social bonding, it is probably female based. The activation of opiates in the context of mammalian mother–infant bonding is well recognized and may have extended its function to further serve as a substrate for social bonding in the monkey group. The reciprocal relationship between grooming behavior and cerebral β-endorphin levels in monkeys would lend support to this viewpoint. In this way, the evolution of sociality has capitalized on existing neural systems. However, because complex social relationships require information-processing at a higher cortical level, rostral telencephalic functioning must somehow gain influence to limbic motivational reward systems. The increased development of the primate amygdala fulfills this role by serving as a relay for corticolimbic communication. Moreover, this cortical influence is all the more profound as a result of the motivational systems themselves becoming emancipated from gonadal hormones.Hence, the consequences of social exclusion in monkeys are remarkably similar to the consequences of mother–infant separation, a cascade of malfunctions at the motivational level paralleled by endocrine and autonomic changes influencing health and well-being.

Acknowledgments

This work was supported by MRC program grants in collaboration with my colleagues Joe Herbert and Barry Everitt. The work could not have been completed without the help of post docs (Nick Martensz, Sandra Vellucci, and Dave Abbott), graduate students (Rachel Meller, Jerry Eberhart, and Usanec Yodyingyuad), and technical assistance (Leslie Bowman, Sue Dilley, Carlos de la Riva, Helen Shiers, Pam Stacey, and Bernadette Tuite).

References

Abbott, D. H., Keverne, E. B., Moore, G. F., and Yodyingyuad, U. (1987). Social suppression of reproduction in subordinate talapoin monkeys, *Miopithecus talapoin*. *In* "Primate Ontogeny, Cognition and Social Behaviour" (Else and Lee, eds.). Proc. 10th Congr. Int. Primatol. Soc., Vol. 3. Cambridge Univ. Press, Cambridge, U.K.

Appleton, J. P., and Mishkin, M. C. (1986). The amygdala: Sensory gateway to the emotions. *In* "Emotion: Theory, Research and Experience" Vol. 3, pp. 281–299. Academic Press, Orlando, Florida.

Bardo, M. T., and Risner, M. E. (1985). Biochemical substrates of drug abuse. *In* "Determinants of Substance Abuse" (Galizis and Marsto, eds.), pp. 65–99. Plenum, New York.

Berenstain, L., and Wade, T. D. (1983). Intrasexual selection and male mating strategies in baboons and macaques. *Int. J. Primatol.* **4**, 201–235.

Bertram, B. C. R. (1978). Living in groups: Predators and prey. *In* "Behavioural Ecology: An Evolutionary Approach" (N. B. Davies and J. R. Krebs, eds.), pp. 269–285. Blackwell, Oxford.

Bowman, L. A., Dilley, S. R., and Keverne, E. B. (1978). Suppression of oestrogen-induced LH surges by social subordination in talapoin monkeys. *Nature (London)* **275**, 56–58.

Bridges, R. S., and Grimm, C. T. (1982). Reversal of morphine disruption of maternal behaviour by concurrent treatment with the opiate antagonist naloxone. *Science* **218**, 166–168.

Bronson, F. H. (1989). "Mammalian Reproductive Biology." Univ. of Chicago Press, Chicago, Illinois.

Buckingham, J., and Cooper, T. (1987). Interrelationships of opioidergic and adrenergic mechanisms controlling the secretion of CRF in the rat. *Neuroendocrinology* **46**, 199–206.

Chapais, B. (1983). Reproductive activity in relation to male dominance and the likelihood of ovulation in rhesus monkeys. *Behav. Ecol. Sociobiol.* **12**, 215–228.

Clement-Jones, V., McLoughlin, L., Tomlin, S., Besser, G. M., Rees, L. H., and Wren, H. L. (1980). Increased β-endorphin but not metencephalin levels in human CSF after acupuncture for recurrent pain. *Lancet 2*, 946–949.

Clutton-Brock, T. H., and Harvey, P. H. (1977). Primate ecology and social organisation. *J. Zool.* **183**, 1–39.

Crook, J. (1989). The behavioural ecology of humans and other mammals. *In* "Comparative Socioecology" (V. Standen and R. A. Foley, eds.), pp. 1–36. Blackwell, Oxford.

Datta, S. B. (1983). Relative power and the acquisition of rank. *In* "Primate Social Relationships: An Integrated Approach" (R. A. Hinde, ed.), pp. 93–103. Blackwell, Oxford.

de Kloet, E. R., Palkovits, M., and Mezey, E. (1981). Opiocortin peptides: Localisation, source and avenues of transport. *Pharmacol. Ther.* **12**, 321–351.

Dixson, A. F. (1983). The hormonal control of sexual behavior in primates. *In* "Oxford Reviews of Reproductive Biology" (C. A. Finn, ed.), pp. 151–219. Oxford Univ. Press, London.

Dixson, A. F., and Herbert, J. (1977). Gonadal hormones and sexual behavior in groups of adult talapoin monkeys (*Miopithecus talapoin*). *Horm. Behav.* **8**, 141–154.

Dixson, A. F., Scruton, D. M., and Herbert, J. (1975). Behaviour of the talapoin monkey (*Miopithecus talapoin*) (studied in groups in the laboratory). *J. Zool.* **176**, 177–210.

Dunbar, R. (1989). Functional significance of social grooming in primates. *Folia Primatol.* **49**, 1–23.

Dunbar, R. I. M. (1988). "Primate Social Systems." Croom Helm, London.

Eberhart, J., Yodyinyuad, U., and Keverne, E. B. (1985). Subordination in male Talapoin monkeys lowers sexual behaviour in the absence of dominants. *Physiol. Behav.* **35**, 673–678.

Eberhart, J. A., Keverne, E. B., and Meller, R. E. (1980). Social influences on plasma testosterone levels in male talapoin monkeys. *Horm. Behav.* **14**, 247–266.

Eberhart, J. A., Keverne, E. B., and Meller, R. E. (1983). Social influences in circulating levels of cortisol and prolactin in male talapoin monkeys. *Physiol. Behav.* **30**, 361–369.

Everitt, B. J., and Herbert, J. (1975). The effects of implanting testosterone propionate into the central nervous system on the sexual behaviour of adrenalectomised female rhesus monkeys. *Brain Res.* **86**, 109–120.

Everitt, B. J., Herbert, J., and Hamer, J. D. (1972). Sexual receptivity of bilateral adrenalectomised female rhesus monkeys. *Physiol. Behav.* **8**, 409–415.

Fabre-Nys, C., Meller, R. E., and Keverne, E. B. (1982). Opiate antagonists stimulate affiliation behaviour in monkeys. *Pharmacol., Biochem. Behav.* **16**, 653–659.

Ford, C. S., and Beach, F. A. (1951). "Patterns of Sexual Behaviour." Harper (Hoeber) New York.

Fossey, D. (1982). Reproduction among free-living mountain gorillas. *Am. J. Primatol., Suppl.* **1**, 97–104.

Gaffan, D., and Harrison, S. (1987). Amygdalectomy and disconnection in visual learning for auditory secondary reinforcement in monkeys. *J. Neurosci.* **7**, 2285–2292.

Gautier-Hion, A. (1966). L'ecologie et l'ethologie du talapoin. *Miopithecus talapoin. Biol. Gabonica* **2**, 311–329.

Gautier-Hion, A. (1970). L'organisation social d'un bande de talapoins (*Miopithecus talapoin*) dans le nord-est du Gabon. *Folia Primatol.* **12**, 116–141.

Gautier-Hion, A. (1973). Social and ecological features of talapoin monkeys: Comparisons with sympatric cercopithecines. *In* "Comparative Ecology and Behaviour of Primates" (R. P. Michael and J. H. Crook, eds.). Academic Press, New York.

Gautier-Hion, A. (1978). Food niches and coexistence in sympatric primates in Gabon. *Recent Adv. Primatol.* **1**, 269–286.

Gessa, G. L., and Paglietti, E. (1979). Induction of copulatory behavior in sexually inactive rats by naloxone. *Science* **204**, 203–205.

Grossman, A., and Rees, L. H. (1983). The neuroendocrinology of opioid peptides. *Br. Med. Bull.* **39**, 83–88.

Gruber, G. C., and Kristal, M. B. (1977). Uterine distention and the onset of maternal behaviour in pseudopregnant but not in cycling rats. *Physiol. Behav.* **19**, 133–37.

Haertzen, E. A., Kocher, T. R., and Miyasato, U. (1983). *Drug, Alcohol Depend.* **11**, 147–165.

Hakan, R. I., and Henrikson, S. J. (1987). Brain pathways in drug dependence. *Soc. Neurosci. Abstr.* **13**, 1282.

Halbreich, U., Asnis, G. M., Shindledecker, R., Zumoff, B., and Nathan, S. (1985). Cortisol secretion in endogenous depression. I. Basal plasma levels. *Arch. Gen. Psychiatry* **42**, 904–908.

Hausfater, G. (1975). Dominance and reproduction in baboons. *Contrib. Primatol.* **7**.

Herbert, J., Keverne, E. B., and Yodyingyuad, U. (1986). Modulation by social status of the relationship between cerebrospinal fluid and serum cortisol levels in male talapoin monkeys. *Neuroendocrinology* **42**, 436–442.

Hinde, R. A. (1983). Description of the proximate factors influencing social structure. *In* "Primate Social Relationships" (R. A. Hinde, ed.), pp. 176–181, Blackwell, Oxford.

House, J. S., Landis, K. R., and Umberson, D. (1988). Social relationships and health. *Science* **241**, 540–545.

Kalin, N. H., and Shelton, S. E. (1989). Defensive behaviours in infant rhesus monkeys: Environmental cues and neurochemical regulation. *Science* **243**, 1718–1721.

Kendrick, K., and Keverne, E. B. (1989). Intracerebroventricular infusions of naltrexone and phentolamine on central and peripheral oxytocin release and on maternal behaviour induced by vaginocervical stimulation in the ewe. *Brain Res.* **505**, 329–332.

Keverne, E. B. (1976). Sexual receptivity and attractiveness in the female monkey. *Adv. Study Behav.* **7**, 155–200.

Keverne, E. B. (1979a). Sexual and aggressive behaviour in social groups of talapoin monkeys. *Ciba Found. Symp.* **62**, 271–286.

Keverne, E. B. (1985). Hormones and the sexual behaviour of monkeys. *In* "Neurobiology and Behaviour" (R. Gilles and J. Balthazard, eds.), pp. 37–47. Springer-Verlag, Berlin.

Keverne, E. B. (1987). Processing of environmental stimuli and primate reproduction. *J. Zool.* **213**, 395–408.

Keverne, E. B. (1988). Central mechanisms underlying the neural and neuroendocrine determinants of maternal behaviour. *Psychoneuroendocrinology,* **13**, 127–141.

Keverne, E. B., and Kendrick, K. (1991). Morphine and CRF potentiate maternal acceptance in multiparous ewes after vaginocervical stimulation. *Brain Res.* **540**, 54–62.

Keverne, E. B., Meller, R. E., and Martinez-Arias, A. M. (1978a). Dominance, aggression and sexual behaviour in social groups of talapoin monkeys. *Recent Adv. Primatol.* **1**, 533–548.

Keverne, E. B., Leonard, R. A., Scruton, D. M., and Young, S. K. (1978b). Visual monitoring in social groups of talapoin monkeys (*Miopithecus talapoin*). *Anim. Behav.* **26**, 933–944.

Keverne, E. B., Eberhart, J. A., and Meller, R. E. (1982). Social influences on behaviour and neuroendocrine responsiveness of talapoin monkeys. *Scand. J. Psychol., Suppl.* **1**, 37–47.

Keverne, E. B., Levy, F., Poindron, P., and Lindsay, D. (1983). Vaginal stimulation: An important determinant of maternal bonding in sheep. *Science* **219**, 81–83.

Keverne, E. B., Eberhart, J. A., Yodyinyuad, U., and Abbott, D. A. (1985). Social influences on sex-differences in the behaviour and endocrine state of talapoin monkeys. *Prog. Brain Res.* **61**, 331–347.

Keverne, E. B., Martensz, N. D., and Tuite, B. (1989). β-Endorphin concentrations in CIF of monkeys are influenced by grooming relationships. *Psychoneuroendocrinology* **14**, 155–161.

Kraemer, G. W., and McKinney, W. T. (1979). Interactions of pharmacological agents which alter biogenic amine metabolism and depression: An analysis of contributing factors in a primate model of depression. *J Affective Disord.* **1**, 33–54.

Kummer, H. (1981). "Primate Societies." Aldine-Atherton, Chicago, Illinois.

Lee, P. C. (1983). Caretaking of infants and mother-infant relationships. *In* "Primate Social Relationships" (R. A. Hinde, ed.), pp. 146–151. Blackwell, Oxford.

Lemmon, W. B., and Allen, M. L. (1978). Continual sexual receptivity in the female chimpanzee (*Pan troglodytes*). *Folia Primatol.* **30**, 80–88.

Levine, S., Coe, C., and Weiner, S. G. (1989). *In* "Psychoendocrinology" (S. Levine and I. Bush, eds.), pp. 341–378. Academic Press, San Diego, California.

Lovejoy, J., and Wallen, K. (1990). Adrenal suppression and sexual initiation in group-living female rhesus monkeys. *Horm. Behav.* **24**, 256–269.

Loy, J. (1987). The sexual behaviour of African monkeys and the question of estrus. *In* "Comparative Behaviour of African Monkeys" (E. Zucker, ed.), pp. 175–195. Alan R. Liss, New York.

Mansour, A., Khachaturian, H., Lewis, M., Akil, H., and Watson, S. (1988). Anatomy of CNS opiate receptors. *Trends Neurosc.* **11**, 308–314.

Maple, T. L., Zucker, E. L., and Dennon, M. B. (1979). Cyclic proceptivity in a captive female orang-utan (*Pongo pygmaeus abelii*). *Behav. Processes* **4**, 53–59.

Marlatt, G. A., and Baer, J. S. (1988). Addictive behaviours: Etiology and treatment. *Annu. Rev. Psychol.* **39**, 223–252.

Martensz, N. D., Vellucci, S. V., Keverne, E. B., and Herbert, J. (1986). β-Endorphin levels in the cerebrospinal fluid of male talapoin monkeys in social groups related to dominance status and luteinizing hormone response to naloxone. *Neuroscience* **18**, 651–658.

Martensz, N. D., Vellucci, S. V., Fuller, L. M., Everitt, B. J., Keverne, E. B., and Herbert, J. (1987). Relationship between aggressive behaviour and circadian rhythms in cortisol and testosterone in social groups of talapoin monkeys. *J. Endocrinol.* **115**, 107–120.

Mayer, A. D., and Rosenblatt, J. S. (1984). Prepartum changes in maternal responsiveness and nest defence in Ratlus norvegiens. *J. Comp. Psychol.* **98,** 177–188.

Mayer, A. D., Faris, P. L., Komisaruk, B., and Rosenblatt, J. S. (1985). Opiate antagonism reduces placentophagin and pup cleaning by parturient rats. *Pharmacol., Biochem. Behav.* **2,** 1035–1044.

McGuire, M. T., Brammer, G. L., & Raleigh, M. J. (1986). Resting cortisol levels and the emergence of dominant male status in vervet monkeys. *Horm. Behav.* **20,** 106–117.

Meller, R. E., Herbert, J., and Keverne, E. B. (1980). Behavioural and endocrine effects of naltrexone in male talapoin monkeys. *Pharmacol., Biochem. Behav.* **13,** 663–672.

Michael, R. P., and Wilson, M. I. (1973). Effects of castration and hormone replacement in fully adult male rhesus monkeys. *Endocrinology (Baltimore)* **95,** 150–159.

Michael, R. P., Herbert, J., and Welegalla, J. (1966). Ovarian hormones and grooming behaviour in the rhesus monkey (*Macaca mulatta*) in the laboratory. *J. Endocrinol.* **36,** 263–279.

Miller, R. L., and Baum, M. J. (1987). Naloxone inhibits mating and conditioned place preference for an estrous female in male rats soon after castration. *Pharmacol., Biochem. Behav.* **26,** 781–789.

Nadler, R. D. (1977). Sexual behaviour of captive orang-utans. *Arch. Sex. Behav.* **6,** 457–475.

Nadler, R. D., Collins, D. C., Miller, L. C., and Graham, C. E. (1983). Menstrual cycle patterns of hormones and sexual behavior in gorillas. *Horm. Behav.* **17,** 1–17.

Olds, M. E., and Forbes, J. C. (1981). Central basis of motivation: Self-stimulation studies. *Annu. Rev. Psychol.* **32,** 527–574.

Panksepp, J. (1986). The psychobiology of prosocial behaviours: Separation distress, play and altruism. *In* "Altruism and Aggression: Biological and Social Origins" (C. Zahn-Waxler, E. M. Cummings, and R. Jannotti, eds.), pp. 19–57. Cambridge Univ. Press, Cambridge, U.K.

Panksepp, J., Herman, B. H., Connor, R., Bishop, P., and Scott, J. P. (1978). The biology of social attachment: Opiates alleviate separation distress. *Biol. Psychiatry* **13,** 607–618.

Pannen, S., and Sapru, H. N. (1986). Cardiovascular responses to medullary microinjections of opiate agonists in anaesthetized rats. *J. Cardiovasc. Pharmacol.* **8,** 950–956.

Poindron, P., LeNeindre, P., Levy, F., and Keverne, E. B. (1984). Les mécanisms physiologiques de l'acceptation du nouveau-né chez la brebis. *Biol. Behav.* **9,** 65–88.

Roberts, A. C., Martensz, N. D., Hastings, M. H., and Herbert, J. (1985). Changes in photoperiod alter the daily rhythm of pineal melatonin content, hypothalamic β-endorphin content and the LH response to naloxone in the male Syrian hamster. *Endocrinology (Baltimore)* **117,** 141–148.

Rose, R. M., Holaday, J. W., and Bernstein, I. S. (1971). Plasma testosterone, dominance rank and aggressive behaviour in male rhesus monkeys. *Nature (London)* **231,** 366–368.

Rose, R. M., Bernstein, I. S., and Gordn, T. P. (1975). Consequences of social conflict on plasma testosterone levels in rhesus monkeys. *Psychosom. Med.* **37,** 50–61.

Rowell, T. E. (1972). Female reproductive cycles and social behaviour in primates. *Adv. Study Behav.* **4,** 69–105.

Rowell, T. E., and Dixson, A. F. (1975). Changes in social organisation during the breeding season of wild talapoin monkeys. *J. Reprod. Fertil.* **43,** 419–34.

Rubin, R. T., Poland, R. E., Lesser, I. M., Winston, B. A., and Blodgett, A. L. N. (1987). Neuroendocrine aspects of primary endogenous depression. *Arch. Gen. Psychiatry* **44,** 328–336.

Rutter, M. (1985). Resilience in the face of adversity: Protective factors and resistance to psychiatric disorder. *Br. J. Psychiatry* **147,** 598–611.

Sapolsky, R. M. (1982). The endocrine stress-response and social status in the wild baboon. *Horm. Behav.* **16,** 279–292.

Scallet, A. C., Suomi, S. J., and Bowman, R. E. (1981). Sex differences in adrenocortical response to controlled agonistic encounters in rhesus monkeys. *Physiol. Behav.* **26,** 385–390.

Schurmann, C. L. (1982). Mating behaviour of wild orang-utans. *In* "Biology and Conservation of the Orangutan" (L. E. M. de Boer, ed.), pp. 269–284. Dr. W. Junk, The Hague.

Seyfarth, L. M., Cheney, D. L., and Hinde, R. A. (1978). Some principles relating social interactions and social structure among primates. *In* "Recent Advances in Primatology" (J. Herbert and D. Chivers, eds.), pp. 39–51. Academic Press, New York.

Seyfarth, R. M. (1983). Grooming and social competition in primates. *In* "Primate Social Relationships" (R. A. Hinde, ed.), pp. 182–189. Blackwell, Oxford.

Shor-Posner, G., Azar, P., Filart, D., Tempel, D., and Liebowitz, S. F. (1986). Morphine stimulated feeding. *Pharmacol. Biochem. Behav.* **24,** 931–939.

Simpson, M. J. A. (1973). The social grooming of male chimpanzees. *In* "The Comparative Ecology of Behaviour of Primates" (R. P. Michael and J. H. Crook, eds.), pp. 411–506. Academic Press, New York.

Simpson, M. J. A., and Howe, S. (1986). Group and matriline differences in the behaviour of rhesus monkey infants. *Anim. Behav.* **34,** 444–459.

Simpson, M. J. A., and Simpson, A. E. (1982). Birth/sex ratios and social rank in rhesus monkey mothers. *Nature (London)* **300,** 440–441.

Sirinathsinghji, D. J. S. (1984). Modulation of lordosis behaviour of female rats by naloxone β-endorphin and its antiserum in the mesencephalic central gray: Possible mediation via GnRH. *Neuroendocrinology* **39,** 222–230.

Siviy, S. M., Calcagnetti, D. J., and Reid, L. D. (1982). Opioids and palatability. *In* "Neural Basis of Feeding and Reward" (B. G. Hoebel and D. Noven, eds.), pp. 517–524. Haer Institute for Electrophysiological Research, Brunswick, Maine.

Stanton, M. E., Patterson, J. M., and Levine, S. (1985). Social influences on conditioned cortisol secretion in the squirrel monkey. *Psychoneuroendocrinology* **10,** 125–134.

Stein, L. (1978). Brain endorphins: Possible mediators of pleasure and reward. *Neurosci. Res. Program Bull.* **16,** 556–567.

Suomi, S. J. (1987). Perinatal development: A psychobiological perspective. *In* "Psychobiological Aspects of Behavioural Development" (N. A. Krasnegor, E. M. Blass, M. A. Hofer, and W. P. Smotherman, eds.), pp. 397–420, Academic Press, San Diego, California.

Suomi, S. J., and Harlow, H. F. (1978). Production and alleviation of depressive behaviours in monkeys. *In* "Social and Personality Development" (M. Lamb, ed.), pp. 325–349. Holt, Rinehart & Winston, New York.

Suomi, S. J., Seaman, S. F., Lewis, J. K., de Lizio, R. D., and McKinney, W. T. (1978). Effects of imipramine treatment of separation induced social disorders in rhesus monkeys. *Arch. Gen. Psychiatry* **35,** 321–325.

Tim, G. K. W., and Lowry, M. T. (1984). Opioids, feeding and anorexias. *Fed. Proc., Fed. Am. Soc. Exp. Biol.* **43,** 2893–2897.

van Schaik, C. P. (1983). Why are diurnal primates living in groups? *Behaviour* **87,** 120–144.

Wardlaw, S. L. K., and Frantz, A. G. (1983). Brain β-endorphin during pregnancy, parturition and the postpartum period. *Endocrinology (Baltimore)* **113,** 1664–1668.

Wilkes, M. M., Watkins, W. B., Stewart, R. D., and Yen, S. S. C. (1980). Localisation and quantitation of β-endorphin in human brain and pituitary. *Neuroendocrinology* **30,** 113–121.

Wise, R. A., and Raptis, L. (1986). Effects of naloxone and pimozide on initiation and maintenance measures of free feeding. *Brain Res.* **368,** 62–68.

Wrangham, R. W. (1980). An ecological model of female bonded groups. *Behaviour* **75,** 262–300.

Wrangham, R. W. (1983). Ultimate factors determining social structure. *In* "Primate Social Relationships" (R. A. Hinde, ed.), pp. 255–261. Blackwell, Oxford.

Wrangham, R. W., and Smuts, B. B. (1980). Sex differences in the behavioural ecology of chimpanzees in Gombe National Park, Tanzania. *J. Reprod. Fertil.* **28,** Suppl., 1–20.

Yen, S. S., and Jaffe, R. B. (1986). "Reproductive Endocrinology," pp. 500–545. Saunders, Philadelphia, Pennsylvania.

Yeo, J., and Keverne, E. B. (1986). The importance of vagino-cervical stimulation for maternal behaviour in the rat. *Physiol. Behav.* **37,** 23–26.

Yodyingyuad, U., Eberhart, J. A., and Keverne, E. B. (1982). Effects of rank and novel females on behaviour and hormones in male talapoin monkeys. *Physiol. Behav.* **28,** 995–1005.

Yodyingyuad, U., de la Riva, C., Abbott, D. H., Herbert, J., and Keverne, E. B. (1985). Relationship between dominance hierarchy, cerebrospinal fluid levels of amine transmitter metabolites (5-hydroxyindole acetic acid and homovanillic acid) and plasma cortisol in monkeys. *Neuroscience* **16,** 851–858.

Zieglgansberger, W. (1984). Opioid actions on mammalian spinal neurons. *Int. Rev. Neurobiol.* **25,** 243–76.

Zuckerman, S. (1932). "The Social Life of Monkeys and Apes." Kegan Paul, London.

The Role of Parasites in Sexual Selection: Current Evidence and Future Directions

MARLENE ZUK

DEPARTMENT OF BIOLOGY
UNIVERSITY OF CALIFORNIA, RIVERSIDE
RIVERSIDE, CALIFORNIA 92521

I. INTRODUCTION

A basic problem in sexual selection is the evolution of secondary sexual characters, such as the classic example of the peacock's tail or the more humble case of the croaking frog. These traits appear to be costly in several respects; they may be physiologically or energetically expensive to produce, requiring expenditure of extra calories or the procurement of particular compounds such as carotenoids. Once developed, they may be detrimental to the viability of their bearer by reducing agility or increasing conspicuousness to predators. In social interactions, the possession of such ornaments may invite competition from other conspecific individuals that may likewise interfere with daily activities.

Nonetheless, morphological and behavioral secondary sex characters are abundant in nature. Efforts to explain the proximate and ultimate causes responsible for their development, and the mating patterns with which they are found, have been at least as prolific. After a period of doubt lasting with a few exceptions for nearly a century, from Darwin's era to the 1960s, most evolutionary biologists are now convinced that many of the elaborate showy displays in males are the result of female preference for them. Likewise, in those relatively fewer species in which females have more colorful or flamboyant attributes, the traits are supposed to be the result of male mate choice.

Having reached that point, the next question is what females prefer and why. How these preferences might be manifested and what they might "mean" in terms of the male's qualities other than simply possessing the trait in question continue to be the focus of much research effort. Models for the evolution of male ornaments can be divided into two groups, although the dichotomy may be misleading because, like most dichotomies, it implies that if one alternative is true the other must necessarily be false.

The first group consists of the "arbitrary" models first proposed by Fisher

39

(1958) and later expanded and further explored by Lande (1981), Kirkpatrick (1982), Pomiankowski (1988), and others. Fisher suggested that mating preferences could develop because they increased mating success of offspring. Both Fisher and the more recent models suggest that although female choice has driven the evolution of exaggerated male ornaments, their elaboration has come about because of genetic correlation between the genes for the trait in males and genes for preferring such a trait in females. Exactly what the female prefers, whether a long tail, a red patch of skin, or a noise like a cement mixer, has no significance beyond the fact that the female, perhaps through sensory predisposition (Ryan and Rand, 1990) or other factors, prefers it. The trait signifies nothing about the viability of the male in question.

A problem with many of the arbitrary models for the evolution of ornaments is that they do not take into account the possibility that female choice itself may be costly (Pomiankowski, 1987). If females must pay in time, energy, or other currency for the privilege of choosing among several males, sexual selection is unlikely to simply drift along in a neutral equilibrium, balancing the degree of female preference with the degree of trait development (Pomiankowski, 1987, 1988).

This combination of an expensive process with an expensive character has led many researchers to suggest that, at least in some circumstances, females may be choosing traits that signify male quality rather than on an arbitrary basis. Because many of the species that exhibit these showy traits have no male parental care, the quality so indicated is assumed to be genetic; females are in effect shopping for "good genes" to pass on to their offspring (Arnold, 1983). Secondary sex characters are therefore expected to be indicators of fitness in the male that bears them.

The notion that female choice for gaudy traits like peacock trains is adaptive has intuitive appeal—some might say dangerously so, given the paucity of empirical support—and the idea has appeared in various forms over the past two decades. Zahavi's (1975) handicap model proposed that males with elaborate ornaments were showing their ability to survive despite such encumbrances and, by implication, must therefore be extremely fit. Despite subsequent squabbles over the operation of the handicap principle (Maynard Smith, 1976; Kirkpatrick, 1986a; Pomiankowski, 1987; Grafen, 1990a,b), versions of the idea that ornaments were only able to be produced by robust individuals able to sequester nutrients, fend off predators, or resist disease have been proposed several times (Kodric-Brown and Brown, 1984; Nur and Hasson, 1984; Hamilton and Zuk, 1982). For the notion to work, female preference must come to emphasize signs of health or vigor that cannot be faked (because they are costly to produce), and those signs are then elaborated by males, perhaps in the short run via arbitrary processes such as Fisher's runaway sexual selection.

This last suggestion, that ornaments are indicators of health and resistance to parasites, is the subject of this article. It is an idea that has attracted increasing interest since it was proposed by W. D. Hamilton and myself in 1982, and it has been the subject of several reviews (Read, 1988; Moller, 1990a,b; McLennan and Brooks, 1992). Here, I will examine the role of parasites in sexual selection by providing a review of current research in the area, but I will do so in a different and somewhat broader context than usual. The host–parasite genetic interactions that provided a rationale for continued female choice in our original hypothesis are only part of the impetus for the current parasite–sexual-selection enthusiasm. The rest comes from a variety of disciplines, including population and community ecology, endocrinology, immunology, and animal behavior, with aspects of each pointing in complementary directions. I will discuss the original predictions based on our hypothesis and suggest some new directions for fruitful research by placing them in a context that asks, far more generally than we first did, "Why parasites?"

II. Original Predictions of the Hamilton–Zuk Hypothesis

If females choose males based on evidence of good health or vigor, a continuing source of heritable genetic variation in fitness must be present in the population (Falconer, 1981); otherwise, the genes for this vigor will eventually go to fixation, and males with long tails will only differ from those with short tails because of nonheritable environmental factors. Parasites and other disease-causing organisms, such as bacteria or viruses, can provide such fitness variation because they can evolve rapidly and dynamically with their hosts (Eshel and Hamilton, 1984; Hamilton, 1982). This capacity for antagonistic coevolution is also the key to several models for the evolution of sexual reproduction itself and was the original impetus for the hypothesis.

If parasites are critical in the evolution of secondary sex characters, two types of predictions can be made: (1) how pressure from parasites has resulted in differing intensities of sexual selection among different species, giving rise to variation in the degree of development of these secondary sex characters; and (2) how female choice operates within a species to select for males most resistant to prevalent parasites.

In our original article, we suggested that intense pressure from parasites makes the need for female choice of resistant mates more acute. Preference for the ornaments that indicate this resistance then leads to greater showiness in more parasitized species. The factors initially creating the differences in parasite level (whether intensity, burden, or prevalence) are left open. Within species, the inability of a male to resist disease should also prevent him from producing the costly ornament preferred by females. Thus, parasite-ridden males will be drab, rather than showy.

In the following section, I discuss each of these predictions, examining new studies and the controversy surrounding the first, and placing the second in a context that will hopefully allow us to distinguish the Hamilton-Zuk hypothesis from other, more general ideas about the effect of parasites on host ecology and behavior.

III.   INTERSPECIFIC TESTS

Comparative analyses such as those required to test the first prediction of the hypothesis about parasites and sexual selection have several advantages. First, as Ridley (1983) points out, the comparative method may be our only opportunity to test general hypotheses about adaptation; we simply cannot tell much about the evolution of a structure or behavior by examining it in a single species. Second, by using the many different manifestations of a trait in different species, whether the trait is parasite burden or length of tail feathers, the likelihood of special cases misleading conclusions is minimized. Third, it is possible to suggest relationships that are tailored to the prediction, but that are made without foreknowledge of the general trends that may be present, giving some of the advantages of a "blind" experiment. Finally and pragmatically, in our case at least the data were already present in the vast literature about parasites in netted or trapped birds from all over the world, obviously collected without any regard for our hypothesis.

Along with these strengths, of course, come weak points. The very disregard for a particular theory that makes the data so objective may also render them unsuitable, if potential confounding variables are ignored. Sample sizes must be very large to compensate for the statistical "noise" that accompanies such broad surveys. And as numerous authors have pointed out, comparative analyses may be complicated by variation in recency of shared ancestry among the taxa studied; does a pattern exist because it arose independently in several different groups, or did it arise once, with subsequent speciation events merely pseudo-replicating the relationship (Pagel and Harvey, 1988; Felsenstein, 1985; Clutton-Brock and Harvey, 1984)?

A.   PARASITES AND PLUMAGE BRIGHTNESS

Probably because of the plethora of published data available, most comparative tests of the Hamilton-Zuk hypothesis have been done on birds. Birds are also often candidates for sexual selection studies, because being visual creatures themselves they attract the attention of likewise sensitive human vision, and they seem to vary intelligibly in showiness.

In our original attempt to see whether the hypothesis was worth pursuing, I scored North American passerines on a scale of 1 to 6, with 1 being very drab and 6 very showy, before seeing the list of blood parasites associated with each species (Hamilton and Zuk, 1982). I consulted several field guides but relied heavily on experience with many of the species in the field. A colleague who was similarly unfamiliar with the parasite list ranked the songs of all the species, working mainly from memory. A positive association was found between parasite prevalence (the proportion of individuals sampled that were infected) and both male brightness and the complexity of male song (Hamilton and Zuk, 1982).

Although provoking interest in doing further research on the topic, as was the intent, this analysis was rough in several respects. It ignored possible confounding effects of ecological variables such as nest height, diet, and flock size, and it did not take into account the problem of taxonomic nonindependence mentioned earlier, because bird species from all families were pooled. A subsequent analysis by Read (1987) examined a dataset on European birds, in addition to reexamining the North American data, and used a method for scoring showiness devised by Baker and Parker (1979) to rank the European species. Read (1987) also controlled for ecological variables as well as taxonomic effects, and found that, if anything, the correlation between parasites and showiness was strengthened by these refinements.

Yet another reanalysis, however, was not so supportive. Read and Harvey (1989a) had a group of colleagues rescore both the North American and European birds; using these rankings, the parasite–brightness relationship, though still positive, became nonsignificant in North American species once taxonomic effects were taken into account. They also noted an unexpected relationship between sample size and the strength of the correlation, with rarer species supporting the hypothesis more strongly than species sampled in greater abundance (Read and Harvey, 1989b).

Other studies have largely supported the hypothesis, although the results are sometimes complicated when methods for determining both the parasite data and extent of sexually selected character development are dissected carefully. A survey of Neotropical birds using a different statistical analysis and subdividing the species into migrants and residents upheld the prediction that resident species, because of their greater capacity for forming close coadaptations with parasites, should show the relationship between parasites and brightness more strongly than would migrant species (Zuk, 1991). Several studies of both endoparasites and ectoparasites in New Guinea birds used data specifically collected to test the hypothesis, rather than relying on previously published surveys (Pruett-Jones et al., 1990, 1991; Pruett-Jones and Pruett-Jones, 1991). Controlling for phylogenetic effects, diet, foraging height, and sample size, and using several different measures of parasite "load" as well as both a "brightness" and a "showiness" measure, Pruett-Jones and colleagues found that most of the predicted positive relationships between parasites and sexually selected traits remained, although one measure of parasitemia (parasite intensity, or the number of different species of parasite harbored by an individual) did not yield significant correlations, and "showiness" was a better predictor of parasites than was "brightness." Weatherhead *et al.* (1991) used a method for scoring coloration that is similar to that of Baker and Parker (1979) to examine blood parasites in 10 North American warbler species; parasitemias were unrelated to the rankings, but as the authors themselves point out, the small sample sizes diminish the power of their test.

B.   Parasites and Acoustic Signals

Only two studies to date have looked for patterns in parasites associated with nonvisual characters. Our original study, as mentioned earlier, pointed to the same relationship between song complexity and parasites in North American birds as we had found using appearance of the birds (Hamilton and Zuk, 1982). After controlling for phylogenetic effects, however, Read and Weary (1990) found that this relationship was no longer significant, and an analysis of European species' songs, using temporal and structural measures rather than subjective rankings, did not reveal any relationship between these measures and parasite load.

C.   Parasites and Sexual Dichromatism in Fishes

Ward (1988, 1989) examined parasite diversity (the number of different genera of parasites) in species of British and Irish freshwater fish ranked according to the degree of difference in coloration between males and females. Across 24 species from 10 families, a positive relationship between diversity and dichromatism was found (Ward, 1988). In a more detailed analysis of parasitism in fishes from isolated bodies of water that contained species from at least four families, the correlation also held (Ward, 1988, 1989). Members of the cyprinid family were least likely to have more parasites when sexual dichromatism was high, perhaps because these fish live in turbid water and visual cues may be less important in mate choice (Ward, 1988, 1989).

D.   Conclusions and Future Directions
for Interspecific Tests

The initial flurry of attempts to test the interspecific hypothesis of Hamilton and Zuk (1982) has settled into the inevitable conclusion that things are more complicated than they seemed at first glance. Despite the controversy over matters of analysis and methodology (Read and Harvey, 1989a,b; Zuk, 1989; Dox, 1989; Hamilton and Zuk, 1989), a large-scale and previously unexpected relationship remains. A pattern of "more parasites" (measured in a variety of ways) occurring with "greater showiness" (measured in a variety of ways) has been detected both in fishes and in birds from four continents spanning a wide range of taxa. This pattern, however, is complex, and elucidating it further, in hopes of understanding the process giving rise to it, will require information at several levels.

1. Promising Groups for Study

First, the arena of testing must be widened to include more organisms besides birds. It is undeniable that birds are conspicuous, possess sexually selected characters (though which characters those may be remains questionable in some cases), and are subject to a wide variety of parasites. Indeed, these features, together with the voluminous available data on unambiguously identified species, drew us to make a preliminary test of our hypothesis on birds in the first place. But as Pruett-Jones et al. (1990, 1991) and others have pointed out, factors such as the existence of parental care in many avian groups makes evaluation of "good genes" models of sexual selection difficult, because females may be choosing males on the basis of direct rather than genetic benefits.

Pruett-Jones et al., unlike most other researchers, collected comparative data specifically for testing the interspecific prediction of the Hamilton-Zuk hypothesis. In so doing, they noted a confounding factor common to all cross-sectional analyses that sample at a single point in time: Parasite levels vary depending on the time at which individual hosts are sampled. This variation has been noted in avian parasites before (Foster, 1969; Weatherhead and Bennett, 1992), but was especially apparent to researchers collecting their own data in the field. The second need, therefore, is for more studies to collect parasite and sexual selection data for the purpose of testing the hypothesis, rather than solely relying on previously published work. The result will hopefully be more uniform sampling, both temporally and with regard to sample sizes of species, the use of an appropriate range of species having differing degrees of showiness, and attention to the most appropriate parasites from the point of view of their effect on the host.

2. Gathering Data about Parasites

This last point, the selection of parasites to study, brings up a problem that all naive behavioral ecologists, including myself, are distressed to realize when they begin this type of work, and that is the paucity of information about the natural history of virtually any pathogenic agent in any natural population of animals. Because parasites have been so little studied in an ecological context (c.f., following paragraph), it can be difficult to know which parasites might be most appropriate for testing the Hamilton-Zuk hypothesis. Even such basic information as whether or not a particular parasite can affect juvenile survival or female fecundity, for example, is often unavailable. Yet, information about the effect of pathogens on the ecology and behavior of their hosts is essential, and for more reasons than merely testing the hypothesis. If parasitological groundwork is required, then it should be sought out.

3. In the Eyes of the Beholder

Equally as important with understanding what being parasitized means in an ecological context is an understanding of what "showiness" really means, not to the investigator but to the animal in question. As Endler and Lyles (1989) point out, bright green parrots may be conspicuous when held in the hand or viewed against the white pages of a field guide, but as anyone who has tried to spot them in a tropical forest knows, they are cryptic in their natural habitat. Other physical conditions such as the quality and direction of light or the time of day when an animal is displaying may also influence the appearance of coloration (J. A. Endler, personal communication).

Coloration alone is almost certainly not the only criterion used by females in choosing males; morphological ornaments such as crests or elongated tails have been demonstrated to be significant predictors of male mating success in several bird species (Andersson, 1982; Moller, 1988, 1990b). Any attempt to evaluate species for the degree of development of sexually selected characters, therefore, needs to take these traits into account. Without studies of mate choice in individual species, it is difficult, however, to know just how much "credit" to assign the different characters. For these reasons, progress in understanding the interspecific prediction of the parasite–sexual-selection hypothesis will best be made in tandem with studies of mate choice within species; as we will discuss, work on the roles of individual characters may lead to insights about why some traits—testosterone-dependent ones, for example, or labile traits with "memory" of the condition of their bearer—are more important than others when females make mating decisions.

Ranking of species by human observers to compare the presumed intensity of sexual selection is clearly a subjective process, perhaps unavoidably so. The use of standardized field guides, although seeming to overcome some of the subjectivity, presents problems of its own. It may be difficult for nonbirders to understand how thoroughly a representation in a bird book may look "nothing like" the same species seen in the field, much to the frustration of the novice. Experience with the species in the field might thus be an asset in scoring. The Baker and Parker (1979) style of evaluating degree of sexual selection by dividing the body of the bird into segments and adding scores together may also provide a useful alternative technique.

Finally, any method of visually evaluating coloration has the flaw that human beings have unknowingly learned to live with: even "normal" human color vision is very variable (Neitz and Jacobs, 1986). It deteriorates markedly with age, reaching a peak of acuity in the early twenties but rapidly worsening by the time many biologists are interested in testing hypotheses about sexual selection. Although this does not imply the necessity for hiring a team of adolescents to score birds, it suggests both that repeated measures over a period of time by the same individual or by different-aged individuals at the same time should not be expected to be consistent, and, more importantly, that we are unlikely to be seeing with a bird's eye no matter when we examine the animals.

A return to my first suggestion, that more attention be paid to animals other than birds, may also provide a partial way out of this difficulty. One of the many reasons why acoustically signaling organisms are such good subjects for behavioral research is that sounds and vibrations readily lend themselves to quantitative analysis and can be captured permanently on tape recordings with fewer of the ambiguities associated with photography of visual signals. Comparative studies of parasites in the many animal taxa that use acoustic signals as the major means of attracting mates (e.g., frogs, orthopteran insects) are at the moment nonexistent, but could both increase the generality of conclusions about the relationship between parasites and sexually selected characters in groups other than birds and eliminate the need for quite so subjective a method for evaluating "showiness."

Problems would still remain, of course; although acoustic signals may be categorized in terms of many temporal and structural elements, an equivalent in kHz to "brilliant scarlet" as opposed to "dull buff" is not immediately obvious. As Kroodsma (1982) and Read and Weary (1990) discuss, possible measures in birds include song duration, song rate, and repertoire size. Sometimes, as with coloration or morphological ornaments, intraspecific studies may suggest the variables of importance in sexual selection of acoustic signals (Searcy and Andersson, 1986; Ryan, 1983; Simmons, 1988; Bailey *et al.*, 1990). In numerous anuran amphibians and singing insects, the energetics of calling have been sufficiently well-studied to permit classification of signals or parts of signals by the energy required to produce them, a meaningful component if females are indeed selecting males on the basis of signals that indicate vigor (Prestwich and Walker, 1981; Taigen and Wells, 1985). Overall, an examination of more acoustically signaling animals, especially those that rely mainly or solely on these signals for mate attraction, should help shed light not only on the Hamilton-Zuk hypothesis but on the meaning of sexual selection on these different sensory modalities. Perhaps "ornaments" in the classic sense of long tails and brilliant plumage do not have counterparts in pheromones, for instance, but the contrast has never been investigated.

4. Taxonomic Facts and Artifacts

The final caveat to interspecific tests, whether on visual, acoustic, or olfactory signals (the latter being completely neglected by investigators) is discussed by Read (1987, 1988) and echoed by numerous other biologists (Felsenstein, 1985;

Read and Harvey, 1989a; Clutton-Brock and Harvey, 1984; Read and Weary, 1990). This complication is, as previously mentioned, the nonindependence of species when each one is used as an individual data point; if a speciose taxon acquired a predisposition to parasites before the speciation events occurred and is also brightly colored, an association between parasites and brightness will emerge as an artifact of the different levels of species richness among taxa if all species are compared.

Taking this difficulty into account usually involves some mechanism for examining species separately within higher taxa such as family or order, or comparing across these higher levels rather than across species alone (Read, 1987; Read and Harvey, 1989b; Pruett-Jones et al., 1990, 1992; Read and Weary, 1990; Zuk, 1991). Sometimes controlling for the taxonomic complication results in weaker correlations; other times it leaves the relationship unaffected. Although some authors take the attitude that a relationship that is more apparent at some levels of taxonomy than others is an artifact, or a misleading complexity that must be "partialled out," this view risks throwing out valuable information for a reason that has likewise attracted the attention of evolutionary biologists interested in sexual selection, albeit in a different context than the role of parasites in mate choice.

The reason is that speciation and sexual selection are not entirely separate processes, as recognized by Lande (1981), West-Eberhard (1979, 1983), and, indeed, early researchers in both topics (Mayr, 1963, 1972; Dobzhansky, 1937). Their relationship is not straightforward, to be sure, but more speciose groups may have gotten that way through the same processes that favor sexual selection, whether those processes include parasites or not. Many families with members exhibiting bizarre and extravagant sexually selected characters are also species-rich, including, for example, bowerbirds and birds of paradise (Diamond, 1972) and Hawaiian Drosophila (Carson et al., 1970). How these groups arose is not clear, but rather than being a confounding factor, sexual selection is part of the evolutionary process. A correlation that exists across species from several families, but that weakens or disappears when families are examined alone, is not necessarily a spurious correlation. Phylogeny must certainly be taken into account in comparative studies, but not to the extent of throwing the baby out with the bathwater. McLennan and Brooks (1991) provide a stimulating discussion of the macroevolutionary implications of parasite-mediated sexual selection.

IV. Why Parasites?

When attempting to test the intraspecific prediction of the Hamilton-Zuk hypothesis, that females should prefer healthy, resistant males as indicated by their well-developed secondary sex characters, researchers are immediately faced with a problem. Even if the results of a test are consistent with the prediction, they are prone to ambiguity, because a relationship between health or vigor and increased mating success can come about for several different reasons, including but not limited to our hypothesis. Indeed, one of the reasons the hypothesis may be getting the attention that it has lies in the belated realization by behavioral ecologists that parasites in general may be important influences on host behavior and evolution.

In this section, therefore, I will first examine in a general sense the rationale for looking at parasites in the context of sexual selection. I will then discuss the intraspecific tests of our hypothesis that have been done to date in this framework and attempt to evaluate their ability to test, not the idea that parasites are important in host reproductive behavior, but that selective pressure from parasites has led to the evolution of sexual ornaments that display disease resistance.

A. BECAUSE IT IS TIME

This consideration may sound a bit facile, but in fact it is not. For a long time, parasitologists were alone in their view that parasites were important influences on host ecology and behavior and that the life history patterns of parasites were more than weird and often distasteful curiosities. Ecologists have traditionally assumed that because they saw their study animals eating and avoiding predation, but not usually obviously fighting off infections, food and avoiding being eaten were the main factors of importance in the animals' lives.

In the past few years, however, ecologists have become increasingly aware of the effect of parasites on the population biology of their hosts (Dobson and Hudson, 1986; Hudson, 1986; Scott and Dobson, 1989; Toft and Karter, 1990). In taxa as diverse as beetles, mice, snails, and birds, parasites have been shown to depress host population growth rates and sometimes fecundity relative to unparasitized populations. For example, a laboratory population of *Tribolium* beetles was consistently smaller when individuals were infected with a cestode parasite (Keymer, 1981). Similar effects may be found in populations naturally infected with parasites, although determining that the infection is indeed causing the depression in growth may be difficult when other variables are uncontrolled (Dobson and Hudson, 1986; Scott and Dobson, 1989).

Other suggestions that parasites are important ecological forces come from studies on how parasites might alter the behavior of their host to make their own transmission and reproduction more likely (Holmes and Bethel, 1972). Moore (1983, 1984) shows that acanthocephalan parasites using isopods as intermediate hosts appear to make infected isopods behave in a manner that exposes them to predation by foraging birds, the definitive host. More general aspects of host behavior that may function to avoid infection by parasites include grooming or preening, alteration of foraging or daily movement patterns, and nest site selection (Hart, 1990). Indeed, Møller (1989) cautioned that use of nest boxes to study cavity-nesting birds may significantly alter results compared with studies of populations using natural holes, because ectoparasites are reduced in the boxes, but under less artificial circumstances have important effects on fitness.

In addition, a wide range of attributes that influence reproductive success, such as behavioral dominance and juvenile growth rate, have been demonstrated to be affected by parasites in both domestic and wild populations of animals (Freeland, 1981; Hart, 1990; Zuk, 1987c; Tinsley, 1989). Until recently, many sublethal parasites were dismissed as unimportant because they did not have the demonstrable economic effect of more dramatic pathogens; it is becoming clear, however, that debilitating pathogens can have significant effects on evolution of their hosts. As Ewald (1983) discusses, the popular belief that long-standing parasitic associations are usually benign is being challenged both by careful work on parameters such as fecundity, which may not be immediately apparent to investigators, and by theoretical considerations that selection will, in fact, often favor pathogens of moderate or extreme virulence, even in the long term.

Finally, sexually transmitted diseases, most recently of course AIDS, have all too tragically reminded us that avoidance of such diseases, and the ability to screen prospective mates for the likelihood of infectivity, may be a crucial factor in sexual interactions. With this awareness, some animal behavior may be reexamined in a new light. For example, many species of birds have a characteristic feather-shaking behavior immediately following copulation; this is especially typical of waterfowl, but occurs in other groups as well. It is possible that this vigorous activity, or other stereotyped postcopulatory cleansing behaviors, serves to dislodge pathogens such as the numerous ectoparasites such as lice that cluster around the cloaca and to which sexual partners are obviously exposed. Research into behavior that serves to reduce transmission of pathogens during sexual contact is only just beginning, but should prove fruitful (Hart et al., 1987; Hart, 1990).

Indeed, the fact that birds, as well as many other vertebrate taxa, possess a cloaca, into which both the gastrointestinal and genitourinary tracts empty, suggests that exposure to gut parasites may also be a danger during copulation. It would be interesting to compare parasite transmission and parasite diversity, as well as some aspects of mating behavior, in groups with and without a cloaca, testing predictions about the relationship between sexual selection, parasites, and possession of a cloaca. Transovarian transmission of pathogens is common in insects (Ewald and Schubert, 1989), but neither it nor its counterpart of sperm-borne disease has been looked for in light of the behavioral ecology of the host.

Most of these considerations of how parasites might be important in host ecology and behavior arose independently of Hamilton's and my ideas about why parasites might influence mate choice. The research previously summarized does suggest that workers from a variety of disciplines and with a variety of viewpoints have created a hospitable atmosphere for the consideration of how para-sites might affect behavioral ecology. One could almost be accused of stating the painfully obvious for asserting that parasites are important in sexual selection; they are so clearly important in virtually every other aspect of behavioral ecology that they must be considered in mate choice as well. We have been neglecting parasites for too long, and it is time—maybe past time—to bring them into current thought about evolution and ecology.

B. HOST–PARASITE GENETIC INTERACTIONS

Parasites do have unique capabilities when it comes to genetic interactions with their hosts, and the potential for these interactions to result in frequency-dependent selection originally suggested that parasites might influence sexual selection as well as the evolution of sexual reproduction itself. In both selection for sex and selection for female choice in sexual selection, the host is involved in so-called evolutionary arms races with the parasite. Analogous to the Red Queen hypothesis, which postulates an advantage for sexual reproduction, genetically determined host–parasite interactions in sexual selection can lead to permanent fitness variation in the genotype of the preferred male (Seger, 1985). This sce-nario, although plausible for other biotic interactions such as predator–prey or plant–herbivore ones, is particularly likely in parasitic relationships because parasites are frequently specific to only one or a very few hosts, setting the stage for fine-tuned antagonisms.

Hamilton (1982) and Eshel and Hamilton (1984), among others, suggest that such antagonisms are very likely to occur in nature and that some version of the handicap principle, especially one using resistance to parasites to generate the dynamic genetic interactions, is feasible. Other theoretical work is equivocal on this point; some theoreticians suggest that the circumstances needed for operation of limit cycles that would account for mate choice under these conditions are too specialized to be of much importance or that the handicap principle in any form simply cannot maintain female choice for ornamented males (Maynard Smith, 1976, 1978; Kirkpatrick, 1986a,b, 1987). Others, by adding some not unrealistic assumptions or conditions such as frequency-dependent costs to female choice or paternal investment, find that the likelihood of stable oscillations of host and parasite genotypes resulting in selection for exaggerated male phenotypes is quite high (Pomiankowski, 1987, 1988; Heywood, 1989).

The discussion about the theoretical plausibility of host–parasite genetic in-teractions maintaining sexual selection is continuing. Although determination of the parameters more or less favorable to generating such interactions is impor-tant, in a sense it does not matter whether cyclic genetic interactions are by themselves sufficient to drive the sexual selection process. They may indeed provide a rationale for continued mate choice, and may act along with other processes such as runaway selection. But parasites are likely to be significant associates of sexual selection in any event, because parasites, in a manner unforeseen by Hamilton and myself at the outset, critically influence two of the major contributors to male ornaments. Attention to the mechanisms by which parasites exert their effect on sexual behavior and morphology is likely to prove a more fruitful means of understanding their role in evolution.

C. PARASITE-MEDIATED MECHANISMS
FOR ORNAMENT PRODUCTION

1. Carotenoid Pigmentation

Carotenoid pigments are responsible for the red and yellow colors seen in many vertebrate and invertebrate animals (Goodwin, 1950). These pigments come from food, rather than being produced by the metabolism; thus, although the distribution of carotenoids on the organism's body is generally inherited (Brush and Siefried, 1968), the intensity of coloration depends on the diet (Goodwin, 1950; Brush, 1978). Carotenoid-pigmented characters, therefore, are condition-dependent, not absolute, and they may play a special role in sexual selection (Kodric-Brown and Brown, 1984; Andersson, 1986).

A study of house finches (*Carpodacus mexicanus*) in Michigan (Hill, 1990) suggests that females may pay close attention to these characters, and argues for increased examination of carotenoid-based secondary sex characters. Male house finches vary considerably in the intensity of the reddish coloration on the breast and head feathers, even within age classes (Hill, 1990). In both field and laboratory work, Hill (1990) showed that females preferred the reddest of four males, whether the coloration occurred as part of natural variation in intensity or was the result of experimental lightening and reddening of the feathers using hair dyes (Fig. 1).

Two implications of this research are relevant here. The first is that females used a condition-dependent trait to make mating decisions, one that indicates a certain level of competence or quality on the part of the male. Condition-dependent traits, because they are costly, prevent "cheating" on the part of a male with bright colors but low fitness. In the context of interest, "fitness" is resistance to parasites. The resistance itself, which is favored by selection, is genetically fixed, not facultative. The trait indicating this fitness, however— bright plumage coloration in this case—is only expressed when its bearer is in good enough condition to do so.

This brings us to the second interesting implication, which is that carotenoids and carotenoid-pigmented structures are particularly affected by parasites. Poultry scientists and breeders have known for many years that skin and comb color in fowl were pigmented with carotenoids obtained in feed, and that the amount of carotenoid pigment observed was related to factors such as fecundity (Palmer and

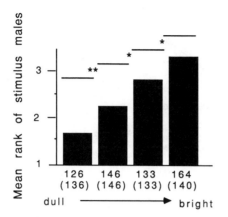

FIG. 1. Response of female house finches to males of different plumage coloration in experimental choice trials. Color variation among males was created with hair dyes and lighteners. Premanipulation plumage scores (derived from adding coloration scores of plumage from seven body regions) are given in parentheses below postmanipulation scores. Lines above the bars indicate which males share statistically similar ranks, where successive levels are statistically different from one another. $* p < .05$, $** p < .01$. $N = 18$. (From Hill, 1990.)

Kempster, 1919a,b,c; Stone et al., 1971). In chickens infected with coccidia, protozoan parasites that can cause severe juvenile mortality, coloration of these carotenoid-dependent tissues was lighter than in uninfected birds, even though the diseased individuals received the same amount of dietary carotenoids as healthy chickens (Ruff et al., 1974). The mechanism by which pathogens interfere with carotenoid metabolism is not fully understood, but the phenomenon appears to be true for parasites other than coccidia (Bird, 1952; Henderson, 1951). In red jungle fowl, females preferred males with more brilliantly colored eyes and combs, both carotenoid-dependent traits and both influenced by nematode gut parasites (Zuk et al., 1990a). Several studies of fishes have shown the influence of carotenoid-derived skin coloration on female choice, with females often preferring the more intensely colored male (Kodric-Brown, 1989; Endler, 1983).

The interaction of these factors of disease and diet to produce condition-dependent ornamental traits is an extremely interesting area and one that deserves more study. If females use a condition-dependent trait such as a carotenoid-pigmented skin patch or feather color as a basis for mate choice, but these characters can only be produced by parasite-resistant males who also obtain the appropriate diet, the females may be getting both a healthy male with so-called "good genes" and one who either knows where to forage, has a good territory, or

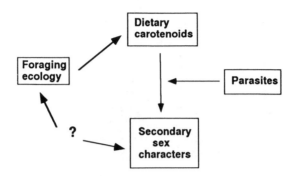

FIG. 2. Hypothetical relationships between carotenoid-pigmented characters, foraging ecology, and parasites. Highly pigmented secondary sex characters may result from either resistance to pathogens, superior ability to sequester dietary carotenoids, or some additive or compensatory combination of the two.

otherwise possesses the capability of transforming carotenoids in the environment into signals (Fig. 2).

It remains to be seen if these two contributors, foraging ecology and parasite resistance, have a compensatory or perhaps additive relationship. Will a male who is exceptionally good at foraging but still susceptible to parasites, for example, be as successful in attracting females as one who is above average in both capacities or one who is exceedingly healthy but not as good at obtaining carotenoids in the diet? At this stage, the nature of the relationships in Fig. 2 can only be speculative, but the potential exists for new links between such previously disparate topics as diet choice and mate choice, with parasites acting as a go-between. In any event, it is important to note that the operation of this mechanism by no means obviates the operation of Hamilton's and my model; it presents a way in which sexual ornaments may be influenced by parasites, but not the reasons behind the process occurring.

2. Testosterone, Ornaments, and the Immune System

A different twist on the concept of condition-dependent traits comes from the relationship between, not diet and parasites, but sex hormones and parasites. Epidemiologists have documented many times that males in several vertebrate species, including humans, show a higher incidence of several kinds of parasites and diseases (Alexander and Stimson, 1989; Bundy, 1989; Zuk, 1990). Sometimes this difference may be attributed to sociological or behavioral differences between the sexes, but much of it is also the result of what may be from the male point of view a rather cruel joke: testosterone, the primary male sex hormone, has a suppressive effect on the immune system, making males more vulnerable to infection.

Testosterone, of course, is required for the production of many morphological sexual characters such as rooster combs and the antlers of deer as well as behavioral attributes important in mating success such as increased territorial behavior during the breeding season (Hutchison and Hutchison, 1983; Alcock, 1979). A study of reindeer, which are both highly sexually dimorphic and highly sexually competitive, revealed an interesting sex difference in infestation with warble flies, a parasite of the muscles and skin that forms nodules visible in the hide of harvested animals (Folstad et al., 1989). A comparison of intact males, castrated males, and females from a population in northern Norway showed that the intact, hormone-producing males suffered from a significantly higher level of larval fly infestation than did either of the other two classes (Fig. 3); the potentially confounding factor of larger male body size presenting a larger target to the flies was controlled for by the use of both intact and castrated males. Folstad et al. (1989) suggest that the difference occurs because the male immune system is compromised by the presence of high levels of circulating testosterone. Other evidence for testosterone-mediated susceptibility is discussed in Folstad and Karter (1992).

Similar sex differences, either directly or indirectly demonstrated to be hormone-mediated, may be seen in several parasitic diseases, including some nematode infections and Chagas' disease (Alexander and Stimson, 1989). Lowered immune competence appears to be the price paid for the sexually selected traits associated with testosterone.

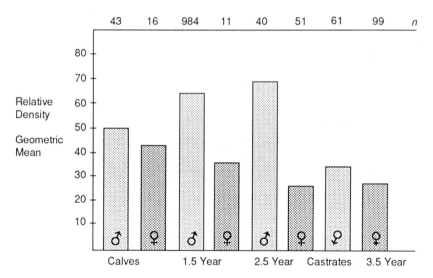

FIG. 3. Geometric mean numbers of warble fly larvae (*Hypoderma tarandi*) in hides of male, female, and castrated male reindeer.

Male epigamic characters and the immune system thus appear to be inextricably entwined. Because the immune system is of course essential in fighting off disease, parasites and epigamic characters are likewise related by a mechanism previously unconsidered. How this dependence manifests itself, and what, then, epigamic characters are "telling" us is a matter of considerable interest but with few concrete data.

As suggested by Folstad and Karter (1992), testosterone level and the immune responses and ornaments that depend on this hormone may be regulated by a feedback loop in response to parasites. According to this view, male ornaments such as antlers and showy plumage are "honest" signals of a male's ability to withstand the obligatory immunosuppressive effects of high testosterone titers (Fig. 4). Cheating is unlikely because the cost of doing so, of presenting showy characters when viability or fitness is low, is an automatic loss of immune function that makes the male too vulnerable to pathogenic effects of parasites for it to be maintained. Males with highly developed secondary sex characters are therefore indicating their capacity to resist the effects of prevalent parasites, even on a compromised immune system, and are expressing a version of a handicap.

This idea does not distinguish between the effect of genetic immunity and that of acquired immunity, the latter being the result of facultative cell-mediated and humoral responses on the part of the host to invasion by a foreign substance. Testosterone presumably affects this second aspect of immunity, because genetic resistance or susceptibility is an inherited all-or-none phenomenon. How is it that some males are better able to afford expenditure of energy and deal with the effects of immune suppression?

Perhaps females benefit most by mating with males that are genetically resistant to parasites. Males with this "bonus" resistance are spared the effort of mounting as complete an acquired immune response as are males that lack such

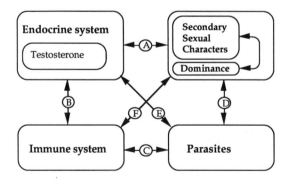

Fig. 4. Predicted interaction of sex hormones and the immune system and their effect on male secondary sexual characters. (From Folstad and Karter, 1992.)

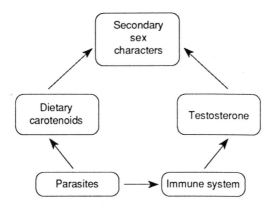

Fig. 5. Summary of combined effects of testosterone and dietary carotenoids on the production of secondary sexual characters, as mediated by parasites.

genetic capability. Females choosing such males are therefore gaining heritable benefits of parasite resistance for their offspring as well as the more immediate benefits of mating with a vigorous male. This heritable fitness gain is of course the advantage to female choice suggested in Hamilton and Zuk (1982), and one that the process may rely on. The relative contributions of genetic and acquired immune responses to the ability of males to withstand pathogens while manufacturing testosterone are again unknown, as is the degree to which corticosteroids, the "stress hormones," mediate their effects (Sapolsky, 1987; A. Cockburn, personal communication). The connections between both parasite-mediated carotenoid pigments and testosterone-mediated immune function, and the effect of both on ornaments, clearly warrant future study (Fig. 5).

V. Intraspecific Tests Reconsidered

An intraspecific relationship of some sort between parasites and sexual selection seems, given the variety of sources pointing to the importance of pathogens in host biology, virtually inevitable. The nature of that relationship, and its reliance on genetic benefits to females choosing resistant males, rather than on a general but vague notion that parasites must be important, now needs to be elucidated. The intraspecific tests of the Hamilton and Zuk hypothesis, summarized in Table I, have attempted such an analysis, with varying success.

As Read (1988) and Møller (1990a) pointed out, intraspecific tests should meet or test the assumptions of the hypothesis and then assess the prediction that females shun a less ornamented male whose shabbiness reflects his susceptibility and parasite burden in favor of a showy resistant male. Many, indeed most, of the

TABLE I
RESULTS OF INTRASPECIFIC TESTS

Host	Parasite	Parasite affects host fitness	Parasite affects male secondary sex characters	Resistance is heritable
Insects				
Field cricket	Gut protozoan	Yes	No	Yes?
Drosophila testacea	Nematode	Yes	?	—
(yellow color of abdomen affected, not known if used by female)				
Fish				
Three-spined stickleback	Ciliate	Yes	Yes	—
Guppy	Gut nematode and ectoparasitic monogenean	Yes	Yes	Yes?
Amphibians				
Gray tree frog	Various	?	No	—
Spadefoot toad	Monogenean	Yes	—	—
Reptiles				
Western fence lizard	Hematozoa (*Plasmodium*)	Yes	Yes	—
Birds				
Ring-necked pheasant	Coccidia	Yes	Yes	Yes
Red jungle fowl	Nematode	Yes	Yes	Yes[a]
Sage grouse	Hematozoa (*Plasmodium*), lice, bacteria	Yes	Yes	—
	Hematozoa (*Haemaproteus*)	—	No	—
Satin bowerbird	Lice	Yes	Yes?	?
Rock dove	Lice	Yes?	?	—
Barn swallow	Fowl mite	Yes	Yes	Yes
Common grackle	Hematozoa	—	Yes	—
Zebra finch	Hematozoa, ectoparasites	—	Yes	—
Red-winged blackbird	Hematozoa	No	Yes	—

[a]Resistance had already been demonstrated in earlier studies by Ackert *et al.* (1935) and Borkakoty and Tewari (1984).

TABLE I (*Continued*)

Predictions		Mechanism		
Females prefer males with fewer parasites	Parasites have disproportionately larger effect on secondary sex characters	Carotenoid-dependent trait	Testosterone-mediated trait	References
Yes/No	—	No	No	Zuk (1987a,b,c; 1988) Simmons (1990)
Yes	—	Yes?	No	Jaenike (1988)
Yes	—	Yes	?	Milinski and Bakker (1990)
Yes	—	No	?	Kennedy et al. (1987)
No	—	No	?	McMinn (1990)
No	—	No	No	Tinsley (1990)
—	—	No	No	Ressel and Schall (1989)
Yes	—	Yes	Yes	Hillgarth (1990a,b)
Yes	Yes	Yes	Yes	Zuk et al. (1990a,b)
Yes	—	Yes	Yes	Johnson and Boyce (1991) Spurrier et al. (1991) Boyce (1990)
No	—	—	Yes	Gibson (1990)
Yes	—	No	?	Borgia and Collis (1989, 1990); Borgia (1986)
Yes	—	No	?	Clayton (1990)
Yes	—	No	Yes	Møller (1990a)
—	—	No	?	C. E. Kirkpatrick et al. (1991)
—	—	Yes	—	Burley et al.(1991)
No	—	Yes	Yes	Weatherhead (1990)

studies listed in Table I support this prediction, and the exceptions are instructive. Although the sample sizes are too small (and the suggestions too *post hoc*) for definitive conclusions, several observations are worth noting.

First, none of the tests with acoustically signaling animals unequivocally supported the hypothesis. Although gregarine gut parasites do influence sexual selection in the field crickets *Gryllus veletis, G. pennsylvanicus,* and *G. bimaculatus,* it appears that females receive more spermatophores from less infected males and may stay with them longer after initial courtship, but are not differentially attracted to males depending on the characteristics of the calling song (Zuk, 1987a,b,c, 1988; Simmons, 1990). The male "ornament," the call, seemed unaffected by parasite burden. Evaluation of the other tests of the hypothesis using anuran amphibians is partly hindered by lack of knowledge of the effects of many parasites on host fitness (Hausfater *et al.,* 1990). Several authors, nonetheless, noted the threshold nature of many frog and toad mating systems, with a large initial energetic investment necessary for males to enter into a breeding aggregation (Arak, 1983; Howard, 1988). The same may be true of acoustically signaling orthopterans. Perhaps parasites exert their major effect (when they have one) early in the sexual selection process, with this minimum level of energy required for sexual competition being attained only by healthy males. After this time, parasites may no longer be important, or acquiring them may be a necessary price for exposure in the breeding arena (Tinsley, 1989, 1990). Alternatively, the association may be spurious; parasites of acoustically signaling animals may be genetically unsuitable for the kinds of parasite–host interactions postulated in the Hamilton-Zuk hypothesis, or female choice may be canalized by sensory constraints in these species (Ryan and Rand, 1990).

Another explanation lies in the second observation about the results listed in Table I. The best support for the hypothesis comes from those systems where the ornament is either carotenoid-derived, such as the sticklebacks (Milinski and Bakker, 1990), or is mediated by testosterone, either behaviorally or structurally, as in the red jungle fowl (Zuk *et al.,* 1990a,b), or both. Perhaps the Hamilton and Zuk model can operate only where the mechanism for ornamentation readily allows interference by parasites. This idea is highly speculative but warrants further consideration, both through investigation of the endocrinological basis of secondary sex characters and the interaction of hormones other than testosterone with the immune system. The effect of parasites on noncarotenoid coloration, such as structural blues or iridescent colors, is also unknown but deserving of study. In the meantime, carotenoid- and testosterone-mediated secondary sex characters occur in a wide range of taxa, and tests of the Hamilton and Zuk model in those systems might prove particularly fruitful.

Viewed in this context, that is, by mechanism, it may be easier to distinguish between the "idea whose time has come" basis for the interpretation of results and one that truly results from ornaments having evolved to reveal male health.

In two studies, the effects of parasites were disproportionately greater on sexually selected characters than on nonsexually selected characters (Zuk *et al.*, 1990b; McMinn, 1990); this argues against the notion that females and ornaments are merely responding to a generalized deleterious effect of disease, with sick males looking worse and attracting less attention from potential mates. None of the other studies were designed to examine this idea, but such evaluation of parasite influence on multiple aspects of host biology can help to distinguish the operation of the Hamilton and Zuk hypothesis from either a direct parasite avoidance behavior on the part of females (Clayton, 1990; Borgia and Collis, 1990) or the general reasoning that because pathogens affect most aspects of behavior, they affect sexual selection as well.

Finally, although again the sample is small, support for the hypothesis appears to depend on the type of parasite examined, with blood parasites presenting the most equivocal results (e.g., C. E. Kirkpatrick *et al.*, 1991; Weatherhead, 1990; Ressel and Schall, 1989). Gut nematodes, for example, were more likely to both uphold the assumptions and support the predictions. Hematozoa, while relatively easy to assess in blood smears, may pose too many difficulties for determination of their effect on secondary sex characters and mate choice. They may influence fitness at certain parasitemias but not others; they may vary enormously in number over the course of a season or even a day within individuals (Pruett-Jones *et al.*, 1992; Foster, 1969). Although the utility of malarias and other blood parasites made them attractive for initial analyses, consideration of parasite biology may argue for caution in the future (Toft and Karter, 1990). Unfortunately, it is premature to characterize an "ideal parasite," but one with less intrahost variation than hematozoa is likely to fall into such a category.

VI. Conclusions

Data and theory often do not advance in tandem, and the evidence about the Hamilton and Zuk hypothesis on the role of parasites in sexual selection is no exception in this regard. Work in both areas is needed, but I suggest that in this case we allow the mechanisms to direct theory. As writers of other reviews have concluded, too few controlled studies have been done to permit firm support or falsification of the hypothesis, but the data that exist are intriguing and certainly support further research (McLennan and Brooks, 1992; Moller, 1990b). Knowledge of the means by which parasites are logically expected to influence sexually selected traits should allow us to make intelligent decisions about the kinds of tests that are most useful. All secondary sex characters are not equivalent, and picking a trait out of the air is as unlikely to represent the best test as the random choice of a parasite. A valuable by-product of such attention to mechanisms is the linking of previously disparate fields of study, such as foraging ecology and parasites (via carotenoids) or immunology and sexual selection (via sex hormones).

The final suggestion is, again as other authors have recognized, a call for greater diversity in the systems of host and parasite used, the inclusion of both laboratory and field data, and the length of time the systems are studied under each circumstance. Genetic cycles of coadaptation cannot be evaluated over the course of a single generation, let alone a cross-sectional sample, and so multigenerational studies are badly needed. Use of a variety of organisms—especially those other than birds—will help to increase the generality of the tests. The Hamilton and Zuk hypothesis will, of course, not account for the evolution of every secondary sex character in every species any more than the runaway process can. The hope is that attention to the mechanisms by which parasites may affect ornaments will provide a more synthetic and multidisciplinary approach to sexual selection.

VII. SUMMARY

The Hamilton and Zuk hypothesis suggests that parasites may play an important role in sexual selection by providing a basis for female choice of males with exaggerated secondary sexual characters. Hamilton and Zuk made two predictions in their 1982 work: (1) Pressure from parasites makes the need for female choice of resistant males more acute, leading to a greater degree of development of ornaments in species where sexual selection is most intense; and (2) Within species, the inability of a male to resist disease should also prevent him from producing the costly ornament preferred by females. Thus, parasite-ridden males will be drab, rather than showy. Interspecific tests, while sometimes problematical, have been largely supportive of the hypothesis. Future work should include surveys of hosts other than birds and parasites other than hematozoa and should carefully consider the meaning of "showiness" in the context of the animal.

Parasites may feature in the evolution of ornaments for several reasons. First, biologists are beginning to acknowledge their neglect of parasites as a force in ecology and evolution in general and, thus, to consider the importance of pathogens in mate choice as well. Second, host–parasite genetic interactions may create situations favorable to "good genes" sexual selection. Third, two crucial mechanisms in the development of many secondary sex characters in a wide variety of groups, carotenoid pigmentation and testosterone, are uniquely affected by parasites, providing a means for the Hamilton and Zuk hypothesis to operate in nature. They also provide links between such diverse fields as foraging ecology, immunology, endocrinology, and behavior.

Acknowledgments

This article is based on a talk presented at the Third International Conference of Behavioural Ecology held in Uppsala, Sweden in August 1990. I am most grateful to Staffan Ulfstrand for inviting me to speak at the conference and to him and all the other attendees who supplied valuable comments, including Andrew Cockburn, Ivar Folstad, Nigella Hillgarth, Manfred Milinski, and Paul Ward. John T. Rotenberry, Beth Braker, Jon Seger, and Len Nunney also provided useful discussion.

References

Ackert, J. E., Eisenbrandt, L. L., Wilmoth, J. H., Glading, B., and Pratt, I. (1935). Comparative resistance of five breeds of chickens to the nematode *Ascaridia lineata* (Schneider). *J. Agric. Res. (Washington, D.C.)* **50,** 607–624.

Alcock, J. (1979). "Animal Behavior: An Evolutionary Approach," 2nd ed. Sinauer, Sunderland, Massachusetts.

Alexander, J., and Stimson, W. H. (1989). Sex hormones and the course of parasitic infection. *Parasitol. Today* **4,** 189–193.

Andersson, M. (1982). Female choice selects for extreme tail length in a widowbird. *Nature (London)* **299,** 818–820.

Andersson, M. (1986). Evolution of condition-dependent sex ornaments and mating preferences: Sexual selection based on viability differences. *Evolution (Lawrence, Kans.)* **40,** 804–816.

Arak, A. (1983). Male-male competition and mate choice in anuran amphibians. *In* "Mate Choice" (P. Bateson, ed.), pp. 181–210. Cambridge Univ. Press, Cambridge, U.K.

Arnold, S. J. (1983). Sexual selection: The interface of theory and empiricism. *In* "Mate Choice" (P. Bateson, ed.), pp. 67–108. Cambridge Univ. Press, Cambridge, U.K.

Bailey, W. J., Cunningham, R. J., and Lebel, L. (1990). Song power, spectral distribution and female phonotaxis in the bushcricket *Requena verticalis* (Tettigoniidae: Orthoptera): Active female choice or passive attraction. *Anim. Behav.* **40,** 33–42.

Baker, R. R., and Parker, G. A. (1979). The evolution of colouration in birds. *Philos. Trans. R. Soc. London, Ser. B* **287,** 63–130.

Bird, F. H. (1952). The problem of pigmentation in broilers. *Coop. Poultryman* **17,** 8–9, 34–35.

Borgia, G. (1986). Satin bowerbird parasites: A test of the bright male hypothesis. *Behav. Ecol. Sociobiol.* **19,** 355–358.

Borgia, G., and Collis, K. (1989). Female choice for parasite-free male satin bowerbirds and the evolution of bright male plumage. *Behav. Ecol. Sociobiol.* **25,** 445–454.

Borgia, G., and Collis, K. (1990). Parasites and bright male plumage in the satin bowerbird (*Ptilorhynchus violaceus*). *Am. Zool.* **30,** 279–286.

Borkakoty, M. R., and Tewari, H. C. (1984). Experimental studies of mechanism of resistance of heavy breeds of chicken against *Ascaridia galli* infection. *Pak. Vet. J.* **4,** 210–214.

Brush, A. H. (1978). Avian pigmentation. *Chem. Zool.* **10,** 141–161.

Brush, A. H., and Siefried, H. (1968). Pigmentation and feather structure in genetic variants of the Gouldian finch, *Poephila gouldiae. Auk* **85,** 416–430.

Bundy, D. A. P. (1989). Gender-dependent patterns of infection and disease. *Parasitol. Today* **4,** 186–189.

Burley, N., Tidemann, S. C., and Halupka, K. (1991). Bill colour and parasite levels of zebra finches. *In* "Bird-Parasite Interactions: Ecology, Evolution and Behaviour" (J. Loye and M. Zuk, eds.), pp. 359–376. Oxford Univ. Press, Oxford.

Carson, H. L., Hardy, D. E., Spieth, H. T., and Stone, W. S. (1970). The evolutionary biology of the

Hawaiian Drosophilidae. *In* "Essays in Evolution and Genetics in Honor of Theodosius Dobzhansky" (M. K. Hecht and W. C. Steere, eds.), pp. 437–543. Appleton-Century-Crofts, New York.

Clayton, D. H. (1990). Mate choice in experimentally parasitized rock doves: Lousy males lose. *Am. Zool.* **30**, 251–262.

Clutton-Brock, T. H., and Harvey, P. H. (1984). Comparative approaches to investigating adaptation. *In* "Behavioural Ecology: An Evolutionary Approach" (J. R. Krebs and N. B. Davies, eds.), 2nd ed., pp. 7–29. Sinauer, Sunderland, Massachusetts.

Cox, F. E. G. (1989). Parasites and sexual selection. *Nature (London)* **341**, 289.

Diamond, J. M. (1972). "Avifauna of the Eastern Highlands of New Guinea." Nuttal Ornithol. Club, Cambridge, Massachusetts.

Dobson, A. P., and Hudson, P. J. (1986). Parasites, disease and the structure of ecological communities. *Trends Ecol. Evol.* **1**, 11–15.

Dobzhansky, T. (1937). "Genetics and the Origin of Species." Columbia Univ. Press, New York.

Endler, J. A. (1983). Natural and sexual selection on color patterns in poeciliid fishes. *Environ. Biol. Fishes* **9**, 173–190.

Endler, J. A., and Lyles, A. M. (1989). Bright ideas about parasites. *Trends Ecol. Evol.* **4**, 246–248.

Eshel, I., and Hamilton, W. D. (1984). Parent-offspring correlation in fitness under fluctuating selection. *Proc. R. Soc. London, Ser. B* **222**, 1–14.

Ewald, P. W. (1983). Host-parasite relations, vectors, and the evolution of disease severity. *Annu. Rev. Ecol. Syst.* **14**, 465–485.

Ewald, P. W., and Schubert, J. (1989). Vertical and vector-borne transmission of insect endocytobionts and the evolution of benignity. *In* "Insect Endocytobiosis: Morphology, Physiology, Genetics, Evolution" (W. Schwemmler and G. Gassner, eds.), pp. 21–35. CRC Press, Boca Raton, Florida.

Falconer, D. S. (1981). "Introduction to Quantitative Genetics." Longman, London.

Felsenstein, J. (1985). Phylogenies and the comparative method. *Am. Nat.* **125**, 1–15.

Fisher, R. A. (1958). "The Genetical Theory of Natural Selection." Dover, New York.

Folstad, I., and Karter, A. J. (1992). Parasites, bright males and the immunocompetence handicap. *Am. Nat.* (in press).

Folstad, I., Nilssen, A. C., Halvorsen, O., and Anderson, J. (1989). Why do male reindeer (*Rangifer t. tarandus*) have higher abundance of second and third instar larvae of *Hypoderma tarandi* than females? *Oikos* **55**, 87–92.

Foster, M. S. (1969). Synchronized life cycles in the orange-crowned warbler and its Mallophagan parasites. *Ecology* **50**, 315–323.

Freeland, W. J. (1981). Parasitism and behavioral dominance among male mice. *Science* **213**, 461–462.

Gibson, R. M. (1990). Relationships between blood parasites, mating success and phenotypic cues in male sage grouse *Centrocercus urophasianus*. *Am. Zool.* **30**, 271–278.

Goodwin, T. W. (1950). Carotenoids and reproduction. *Biol. Rev. Cambridge Philos. Soc.* **25**, 391–413.

Grafen, A. (1990a). Sexual selection unhandicapped by the Fisher process. *J. Theor. Biol.* **144**, 473–516.

Grafen, A. (1990b). Biological signals as handicaps. *J. Theor. Biol.* **144**, 517–546.

Hamilton, W. D. (1982). Pathogens as causes of genetic diversity in their host populations. *In* "Population Biology of Infectious Diseases" (R. M. Anderson and R. M. May, eds.), pp. 269–296. Springer-Verlag, New York.

Hamilton, W. D., and Zuk, M. (1982). Heritable true fitness and bright birds: A role for parasites? *Science* **218**, 384–387.

Hamilton, W. D., and Zuk, M. (1989). Parasites and sexual selection: Hamilton and Zuk reply. *Nature (London)* **341**, 289–290.

Hart, B. L. (1990). Behavioral adaptations to pathogens and parasites: Five strategies. *Neurosci. Biobehav. Rev.* **14**, 273–294.

Hart, B. L., Korinek, E., and Brennan, P. (1987). Postcopulatory genital grooming in male rats: Prevention of sexually transmitted infections. *Physiol. Behav.* **41**, 321–325.

Hausfater, G., Gerhardt, H. C., and Klump, G. M. (1990). Parasites and mate choice in gray treefrogs, *Hyla versicolor. Am. Zool.* **30**, 299–312.

Henderson, P. D. (1951). Pigmentation studies in broilers. *Feedstuffs* Aug. 25, pp. 36–37.

Heywood, J. S. (1989). Sexual selection by the handicap mechanism. *Evolution (Lawrence, Kans.)* **43**, 1387–1397.

Hill, G. E. (1990). Female house finches prefer colourful males: Sexual selection for a condition-dependent trait. *Anim. Behav.* **40**, 563–572.

Hillgarth, N. (1990a). Parasites and female choice in the ring-necked pheasant. *Am. Zool.* **30**, 227–234.

Hillgarth, N. (1990b). Sexual selection and parasites in pheasants. Ph.D. Thesis, University of Oxford, Oxford, England.

Holmes, J. C., and Bethel, W. M. (1972). Modification of intermediate host behavior by parasites. *J. Linn. Soc., Suppl.* **1**, 123–149.

Howard, R. D. (1988). Reproductive success in two species of anurans. *In* "Reproductive Success" (T. H. Clutton-Brock, ed.), pp. 99–113. Univ. of Chicago Press, Chicago, Illinois.

Hudson, P. J. (1986). The effect of a parasitic nematode on the breeding production of red grouse. *J. Anim. Ecol.* **55**, 85–92.

Hutchison, J. B., and Hutchison, R. E. (1983). Hormonal mechanisms of mate choice in birds. *In* "Mate Choice" (P. Bateson, ed.), pp. 389–405. Cambridge Univ. Press, Cambridge, U.K.

Jaenike, J. (1988). Parasitism and male mating success in *Drosophila testacea. Am. Nat.* **131**, 774–780.

Johnson, L. L., and Boyce, M. S. (1991). Female choice of males with low parasite loads in sage grouse. *In* "Bird-Parasite Interactions: Ecology, Evolution and Behaviour" (J. Loye and M. Zuk, eds.), pp. 377–388. Oxford Univ. Press, Oxford.

Kennedy, C. E. J., Endler, J. A., Poynton, S. L., and McMinn, H. (1987). Parasite load predicts mate choice in guppies. *Behav. Ecol. Sociobiol.* **21**, 291–295.

Keymer, A. (1981). Population dynamics of *Hymenolepis diminuta* in the intermediate host. *J. Anim. Ecol.* **50**, 941–950.

Kirkpatrick, C. E. J., Robinson, S. K., and Kitron, U. D. (1991). Phenotypic correlates of blood parasitism in the common grackle. *In* "Bird-Parasite Interactions: Ecology, Evolution and Behaviour" (J. Loye and M. Zuk, eds.), pp. 349–358. Oxford Univ. Press, Oxford (in press).

Kirkpatrick, M. (1982). Sexual selection and the evolution of female choice. *Evolution (Lawrence, Kans.)* **36**, 1–12.

Kirkpatrick, M. (1986a). The handicap mechanism of sexual selection does not work. *Am. Nat.* **127**, 222–240.

Kirkpatrick, M. (1986b). Sexual selection and cycling parasites: A simulation study of Hamilton's hypothesis. *J. Theor. Biol.* **119**, 263–271.

Kirkpatrick, M. (1987). Sexual selection by female choice in polygynous animals. *Annu. Rev. Ecol. Syst.* **18**, 43–70.

Kodric-Brown, A. (1989). Dietary carotenoids and male mating success in the guppy: An environmental component to female choice. *Behav. Ecol. Sociobiol.* **25**, 393–401.

Kodric-Brown, A., and Brown, J. H. (1984). Truth in advertising: The kinds of traits favored by sexual selection. *Am. Nat.* **124**, 309–323.

Kroodsma, D. E. (1982). Song repertoires: Problems in their definition and use. *In* "Acoustic Communication in Birds" (D. E. Kroodsma and E. H. Miller, eds.), Vol. 2, pp. 125–146. Academic Press, New York.

Lande, R. (1981). Models of speciation by sexual selection on polygenic traits. *Proc. Natl. Acad. Sci. U.S.A.* **78**, 3721–3725.

Maynard Smith, J. (1976). Sexual selection and the handicap principle. *J. Theor. Biol.* **57,** 239–242.

Maynard Smith, J. (1978). The handicap principle—A comment. *J. Theor. Biol.* **115,** 1–8.

Mayr, E. (1963). "Animal Species and Evolution." Harvard Univ. Press, Cambridge, Massachusetts.

Mayr, E. (1972). Sexual selection and natural selection. *In* "Sexual Selection and the Descent of Man 1871–1971" (B. Campbell, ed.), pp. 87–104. Aldine, Chicago, Illinois.

McLennan, D. A., and Brooks, D. R. (1991). Parasites and sexual selection: Parasite biology, macroevolutionary information and the Hamilton-Zuk hypothesis. *Q. Rev. Biol.* **66,** 255–286.

McMinn, H. (1990). Effects of the nematode parasite *Camallanus cotti* on sexual and non-sexual behaviors in the guppy (*Poecilia reticulata*). *Am. Zool.* **30,** 245–250.

Milinski, M., and Bakker, T. C. M. (1990). Female sticklebacks use male colouration in mate choice and hence avoid parasitized males. *Nature (London)* **344,** 330–333.

Møller, A. P. (1988). Female choice selects for male sexual tail ornaments in the monogamous swallow. *Nature (London)* **332,** 640–642.

Møller, A. P. (1989). Parasites, predators and nest boxes: Facts and artifacts in nest box studies of birds? *Oikos* **56,** 421–423.

Møller, A. P. (1990a). Parasites and sexual selection: Current status of the Hamilton and Zuk hypothesis. *J. Evol. Biol.* **3,** 319–328.

Møller, A. P. (1990b). Male tail length and female mate choice in the monogamous swallow *Hirundo rustica. Anim. Behav.* **39,** 458–465.

Moore, J. (1983). Responses of an avian predator and its isopod prey to an acanthocephalan parasite. *Ecology* **64,** 1000–1015.

Moore, J. (1984). Altered behavioral responses in intermediate hosts—An acanthocephalan parasite strategy. *Am. Nat.* **123,** 572–577.

Neitz, J., and Jacobs, G. H. (1986). Polymorphism of the long-wavelength cone in normal human colour vision. *Nature (London)* **323,** 623–625.

Nur, N., and Hasson, O. (1984). Phenotypic plasticity and the handicap principle. *J. Theor. Biol.* **110,** 275–297.

Pagel, M. D., and Harvey, P. H. (1988). Recent developments in the analysis of comparative data. *Q. Rev. Biol.* **63,** 13–40.

Palmer, L. S., and Kempster, H. (1919a). Relation of plant carotinoids (sic) to growth, fecundity, and reproduction of fowls. *J. Biol. Chem.* **39,** 299–312.

Palmer, L. S., and Kempster, H. (1919b). The physiological relation between fecundity and the natural yellow pigmentation of certain breeds of fowl. *J. Biol. Chem.* **39,** 313–329.

Palmer, L. S., and Kempster, H. (1919c). The influence of specific feeds and certain pigments on the color of the egg yolk and body fat of fowls. *J. Biol. Chem.* **39,** 331–337.

Pomiankowski, A. N. (1987). The costs of choice in sexual selection. *J. Theor. Biol.* **128,** 195–218.

Pomiankowski, A. N. (1988). The evolution of female mate preference for male genetic quality. *Oxford Surv. Evol. Biol.* **5,** 136–184.

Prestwich, K. N., and Walker, T. J. (1981). Energetics of singing in crickets: Effects of temperature in three trilling species (Orthoptera: Gryllidae). *J. Comp. Physiol., B* **143,** 199–212.

Pruett-Jones, M. A., and Pruett-Jones, S. G. (1991). Analysis and ecological correlates of tick burdens in a New Guinea avifauna. *In* "Bird-Parasite Interactions: Ecology, Evolution, and Behaviour" (J. E. Loye and M. Zuk, eds.), pp. 154–176. Oxford Univ. Press, Oxford (in press).

Pruett-Jones, S. G., Pruett-Jones, M. A., and Jones, H. I. (1990). Parasites and sexual selection in birds of paradise. *Am. Zool.* **30,** 287–298.

Pruett-Jones, S. G., Pruett-Jones, M. A., and Jones, H. I. (1991). Parasites and sexual selection in a New Guinea avifauna. *Curr. Ornithol.* **8,** 213–246.

Read, A. F. (1987). Comparative evidence supports the Hamilton and Zuk hypothesis on parasites and sexual selection. *Nature (London)* **327,** 68–70.

Read, A. F. (1988). Sexual selection and the role of parasites. *Trends Ecol. Evol.* **3,** 97–102.

Read, A. F., and Harvey, P. H. (1989a). Reassessment of evidence for Hamilton and Zuk theory on the evolution of secondary sex characters. *Nature (London)* **339**, 618–620.

Read, A. F., and Harvey, P. H. (1989b). Validity of sexual selection in birds: Read and Harvey reply. *Nature (London)* **340**, 105.

Read, A. F., and Weary, D. M. (1990). Sexual selection and the evolution of bird song: A test of the Hamilton-Zuk hypothesis. *Behav. Ecol. Sociobiol.* **26**, 47–56.

Ressel, S., and Schall, J. J. (1989). Parasites and showy males: Malarial infection and color variation in fence lizards. *Oecologia* **78**, 158–164.

Ridley, M. (1983). "The Explanation of Organic Diversity: The Comparative Method and Adaptations for Mating." Oxford Univ. Press, Oxford.

Ruff, M. D., Reid, W. M., and Johnson, J. K. (1974). Lowered blood carotenoid levels in chickens infected with coccidia. *Poult. Sci.* **53**, 1801–1809.

Ryan, M. J. (1983). Sexual selection and communication in a neotropical frog, *Physalaemus pustulosus. Evolution (Lawrence, Kans.)* **37**, 261–272.

Ryan, M. J., and Rand, S. (1990). The sensory basis of sexual selection for complex calls in the Tungara Frog, *Physalaemus pustulosus* (Sexual selection for sensory exploitation). *Evolution (Lawrence, Kans.)* **44**, 305–314.

Sapolsky, R. M. (1987). Stress, social status, and reproductive physiology in free-living baboons. *In* "Psychobiology of Reproductive Behavior: An Evolutionary Perspective" (D. Crews, ed.), pp. 292–322. Prentice-Hall, Englewood Cliffs, New Jersey.

Scott, M. E., and Dobson, A. (1989). The role of parasites in regulating host abundance. *Parasitol. Today* **5**, 176–183.

Searcy, W. A., and Andersson, M. (1986). Sexual selection and the evolution of song. *Annu. Rev. Ecol. Syst.* **17**, 507–533.

Seger, J. (1985). Unifying genetic models for the evolution of female choice. *Evolution (Lawrence, Kans.)* **39**, 1185–1193.

Simmons, L. W. (1988). The calling song of the field cricket *Gryllus bimaculatus* (De Geer): Constraints on transmission and its role in intermale competition and female choice. *Anim. Behav.* **36**, 380–394.

Simmons, L. W. (1990). Post-copulatory guarding, female choice and the levels of gregarine infections in the field cricket, *Gryllus bimaculatus. Behav. Ecol. Sociobiol.* **26**, 403–407.

Spurrier, M. F., Boyce, M. S., and Manly, B. F. J. (1991). Effects of parasites on mate choice by captive sage grouse. *In* "Bird-Parasite Interactions: Ecology, Evolution and Behaviour" (J. Loye and M. Zuk, eds.), pp. 389–398. Oxford Univ. Press, Oxford (in press).

Stone, H. A., Collins, W. M., and Urban, W. E., Jr. (1971). Evaluation of carotenoid concentration in chicken tissues. *Poult. Sci.* **50**, 675–681.

Taigen, T. L., and Wells, K. D. (1985). Energetics of vocalization by an anuran amphibian (*Hyla versicolor*). *J. Comp. Physiol.* **155**, 163–170.

Tinsley, R. C. (1989). Effects of host sex on transmission success. *Parasitol. Today* **5**, 190–196.

Tinsley, R. C. (1990). The influence of parasite infection on mating success in spadefoot toads, *Scaphiopus couchii. Am. Zool.* **30**, 313–324.

Toft, C. A., and Karter, A. J. (1990). Parasite-host coevolution. *Trends Ecol. Evol.* **5**, 326–329.

Ward, P. I. (1988a). Sexual dichromatism and parasitism in British and Irish freshwater fish. *Anim. Behav.* **36**, 1210–1215.

Ward, P. I. (1988b). Sexual showiness and parasitism in freshwater fish: Combined data from several isolated water systems. *Oikos* **55**, 428–429.

Weatherhead, P. J. (1990). Secondary sexual traits, parasites and polygyny in red-winged blackbirds *Agelaius phoeniceus. Behav. Ecol.* **1**, 125–130.

Weatherhead, P. J., and Bennett, G. F. (1992). Ecology of red-winged blackbird parasitism by haematozoa. *Can. J. Zool.* (to be published).

Weatherhead, P. J., Bennett, G. F., and Shutler, D. (1991). Sexual selection and parasites in wood warblers. *Auk* **108**, 147–152.

West-Eberhard, M. J. (1979). Sexual selection, social competition, and evolution. *Proc. Am. Philos. Soc.* **123**, 222–234.

West-Eberhard, M. J. (1983). Sexual selection, social competition, and speciation. *Q. Rev. Biol.* **58**, 155–183.

Zahavi, A. (1975). Mate selection—A selection for a handicap. *J. Theor. Biol.* **53**, 205–214.

Zuk, M. (1987a). Variability in attractiveness of male field crickets (Orthoptera: Gryllidae) to females. *Anim. Behav.* **35**, 1240–1248.

Zuk, M. (1987b). The effects of gregarine parasites, body size, and time of day on spermatophore production and sexual selection in field crickets. *Behav. Ecol. Sociobiol.* **21**, 65–72.

Zuk, M. (1987c). The effects of gregarine parasites on longevity, weight loss, fecundity and developmental time in the field crickets *Gryllus veletis* and *G. pennsylvanicus*. *Ecol. Entomol.* **12**, 349–354.

Zuk, M. (1988). Parasite load, body size, and age of wild-caught male field crickets (Orthoptera: Gryllidae): Effects on sexual selection. *Evolution (Lawrence, Kans.)* **42**, 969–976.

Zuk, M. (1989). Validity of sexual selection in birds. *Nature (London)* **340**, 104.

Zuk, M. (1990). Reproductive strategies and sex differences in disease susceptibility: An evolutionary viewpoint. *Parasitol. Today* **6**, 231–233.

Zuk, M. (1991). Parasites and bright birds: New data and a new prediction. *In* "Bird-Parasite Interactions: Ecology, Evolution and Behaviour" (J. Loye and M. Zuk, eds.), pp. 317–327. Oxford Univ. Press, Oxford.

Zuk, M., Thornhill, R., Johnson, K., and Ligon, J. D. (1990a). Parasites and mate choice in red jungle fowl. *Am. Zool.* **30**, 235–244.

Zuk, M., Johnson, K., Thornhill, R., and Ligon, J. D. (1990b). Parasites and male ornaments in free-ranging and captive red jungle fowl. *Behaviour* **114**, 232–248.

Conceptual Issues in Cognitive Ethology

Colin Beer

INSTITUTE OF ANIMAL BEHAVIOR
RUTGERS UNIVERSITY
NEWARK, NEW JERSEY 07102

I. Historical Introduction

To begin with, why *cognitive* ethology? The short historical answer is that Donald Griffin (1976, p. 102) picked the term as his name for the study of mental experience in animals, in a provoking book in which he argued that such study was due for revival. He was reacting to the prohibition that behavioristic doctrine was continuing to place on serious consideration of the possibility that subjective states might exist in animals and have significant causal efficacy in their behavior, and persuaded that new evidence demanded a reopening of what he called "the question of animal awareness." Is ethological concern with this matter aptly described as cognitive?

David Premack has complained that talk of cognition in invertebrates, even in the context of the remarkable communication capacities of honeybees, verges on the oxymoronic: "Griffin's phrase 'cognitive ethology' (Griffin, 1976), when applied to invertebrates, is a colorful misnomer, rather like 'equatorial Norway' or the 'nautical jungle' " (Premack, 1986, p. 137). But denying cognition to insects is just as question-begging as ascribing it to them, unless there is some clear and explicit specification of what cognition is supposed to include and entail. Premack's definition—"the construction of mental representations on which one makes computations" (Premack, 1986, p. 136)—is not much help, for the nature of mental representations and computational theories of mind are controversial conceptual issues too much in flux for any confident prediction about how they might bear on animal cases.

Nevertheless, in the terms of current cognitive science, Premack does locate cognition where philosophers have traditionally placed it: in the mind's capacity to deal with information, including its reception, storage, and processing. Thus, courses in cognitive psychology have typically comprised treatments of perception, memory, and thinking. Since antiquity, the capacity to reason has been viewed as something especially human, in contrast to the reception of sensory

69

stimulation and the production of motor response, which are held in common by all animals.

In the middle ages, the doctrines of Plato, and then Aristotle, were recast in theological terms, including the tripartite divisioning of the soul between appetitive, sensitive, and intellectual functions. In the eighteenth century, in the context of a disquisition on beauty, Moses Mendelssohn sorted the activities of the soul into the categories implicit in Plato: knowing, feeling, and willing. Kant, in *The Critique of Judgement* and the *Anthropologie,* adopted Mendelssohn's three-faculty doctrine, but in a psychology couched in terms of consciousness and mental life rather than soul. In the nineteenth century the subject matter of psychology was frequently sorted under the headings of cognition, volition, and affection, or equivalent terms, and many modern textbooks of psychology still divide their subject matter between thinking, motivation, and sensation. In the "hormic psychology" of William McDougall (1908) the concepts of cognition (thinking), conation (willing), and affection (feeling) formed the basis of an influential theory of instinct, and Freudian psychoanalytic theory is similarly in the tradition of distinguishing reason from appetite and feeling.

If cognitive ethology were also following this tradition, one would expect it to be mainly concerned with animal intelligence. But this would be to place it in what has been one of the main streams of comparative psychology, at least since Romanes published a book entitled *Animal Intelligence* in 1881. For much of this century, this stream flowed between banks more or less confining it to studies of learning and excluding consideration of mentalistic conceptions of mind. It has now broadened out to include much more than it used to, but the main channel remains bedded in concern with such things as problem solving, memory, and discrimination capacities, at least if my sampling of what is called "animal cognition" is anything to go by.

The title Griffin chose for his second book on cognitive ethology was *Animal Thinking* (Griffin, 1984). As this suggests, he includes the traditional field of cognition in his area of concern, but there is much more besides and the heart of the matter is elsewhere. Indeed the title of the earlier book—*The Question of Animal Awareness* (Griffin, 1976)—more accurately announced what cognitive ethology was to be about, and the book cast the behavioristic-learning theorists as part of the opposition. Griffin's main concern has been the issue of whether animals other than humans have subjective mental experiences, and, if so, how we might try to find out what such experiences are like. It thus includes sensation and conation at least as much as cognition in the traditional sense, and the latter is of interest mainly to the extent that it is consciously entertained.

The "question of animal awareness" has a long and tangled history. Indeed, people have probably always had to face it in some form. They have done so by adopting one of two contrasting positions: either they argued that animals are mindless and devoid of feelings, thoughts, beliefs, and desires or they regarded animals as having minds and therefore being cognitively and affectively aware in the ways in which we are, at least to some degree. This latter view appeals to common sense, making it by far the more widely held by people at large, now and in the past. Of Descartes' argument that animals are automata, lacking consciousness, Malcolm (1973) wrote that readers are astonished when they come upon it, and Vendler (1972, p. 152) said that "the notorious doctrine of the automatism of brutes [is] perhaps the most counterintuitive item" in the whole of Descartes' philosophy. Nevertheless, this "notorious doctrine" probably has the majority of scientists on its side, because it is the one more consistent with materialism, the dominating philosophy of science.

Materialism provides one kind of answer to another and even deeper issue raised by Descartes' philosophical system, which was a rational reconstruction of knowledge from what was left after the deconstruction wrought by his pursuit of truth using the method of systematic doubt. The issue is the equally notorious mind–body problem. The Cartesian ontology is a dualism of mental and material substances—two fundamentally different kinds of stuff having no properties in common and therefore perplexing with regard to the relationship holding between them. Descartes' answer to the problem was interactionism: mind and body mutually influence one another. How this could possibly be, given their disparate natures, has had philosophers looking for alternatives ever since. The alternative offered by materialism consisted of discarding one of Descartes' substances: according to materialism only matter exists, and what we call mind is merely a by-product or emanation of matter.

In eighteenth-century France, most of the philosophers and scientists associated with the revolution and its aftermath were materialists, partly because their anticlerical position seemed to entail it. However, they also illustrate the difficulty of sustaining a consistent materialism. That human beings have sensations and ideas, beliefs and desires, which can be efficacious in causing action, could hardly be denied, and according to a number of authorities (e.g., Gassendi, 1658; de la Chambre, 1685; see Rosenfield, 1968; Richards, 1988), comparison and logic argued that the same must be true of animals. There were Cartesians who tried to maintain a purely mechanistic conception of the control of animal action, but even they tended to slip into mentalistic attribution when instinctive machinery appeared inadequate to account for performance. For example, de Condillac (1755) criticized Buffon for inconsistency in maintaining on the one hand that animals are mindless machines, and on the other allowing that they can perceive objects and experience pleasure and pain. To sustain a materialist position and at the same time do justice to the testimony of experience, de la Mettrie (1748/1960) and others of his persuasion reconceptualized matter as sentient and active in the production of bodily action rather than insentient and inert as the Cartesians assumed. This enabled the sensationalists, as they have been called (Richards, 1988), to apply the empiricist epistemology of Locke to the understanding of animal behavior. According to the sensationalists, the effects of stimulation are registered in an animal as ideas, the associations of which in memory and imagination give rise to reasoned judgments guiding choice of action. Instinct was thus construed as grounded in habit, an idea that anticipated the evolutionary associationism of Herbert Spencer.

The nineteenth century has been described as "the age of philosophical materialism" (Mandelbaum, 1974, quoted by Richards, 1988, p. 333). A typical and often mentioned instance supporting this description is the position taken by a group of physiology students, which included such famous names as Helmholtz, Virchow, Ludwig, du Bois Reymond, and Brücke, in opposition to the vitalism of their teacher in Berlin in the 1840s, Johannes Müller. In a letter to a friend, du Bois Reymond said that he and Brücke had sworn an oath that they would adhere to the principle that "no other forces than common physico-chemical ones are active within the organism" (quoted in Boring, 1950, p. 708). Later in the century, Sechenov put Russian physiology on a materialistic and deterministic footing (see Yaroshevsky, 1971) that included sensation and consciousness within its compass. It was in the nineteenth century that the term "scientist" became current (coined in 1840 according to the Oxford English Dictionary), and science began seriously to usurp the authority of religion.

However, science and religion were not always seen as antithetical. For example, the implications of early nineteenth-century geology for the question of the age of the earth were accepted by the more intellectually respected divines of the time (Gillispie, 1951), some of whom, such as Adam Sedgwick, participated in the collection of the scientific evidence (Rudwick, 1985). And several of the contributors to the natural theology of the Bridgewater Treatises, such as Buckland and Bell, were eminent scientists.

In the fifth of the Bridgewater Treatises, Roget (1834) maintained that "the brain is the material instrument by which we retrace and combine ideas, and by which we remember, we reason, we invent" (Roget, 1834, Vol. 2, p. 510). This idea that matter can be sentient and so organized as to produce thought, essentially the view of Locke and the eighteenth-century sensationalists, was regarded as reasonable by a number of respected authorities in Britain at the time when Darwin was developing his theory of evolution. Darwin presumably accepted the idea, for he saw no inconsistency in declaring himself a materialist and at the same time writing at length about the mental powers of animals, including curiosity, attention, imagination, reason, abstraction, and self-consciousness, as he did in *The Descent of Man* (1871). Ghiselin (1969) has argued that most of Darwin's writing in this anthropomorphic vein was merely metaphorical, but this reading cannot be sustained where Darwin was expressly seeking to establish continuities between animal and human mental capacities. In any case, the defense is unnecessary if one accepts that materialism is compatible with mentalism.

However for most Victorians, materialism was associated with denial of mind, morality, and human values, and this led them to repudiate it. For example, Spencer, in spite of his hostility to received religious doctrine, emphatically denied being a materialist (see Richards, 1988, pp. 331–332). Perhaps more surprising is the case of T. H. Huxley, who is generally thought of as materialism personified. In an essay of 1874, Huxley returned to Descartes' view that animals are automata. "What proof is there," he asked, adapting a passage from Malebranche, "that brutes are other than a superior race of marionettes, which eat without pleasure, cry without pain, desire nothing, know nothing, and only simulate intelligence as a bee simulates a mathematician?" (Huxley, 1893, p. 218) After reviewing the more recent arguments and evidence for the automaton view, Huxley concluded that it was far more defensible than when Descartes promulgated it. Even so he ended up rejecting the idea:

> The doctrine of continuity is too well established for it to be permissible to me to suppose that any complex natural phenomenon comes into existence suddenly, and without being preceded by simpler modifications; and very strong arguments would be needed to prove that such complex phenomena as those of consciousness, first make their appearance in man (Huxley, 1893, p. 236).

Huxley thus granted consciousness to animals, but then denied that it is efficacious in the causation of action:

> The consciousness of brutes would appear to be related to the mechanism of their body simply as a collateral product of its working, and to be as completely without power of modifying that working as the steamwhistle which accompanies the work of a locomotive engine is without influence upon its machinery. Their volition, if they have any, is an emotion indicative of physical changes, not a cause of such changes (Huxley, 1893, p. 245).

Now the doctrine of continuity came into play again, although in the reverse direction: Huxley accepted that "the argumentation which applies to brutes holds equally good for man"; so we too are conscious automata. Anticipating that such a conclusion would brand him a materialist, he disavowed the charge, saying that "I am utterly incapable of conceiving the existence of matter if there is no mind in which to picture that existence" (Huxley, 1893, p. 245).

A more active role for mind in relation to matter has been found in the thinking of other nineteenth-century evolutionists. In a book on which I have already drawn several times, *Darwin and the Emergence of Evolutionary Theories of Mind and Behavior,* Robert Richards (1988) has worked through the writings of a number of the foremost figures in nineteenth-century biology and psychology and found them to be anything but materialistic, if materialism is taken to be the doctrine that only inert matter exists, mind being merely a material epiphenomenon. On the contrary, according to Richards: "Spencer, Haeckel, Romanes,

Morgan, James and Baldwin spun out a monistic metaphysics that made matter epiphenomenal to mind" (Richards, 1988, p. 543). That is to say, these evolutionists conceived changes in the structure and functioning of mind as preceding and hence guiding changes in the structure and functioning of the body, in the course of animal evolution (cf. Gottlieb, 1987).

It would take more space than would be appropriate to try to cover Richards's story here, so I refer the interested reader to his book. My purpose has been achieved if these historical reflections serve to illustrate the variety of conceptions of animal mind and of the relationship between mind and matter, all of them preconceived rather than derived from observation, that preceded and gave rise to twentieth-century attitudes on the issues. In particular, the evidence shows that materialism, which is assumed by modern science, was often taken to be compatible with mentalism. Also, in spite of the traditional distinctions drawn between thought, affect, and will, it was common to assume, in discussion of animal mentality, that they were tied up together, that grounds for ascribing thought entailed feeling and volition as well. For instance, Descartes reasoned that lack of speech meant absence of thought, which includes true feeling or passion and volition, so because animals are speechless they must also be mindless, desireless, and senseless (Malcolm, 1973). With the revival of interest in animal mentality, as well as in cognitive and humanistic psychology, some of the past issues and ideas have resurfaced in new forms that have yet to be clearly articulated.

As talk of *the* question of animal awareness suggests, cognitive ethology has tended to conflate separable aspects of animal mentality and, thus, followed Descartes' example. Consequently, cognition for a cognitive ethologist has to be understood as including concern about sensation and feeling, intention and desire, along with thought and belief.

Cognitive ethologists also, at least tacitly, assume that the answers to their questions can be sought within a materialistic framework. In part, this framework comes from the kinds of naturalistic and biological perspectives that give ethology whatever distinctness it has from the other behavioral sciences (cf. Hinde, 1982).

But questions of animal mind can hardly avoid being involved with questions of human mind as well. Many of the problems posed by animal mentality are posed by human mentality also, and the kinds of problems are both psychological and philosophical. Cognitive ethology would thus appear to be in a position calling for close ties to cognitive psychology and the philosophy of mind and to the alliance of these two with computer science, linguistics, neuroscience, and artificial intelligence in the enterprise called cognitive science. However, such ties as there are have so far been few and loose.

Cognitive ethologists have, by and large, drawn on common sense psychology and philosophy for the premises on which they formulate their questions, base their arguments, and design their experiments. Such "folk psychology" has been called in question in ways bearing on the cognitive ethological enterprise. For this reason, and because of a long-standing concern about the inescapable coercion of preconceived ideas in science (e.g., Beer, 1980), I chose to embark on this essay on what I see as some of the conceptual issues in cognitive ethology. My aim is to draw attention to the relevance of philosophy, and to the relevant philosophy, rather than to try to provide answers to the conceptual questions. Modern philosophers generally seem more interested in raising questions than in answering them. Though no philosopher myself, I can at least imitate them in this regard.

I divide my discussion between four intertwined themes: the varieties of awareness and consciousness; language and thought; intention and action; intentionality and folk psychology.

II. Awareness, Consciousness, and Imagery

A. Looking Inward

"*Awareness* is the whole set of interrelated mental images of the flow of events . . . ." (Griffin, 1976, p. 5). Griffin also defined intention and consciousness in terms of mental imagery. In thus putting imagery in the forefront of his conception of animal mental life, he again conformed to an old model.

At least since the time of St. Augustine, the mind has been "visualized" as an inner eye perceiving reflections of the world as if in a mirror or, later, as scanning an analogue of a cinema screen or television monitor, and philosophers have taken up the image in the pursuit of epistemology. From Descartes onward, this view of the acquisition of knowledge, in which "the intellect *inspects* entities modeled on retinal images" (Rorty, 1980, p. 45), has influenced how people have thought about what it is like to be mindful and sought certainty for the grounding of belief. The "ideas" of Locke, the "impression" of Hume, the "Vorstellungen" of Wundt, and the "sense data" of Russell exemplify repeated efforts to establish the foundations of knowledge on sure ground—the immediately "given" content of consciousness. The analysis of this content into its components, and elucidation of the principles governing their combination in experience, constituted the primary business of the "new," experimental psychology, according to Wundt who "founded" this psychology (Boring, 1950, p. 316) in Germany in the latter part of the nineteenth century and Titchener who later brought a British version of it to America. Both Wundt and Titchener claimed that introspective observations by adequately trained human subjects empirically verified the view that thought always consists of sequences of images, sensations, or feelings (e.g., Titchener, 1909).

However, the deliverances of introspection were anything but unanimous on this issue. In France, for example, Binet (1903) reported that his subjects often denied consciousness of any imagery when they were given problems to solve in their heads, and described their thoughts in purely propositional terms, such as that they were thinking of such and such or that so and so. In Germany, Külpe and his colleagues at Würzburg likewise claimed experimental evidence for the existence of "imageless thoughts." In America, James (1890) maintained that mental life is experienced as continuous flow—a "stream of consciousness"— rather than a succession of discrete events or sensation states, as Titchener and his "structuralist" school assumed.

Such lack of agreement on what psychology was supposed to be about, its ostensible phenomena, redounded to critics of the new science. Earlier in the century, Comte (1830–1842) had already objected to introspection as a method and ridiculed the inconsistency of its reports (see Lyons, 1986). For Comte, the idea that one can observe one's experience while it is being had implies a division in consciousness between the observer and the observed that he believed to be "a manifest impossibility." To catch consciousness on the fly, as it were, is like trying to turn quickly enough to glimpse the back of your head in the mirror: "We cannot catch ourselves in any particular occurrent state of consciousness because the shift of consciousness to the act of catching involves abandoning the state of consciousness that we would catch" (Lloyd, 1989, p. 187). Mill (1882) and James (1890) tried to meet this objection by arguing that introspection is a form of retrospection: the mind reports inspection of what it has stored from its experience in the immediate past and, hence, in what James, following a Mr. E. R. Clay, called "the specious present" (James, 1890, Vol. I, p. 609). But this seemed to mean that introspection can inform only about what we were conscious of, never what we are conscious of, which is counterintuitive; and, for introspection to do even this, the content of immediate past experience must surely have to be returned from memory to consciousness, and with it the problem of achieving distance between subject and object (Lyons, 1986, p. 14). The problem was part of the legacy of the metaphor of mind as divided between inner eye and mirror.

James's response to Comte's other charge, the inconsistency of the "data" of introspection, was to say that introspection, like any form of observation, is fallible and, as with observation in general, can be improved by taking steps to increase its precision, accuracy, and reliability. It was to achieve such improvement that Wundt, Titchener, and the other "new" psychologists devised standard experimental test procedures and rigorous training programs for their human subjects. But when even these methods failed to reach consensus on such issues as the question of imageless thought, and this failure led to nasty public accusations of bad science, the introspective approach, which James had said "we have to rely on first and foremost and always" (1890, Vol. I, p. 185), fell into disrepute. So was the way opened for behaviorism, a psychology with consciousness left out and animals drawn in.

Now that the power and persuasiveness of behaviorism have waned, talk of consciousness, awareness, and other mental attributions is again psychologically respectable, even in reference to animal behavior. Indeed, it can be argued that belief in animal mentality never really disappeared, but only went into hiding, or submerged into implicitness in some of the language used to describe animal action, during the years of behaviorist dominance (e.g., Mason, 1976). However, conceptions of mentality did not go unchanged in their period of psychological exile. Behaviorism left its mark on them, and philosophy continued to concern itself with the issues they entailed. As a consequence, consciousness has come to be viewed as covering a variety of mental states, none of which is adequately represented by the metaphor of inner eye and mirror.

The inner eye image can be said to add complication without solving any problem. Why interpose this screening of reflections, or sense data, or immediate experiences, or images between seeing and its object, between hurting and the pain, between thinking and the thought? There is, of course, a sequence of sensory and neurophysiological events that somehow mediates between stimulation and experience or underlies the cognitive process; but this is irrelevant to the phenomenological case. We do not, for instance, perceive retinal images (if we did, would the world look upside down?) or their projections to the occipital cortex. No: we see the red light, or suffer toothache, or think that tomorrow is Thursday, and the immediacy between these mental states and their contents leaves no phenomenological room for extras discoverable by introspection (for a recent and detailed discussion along these lines, see Lyons, 1986; earlier forms of the argument can be found in phenomenological and Gestalt psychology, e.g., Wertheimer, 1922). But even if the inner eye and its ghostly screen could be fitted in, they would merely repeat rather than answer the question they were supposed to deal with, namely, how the mind can come to know about the world. For if the inner eye is modeled on the outer eye, then all it provides are images, which in turn must be scanned to be experienced, presumably by a still more interior eye, which provides further images, and so on without end. Putting "a ghost in the machine" leads one into an infinite regress (Ryle, 1949, e.g., p. 213).

However, in spite of these criticisms, of which I have given only an impressionistic sketch, introspection continues to be a term of art in psychology and the philosophy of mind, where it picks out a way in which we can be conscious of ourselves or self-conscious. Even if the conception of introspection as "examination of the contents of consciousness" (Humphrey, 1983, p. 30) as classically conceived is mistaken, we do from time to time turn our attention inward, as it were, to dwell on the sensible qualities of what we are observing, the affective qualities of what we are feeling, the subjective qualities of what we are thinking. Thus, a wine taster tries to concentrate on and discriminate among the savors mingled on his palate; a patient tries to answer the doctor's question about whether the pain is dull or sharp, diffuse or localized; and when trying to recall a name, we may wonder at how success comes only after we have backed off from what seemed like groping toward something dimly apprehended but just out of reach (cf. Proust, 1913, Vol. I, pp. 58–62). Different from these examples of reflection on subjective experience are the sorts of state in which one might be said to be engaged in a debate with oneself over a course of action or critical of oneself for moral laxity, lack of sensitivity, or weakness of will. Here, an explicit sense of self is involved, or what Mead (1964) and Oatley (1988) refer to as a model of the self.

B. THE VARIETIES OF CONSCIOUS AWARENESS

These introspective states exemplify what people often mean when they talk of consciousness and being consciously aware. But consciousness and awareness can cover other kinds of states as well; indeed, the diversity in usage of the terms boggles the tidy mind. Writers differ on what the criteria of consciousness are, on where to draw the lines between categories of consciousness, and on whether these categories constitute a natural kind (e.g., Ryle, 1949; Natsoulas, 1978; Bisiach, 1988; Churchland, 1988; Oatley, 1988; Lloyd, 1989). A sampling of the diversity includes the following. Consciousness can refer simply to the state of being awake, as opposed to being asleep or knocked out, as when we refer to someone's regaining consciousness after being in a coma. One can have consciousness of, or be conscious of, the presence of something in the sense of being alert to it in the present moment, as one might say that one was aware of or had awareness of the man crouching in the shrubbery. But consciousness and awareness are not always synonymous, for one can be aware of a certain fact without that fact's having to be in consciousness here and now; and we should be likely to say that in our dream we were more aware of something than that we were conscious of it. Being in pain and feeling dizzy are conscious experiences, but they are not experiences *of* anything apart from themselves. In contrast, conscious perceptual states are always of or about something; they have content; we see an object or hear a sound. You cannot simply see or hear in the way you can simply hurt or tingle. On the other hand, both sensation and perception are dependent on something impinging or seeming to impinge on the mind from without. Even an hallucination is experienced as situated elsewhere than in the mind itself. In other words, sensations, perceptions, and hallucinations, other than those we bring about by deliberately seeking them, are passively received, not under voluntary control. Differing from this is what goes on when one engages in a bit of planning, calculating, deliberating, or such like. Here the mind does take an active part and is, at least to some extent, in voluntary control. In much human cognition, the content of consciousness is tied to linguistic or other symbolic formulation, as in reading a text or comprehending Fermat's last theorem. Finally, there is consciousness of self as implicitly or explicitly involved in introspection.

Given this diversity, Churchland (1988) argued that we are probably mistaken to ask for *the* definition or *the* concept or *the* problem of consciousness (see also Lycan, 1987; Allport, 1988). Similarly, one can question the soundness of talking about *the* question of animal awareness. Churchland (see also Wilkes, 1989) thinks that consciousness is no more likely to be a "natural kind" for the cognitive scientist than weeds are for the botanist or jewels for the mineralogist. Just as weeds comprise plants from several different botanical taxa and so do not constitute a unified category by botanical criteria, so the phenomena of consciousness may consist of several different kinds of mental state requiring separate psychological consideration. She speculates that when neurobiology is sufficiently advanced, we may find it possible to reconfigure cognitive categories on the basis of neurological substrate. In the meantime, she recommends that work focus on particular kinds of consciousness that can be given firm empirical anchorage from which theoretical connections to neuroscience seem feasible. Whether one goes along with this view or sides with functionalist philosophers like Fodor (e.g., 1981), who maintain that mental types cannot be mapped onto neural types and, hence, that psychology will never be reduced to physiology, the recognition that consciousness is heterogeneous carries with it the possibility that animals may be conscious in some ways but not in others.

Dan Lloyd has made this point explicitly. In the course of developing a minimalist theory of mental representation (Lloyd, 1989), he too finds consciousness to be a mixed bag: "The concept of consciousness, as wielded by ordinary folk and spruced up by philosophers, seems to include four disparate phenomena: sensation, perception, reflection, and introspection" (Lloyd, 1989, p. 179). Earlier he had used some physiological research on the vision of toads to flesh out his model of representation. From this and some other considerations, such as the fact that we regard an anesthetized toad as unconscious, he is persuaded that toads are perceptually aware but incapable of reflecting on their experience or being introspective about it. Like Danto (1985), whom he quotes, he envisions animal consciousness as bound to the moment of experience, the "present and particular" (Bennett, 1989, p. vii), and lacking in the ability to "metarepresent" such experience as happening in the past or future. And because animals are thus bereft of reflection in general, they are denied that special kind of reflection that generates introspective consciousness of self in relation to experience and the world, the capacity to think of themselves as persisting egos, each located at an existential crux in time and space—"at the still point of the turning world." I expect that even tough-minded critics would be more receptive to cognitive ethology if its claims for animal awareness were limited to sensation and perception rather than encompassing the whole package.

C. THE PRIVACY OF EXPERIENCE

Although limiting the question of animal awareness to sensation and perception might simplify the matter in some respects, it also makes the prospect of investigation murky, both in the sense of clouding the view and in the sense of dimming heuristic hopes. From its beginnings, ethology has been concerned about what features of its world an animal can perceive. Experimental studies revealed differences in the stimulus modalities to which different species are receptive, in the ranges of receptivity within a modality, and in discrimination within these ranges. And even when these dimensions of sensory capacity have been determined for a particular kind of animal, the knowledge has sometimes proved insufficient for inference to what such an animal is reacting to in a particular situation, as in the cases of the classic studies of Lack (1943) and Tinbergen (e.g., 1951) on sign stimuli. When the receptive capacities of animals differ from ours in these ways, we can only blankly wonder about what their sensory and perceptual experiences might be like. For instance, I find it impossible to imagine being visually unable to tell the difference between N and its mirror image, as is the case for an octopus, or to visualize a color outside the sensible spectrum so as to assimilate a bee's sensation of ultraviolet. Similarly the auditory world of a bat is phenomenologically beyond our ken.

The question of what it is like to be a bat gave title to a well-known article in which Thomas Nagel (1974) argued that consciousness "makes the mind–body problem really intractible." The best we can do, Nagel said, is to try to imagine what it would be like for oneself to be equipped like a bat and behave like one. This is the old ejective approach of mentally projecting oneself into the situation of the animal, with its dimensions, sensory equipment, motor capacities, and so on, that was used by Romanes and some of the functionalist psychologists of the Chicago School who worked with animals. The problem, according to Nagel, is that imagining in this way will not tell you "what it is like for a *bat* to be a bat." For one thing, it is beyond the capacities of our sensory and nervous systems to provide phenomenal experience of ultrasonic echoes and, hence, for us to perceive objects at a distance by their means. More generally, the argument is that, unless we can occupy the subjective point of view of the being whose awareness we wonder about, the quality of that awareness must remain forever inaccessible, no matter how much we may get to know about the relevant neurophysiology.

Some philosophers have taken issue with Nagel and those who think like him, such as Jackson (1982), Robinson (1982), and Campbell (1983). For example, P. S. Churchland (1985) uses several arguments to counter Nagel's case for saying that qualia—phenomenologically experienced sensation states—are irreducible to accounts in terms of brain states. He begins by setting out the conditions for successful intertheoretic reduction in science, and then argues, first, that qualia present no exception to the possibility of such reduction and, second, that the contrary position depends on either equivocation or false premises. Take the argument that someone could know all that there is to know about brain states, yet not know what it is like to experience the color red, and hence, by Leibniz's law, the experience of red cannot be equivalent to a brain state. Churchland replies that two different types of knowledge are involved here—knowledge by description (e.g., what botany can tell you about peaches) and knowledge by acquaintance (e.g., what you learn about a peach from biting into one) (Russell, 1956)—and there is no reason for denying that they can be about exactly the same thing. Nevertheless, when he comes to consider the bat, Churchland has to admit that "if a bat's brain includes computational machinery that the human brain simply lacks (which seems likely), then the subjective character of *some* of the bat's internal states may well be beyond human imagination" (P. S. Churchland, 1985, p. 27).

Another line of criticism against arguments that appeal to the privacy of qualia takes a linguistic turn. Roughly speaking, it says that for words like "pain," "yellow," and "sour" to serve for communication, they must get their meanings in some way other than or additional to each person's attaching them to individually and subjectively discriminated sensation states. If private assignment were the whole story, we should have no reason for believing that when other people use sensation words they refer to experiences that are the same as our own. A bit farther down this road lies skepticism about the existence of any other minds than our own—the dead end of solipsism. A defense of common sense takes the private assignment story to be incoherent. Wittgenstein (1958) argued that for words to mean the same thing on different occasions, there must be some way of checking that they have been used consistently. The private assignment account provides for no such checking: using a word consistently with definition and seeming to use a word consistently with definition will be indistinguishable—"whatever is going to seem right to me is right. And that only means that here we can't talk about 'right' " (Wittgenstein, 1958, p. 92; for discussions of the issue of a private language, see Jones, 1971). Wittgenstein's position was that a private language is impossible; for words to have meaning they stand in need of "outward criteria."

This view was developed into what has become known as philosophical behaviorism, most notably in Gilbert Ryle's *The Concept of Mind* (1949). For Ryle, references to mental states amounted to (could be "cashed" for) statements about behavioral dispositions. For me to say that I am tired, for example, would mean that if a bed were available and nothing prevented me from doing so, I should lie down on it and rest. In general, Ryle maintained, talk about states of mind can be translated into talk about what a person would do under certain circumstances. If such translation could be carried out consistently and comprehensively, cognitive ethology would be much less problematic than it is, for much of the objection to ascribing mental states to animals would fall away.

However, philosophers are now generally agreed that the program of rewriting mental states as behavioral dispositions cannot be carried through. In addition to its being impossible to enumerate all the circumstances in which a particular mental state attribution will be predictive of behavior, the circumstances can rarely be specified without invoking other mental states. Thus, my being tired will mean that if I have a bed I shall be disposed to lie down on it, but only provided that I do not think there are poisonous spiders under the covers, or fear that I shall be caught napping when I should be on guard, or want to stay awake to make sure that my children get in safely, and so on. To translate these qualifications into behavioral terms would generate yet others containing still further mental references, and so on endlessly. Likewise, to ascribe a belief to a dog might be to say what the animal would do if such and such were the case, but only given certain assumptions about its wants, fears, perceptions, and conflicting interests.

D.   DOES SENSORY RECEPTIVENESS ENTAIL CONSCIOUSNESS?

Do we have to ascribe conscious states to an animal, even if we limit the possibilities to sensations and perceptions? Descartes' case for denying even minimal consciousness to animals has recently received empirical support from a rhesus monkey and, unlikely as it may seem, some human clinical evidence. The monkey was called Helen. In 1966, she had her visual cortex surgically removed in an experiment intended to throw light on brain damage in humans (Humphrey, 1983). Following the operation, Helen appeared to be totally blind. Nevertheless, there was reason to think that the monkey's visual functioning had not been completely wiped out, and so Nicholas Humphrey continued to work with Helen in an effort to see if use of her eyes could be restored. In the course of the next 7 years, during which Humphrey coaxed and cajoled her in numerous ways, Helen gradually returned to behaving as though she could see (Weiskrantz, 1972, 1980; Humphrey, 1974). However, in some respects she remained persistently different from normally sighted animals, and Humphrey was led to the conclusion that, although she was receiving and using visual information, she lacked any accompanying conscious visual imagery. Appearances to the contrary, Helen was, paradoxically speaking, limited to the experience of sightless vision. For most of us, it is beyond our reach to imagine what sightless vision might be like. However, since Helen's case became known, "blindsight" has been discovered in people with damage to the visual cortex. Larry Weiskrantz, who initiated the work on Helen, has reviewed studies that he and others have made of patients suffering from "hemianopia": phenomenal blindness on one side of the visual field due to a lesion in the corresponding half of the striate cortex (Weiskrantz *et al.*, 1974; Weiskrantz, 1980). When such patients were asked to "guess" the location or shape of an object placed in the blind half of their visual fields, they did so with remarkable accuracy, in spite of reporting that they could see nothing there. The human instances of blindsight are comparable to the sightless vision of Helen and other monkeys subjected to striate cortex removal (Weiskrantz, 1988). The general point made by Humphrey is that animal behavior guided by sensory information does not entail that the information is available to conscious awareness in the form of imagery or anything else: there need be no inner viewing screen, and nobody at home to monitor it if there were. There may be nothing that it is like to be a bat, nothing that it is like to experience the color of ultraviolet light subjectively.

To account for consciousness in humans, Humphrey turns to an evolutionary argument. He asks what consciousness might be for in terms of adaptive function, and finds the answer in the nature of our social life. People live in groups in which they compete and cooperate with one another in complex ways requiring profound degrees of mutual psychological understanding to manage. Such understanding, according to Humphrey, depends on our being able to consult our own experience so as to be able to put ourselves imaginatively into the place of the other person and so anticipate that person's action, empathize with how they feel, construe what they intend, perceive how they might be manipulated, mollified, encouraged, enlisted in the service of our interests (Humphrey, 1976, 1983, 1986). Only among the higher primates and cetaceans does one find social sophistication of an order calling for this capacity to be a "natural psychologist"; only for a natural psychologist do consciousness, introspection, and intellect make functional evolutionary sense. So Humphrey argues that consciousness of even the most rudimentary sort is probably of relatively recent evolutionary origin and tied to the elite reaches of vertebrate sociality.

E. THE COHERENCE OF CONSCIOUSNESS

Some philosophers have questioned whether even rudimentary consciousness is a coherent and useful concept applying to humans, let alone animals. They oppose a deeply entrenched position, which I alluded to earlier, and which has persisted at least since Locke's *An Essay Concerning Human Understanding* (1690/1965). According to this, all thought is built on a foundation of elementary states of sensory awareness or bodily feeling by means of association, reflection, generalization, abstraction, and so forth. These elementary components of experience were supposed to carry their own guarantee of indubitability in being ineffable, unitary, subjective, and immediately or directly present to consciousness (cf. Dennett, 1988). To have such immediate experiences, such qualia, is to know what it is like to be you. But, as we have noted, the intimacy, privacy, particularity, and incommunicable qualities of qualia are supposed to put them beyond access to any but the subject experiencing them. Consequently, we can never know for sure what it is like to be someone else, let alone what it is like to be a creature equipped with sensory apparatus very different from ours. A number of writers have taken issue with this epistemological tradition as a whole (e.g., Austin, 1962; Rorty, 1980). Daniel Dennett (1988) cut loose on qualia in particular.

Dennett takes each of the supposed properties of qualia—ineffability, seamlessness, privacy, and immediacy—and finds them to be as slippery as soap when philosophical analysis tries to pin them down or fix them to the facts of cognition. For instance, if one now enjoys the taste of a cheese that one hated as a child, is it because the quale produced by the cheese is qualitatively different or because the palate responds to the same quale differently? Direct phenomenal access to the experience should provide the answer but does not. To the child all cheeses taste the same, but to the adult even cheeses of the same type can be distinguished by complex differences in their compound savor; what seems unitary to the uninitiated can be composite to the connoisseur. Instead of being the bedrock of certainty for the acquisition of knowledge, sensations turn out to be ambiguous and our judgements of them fallible; so much so that Dennett (1988, p. 49) pronounces that "'qualia' is a philosophers' [sic] term which fosters nothing but confusion, and refers in the end to no properties or features at all." He thus concurs with Lyons (1986) on the speciousness of the classical conception of introspection. He also agrees with Austin (1962, p. 104) who said that "The pursuit of the incorrigible is one of the most venerable bugbears in the history of philosophy." Dennett thinks that we should be well advised to give up such pursuit.

However, Dennett does not go so far as to dispense with consciousness altogether. He says, "I do not deny the reality of conscious experience" (1988, p. 42). Other philosophers think that the behaviorists were right to try to leave consciousness out of psychology. They maintain that the concept is so shot through with multiple meaning that it is worse than useless, a cause of confusion and muddle comparable to the mischief of ambiguity perpetrated by the concept of instinct. Wilkes (1984, 1988) takes this position, and also points out that in languages other than English there may be nothing with the same range and scope as our words "conscious" and "consciousness." She would have us forget them for scientific and philosophical purposes.

Yet in spite of all the objections to consciousness as a coherent concept, there are people who believe some concept of consciousness to be indispensible to psychology. For example, one of the editors of a book entitled *Consciousness in Contemporary Science* writes: "consciousness in psychological science is demanded, legitimate, and necessary . . . Psychology without consciousness, without phenomenal experience or the personal level, may be biology or cybernetics, but it is not psychology" (Marcel, 1988, p. 121). Likewise Lloyd, while recognizing that philosophical problems plague each of his categories of consciousness, nevertheless thinks that we have too much invested in "good old-fashioned consciousness" to try to do without it: "concepts of consciousness, in all four guises, are woven into our ethics, our art, our conception of human nature and civilization" (Lloyd, 1989, p. 189). Faced with the prospect of having to dismantle much of our conceptual scheme if consciousness were discarded, Lloyd opts for making do with the concepts that we have and treating the problems as obstacles around which the concepts can be maneuvered. If human consciousness is thus here to stay, can animal consciousness be far behind?

As I have noted already, people, apart from behaviorists and their ilk, tend to think it natural to think that animals think like us. Humphrey (1986) explains this as a consequence of our extending our "natural psychology" beyond its original biological function of reading the minds of others in social competition, to a way of dealing with the world in general, to an inveterate tendency for us to assume a conscious model of the universe, anthropomorphically or animistically attributing moods and motives to everything from animals and plants to scenery and weather, which works well enough enough of the time to be pragmatically justified or even naturally selected. No doubt much of this is only in a manner of speaking, but when we talk of animal behavior, especially when the animals are phylogenetically close to us or our domesticated companions, we are likely to mean consciousness and its cognates literally—in the same ways that we use them of ourselves.

However, a little reflection will make us realize that it must often be the case that whatever state of consciousness or awareness an animal might be in, it must be different from what ours would be in the same situation. Take, for example, the situation of a bird becoming aware of a cat creeping up on it. When we are in the situation of being aware of a cat, we are also at least potentially aware of a furry feline, a carnivorous mammal, a warm-blooded vertebrate, an animal, an organism, and a host of other connotations connected with catness (cf. Stich, 1983, pp. 104–105). Clearly, the bird will have few, if any, of these actually or potentially in mind. What then is it for the bird to be aware of the cat? If the bird has some concept of catness, it must be very different from ours. Perhaps it consists in no more than the perceived features identifying cats as a class of thing innately or experientially associated with fear or danger. In a case like this, the difference between the animal and the human is one that possession of language makes. The rich network of concepts within which our thought of a cat is placed is unthinkable in the absence of the kind of thinking that language makes possible. I now turn to discussion of awareness and language.

III. AWARENESS AND LANGUAGE

In a letter to an Englishman, Henry More, Descartes wrote that the main reason for denying thought to animals is that they have no "real speech . . . such speech [being] the only certain sign of thought hidden in a body" (Kenny, 1970, pp. 277–278). Norman Malcolm (1973) took up this point and argued that although linguistic expression may be necessary to establish that an animal is thinking about something or other, there is no such requirement for inferring that an animal thinks that something or other is the case. The distinction between having the thought that P and thinking that P, that is, believing that P, is a real one, for I can, on the one hand, entertain the thought that unicorns exist without believing it to be true and, on the other hand, think (believe) that unicorns are mythological fictions without having to have that thought in mind. But while we can often judge what people think (believe) from what they do, Malcolm goes along with Descartes in holding that we can know their thoughts only from what they say. Therefore, because animals cannot talk, we can form no idea of what it might be for them to have a thought. Not that thoughts are to be identified with their linguistic expression; many thoughts go unexpressed. Nevertheless, in Malcolm's view, thoughts are dependent on language for both their instantiation and their revelation. As E. M. Forster reported an old lady as complaining, "How can I know what I think till I see what I say?" (Auden, 1962, p. 22).

Malcolm also argued, contra Descartes, that there is more to mental life than having thoughts—that there are many occasions of thinking, recognizing, perceiving, being aware of something, being averse to something, the experience of which is devoid of propositional content. And if, say, I can tell that a certain bird is a finch without formulating the thought "That is a finch," it does not follow that the recognition is unconscious, any more than my discomfort from having a sore throat must be unconscious unless attended by the thought "I have a sore throat." Malcolm takes the common sense view that at least some animals share with us at least some kinds of thought-free consciousness and says, "It is the prejudice of philosophers that only propositional thoughts belong to consciousness, that stands in the way of our perceiving the continuity of consciousness between human and animal life" (Malcolm, 1973, p. 20).

Gareth Matthews (1978) differed from Malcolm on the issue that thought is dependent on language. Matthews uses Köhler's (1925) account of how the chimpanzee Sultan arrived at the solution of joining two sticks together to get a banana placed otherwise out of reach. To Matthews, the description of events suggested that (A) "The thought that the two sticks can be put together to make one stick occurs to Sultan," and (B) "The thought that the double stick can be used to fetch a banana occurs to Sultan" (Matthews, 1978, p. 448). Because these thoughts were had in the absence of the possibility of their verbal expression, Matthews took Malcolm to have been refuted. But what went on in Sultan's head might just as plausibly have been (A) the perception that the two sticks could be joined, and (B) the realization that the double stick could reach the banana. Neither of these implies thought in propositional form. Both exemplify nonpropositional awareness of the kind that Malcolm believed to be continuous between human and animal life.

Malcolm, Matthews, and others who think along similar lines about the mentality of animals (e.g., Vendler, 1972) take it for granted, like Descartes, that animals lack anything like linguistic capacity and, hence, assume that the brutes are truly dumb. In contrast, Griffin (1976, 1984), with his fancy for King Solomon's ring, rejects any such assumption. As a Darwinian biologist, he takes the position that there must be evolutionary continuity between whatever cognitive equipment underlies human language and the cognitive equipment of ancestral and cognate forms, the differences being of degree rather than of kind. He discusses the comparison of human and animal communication systems with regard to their "design features" (Hockett, 1959; Hockett and Altmann, 1968; Thorpe, 1974) and is unpersuaded that any feature of human language is peculiar to it. He welcomes the work devoted to teaching higher vertebrates—apes, dolphins, sea lions, and a parrot (for a recent review, see Ristau, 1992)—language-like sign systems, as providing evidence of kinds of cognitive capacity consistent with the principle of evolutionary continuity. He contemplates the possibility that animal communication systems will provide a "window on the minds of animals" (Griffin, 1976, p. 87) when we come to understand them sufficiently to enable us to "eavesdrop" and so discover what animals are expressing about their mental lives and whether they make reference to things in the outside world.

There are highly controversial issues here. For example, David Premack (1986), one of the major figures in the animal language arena, has criticized the claims and conclusions of much of the work of other participants, and argued that, while his own experiments have demonstrated that a chimpanzee can use an acquired system of signs and rules in ways that reveal referential and inferential capacity beyond what apes used to be thought capable of, these experiments also show limitations implying deep-seated differences between simian and human intelligence. Whereas the ape's command of syntax is bound to the training it has received, the human child goes beyond experience to generate rules that bespeak contribution from a "hard wired" basis for language acquisition (cf. Chomsky, 1980). Moreover, the ape appears to lack both the kind of inductive capacity that enables the child to arrive at the rules of a linguistic grammar and the syntactic categories, such as "noun phrase" and "verb phrase," which according to a consensus among linguists, are necessary for the formulation of such rules. Premack goes on to consider how human language is only one among a number of characteristically human cognitive and social attributes, to which it is intimately connected and with which it contributes to the basic nature of the human mind. He even suggests that preoccupation with language without taking these related attributes into account may be distorting our view of that nature.

The main title of Premack's book is *Gavagai!*, which alludes to a device used by W. V. Quine (1960) in a discussion of "the indeterminacy of radical translation." Quine pictured a linguist in a strange country trying to understand the utterly foreign language of one of the natives, who says "gavagai" when a rabbit runs by. Once the linguist has established a way of getting the native to assent or dissent in response to pointing gestures he is able to determine the "stimulus meaning" of an utterance like "gavagai"—the external circumstances in which the expression does and does not apply. But, Quine argued, even if the native says or assents to "gavagai" when and only when there is a rabbit in the offing, the linguist is in no position to conclude that "gavagai" means "rabbit," for all sorts of other possibilities are consistent with the division of situations established by the responses to pointing: "Who knows but what the objects to which this term applies are not rabbits at all, but mere stages, or brief temporal segments, of rabbits?" (Quine, 1960, p. 51). What might be in a person's head is undetermined by what is out at their finger tips. Translation from a language radically different from one's own is thus bound to be indeterminate. Likewise, when an animal has been taught some version of a linguistic sign system, there can be indeterminacy about just what the animal has learned in terms of mental representation, although Premack thinks that tests can be devised to get beyond the point where Quine left the question. The situation is even worse when one is trying to deal with an animal's own sign system, especially in the more complex cases where semantic indeterminacy may be shrouded in syntactic indeterminacy: doubt about what the units or dimensions of signal significance are and, hence, what rules of order or combination might apply (Beer, 1977).

The preceding considerations are consistent with Wittgenstein's comment: "If a lion could talk, we could not understand him" (1958, p. 223). Wittgenstein made this remark in the course of some reflections on how enigmatic people can be to one another, especially when they come from radically different cultures. He viewed a language as part of a "form of life" (Wittgenstein, 1958, pp. 11, 226), which meant that the understanding of a concept in the language requires knowing how the concept relates to the customs, beliefs, and other expressions surrounding its use, the rules of the "language game" in which it plays a part. This emphasis on language as activity went with a conception of meaning as use (e.g., "What we call *"descriptions"* are instruments for particular uses," Wittgenstein, 1958, p. 99): how a word is to be used is governed by the rules of the language game that furnish the "outward criteria" for its application. For example, a criterion for "pain" is pain behavior. Wittgenstein was thus led to a kind of operationalism, which, as I have noted, was a forerunner of the philosophical behaviorism developed by Ryle.

Operationalism and verificationism can be viewed as versions of the traditional philosophical preoccupation with grounding knowledge on sure foundations impervious to erosion by doubt, a pursuit that has been described as foundationalism (e.g., Rorty, 1980). As Dennett's questions about qualia exemplified, many philosophers are now persuaded that foundationalism will not work. For instance, Quine (1953) argued that the verification principle of logical positivism, and the analytic/synthetic distinction on which it depends, are dispensable dogmas incapable of being rigorously sustained. Sellars (1956) portrayed empiricist foundationalism as "the myth of the given," with the sense datum theories of knowledge resting on shifting sand. He took the position that words have sense by virtue of their relationships to one another in a coherent conceptual framework. Chihara and Fodor (1965) concentrated on Wittgenstein's claim about criteria. They argued that it has some implausible implications, and that Wittgenstein's reasoning on its behalf is inconclusive. Like Sellars, they appeal to the notion of a conceptual scheme, comparable to a scientific theory, as governing everyday language and thought about mental states.

We thus have two related conceptions of considerable relevance to cognitive ethology: a network notion of meaning and the idea that the ways in which we use concepts like belief and desire constitute a theory. I have already alluded to the network theory in commenting on the case of crediting a bird with having a belief about a cat: so many of the connections that our having a belief about a cat has to other beliefs are missing in the case of the bird that is not at all clear what the bird can be said to believe. In a subsequent section, I shall discuss the issue of whether our use of mentalistic terms constitutes a theory. I also postpone till then some consideration of a further twist of the issue of how language is related to thought, but one in which questions of consciousness are set aside. In the meantime, I turn to another set of issues in which how the questions are construed and pursued can depend on how behavior is conceived and described.

IV. Actions, Intentions, and Functions

In 1964, Charles Taylor published a book entitled *The Explanation of Behaviour* in which he contrasted the kind of explanation we give of behavior categorized as action with the kind of explanation we give of behavior categorized as movement. Compare "he waved" with "his arm went up"—two descriptions of the one piece of behavior. An explanation of the action of waving might be that the man wanted to attract the attention of a friend; an explanation of the movement of arm extension upward would be that certain neurons fired and certain muscles contracted. As a rule, Taylor maintained, actions call for explanations in terms of intentions, and movements call for explanations in terms of causes, and the logical relations between an intention and an action is different from that between a cause and a movement. For a purported intention to explain an action, the action must be such as to conduce toward satisfaction of the intention—there must be a rational teleological connection between the intention and the action. The connection between a movement and its cause, on the other hand, is merely contingent—a matter of brute fact about what follows what, devoid of logical constraint or necessity [cf. Hume (1739): "necessity is something that exists in the mind, not in objects . . . ."]. Taylor argued that, although behavioristic psychology sought to account for animal behavior solely in causal terms, it could not avoid categorizing much of the behavior as action and so implying that animals have intentions.

Taylor's argument led to much discussion. A group of philosophers and scientists at Oxford continues to meet on the issues and in 1989 produced a book, *Goals, No-Goals and Own Goals* (Montefiore and Noble, 1989), containing essays and debate representative of the discussion. Central to this collection is a study by McFarland that maintains that a scientific approach to apparent purposiveness in behavior has to distinguish critically between goal-achieving behavior, goal-seeking behavior, goal-directed behavior, and intentional behavior. McFarland argues that the purposiveness of behavior can generally be accounted for by the evolutionarily constructed design of an organism, without need for invoking goal directedness or intention, with their implied internal representations of the goals sought and achieved by such design. Other contributors defended positions closer to Taylor's, to the effect that how you describe behavior affects how you try to explain it.

However, philosophical usage has not upheld Taylor's dichotomy between intentions and causes: intentions, along with beliefs and desires and other "propositional attitudes," have been regarded as mental causes of the actions to which they give rise. Nevertheless, Taylor's point that the questions raised by behavior can depend on how it is described, in particular that behavior may call for explanation in terms of intention under some descriptions but not others, has been taken up by a number of writers. For example, Anscombe (1963) described a man sawing wood as, at the same time, sawing a plank, sawing an oak plank, making a pile of sawdust, and creating a din, only some of which descriptions could be said to represent his intention. In a similar vein, Millikan (1986) argued that of the majority of the many descriptions that might be given of a piece of animal behavior, only a narrow selection will be biologically significant, namely, those representing the behavior in a way that bears on its function. Thus, a gull performing a display may be making its shadow go up and down, but that will be beside the point of what it is doing. Ethologists concerned with communication studies are often presented with the problem of sorting out the features of a signal that constitute its "sign vehicle" (Morris, 1946), the attributes conducive to effecting change in a recipient animal's response tendencies.

Of course functions and intentions present two very different kinds of explanation of behavior. Nevertheless, the same terms can be used for either attribution in many cases, and this sometimes causes confusion. Take "deception" for example: it can describe the consequences of an action (or of a physical feature such as the wasplike appearance of the flowers of some *Ophrys* orchids) or the intention with which an action is carried out. Often there is no ambiguity: to say that the eyespot display of a saturnid moth fools a flycatcher into thinking that it is faced with an owl is not to say, and is not taken to be saying, that the insect deliberately put the eyespots on its wings and had the deceptive end in view when it exposed them at the critical moment. But when a plover performs a broken wing display in the presence of a predator (Simmons, 1955; Armstrong, 1956; Skutch, 1976; Ristau, 1991), with all the appearance of attempting to lead the predator away from its clutch or brood, description of the performance as distraction behavior is neighbor to the thought that the bird was pretending. Similarly, when, in the absence of a predator, a vervet monkey utters an alarm call during a melee in which its troop is losing ground, and so causes the hostilities to cease as all the combatants take to the trees (Dennett, 1987), the question may be left open whether describing the action as deceptive implies intent to deceive as well as efficacy to deceive.

To avoid the misunderstanding that can result from such ambiguity, some ethologists explicitly disavow any intentionalistic connotation when they describe animal action in terms that usually imply intention when used of people. Richard Dawkins begins *The Selfish Gene* with an emphatic statement about how he is to be read when he uses words like "selfishness" and "altruism":

> It is important to realize that the above definitions of altruism and selfishness are *behavioural*, not subjective. I am not concerned here with the psychology of motives. I am not going to argue about whether people who behave altruistically are 'really' doing it for secret or subconscious selfish motives. My definition is concerned only with whether the *effect* of an act is to lower or raise the survival prospects of the presumed beneficiary (Dawkins, 1976, pp. 4–5).

However, because such words are so wedded to intentionalistic implication in ordinary talk about ourselves, it is perhaps unsurprising that some of the people who picked up Dawkins's book forgot his proviso as they read on and took literally much that was really intended metaphorically. At least this is one way in which Midgley's (1979) shrill criticism of the book can be construed. But Dawkins, in his reply to Midgley, denied that he was being metaphorical:

> When biologists talk about 'selfishness' or 'altruism' we are emphatically not talking about emotional nature, whether of human beings, other animals, or genes. We do not even mean the words in a *metaphorical* sense. We *define* altruism and selfishness in purely behaviouristic ways . . . (Dawkins, 1981, p. 557, his emphases).

Such behavioristic construal of ordinary language for biological purposes has been applied to a selection of intentionalistic terms. Ethologists and sociobiologists write of decision-making, assessment, choice, evaluation, and other terms for mental acts, but usually in quantitatively technical contexts, such as game theory and optimality theory, which give the terms senses that exclude any concern with what might be consciously going on in a mind. In two articles in which they discuss animal communication as informative or manipulative (Dawkins and Krebs, 1978; Krebs and Dawkins, 1984), Dawkins and Krebs include "manipulation," "persuasion," "lying," even "mindreading" and "intention" among the words they use, but with meanings that have to do with functional consequences rather than subjective motives. Here, for example, "intention" amounts to "what the actor will do next" (Krebs and Dawkins, 1984, p. 397). The biological uses of these and like terms thus constitute a network distinct from that of ordinary language and, hence, within which many of the implications of the ordinary language uses do not hold. There is venerable precedent for this usage. In the sixth edition of *The Origin of Species,* Darwin responded to critics of his choice of "natural selection":

> Others have objected that the term selection implies conscious choice in the animals which become modified; and it has even been urged that, as plants have no volition, natural selection is not applicable to them! In the literal sense of the word, no doubt natural selection is a false term; but who ever objected to chemists speaking of the elective affinities of the various elements? - and yet an acid cannot strictly be said to elect the base with which it in preference combines. It has been said that I speak of natural selection as an active power or Diety; but who objects to an author speaking of the attraction of gravity as ruling the movements of the planets? Everyone knows what is meant and implied by such metaphorical expressions; and they are almost necessary for brevity. (Darwin, 1872, p. 64).

However, when the derived use of language goes beyond isolated metaphors to systematic recalibration of whole ways of talking, there is no guarantee that everyone will know what is meant. Hence, there has been much misunderstanding of sociobiological and behavioral ecological writing by readers unlettered in the ways in which evolutionary biologists understand one another. I have even encountered people who have taken kin selection to mean an animal's favoring close kin in situations of choice, rather than the evolution of kin-promoting behavior as a consequence of its contribution to inclusive fitness, for which Maynard Smith (1964) introduced the term.

The problem is exacerbated by the fact that, besides the questions about functions to which terms like "decision," "strategy," "evaluation," and "rule-use" are applied in behavioristic senses, there are questions about the proximal processes underlying performance—how the animal arrives at a decision, chooses a strategy, makes an evaluation, or follows a rule—and the answers that propose themselves to such questions are likely to be couched in the same kinds of terms understood in their everyday senses. Thus, individual decision making suggests an actual inner weighing of the risks and returns, the costs and benefits, the short- and long-term consequences of alternative courses of action, and inferential reasoning taking into account probabilities, preferences, values, and needs. The two networks, behavioristic and intentionalistic, consequently tend to draw together, but are thereby liable to become tangled as the same words shuttle between behavioristic and intentionalistic readings.

V. INTENTIONALITY, FOLK PSYCHOLOGY, AND COGNITIVE SCIENCE

A. INTENTIONALITY

For cognitive ethology, intentionalistic readings of mind-laden words applied to animals should be taken seriously and not set aside as sociobiology stipulates. But by "intentionalistic" here, I mean more than the word usually connotes, and I need to make this explicit. I need to do this because, as Dennett has said, "ethologists . . . persist in conflating the philosophical notion (Brentano's notion—the concept of *aboutness,* in a word) and the more or less everyday notion of intentionality: the capacity to perform intentional actions or frame intentions to act" (Dennett, 1987, p. 271); and because the philosophical notion Dennett refers to is implicitly involved in much that cognitive ethologists say about the minds of animals.

However, this philosophical notion of intentionality appears to be difficult for non-philosophers to get clear. A reader of a previous version of this article found my attempt at explication of intentionality incomprehensible. A recent book on motivation, by an ethologist, represents a special logical feature of intentionalistic idioms—their "referential opacity"—as the "non-translatability of intentional terms into behavioural terms" (Colgan, 1989, p. 67), which is dead wrong. The philosophers do not make things any easier when they vary the spelling between "intentionality" and "intensionality," sometimes using the difference to mark a distinction, and sometimes not. They also use the coupled terms "intension" and "extension" for the distinction between a term's conceptual meaning and what falls within its domain, as in the contrast between sense and reference, connotation and denotation (Cohen and Nagel, 1934). Moreover, intentionality, in the sense deriving from Brentano, continues to be a controversial matter for philosophers of mind (e.g., Dennett, 1969, 1987; Searle, 1980). In spite of these difficulties, I think it necessary to include at least an outline of the concept here, for it could have serious implications for cognitive ethology. Other and fuller treatments can be found in Dennett (1969, Chapter 2), Boden (1972, esp. pp. 47–49), and Lockery (1989, esp. pp. 121–129).

Brentano's (1874) concept of intentionality includes all mental states that are *about* or directed toward something or other (their content). So in addition to intention, which is always intention that something or other come to pass, intentionality includes knowing, which is always knowledge about something or other, desiring, which is always desire for something or other, guessing, which is always guessing that or about something or other; likewise, recognizing, wishing, hoping, remembering, forgetting, doubting, and numerous other terms standing for what philosophers call propositional attitudes. As I pointed out earlier about perception, which is another example of intentionality, an intentional state is unlike a state like tiredness or lassitude in that you cannot, for example, just believe or desire purely and simply, empty of content. Brentano thought that only mental states could have this property of aboutness, that intentionality is "what distinguishes the mental of psychological from the physical" (Chisholm, 1967, p. 201). If this were so, then to talk of animals as perceiving, recognizing, remembering, forgetting, and so forth, would be tantamount to assuming them to have mentality. The exclusiveness of intentionalistic properties to mental states is one of the issues that philosophers continue to debate.

To support the thesis that intentionality is "the mark of the mental," philosophers have sought logical criteria that apply to sentences describing mental states but not sentences describing physical phenomena. Among these criteria are referential opacity (Quine, 1960, p. 144) and existential generalization. Referential opacity obtains when substitution of coreferring terms in a sentence may not preserve its truth. Take the sentence "John believes that George Eliot wrote *Middlemarch*," and assume it to be true. If you substitute "Mary Ann (or Marian) Evans" for "George Eliot," the resulting sentence could be false, for John might not know that George Eliot and Mary Ann Evans are one and the same. Contrast this with "George Eliot wrote *Middlemarch*," which states a nonpsychological fact. Now the substitution makes no difference to the truth of the sentence.

For "George Eliot wrote *Middlemarch*" to be true, there must have been a writer called George Eliot and a book called *Middlemarch*. Neither of these need be the case for the sentence about John's belief to be true. This exemplifies the test of existential generalization. As a rule, sentences concerning nonpsychological facts (extensional sentences) assume the existence of what they refer to; intentional sentences need not.

Although these and related logical criteria generally differentiate sentences about intentional states from sentences about physical facts, there are exceptions (see Chisholm, 1967; Kneale and Prior, 1968), especially cases of nonintentional description that slip past the logical tests for intentionality (e.g., the nonintentional sentence "three is the square root of nine" appears to be referentially opaque; try substituting "the number of the planets" for "nine"). Philosophers are still seeking ways of refining the logical rules so that they pick out all and only statements about intentional states. In the meantime, we can ask whether and how these logical tests apply to ascriptions of intentional states to animals.

The answer seems to be that it is doubtful whether there can ever be a straightforward application of any of the logical tests for intentional ascription in animal cases. Take the possibility that an animal might believe in or desire something that does not exist. For this to be judged seriously, there must surely be some observable or empirical consequences. It is difficult to think of any cases for which what might be construed as observable consequences of such a belief or desire cannot be interpreted in simpler terms, making no appeal to intentionality. For example, when a gull or a fish reacts to its mirror image as though it believed it were faced by another of its kind, an ethologist can fall back on the classical story of how sign stimuli elicit patterns of aggressive or courtship behavior. Even the bees that Gould (Gould and Gould, 1986) tricked into passing false information to their hive mates can be accommodated by a causal account needing no importation of intentionality. Millikan has viewed the bee dancing as referentially opaque: "Von Frisch knew what bee dances are about, but it is unlikely that bees do. Bees just react to the bee dances appropriately" (Millikan, 1984, p. 13). But this way of deploying referential opacity is hardly a test for intentional ascription comparable to a human case. If it were, we could credit a clock with intentionality, because we know what the position of the hands on the clock face are about, but the clock does not. Unless the bees have alternative ways of representing the same state of affairs and, hence, are in a position to be acquainted with this state of affairs under one representation but not under another, they cannot be capable of being in referentially opaque states in the way that we are. Indeed, when Millikan says that the bees merely react appropriately, she admits as much.

We have alternative mental representations of the same things because we know them by different signs, different names, different descriptions. So we can refer to the same heavenly body as "the morning star," "the evening star," or "the planet Venus"; whether we know that these alternatives refer to the same thing will affect how they enter into our beliefs. Because animals, with the possible exception of some specially trained instances, lack anything like our cognitive manifold of names and descriptions, little if anything of what logically applies to intentional ascription in the human case carries straightforwardly over to intentional ascription in animal cases.

B. THE LANGUAGE OF THOUGHT

As in the case of thought discussed earlier (Malcolm, 1973), part of the problem of ascribing intentional states to animals is that intentional talk is fully articulate only where talk is a means of expressing intentionality or settling questions about intentionality. "it is the *possibility* of our declaring, or expressing, our intentions from moment to moment, and if the question is asked, that gives sense to the notion of intention itself" (Hampshire, 1960, p. 97). The same may be said of beliefs and desires and their entailment relations. Even the Freudian notion of unconscious desires becomes operative only through application of the "talking cure." We are again presented with a network conception of meaning: ascribing intentional states to an agent is normally tied into the agent's being able to say what the intentionality is about.

However, Fodor (1975) has developed a theory that makes cognition dependent on language, even where there is no possibility of the agent's giving tongue to the thinking. According to this argument, intelligent behavior is a product of thought, thought requires representation, and representation is possible only within a system having linguistic properties: a "language of thought" (cf. Dennett, 1978, p. 90). This purportedly innate mental code is prior to and necessary for acquisition of spoken natural language and is operative in prelinguistic children and intelligent animals. The idea is that features of the experienced world are mapped onto the mind in the terms of the code, which implies a preexisting structural correspondence between the world and the code. Because such correspondence is a prerequisite of the encoding, its foundations must be prior to any experience. Fodor, therefore, appeals to an evolutionary origin for the representational system. We can think of representations as sentences in the head from which syntactic computation can generate other sentences and, hence, decisions about actions. The formal properties of the representations and algorhythmic transformation rules, thus, govern thinking, the semantic content of which is read in and out via the mapping relations. However, these mapping relations— the relations between the syntactic and semantic sides of representation—present what Fodor (1981, p. 203) describes as "*the* problem for representational theories to solve."

All this may seem a farfetched philosophical concoction, and numerous critics have taken issue with it (e.g., Dennett, 1978; Churchland, 1978; Campbell and Bickhard, 1987). Yet, Fodor's representational theory of mind is an explicit working out of what is implicit in much philosophy of mind, and even the commonsense kind of psychology that people in general assume when they use such terms as belief and desire, knowing and thinking. Indeed, Fodor has claimed that commonsense belief-desire psychology, and the representational theory of mind elaborated from it, offer the only plausible accounts of intelligent behavior. For example, in his recent book *Psychosemantics* he starts out by describing some behavior of his cat as resulting from beliefs and desires:

> I have no serious doubt that this theory (what I call 'commonsense belief/desire psychology') is pretty close to being true. My reason for believing this . . . . is that commonsense belief/desire psychology explains vastly more of the facts about behavior than any of the alternative theories available. It could hardly fail to do so: there *are* no alternative theories available (Fodor, 1987, p. x; his emphasis).

Toward the end of the book he says, "As things stand now, the cost of not having a Language of Thought is not having a theory of thinking" (Fodor, 1987, p. 147).

Among the rival theories that Fodor dismisses as no alternatives to a representational theory of mind are Rylean philosophical behaviorism and mind–brain identity theory. I have mentioned the difficulties encountered by philosophical behaviorism. Mind–brain identity theorists (e.g., Place, 1956; Smart, 1959; Lewis, 1966) take the position that mental events are brain events, and so processes in the former reduce to processes in the latter. Fodor, and other philosophers who think like him, can accept that each instance of a mental event is an instance of a brain event, that is, that there is token-to-token identity (and substance dualism of the Cartesian sort is false), but they have several arguments against the stronger claim that kinds of mental events map onto kinds of brain events, that is, type-to-type identity. You and I probably share the same belief that table salt is sodium chloride, but does that entail that in corresponding sites in our brains, we each have a five part embodiment of the proposition? What of the German who believes that Kochsalz ist Chlornatrium, and the Frenchman who believes that sel de table est chlorure de sodium? Do they or do they not share our belief given that the engram for it would be of three parts for the one and seven parts for the other? And what of the possibility of a computer's holding the proposition in a manner construable as belief? Because the machine is made of stuff different from outs, there could not be physical type identity, yet propositional content identity there certainly would be.

From arguments like these philosophers have built a case for holding that cognitive science constitutes a domain distinct from and not collapsible into neuroscience. The categories of mind are functionally rather than ontologically related to their physical instantiations and so have to be dealt with in their own terms, not those of neurophysiology or physics. For this reason, the philosophers who take this sort of stand on the autonomy of cognitive study are generally referred to as functionalists. Although varying among themselves on numerous issues, they constitute a major force among current philosophers of mind (see Cummins, 1983).

C. Contra Folk Psychology

However functionalism, in this latterday sense (cf. the functionalist psychology of Angell, Dewey, and company), has its opponents. Among these are philosophers who take issue with functionalism's basis in common-sense belief/desire psychology, or what they more tersely call folk psychology. Folk psychology is regarded as a theory, and so, like any theory, can be subjected to examination for internal coherence and capacity to accommodate the facts falling in its domain. Stephen Stich (1983) found folk psychology to be wanting in coherence; the Churchlands question its explanatory capability (P. M. Churchland, 1981, 1985; P. S. Churchland, 1985).

Stich argues that folk psychology is a semantic theory of the mind, one in which the mental code has representational meaning affecting cognitive processing, as when reading the menu contributes to one's decision about what to order. He contrasts this with a causal or syntactic theory, in which the cognitive processing depends solely on formal features and relations of the code, as in algebraic inference. Stich holds that only the latter can provide a sound basis on which to ground cognitive science. Part of the reason is that the content internally represented according to the semantic theory is affected by the circumstances and ideological context in which an individual is situated. This has the consequence that formally identical belief tokens—mental sentences, perhaps—in different individuals could differ in reference and in how what they represent is connected to other content in a network of relationships. Such lack of consistency between formal and representational aspects of the code raises problems for the individuation of types of belief states and generalization about them. For instance, whatever the generalizations folk psychology might generate about belief states, they will not extend to prelinguistic children, brain-impaired patients, intelligent animals, and other exotic cases that should come within the scope of a mature cognitive science.

In Stich's view, such a science needs to deal with autonomous mental states free of the vagaries of external circumstance and ideological context and emanating from brain states. So Stich proposes to do away with belief and the other propositional attitudes and put in their place a purely syntactic theory of mind as the psychological basis on which to build cognitive science. This, he claims, will capture all the generalizations of a representational theory of mind in a precise manner and also take in the exotic cases falling outside the purview of the representational theory.

However, Stich does not show how this translation might be effected for any folk psychological generalizations or how, for example, the description of behavior might be consistently overhauled, as it would have to be, to replace action terms like "fleeing," which imply intentionality, with movement terms like "running," without losing the point of what the commonsense language is about. This latter, the Watsonian behaviorists tried to do, but it is now generally agreed that they failed for reasons that Tolman made evident when he argued his distinction between molar and molecular categorization of behavior. Critics (e.g., Horgan and Woodward, 1985; Sanford, 1986–1987) have remarked that the examples from social psychology used by Stich to support his argument are all couched in folk psychological terms. Stich admits as much (1983, p. 230), yet he makes no attempt to show how the implications of these examples might be otherwise stated. Others (Marras, 1987; Russow, 1987) contended that the context relativity affecting a semantic content account of the mind must apply also to a causal account, because "the causal potential of a mental token is . . . affected by the presence or absence of other tokens" (Marras, 1987, p. 118). Stich's case against belief has thus been represented as less than compelling.

Stich himself admits sympathizing with people who quail at the prospect of having to try to renounce folk psychology, for such renunciation would entail the loss of much that is central to our conception of ourselves as moral agents and as persons (cf. Lloyd, 1989, p. 189, quoted earlier). He holds out the possibility that even if folk psychology cannot be the basis of cognitive science, it might still continue to provide at least a rough and ready means of expressing truths other than those that are the business of cognitive science but that are the business of the social sciences and the humanities. However, he is less than sanguine about even this prospect. He reviews a number of experiments by social psychologists on dissonance and self-attribution (e.g., Nisbett and Wilson, 1977), the results of which are inconsistent with expectation according to folk psychology. There are, he says, empirical assumptions involved in belief attribution, which could well turn out to be false. He also makes the point that folk psychology is more or less a singular exception to the rule that folk theories have fallen victim to the advancement of science. Folk chemistry, folk medicine, folk physics, and so on, have all been shown to be wrong. Stich asks, "is there any reason to think that ancient camel drivers would have greater insight or better luck when the subject at hand was the structure of their own minds rather than the structure of matter or the cosmos?" (1983, pp. 229–230).

The Churchlands also make the point that current folk psychology has remained virtually unchanged since the time of Aristotle, in contrast to what has happened in other sciences. In addition to this "stagnation," they charge folk psychology with ineptness and insularity. The ineptness consists in the failure of folk psychology to account for a great deal of what an adequate theory of mental life should be expected to cover:

As examples of central and important mental phenomena that remain largely or wholly mysterious within the framework of [folk psychology], consider the nature and dynamics of mental illness, the faculty of creative imagination, or the ground of intelligence differences between individuals. Consider our utter ignorance of the nature and psychological functions of sleep, that curious state in which a third of one's life is spent. Reflect on the common ability to catch an outfield fly ball on the run, or hit a moving car with a snowball. Consider the internal construction of a 3-D visual image from subtle differences in the 2-D array of stimulations in our respective retinas. Consider the rich variety of perceptual illusions visual and otherwise. Or consider the miracle of memory, with its lightning capacity for relevant retrieval. On these and many other mental phenomena, [folk psychology] sheds negligible light (Churchland, 1981, p. 73).

The insularity of folk psychology places it defiantly outside the integrated account of human nature being assembled from applications of physics and chemistry to material questions, of physiology and biochemistry to functional questions, of genetics and embryology to developmental questions, of ecology and ethology to evolutionary questions. As we have seen, functionalist philosophers of mind argue that it is impossible to reduce the folk psychology of mental states to the neurophysiology of brain states. So much the worse for folk psychology, according to the Churchlands. In any case, they think that it may not be worth reducing to anything—that it is overdue for elimination and replacement by a materialist theory of mind grounded in neuroscience. In addition to progress in the bottom-up approaches of neuroscience itself, they find support for their view in the field of artificial intelligence, where a previously defeated movement has regrouped under a new banner—that of parallel distributed processing or connectionism.

D. MINDS, BRAINS, AND COMPUTERS

When McCulloch and Pitts (1943) devised a way of getting a computer to do symbolic logic, they described their model as a neural net, implying relevance to how real brains work, even though the units out of which their networks were constructed were far simpler than real neurons. Developments of this approach led to Frank Rosenblatt's (1962) invention of "perceptrons": networks of modifiable connections capable of stimulus–response "learning." However, perceptrons proved to have severe limitations as models of how a brain might work (Minsky and Papert, 1969) and, consequently, neural nets were abandoned in favor of information-processing models based on the linear sequential computational operation of conventional digital computers in the Turing (1937) and von Neumann (1958) tradition. For example, when Fodor (1975) claimed for his language of thought that it was based on the only kind of psychological theory we have, he assumed that thought consists of computations over symbols. But the computational approach has problems of its own, such as the problems of "combinatorial explosion" (Dennett, 1987) and "finitary predicament"—the limited information processing capacity of actual brains and computers (Cherniak, 1986, p. 8). Even relatively simple operations, like paired comparison, require astronomical computational capacity once the number of items gets beyond a quite modest figure, and the time needed to carry out the computations serially likewise quickly builds up to durations longer than the life of the universe. Neural conduction is considerably slower than electronic conduction, yet the brain can do swiftly what would hang up a computer for ages. Apparently the brain cannot be a serial processor. An alternative possibility is that the brain is a parallel processor, breaking up each cognitive operation into parts that can be worked on separately and simultaneously in a fraction of the time required for serial computation. Such parallel distributed processing requires a network of connections, and the brain is just such a network. Attention has swung back to neural net models.

To circumvent the limitations of the perceptrons, the new connectionist models have multi-layered instead of single-layered neural nets. They are equipped with a set of sensors for registering stimulus patterns and a set of "motor" units for effecting responses, the input and output units connecting comprehensively to the units of a "hidden" network sandwiched between them. The connections between the input units and the hidden units and between the hidden units and the output units vary in their transmission values or weights, and these weights can be altered as a consequence of "experience" or "training": whenever for a particular input the output tends in the training direction, the connections that were active have their weights strengthened, and, correspondingly, connections tending away from the training goal have their weights weakened, the adjustments being effected by "back propagation" (Rumelhart *et al.,* 1986). Such connectionist network programs have been run, and the results have been greeted with jubilation by those looking for an understanding of the mind in neural terms. Among the more impressive achievements is that of NETtalk, a network that has been trained to read English text aloud (Sejnowski and Rosenberg, 1987).

Connectionist systems differ from classical computational models of the mind in that they apparently include no program—no set of rules in accordance with which input is transformed into output, only a matrix of intervening conduction values determined by progressive adjustment of inner to outer relations. The relations between input and output can be *described* in terms of rules, but seem not to be internally *governed* by such rules (see Lloyd, Chapter 4). The representational order received on the one side and delivered in translated form at the other is dispersed in between, scattered among the shuttling threads of the neural loom. Indeed, it is an open question whether and how connectionist networks can be representational at all, except as their inputs and outputs are interpreted externally. This contrasts with a theory like Fodor's language of thought, which makes internal or mental representation, including the representation of syntactic rules, the heart of the matter. Indeed, connectionist models appear to have no place in them for such folk psychological states as belief and desire, the propositional attitudes of representational theories of mind. NETtalk is remarkable in being able to develop the ability to turn text into talk, but it is totally incapable of comprehending the meanings of the strings of symbols it translates. All this is fine in the eyes of the eliminative materialists, who think it unlikely that the categories of folk psychology will survive the development of a fully mature neuroscience.

For the defenders of a representational theory of mind, these contrasts imply that connectionism cannot constitute a theory of mind. Fodor continues to insist that commonsense psychology is the only theory of mind that we have: "We have no idea of how to explain ourselves to ourselves except in a vocabulary which is *saturated* with belief/desire psychology" (Fodor, 1987, p. 9). At best, according to Fodor and Pylyshyn (1988), connectionism offers suggestions about how belief/desire psychology might be implemented in the neural networks of brains, the syntactic computational rules of the language of thought being somehow distributively represented in the matrixes of weighted connections. The compatibility of computational and connectionist configurations is manifest in the fact that, so far, the testing of connectionist programs has all been done on conventional serially processing digital computers. On the other hand, although connectionist architecture is inspired by neural organization, there are differences between connectionist units and real neurons and these differences are likely to be important for claims that connectionist networks model the brain. For instance, there is wide variation in neuronal and synaptic characteristics, in contrast to the uniformity of connectionist units, and the back propagation by which training effects adjustment in connectionist networks contrasts with the prevalence of unidirectional transmission in neural networks. No doubt refinements in the designs and details of connectionist architecture can reduce these differences; but neuroscience has yet to arrive at an understanding of the fine-grained functioning of nervous systems sufficient to tell what the crucial differences are likely to be. An alternative to attempting "total brain simulation" (Lloyd, 1989, p. 93) is to let connectionism develop along its own lines in the hope that general principles might be forthcoming of a sort illuminating to brain function, after the fashion of cybernetics and systems theory or similar to the way in which games theory has been applied to questions of behavioral evolution.

Wherever the currently volatile relationships between computational theories of the mind and connectionism end up, the two approaches share what might be called the problem of meaning or semanticity. As we have noted, NETtalk cannot be said to understand the words it reads and utters. Likewise, classical artificial intelligence programs manipulate symbols without having a clue as to what they stand for. John Searle (1980) has likened the situation to that of a man who is put in a room into which Chinese characters are passed, for each of which he has to select and deliver another character according to a correspondence list he has. If the characters he receives are questions to which the characters he delivers are answers, it will appear to someone looking on from outside that the man in the room understands Chinese. This, of course, is not the case at all: the man in the room is simply shuffling squiggly marks according to a set of rules. Likewise with computer programs. But minds deal with meanings. Therefore, Searle concludes, minds cannot be programs as proponents of "strong" artificial intelligence maintain. Neither can they be connectionist networks, by this sort of argument. Fodor and the functionalists recognize the problem, accept it as a challenge, admit that they are still in want of a solution [e.g., "What we need now is a semantic theory for mental representations; a theory of how mental representations represent. Such a theory I do not have" (Fodor, 1981, p. 31)]. Folk psychology blithely goes on as though the problem of meaning is of no concern to it.

If folk psychology, as practiced by people at large, can thus ignore one of the central questions about how minds are related to brains, there is surely something odd about regarding it as a theory on a par with theories in the physical and biological sciences. True, it furnishes functionalism and the representational and computational theories of mind with their basic intentionalistic concepts and generalizations, but its main business would appear to be other than to give the sorts of philosophical and scientific explanations of mentality sought by cognitive science (cf. Wilkes, 1988, p. 33: "common sense [psychology] and science have such dramatically different aims that it seems absurd to compare them as theories"). Ordinary folk psychology provides people with a means of dealing with one another, making sense of their own and others' actions, competing and cooperating effectively in a world demanding finesse in social skills and sensitivity. For most of the time it works well enough, as well as one might expect a product of evolutionary adaptation to work. Andy Clark (1987) likened folk psychology, which he prefers to call *naive* psychology, to Hayes's (1979) notion of naive physics. In our dealings with the physical world, we deploy an understanding of how objects and forces commensurate with our middle-sized place in reality comport themselves. Without appreciation of properties like solidity, relations like support, dimensions like time, we should come to grief as soon as we tried to move about in or act on the world. Such an everyday science of the material is a far cry from quantum mechanics and relativity theory, but it works for everyday getting about, for which quantum mechanics and relativity theory are useless. Similarly, one can argue, our commonsense everyday sort of psychology constitutes a kind of competence without which we should come to social disaster, however different from it cognitive scientific theories might turn out to be.

Such pragmatic justification for folk psychology is similar to a position adopted by Daniel Dennett (e.g., 1978, 1987), which he calls the intentional stance. Dennett introduced the idea in the context of coping with a chess-playing computer. You can regard the computer as a physical object with such and such parts in such and such states. This is to adopt a *physical* stance toward it, which is useful when something goes wrong and has to be mended. Then to understand how the thing functions, you need to know about its design, including the way in which it has been programmed. This is to adopt a *design* stance, which is useful if you want to know how the machine will work or the input/output patterns to be expected from it. But if you want to play the computer at chess, neither the physical stance nor the design stance will get you very far; you need to treat it as though it knows the rules of the game, comprehends the state of play, draws rational inferences, and wants to win. Only by ascribing belief/desire psychology to the machine will you be able to try to anticipate its moves in developing your position. This is to adopt the *intentional* stance. We do it all the time in our interactions with people. More recently, Dennett (1983) has extended his intentional system strategy to animal behavior.

As far as Dennett is concerned, questions about whether a computer or an animal really has beliefs and desires, and the awareness that goes with these intentional states as we experience them, are beside the point. The point is that the intentional stance is essentially an instrumental strategy; the beliefs and desires and other intentional states imputed to the machine or the animal are, if you like, useful fictions: they afford a means of predicting and making sense of the moves of the machine and the behavior of the animal. Dennett seems to think that a scientific understanding of animal behavior and human psychology will ultimately come down to what is revealed by the design stance and the physical stance, and hence that the intentional stance will be dispensable, as eliminative materialism maintains. In the meantime, however, and for practical purposes, we are stuck with it for dealing with one another, with complex computers, and, at least some of the time, with animal behavior.

If folk psychology is no more than a kind of toolkit for coping with the cognitive and conative demands and tensions of human life in society and the physical world, albeit with an evolutionary provenance, rather than a soundly principled theory of how mind and brain are somehow one, cognitive ethology may need to reconsider some of its premises. The question, or questions, of animal awareness have been unquestioningly predicated on commonsense belief/desire psychology, but presumably we are seeking a sound scientific rather than or in addition to a pragmatically effective understanding of animal mentality.

For pragmatic effectiveness we still regard the sun as though it circles the earth, but can switch to the Copernican view when we need to be scientific about it. As yet, we have no parallel to the Copernican view when it comes to cognitive psychological theory. If the supporters of folk psychology and the philosophical positions grounded in it are right, we shall not need one. But the doubts about folk psychology are serious enough for cognitive ethology to be concerned about them if it wants to avoid the possibility of becoming the equivalent of a flat earth sect. There is, thus, good reason for cognitive ethology to keep track of developments in cognitive science and the philosophy of mind.

VI. SUMMARY CONCLUSIONS

1. The history of thought about animal mentality includes a variety of conceptions and issues, which tend to get conflated in cognitive ethology.
2. The terms awareness and consciousness cover a variety of mental states, which probably do not constitute a natural kind, and differ in the likelihood of animals having them.
3. Concepts like thought and belief are so enmeshed in a network involving language that applying them to animals lacking language is highly problematic.
4. The way in which behavior is described can affect the kinds of questions raised by it, for example, action terms usually imply intention. Denial of such implication in sociobiological accounts does not dispose of questions of animal intentionality.

5. The concept of intentionality in the philosophy of mind covers all mental states that are about something and, hence, includes belief, hope, perception, remembering, and so forth, as well as desire and intent.

6. The way people use the concepts of intentionality constitute what some philosophers regard as a psychological theory—folk psychology—on the basis of which the more sophisticated representational theories of the mind have been constructed.

7. Folk psychology has come under serious criticism. This should be of concern to cognitive ethology, which takes folk psychology for granted in formulating its questions.

Advances in science have sometimes resulted from stepping back to a previously discarded position. Perhaps cognitive ethology will prove to be an advance in the study of behavior in consequence of resuscitating questions of animal awareness. How far back it will be necessary to go to find the more fruitful formulation of these questions remains open to doubt, however: to Darwin and Romanes who believed in animal awareness? or to Descartes, who did not?

Acknowledgments

I thank Carolyn Ristau, Jay Rosenblatt, and Peter Slater for their helpful comments on an earlier draft of this article.

References

Allport, A. (1988). What concept of consciousness? In "Consciousness in Modern Science" (A. J. Marcel and E. Bisiach, eds.), pp. 159–182. Oxford Univ. Press (Clarendon), Oxford.

Anscombe, G. E. M. (1963). "Intention." Blackwell, Oxford.

Armstrong, A. E. (1956). Distraction display and the human predator. Ibis 98, 641–654.

Auden, W. H. (1962). "The Dyer's Hand." Vintage, New York.

Austin, J. L. (1962). "Sense and Sensibilia." Oxford Univ. Press, Oxford.

Beer, C. G. (1977). What is a display? Am. Zool. 17, 155–165,

Beer, C. G. (1980). Perspectives on animal behavior comparisons. In "Comparative Methods in Psychology" (M. H. Bornstein, ed.), pp. 17–64. Erlbaum, Hillsdale, New Jersey.

Bennett, J. (1989). "Rationality." Hacket, Indianapolis, Indiana.

Binet, A. (1903). "L'étude éxperimentale de l'intelligence." Schleicher, Paris.

Bisiach, E. (1988). The (haunted) brain and consciousness. In "Consciousness in Modern Science" (A. J. Marcel and E. Bisiach, eds.), pp. 101–120. Oxford Univer. Press (Clarendon), Oxford.

Boden, M. A. (1972). "Purposive Explanation in Psychology." Harvard Univ. Press, Cambridge, Massachusetts.

Boring, E. G. (1950). "A History of Experimental Psychology." Appleton-Century-Crofts, New York.

Brentano, F. (1874). "Psychology vom empirischen Standpunkt." Meiner, Leipzig.

Campbell, K. (1983). Abstract particulars and the philosophy of mind. Aust. J. Philos. 61, 129–141.

Campbell, R. L., and Bickhard, J. H. (1987). A deconstruction of Fodor's anticonstructivism. Hum. Dev. 30, 48–59.

Cherniak, C. (1986). "Minimal Rationality." MIT Press, Cambridge, Massachusetts.

Chihara, C. S., and Fodor, J. (1965). Operationalism and ordinary language: A critique of Wittgenstein. *Am. Philos. Q.* **2,** 281–295.

Chisholm, R. M. (1967). Intentionality. *In* "The Encyclopedia of Philosophy" (P. Edwards, ed.), Vol. 4, pp. 201–204. Macmillan and Free Press, New York.

Chomsky, N. (1980). "Rules and Representations." Columbia Univ. Press, New York.

Churchland, P. M. (1981). Eliminative materialism and propositional attitudes. *J. Philos.* **78,** 67–90.

Churchland, P. M. (1985). Reduction, qualia, and the direct introspection of brain states. *J. Philos.* **82,** 8–28.

Churchland, P. S. (1978). Fodor on language learning. *Synthese* **38,** 149–159.

Churchland, P. S. (1985). "Neurophilosophy." MIT Press, Cambridge, Massachusetts.

Churchland, P. S. (1988). Reduction and the neurobiological basis of consciousness. *In* "Consciousness in Modern Science" (A. J. Marcel and E. Bisiach, eds.), pp. 273–304. Oxford Univ. Press (Clarendon), Oxford.

Clark, A. (1987). From folk psychology to naive psychology. *Cognit. Sci.* **11,** 139–154.

Cohen, M. R., and Nagel, E. (1934). "An Introduction to Logic and Scientific Method." Routledge & Kegan Paul, London.

Colgan, P. (1989). "Animal Motivation." Chapman & Hall, London

Comte, A. (1830–1842). "Cours de philosophie positive," 6 vols. Bachelier, Paris.

Cummins, R. (1983). "The Nature of Psychological Explanation." MIT Press, Cambridge, Massachusetts.

Danto, A. C. (1985). "Narration and Knowledge." Columbia Univ. Press, New York.

Darwin, C. (1871). "The Descent of Man and Selection in Relation to Sex." Murray, London.

Darwin, C. (1872). "The Origin of Species," 6th ed. Murray, London.

Dawkins, R. (1976). "The Selfish Gene." Oxford Univ. Press, Oxford.

Dawkins, R. (1981). In defence of selfish genes. *Philosophy* **54,** 556–573.

Dawkins, R., and Krebs, J. R. (1978). Animal signals: information or manipulation. *In* "Behavioural Ecology—An Evolutionary Approach" (J. R. Krebs and N. B. Davies, eds.), pp. 282–309. Blackwell, Oxford.

de Condillac, E.-B. (1755). "Traité des animaux." Marcel, Amsterdam.

de la Chambre, C. (1685). "Les caractères des passion," 2nd ed. Michel, Amsterdam.

de la Mettrie, J. O. (1748). "L'homme machine" (A. Vartanian, ed. Princeton Univ. Press, Princeton, New Jersey, 1960).

Dennett, D. C. (1969). "Content and Consciousness." Routledge & Kegan Paul, London.

Dennett, D. C. (1978). "Brainstorms." Bradford Books, Montgomery, Vermont.

Dennett, D. C. (1983). Intentional systems in cognitive ethology: The "Panglossian Paradigm" defended. *Behav. Brain Sci.* **6,** 343–390.

Dennett, D. C. (1987). "The Intentional Stance." MIT Press, Cambridge, Massachusetts.

Dennett, D. C. (1988). Quining qualia. *In* "Consciousness in Modern Science" (A. J. Marcel and E. Bisiach, eds.), pp. 42–77. Oxford Univ. Press (Clarendon), Oxford.

Fodor, J. A. (1975). "The Language of Thought." Crowell, New York.

Fodor, J. A. (1981). "Representations." MIT Press, Cambridge, Massachusetts.

Fodor, J. A. (1987). "Psychosemantics." MIT Press, Cambridge, Massachusetts.

Fodor, J. A., and Pylyshyn, Z. W. (1988). Connectionism and cognitive architecture: A critical analysis. *In* "Connections and Symbols" (S. Pinker and J. Mehler, eds.), pp. 3–71. MIT Press, Cambridge, Massachusetts.

Gassendi, P. (1658). "Opera Omnia," 6 vols. Anisson and Devenet, Lugduni.

Ghiselin, M. (1969). "The Triumph of the Darwinian Method." Univ. of California. Press, Berkeley.

Gillispie, C. (1951). "Genesis and Geology: The Impact of Scientific Discoveries upon Religious Beliefs in the Decades before Darwin." Harper, New York.

Gottlieb, G. (1987). The developmental basis of evolutionary change. *J. Comp. Psychol.* **101,** 262–271.

Gould, J. L., and Gould, C. G. (1986). Invertebrate intelligence. *In* "Animal Intelligence" (R. J. Hoage and L. Goldman, eds.). Smithson. Inst. Press, Washington, D.C.

Griffin, D. R. (1976). "The Question of Animal Awareness." Rockefeller Univ. Press, New York.

Griffin, D. R. (1984). "Animal Thinking." Harvard Univ. Press, Cambridge, Massachusetts.

Hampshire, S. (1960). "Thought and Action." Chatto and Windus, London.

Hayes, P. (1979). The naive physics manifesto. *In* "Expert Systems in the Micro-electronic Age" (D. Michie, ed.). Edinburgh Univ. Press, Edinburgh.

Hinde, R. A. (1982). "Ethology." Oxford Univ. Press, Oxford.

Hockett, C. F. (1959). Animal "languages" and human language. *In* "The Evolution of Man's Capacity for Culture" (J. N. Spuhler, ed.), pp. 32–39. Wayne State Univ. Press, Detroit, Michigan.

Hockett, C. F., and Altmann, S. A. (1968). A note on design features. *In* "Animal Communication" (T. A. Sebeok, ed.), pp. 61–72. Indiana Univ. Press, Bloomington.

Horgan, T., and Woodward, J. (1985). Folk psychology is here to stay. *Philos. Rev.* **44,** 197–226.

Hume, D. (1793). "Treatise of Human Nature." (Modern edition by L. A. Selby-Bigge. Oxford Univ. Press (Clarendon), Oxford, 1888).

Humphrey, N. (1974). Vision in a monkey without striate cortex: A case study. *Perception* **3,** 241–255.

Humphrey, N. (1976). The social function of intellect. *In* "Growing Points in Ethology" (P. P. G. Bateson and R. A. Hinde, eds.), pp. 303–318. Cambridge Univ. Press, Cambridge, U.K.

Humphrey, N. (1983). "Consciousness Regained." Oxford Univ. Press, Oxford.

Humphrey, N. (1986). "The Inner Eye." Faber & Faber, London.

Huxley, T. H. (1874). On the hypothesis that animals are automata and its history. *Fortnightly Rev.* **22,** 555–589.

Huxley, T. H. (1893). "Collected Essays. Vol. I. Method and Results." Macmillan, London.

Jackson, F. (1982). Epiphenomenal qualia. *Philos. Q.* **32,** 127–136.

James, W. (1890). "Principles of Psychology," 2 vols. Holt, New York.

Jones, O. R., ed. (1971). "The Private Language Argument." Macmillan, London.

Kenny, A., ed. (1970). "Descartes, Philosophical Letters." Oxford Univ. Press, Oxford.

Kneale, W., and Prior, A. N. (1968). Intentionality and intensionality. *Proc. Arist. Soc., Suppl.* **42,** 73–105.

Kohler, W. (1925). "The Mentality of Apes." Kegan Paul, Trench & Trubner, London.

Krebs, J. R., and Dawkins, R. (1984). Animal signals: Mind reading and manipulation. *In* "Behavioral Ecology—An Evolutionary Approach" (J. R. Krebs and N. B. Davies, eds.), 2nd ed., pp. 380–402.

Lack D. (1943). "The Life of the Robin." Penguin, London.

Lewis, D. (1966). An argument for the identity theory. *J. Philos.* **63.**

Lloyd, D. (1989). "Simple Minds." MIT Press, Cambridge, Massachusetts.

Locke, J. (1690). "An Essay Concerning Human Understanding." (J. Yolton, ed., 2 vols, 5th ed. Everyman, New York, 1965).

Lockery, S. (1989). Representation, functionalism, and simple living systems. *In* "Goals, No-Goals and Own Goals" (A. Montefiore and D. Noble, eds.), pp. 117–158. Unwin Hyman, London

Lycan, W. G. (1987). "Consciousness." MIT Press, Cambridge, Massachusetts.

Lyons, W. (1986). "The Disappearance of Introspection." MIT Press, Cambridge, Massachusetts.

Malcolm, N. (1973). Thoughtless brutes. *Am. Philos. Assoc.* **46,** 5–20.

Mandelbaum, M. (1974). "History, Man & Reason: A Study in Nineteenth Century Thought." Johns Hopkins Univ. Press, Baltimore, Maryland.

Marcel, A. J. (1988). Phenomenal experience and functionalism. *In* "Consciousness in Modern

Science" (A. J. Maecell and E. Bisiach, eds.), pp. 121–158. Oxford Univ. Press (Clarendon), Oxford.

Marras, A. (1987). Stephen Stich's "From folk psychology to cognitive science: The case against belief." *Philos. Sci.* **54**, 115–127.

Mason, W. A. (1976). Review of "The question of animal awareness" by D. R. Griffin. *Science* **194**, 930–931.

Matthews, G. A. (1978). Animals and the unity of psychology. *Philosophy* **53**, 437–454.

Maynard Smith, J. (1964). Group selection and kin selection. *Nature (London)* **201**, 1145–1147.

McCulloch, W. S., and Pitts, W. (1943). A logical calculus of the ideas immanent in nervous activity. *Bull. Math. Biophys.* **5**, 115–133.

McDougall, W. (1908). "An Introduction to Social Psychology." Methuen, London.

Mead, G. H. (1964). The social self. *In* "Selected Writings of George Herbert Mead" (A. J. Reck, ed.), pp. 142–149. Bobbs-Merrill, Indianapolis, Indiana.

Midgley, M. (1979). Gene-juggling. *Philosophy* **54**, 439–458.

Mill, J. S. (1882). "Dissertations and Discussions," 5 vols. Holt, New York.

Millikan, R. G. (1984). "Language, Thought, and Other Biological Categories." MIT Press, Cambridge, Massachusetts.

Millikan, R. G. (1986). Thoughts without laws: Cognitive science with content. *Philos. Rev.* **95**, 47–80.

Minsky, M., and Papert. (1969). "Perceptrons." MIT Press, Cambridge, Massachusetts.

Montefiore, A., and Noble, D., eds. (1989). "Goals, No-Goals and Own Goals." Unwin Hyman, London.

Morris, C. W. (1946). "Signs, Language and Behavior." Braziller, New York.

Nagel, T. (1974). What is it like to be a bat? *Philos. Rev.* **83**, 435–450.

Natsoulas, T. (1978). Consciousness. *Am. Psychol.* **33**, 906–914.

Nisbett, R. E., and Wilson, T. DeC. (1977). Telling more than we know: Verbal reports on mental processes. *Psychol. Rev.* **84**, 231–259.

Oatley, K. (1988). On changing one's mind: A possible function of consciousness. *In* "Consciousness in Modern Science" (A. J. Marcel and E. Bisiach, eds.), pp. 369–389. Oxford Univ. Press (Clarendon), Oxford.

Place, U. T. (1956). Is consciousness a brain process? *Br. J. Psychol.* **47**, 44–50.

Premack, D. (1986). "Gavagai Or the Future History of the Animal Language Controversy." MIT Press, Cambridge, Massachusetts.

Proust, M. (1913). "A la Recherche du Temps Perdu. I. Du Côté de Chez Swann." (English translation by C. K. Scott Moncrieff. "Remembrance of Things Past. I. Swann's Way." Chatto and Windus, London, 1922).

Quine, W. V. (1953). "From a Logical Point of View." Harvard Univ. Press, Cambridge, Massachusetts.

Quine, W. V. (1960). "Word and Object." MIT Press, Cambridge, Massachusetts.

Richards, R. J. (1988). "Darwin and Emergence of Evolutionary Theories of Mind and Behavior." Univ. of Chicago Press, Chicago, Illinois.

Ristau, C. A. (1991). Aspects of the cognitive ethology of an injury-feigning bird, the Piping Plover. *In* "Cognitive Ethology—The Minds of Other Animals" (C. A. Ristau, ed.), pp. 91–126. Erlbaum, Hillsdale, New Jersey.

Ristau, C. A. (1992). "Animal language and cognition projects." *In* "Handbook of Human Symbolic Evolution" (A. Lock and C. R. Peters, eds.). Oxford Univ. Press, Oxford (in press).

Robinson, H. (1982). "Matter and Sense." Cambridge Univ. Press, New York.

Roget, P. M. (1834). "Animal and Vegetable Physiology Considered with Reference to Natural Theology," 2 vols. Pickering, London.

Romanes, G. (1881). "Animal Intelligence." Kegan Paul, Trench, London.

Rorty, R. (1980). "Philosophy and the Mirror of Nature." Blackwell, Oxford.

Rosenblatt, F. (1962). "Principles of Neurodynamics, Perceptrons and the Theory of Brain Mechanisms." Spartan Books, Washington, D.C.

Rosenfield, L. (1968). "From Beast Machine to Man Machine." Octagon Books, New York.

Rudwick, M. J. S. (1985). "The Great Devonian Controversy." Univ. of Chicago Press, Chicago, Illinois.

Rumelhart, D. E., McClelland, J. L., and the PDP Research Group (1986). "Parallel Distributed Processing. Vol. 1. Foundations." MIT Press, Cambridge, Massachusetts.

Russell, B. (1956). "Logic and Knowledge." Allen & Unwin, London.

Russow, L.-R. (1987). Stich on the foundations of cognitive psychology. *Synthese* **70**, 401–413.

Ryle, G. (1949). "The Concept of Mind." Hutchinson, London.

Sanford, D. H. (1986–1987). Review of "From folk psychology to cognitive science: The case against belief" by S. P. Stich. *Philos. Phenom. Res.* **47**, 149–154.

Searle, J. R. (1980). Minds, brains, and programs. *Behav. Brain Sci.* **3**, 417–457.

Sejnowski, T., and Rosenberg, C. (1987). Parallel networks that learn to pronounce English text. *Complex Syst.* **1**, 145–168.

Sellars, W. (1956). Empiricism and the philosophy of mind. *In* "Minnesota Studies in the Philosophy of Science" (H. Feigl and M. Scriven, eds.), vol. 1, pp. 253–329. Univ. of Minnesota Press, Minneapolis.

Simmons, K. E. L. (1955). The nature of the predator-reactions of waders towards humans; with special reference to the role of aggressive-, escape-, and brooding-drives. *Behaviour* **8**, 130–173.

Skutch, A. F. (1976). "Parent Birds and their Young." Univ. of Texas Press, Austin.

Smart, J. C. (1959). Sensations and brain processes. *Philos. Rev.* **68**, 141–156.

Stich, S. P. (1983). "From Folk Psychology to Cognitive Science." MIT Press, Cambridge, Massachusetts.

Taylor, C. (1964). "The Explanation of Behaviour." Routledge & Kegan Paul, London.

Thorpe, W. H. (1974). "Animal Nature and Human Nature." Doubleday, Garden City, New York.

Tinbergen, N. (1951). "The Study of Instinct." Oxford Univ. Press (Clarendon), Oxford.

Titchener, E. B. (1909). "A Textbook of Psychology." Macmillan, New York.

Turing, A. M. (1937). On computable numbers, with an application to the Entscheidungsproblem. *Proc. London Math. Soc.* **42**, 230–265.

Vendler, Z. (1972). "Res Cogitans." Univ. of Cornell Press, Ithaca, New York.

von Neumann, J. (1958). "The Computer and the Brain." Yale Univ. Press, New Haven, Connecticut.

Weiskrantz, L. (1972). Behavioural analysis of the monkey's visual system. *Proc. R. Soc. London, Ser. B* **182**, 427–455.

Weiskrantz, L. (1980). Varieties of residual experience. *Q. J. Exp. Psychol.* **32**, 365–386.

Weiskrantz, L. (1988). Some contributions of neuropsychology of vision and memory to the problem of consciousness. *In* "Consciousness in Modern Science" (A. J. Maecel and E. Bisiach, eds.), pp. 183–199. Oxford Univ. Press (Clarendon), Oxford.

Weiskrantz, L., Warrington, E. K., Sanders, M. D., and Marshall, J. (1974). Visual capacity in the hemianopic field following a restricted occipital ablation. *Brain* **97**, 709–728.

Wertheimer, M. (1922). Untersuchungen zur Lehre von der Gestalt. *Psychol. Forsch.* **1**, 47–58.

Wilkes, K. V. (1984). Is consciousness important? *Br. J. Philos. Sci.* **35**, 223–243.

Wilkes, K. V. (1988).—, yìshì, duh, um, and consciousness. *In* "Consciousness in Modern Science" (A. J. Marcel and E. Bisiach, eds.), pp. 16–41. Oxford Univ. Press (Clarendon), Oxford.

Wilkes, K. V. (1989). Explanation—how not to miss the point. *In* "Goals, No-Goals and Own Goals" (A. Montefiore and D. Noble, eds.), pp. 194–210. Unwin Hyman, London.

Wittgenstein, L. (1958). "Philosophical Investigations." Blackwell, Oxford.

Yaroshevsky, M. F. (1971). "Psychologia v XX Steletti." Political Literature Publishing House, Moscow.

Responses to Warning Coloration in Avian Predators

W. Schuler

II. Zoologisches Institut und Museum der Universität
D-3400 Göttingen, Germany

T. J. Roper

School of Biological Sciences
University of Sussex
Brighton BN1 9QG, England

I. The Problem of Warning Coloration

A. Warning Coloration: An Idea and Its History

Mimicry, warning coloration, and chemical defense in insects constitute especially clear examples of adaptation through mutation and natural selection. As such, they have been of interest to evolutionary biologists since the time of Darwin (Mayr, 1982). They have not only facilitated our practical understanding of the way in which new morphological features arise and are maintained through the action of natural selection, but have also given rise to important new developments within evolutionary theory, in particular to the principle of kin selection (Fisher, 1930; Maynard Smith, 1964).

Although biologists have been occupied with mimicry, warning coloration, and chemical defense for over a century, our knowledge of these phenomena has not been characterized by gradual accumulation of empirical evidence. Rather, ideas were formulated and discussed for decades before any serious attempt was made to test their assumptions and predictions experimentally. Nor did these underlying ideas develop gradually. They originated in the hypothesis of mimicry, that is, of "imitation" of signals. The principles of warning coloration and chemical defense, which refer to the signals themselves and their meaning, were only explicitly formulated later on. This tendency to approach warning coloration via the different and more complex phenomenon of mimicry continues to be common (e.g., Schuler, 1974, 1982; Malcolm, 1990).

The course of evolution can be reconstructed by consideration of any organ-

111

ism, because all organisms bear the marks of their evolutionary histoty. But these marks are especially easy to decipher in the wings of butterflies, where they have been, as it were, explicitly painted in by natural selection. One of the first scientists to attempt to decode such marks was Henry Walter Bates (1862), who discovered the mimetic relationship between pierid and ithomiid butterflies in the Amazon basin. In any one region, he noted, the appearance of certain pierids resembled that of ithomiids, whereas pierids and ithomiids from different regions differed from one another in appearance. Bates concluded that pierids had adapted so as to resemble the appearance of ithomiids, called them mimics of their ithomiid models, and labeled the whole phenomenon "mimicry." To explain the phenomenon, he referred to the theory of natural selection, which was then quite new (Darwin, 1859). He supposed that ithomiids are rejected by birds because they are unpalatable and that the palatable pierids are rejected because of their physical resemblance to ithomiids. Thus, he hypothesized that the similarity between pierids and ithomiids had come about because at any given time, birds and other predators had spared those pierids that, by chance, were more similar to ithomiids than were others of their conspecifics.

Bates's mimicry hypothesis was right but some of its assumptions were not verified until a century later; he himself could only present circumstantial arguments. As evidence that birds reject ithomiids, he cited the fact that he had never seen any of the numerous insectivorous birds of the Amazon hunting ithomiid butterflies, despite the fact that the latter should have been easy prey on account of their frequency, conspicuousness, and slow manner of flying. As a cause of this rejection of ithomiids, Bates postulated unpalatability because, on the one hand, ithomiids have no apparent weapons such as stings or spines and, on the other, they emanated a smell that seemed to him to be mildly unpleasant. In addition, he noted that in his collections ithomiids were unusually immune to attack by mites and other pests.

Subsequent researchers provided corroborative evidence; for example, Haase (1892) noted that papilionid butterflies identified as models in mimicry systems, and hence thought to be unpalatable, ate as larvae from poisonous plants. Important additional proof of the unpalatability of models came from the knowledge that such butterflies contain cardiac glycosides (e.g., Reichstein et al., 1968; Brower, 1969) or other compounds (see Rothschild, 1985) that taste aversive or are poisonous to birds. In this way, the notion of unpalatability was given a palpable material basis.

According to the mimicry hypothesis, birds and other predators reject *on sight* certain insects that they think are unpalatable. This means that some aspect of the appearance of such insects is a visual signal, to the predator, of unpalatability in the prey. Thus, did the logic of the mimicry hypothesis give rise to the hypothesis of warning coloration, which states that insects and other animals (regardless of whether or not they are models in mimicry systems) might also use *conspicuous* color patterns as a visual signal of unpalatability (Wallace, 1867; see Guilford, 1990). Poulton (1890) termed such color patterns "aposematic coloration."

Darwin had previously been occupied with conspicuous color patterns in butterflies and had attributed them to sexual selection, but he saw no possibility of explaining conspicuous coloration in insect larvae in the same terms. Wallace responded by suggesting that the conspicuous coloration of larvae was a signal not to conspecifics but to predators: it indicated unpalatability. Without such an external signal, he argued, a larva could not benefit from its unpalatability because a predator would have to attack and wound it to discover that it tasted bad.

An obvious and important prediction of the warning coloration hypothesis is that conspicuous insects should (unless they are mimics of other unpalatable species) be unpalatable to potential predators. This prediction has been tested by various researchers since about the turn of the century, with mixed results. Alcock (1896), for example, reported that a tame Himalayan bear (*Ursus thibetanus*) enjoyed being fed green and brown palatable grasshoppers by hand but, when offered a black and red one that exuded a pungent smelling fluid, knocked it out of the investigator's hand, just as it had done previously when irritated by means of a burning cigar. If all tests of unpalatability had had such an unequivocal outcome, the warning coloration hypothesis would doubtless soon have been regarded as impregnable. Unfortunately, however, birds, which are less sensitive to chemical signals than mammals, do not always respond as unambiguously. In addition, conflicting results also occurred through lack of sophistication in experimental design, such as offering the same predator different insects under different conditions (e.g., Finn, 1895, 1896). Arguments also arose because opponents of warning coloration, who cited as their primary source of negative evidence the occurrence of conspicuously colored insects in the gut contents of wild birds (McAttee, 1932), were trapped in an all-or-none conception of the hypothesis. For example, Heikertinger (1919; our translation) wrote that "If an insect species is eaten by an insect-eating species then it is effectively not protected against the latter."

Fortunately, however, other experimenters were at the same time developing a more sophisticated view of the available evidence, realizing that there might be differential sensitivity in different predators and that the results of experiments might depend on factors such as the state of hunger of the predator (Swynnerton, 1919). In the end, the controversy over warning coloration, which lasted for decades, was ended by convincing experimental evidence of unpalatability in conspicuous prey, but it also required that opponents accept the notion of differential survival of prey (i.e., the idea that a color pattern protects its bearer if the latter is preyed on merely at a lower rate than different-looking conspecifics).

Relatively well-designed experiments on mimicry and unpalatability were first carried out by Mostler (1935) on hymenopterans and their syrphid fly mimics. He showed, first, that several species of songbirds reject bees and wasps only after having had (unpleasant) experience of them and, second, that birds experienced with bees and wasps subsequently avoid the similar-looking but harmless syrphids. Brower (1958a,b,c) furnished comparable proof of mimicry in several North American butterflies, whereas Brower and Brower (1964) showed that birds learned to avoid the South American ithomiid species thought to be unpalatable to them by Bates. These studies all involved laboratory tests in which captive birds were offered different kinds of prey, but evidence also emerged of the effectiveness of artificial mimics under field conditions (Jeffords et al., 1979).

In some respects, the longstanding controversy about the reliability of tests of unpalatability is still alive; for example, Mallet (1990) argues that because experimental tests can always be criticized in one way or another, Bates's comparative data are still more important as evidence of mimicry than are any subsequent tests of his theory's predictions. We would argue, instead, that the two types of evidence should be regarded, along with genetical studies of the inheritance of mimetic patterns (e.g., Clarke and Sheppard, 1960; Turner, 1977) and biochemical studies of the structure and effects of noxious compounds (e.g., Rothschild, 1985), as complimentary strands of evidence corroborating Bates's original outstanding insight.

The hypothesis of mimicry is based on the idea that predators avoid, on sight, prey that they find aversive. It is usually assumed that avoidance is learned, but the question as to whether naive predators avoid warningly colored prey was also asked at a relatively early stage. Lloyd Morgan (1896) showed that artificially incubated domestic chicks (Gallus gallus domesticus) both pecked at and ate brown geometrid caterpillars, whereas they pecked at, but subsequently rejected, the black-and-yellow ringed caterpillar of the cinnabar moth (Tyria jacobaeae). Windecker (1939) confirmed and extended this result and concluded that the conspicuous coloration of the cinnabar moth larva is not a warning signal to naive predators. Similarly, Mostler (1935) found that hand-raised songbirds accepted wasp-mimicking syrphid flies so long as they had not previously experienced wasps. In view of this evidence, it was generally supposed that the response of predators to warningly colored prey is acquired through learning, and as a result, it was assumed that the only function of warning coloration was to facilitate avoidance learning. For example, Wickler (1968) wrote emphatically that "Warning colors are nothing but a specially significant stimulus for learning" (our translation).

Although the idea that warning coloration facilitates learning is an old one, surprisingly few experiments have been done to test it, and most of those that were done were methodologically inadequate or did not give the expected result. Windecker (1939, p. 124 et seq.) found that domestic chicks learned more rapidly to avoid black-and-yellow painted mealworms than brown ones, but because he used the same chicks for both tests, order of testing was a confounding variable. Eibl-Eibesfeldt (1952) gave small black-and-yellow or blue painted sticks to common toads and found, contrary to his expectation, that his subjects learned to avoid both at the same rate. Better and more recent evidence concerning the effect of conspicuousness on the rate of avoidance learning is discussed later in Section II,D.

Curiously, Wickler's (1968) unambiguous statement about the function of warning coloration provoked few learning experiments; rather, it stimulated work on the unlearned avoidance of poisonous warningly colored prey. Shortly after the appearance of Wickler's book, there appeared the first relatively convincing indications of unlearned avoidance of warningly colored sea snakes (*Pelamis platurus*) by predatory fish (Rubinoff and Kropach, 1970) and of coral snake (*Micrurus fulvius*) models by mammals (Gehlbach, 1972). Subsequently, Smith (1975, 1977) produced clear evidence of unlearned avoidance of coral snake patterns in birds, whereas Caldwell and Rubinoff (1983) found strong avoidance of sea snakes by naive herons (*Butorides striatus*) and egrets (*Casmerodius albus* and *Egretta thula*).

Although early studies suggested that naive birds do attack warningly colored insects (e.g., Morgan, 1896; Mostler, 1935; Windecker, 1939; but see also Davies and Green, 1976), the possibility remained that warningly colored insects might provoke a less vigorous or less complete form of predatory behavior. Coppinger (1970) was the first to provide evidence in support of this idea, showing that naive blue jays (*Cyanocitta cristata*) and other birds attacked the black-and-red butterfly *Anartia amalthea* at a lower rate than the brown-and-white *Anartia jatrophae*. Subsequently, Schuler (1982) showed a similar effect comparing the initial predatory responses of starlings toward black-and-yellow striped versus plain green, brown, or yellow insect dummies, and Schuler and Hesse (1985) showed that naive domestic chicks responded less vigorously toward black-and-yellow painted mealworms than to uniform green ones. Schuler and Hesse concluded that although naive chicks peck equally frequently at striped and unstriped prey, they are more reluctant to handle striped prey intensively or to eat them. These experiments by Schuler and others were the starting point for the studies reviewed later in Sections II,A to II,C.

B. Theories of the Evolution of Warning Signals and the Need for Knowledge about Predators' Responses

The existence of insect larvae that are conspicuously colored and unpalatable, but in other respects physically vulnerable to predators, gave rise not only to the idea of warning coloration but also to the concept of kin selection (Fisher, 1930; Maynard Smith, 1964). Kin selection in turn played an important role in the development of a new view of social behavior (Hamilton, 1964; Wilson, 1975) and, subsequently, became an essential component in the theoretical base of modern sociobiology and behavioral ecology (e.g., Trivers, 1985; Dawkins, 1989). Thus, developments in evolutionary theory that arose initially from considerations of warning coloration have had important and wide-ranging implications.

In his book *"The Genetical Theory of Natural Selection,"* Fisher (1930) asked how unpalatability could evolve in caterpillars through the mechanism of mutation and natural selection. It is easy to imagine a mutation arising that confers some degree of increased unpalatability on its possessor, but if the only possessor of such a mutation is killed or mortally wounded in the course of being sampled by a predator, then the allele in question will immediately be removed from the population. Thus, such a mutation cannot spread by individual selection; a larva gains no fitness benefit from wreaking posthumous revenge on a predator that has already eaten it. Kin selection, however, offers a possible escape from this paradox. If an adult bearing the mutation delivers it to its offspring, then the sacrifice of one member of the family to a predator may enhance the survival of the remaining members, provided that the predator avoids them after its initial experience. Thus, although the sacrificed individual does not benefit from its unpalatability, its close kin do.

If a species is already unpalatable, then the same argument can be applied to the evolution of warning coloration. A single conspicuously colored mutant is likely to attract the attention of predators and will, therefore, quickly be eliminated from the population. However, in a group of mutants of similar appearance, the survivors will profit, once a predator learns to associate their appearance with unpalatability and, hence, to avoid them.

In support of kin selection as a factor in the evolution of unpalatability, Fisher (1930) remarks that egg-clustering in butterflies (i.e., the habit of laying a whole batch of eggs in a single location), if it produces an assemblage of related larvae, will offer favorable conditions for the action of kin selection. But he also stresses that kin selection need only be considered when the predator kills or mortally wounds the insect in the process of tasting it for the first time. This can be assumed to occur in the case of most insect larvae, which die as a consequence of even minor injuries to their integument. But as the entomologists of Fisher's time were aware, and as Poulton informed him, some warningly colored insects are built rather tough and might survive attack by a naive predator. Fisher concluded that, in such cases, an individual could itself profit from being warningly colored, because such coloration would protect the individual from future attacks by the same experienced predator. Thus, both unpalatability and warning coloration could, at least in some cases, succeed by a straightforward mechanism of individual selection.

In more recent discussions of the evolution of warning coloration and unpalatability, the relative importance of kin selection and individual selection has continued to be debated. With the rise of behavioral ecology and sociobiology, kin selection was cited as an explanation for diverse kinds of altruistic behavior (Wilson, 1975). At the same time, not surprisingly, it became the generally accepted explanation of warning coloration (e.g., Krebs and Davies, 1981). But as Wiklund and Järvi (1982) pointed out, no one had actually tested whether predators kill warningly colored insects during the first encounter. When they themselves carried out survival tests with a variety of insect prey and naive avian predators, they found that about 50% of warningly colored insects were not touched by the predator on the first encounter and, of the remaining 50% of prey, a large majority survived the encounter. Wiklund and Järvi declared themselves strongly in favor of individual selection as a mechanism for the evolution of warning coloration, whereas others (e.g., Harvey and Paxton, 1981a,b) continued to argue for kin selection.

Guilford (1985, 1990, 1990b) has clarified the issue by analyzing the conditions under which different types of selection could be expected to operate and by pointing out that what he calls "synergistic selection" (Guilford, 1990b) might operate in addition to individual and kin selection. Synergistic selection, which is similar to the "green beard selection" of Dawkins (1976), occurs if the predator, after attacking a mutant individual, spares other individuals of the same physical type, regardless of whether or not they are kin. Given that predators do discriminate on the basis of prey appearance, synergistic selection is an inevitable concomitant of warning coloration. That is, after attacking a distasteful insect that has a particular physical appearance, the predator will selectively avoid other insects that look the same, regardless of their degree of genetic relatedness.

As Guilford stresses, individual, kin, and synergistic selection are not mutually exclusive mechanisms; after attacking but not severely harming a warningly colored individual, a predator might subsequently avoid the same individual, its kin, and other related individuals that look the same. How important each of these three forms of selection is in a particular case will depend on the properties of prey and predator and, hence, is a matter for empirical investigation.

As regards prey, individual selection will be favored by survival of an initial attack by a naive predator, and this will depend on factors such as the toughness of the cuticle and whether or not the defensive chemical is secreted on the surface of the body. Kin selection will obviously be favored by aggregation of the prey in kin groups, and synergistic selection should be important in the evolution of warning coloration because, by definition, warning coloration is externally visible to a predator.

As regards the predator, a tendency to attack novel prey cautiously will favor individual selection as a mechanism underlying warning coloration. If the predator encounters a group of individuals of an unpalatable species, some of which are conspicuously colored mutants and others of which show the original cryptic phenotype, then the mode of selection that operates will depend on how the predator reacts to its unpleasant experience. If the predator ascribes unpalatability to the whole group and thereafter avoids the place where they aggregate, unadulterated kin selection will operate. On the other hand, if the predator only avoids specimens that physically resemble the sampled prey individual, then synergistic selection will occur. Similar considerations also apply in other scenarios: for example, ones in which frequency dependent selection is important (e.g., Mallet and Singer, 1987) or in which unpalatability evolves via many small mutations (Schuler, 1987, pp. 127 *et. seq.*).

In conclusion, the way in which a naive predator approaches new prey types and the way in which its behavior changes as a result of encounters with unpalatable prey are crucial to the question of how selection operates. Thus, investigations of the responses of predators to warningly colored prey, while not dealing directly with questions of evolution, are vital if we are to understand fully the evolution of warning coloration.

II. RESPONSES OF BIRDS TO WARNINGLY COLORED PREY

A. UNLEARNED RESPONSES IN DOMESTIC CHICKS

After experiencing prey of one type, predators generalize to others of similar appearance (e.g., Coppinger, 1969). Thus, unlearned responses to warningly colored prey can only be studied properly in prey-naive individuals. Besides telling us about predispositions toward different prey types in extant species, the behavior of naive individuals may also offer us a glimpse of how primeval predators may have responded to the first warningly colored prey to evolve. However, any analogy between extant and extinct species depends on the assumption that the behavior of the latter has not altered during the course of evolution as a consequence of exposure to warningly colored prey; that is, we have to distinguish between ontogenetically naive and evolutionarily naive predators. We return to this point later (Section III,A). Here, we describe the reactions of domestic chicks (*Gallus gallus domesticus*) to real and simulated prey of different colors and patterns.

1. *Establishing an Unlearned Response*

Lloyd Morgan (1896) concluded that newly hatched chicks peck at different colored objects with complete impartiality, but this conclusion was based only on qualitative observations. Many subsequent studies have shown that there is, in fact, a quantitative difference in the rate at which chicks peck at objects of different colors, that is, naive chicks do have color preferences (e.g., Fischer *et al.*, 1975). However, the differences in peck rate are often not very pronounced, and different procedures and strains of chick sometimes give different results. Thus, experiments using arbitrary artificial objects in laboratory conditions have not given a clear picture of color preferences and their results do not suggest any consistent functional interpretation.

As already noted (Section I,A), Coppinger (1970) tested hand-reared blue jays with two species of Trinidadian butterflies. The birds rejected the warningly colored black-and-red butterflies but attacked brown-and-white control butterflies. Coppinger attributed rejection of the former species to the novelty of its appearance: his birds were reared on brown food (chick starter crumbs), from which he inferred that black-and-red coloration was more novel than brown-and-white. But as Curio (1976) pointed out, Coppinger's results could equally well be explained in terms of an unlearned tendency to avoid warningly colored prey.

Schuler (1982) attempted to test the novelty hypothesis by giving young starlings (*Sturnus vulgaris*) a choice between black-and-yellow striped insect dummies and plain green, yellow, or brown ones. The birds had been fed on dark brown, light brown, and yellow foods but never on green food and so should, according to Coppinger's hypothesis, have avoided green prey. In fact, the birds rejected the black-and-yellow striped dummies at a greater rate than any of the plain-colored ones, from which Schuler concluded that they had a specific unlearned tendency to avoid warning colors or patterns.

Because altricial species such as blue jays and starlings can only be tested when they are several weeks old, it is difficult to be sure, even when using hand-reared birds, that prey choice has not been influenced by prior experience of the food being eaten. Schuler and Hesse (1985) circumvented this problem by using domestic chicks that, being precocial, can be tested on the first day of hatching, before any experience of food. Rather than using as prey real warningly colored insects, which differ not only in color but also in features such as size, shape, cuticle toughness, and palatability, Schuler and Hesse presented dead mealworms (larvae of *Tenebrio molitor*) that had been painted with nontoxic finger paints. These prey differed in color but were otherwise uniformly edible, and, unlike inanimate models, they were sufficiently realistic to elicit a full range of predatory and ingestive responses. The chicks were tested in pairs for three 5-min sessions, and in each session were given a simultaneous choice between five green and five black-and-yellow striped larvae. (The striped larvae were painted with three transverse black stripes on a yellow background.) Data were recorded from the more active chick in each pair.

During the three sessions, 17 of 20 chicks attacked at least one larva and 11 ate at least one. There was no color preference in the first larva to be pecked, but all 11 chicks that consumed a larva consumed a green one first (Fig. 1a). Thus, the choice behavior of chicks changed between pecking at a larva and eating it. Further analysis showed (Fig. 2a) that in all cases in which a black-and-yellow larva was attacked first, the attack was terminated after pecking, whereas most chicks that attacked a green larva first not only pecked at it, but continued to handle it and often to eat it. ("Handling" in this context means picking the prey

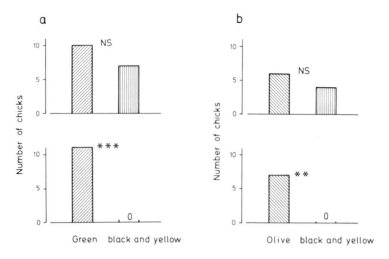

FIG. 1. Responses of prey-naive chicks in choice tests between black-and-yellow striped and green or olive prey. *Upper half:* First type pecked. *Lower half:* First type eaten. (a) Unfed chicks tested on Day 1. (b) Chicks given yellow egg food before testing on Days 3–5. ** $p < .01$; *** $p < .001$ (Binomial test).

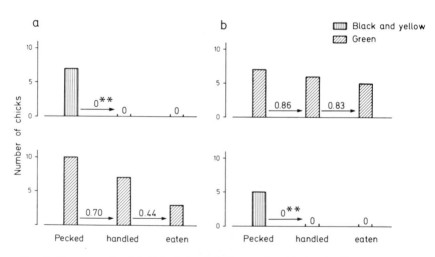

FIG. 2. Responses of unfed chicks during their first attack on black-and-yellow and green prey. *Upper half:* Chicks attacking black-and-yellow larvae first. *Lower half:* Chicks attacking green larvae first. (a) The first attack of each chick. (b) The first attack on the other color type by the same chicks. *Arrows:* Probability of transition to the following phase. ** $p < .01$, Fisher exact probability test. (From Schuler and Hesse, 1985, reproduced with permission of Springer-Verlag.)

up, manipulating it in the beak, carrying it around, or beating it on the ground.) The same result emerged from analysis of the second prey type to be attacked (Fig. 2b). That is, chicks that attacked a green prey first and a black-and-yellow prey second only pecked at the second prey, whereas chicks that attacked a black-and-yellow prey first and a green prey second not only pecked at but also handled the second prey.

Because attack on black-and-yellow prey was only inhibited after the stage of pecking, the possibility arose that it was caused by the black and/or yellow paint smelling or tasting unpleasant. This seemed unlikely, because chicks that did eventually consume black-and-yellow larvae showed no obvious aversive reaction, nor was there any rejection of chick food contaminated with black and yellow paint. However, a mild aversion would not be revealed by these tests. As a further control, therefore, Schuler and Hesse offered chicks mealworms painted with an olive-colored mixture produced by mixing black and yellow paints in the same weight ratio as was used to paint the black-and-yellow striped larvae. These chicks were fed on a mixture of mashed hard-boiled egg and shredded wheat ("egg-food") and were tested in daily sessions from Day 3 to Day 10.

As Fig. 1b shows, the results for the first three sessions were similar to those of the previous experiment. That is, the first peck of chicks was equally likely to be directed toward an olive as toward a striped larva, but the first larva eaten was always an olive one. Because rejection of black-and-yellow prey occurred despite the fact that the chicks had been fed on yellow food, this experiment not only controls for aversive effects of the black and yellow paints but also offers further evidence against Coppinger's (1970) "novelty" hypothesis. Accordingly, Schuler and Hesse concluded that chicks had a genetically fixed predisposition to avoid warningly colored prey. (We return in Section II,C to the question of whether such an avoidance tendency can justifiably be called "innate.")

2. Further Analysis of the Response

a. The Signal Value of Stripes. In all the experiments so far described, the experimental prey were colored with alternating transverse black-and-yellow stripes on the grounds that this is generally considered to be a warning pattern. The comparison between black-and-yellow striped and plain green or brown mealworms, however, leaves open a number of possibilities as to what precise feature of the striped prey is aversive; the aversion could be due to black alone, yellow alone, the presence of two colors, the presence of stripes, or to the entire stimulus configuration encompassing both those particular colors and their arrangement in the form of alternating stripes.

This question of what prey feature inhibits handling was investigated by Roper and Cook (1989), using a testing procedure similar to that of Schuler and Hesse (1985). In the first of Roper and Cook's experiments, four groups of chicks were offered a simultaneous choice between control (plain olive) and experimental mealworms. In Group 1, the experimental prey were painted with alternating black-and-yellow stripes as in Schuler and Hesse's experiment; in Group 2, the experimental prey were painted black all over; in Group 3, they were painted yellow all over; and in Group 4, they were painted black on one half of the body and yellow on the other half (a pattern described as "bicolored"). Two further experiments were also conducted with a similar design but using different color combinations for the experimental prey, namely, red and yellow in Experiment 2 and red and black in Experiment 3. The point of the experiments was to see whether stripes in general, bicolored patterns in general, or any of the single colors black, yellow, and red were aversive. Four measures of behavior were recorded: the type of mealworm (experimental or control) that a chick first pecked; the type that it first picked up; the total number of pecks emitted by each chick to each type of mealworm; and the total number of pickups by each chick to each type of mealworm. The scores for each measure of behavior were expressed as a preference ratio: that is, the number of responses to experimental prey divided by the total number of responses to both types of prey.

In the first experiment (Fig. 3a), chicks offered a choice between black-and-yellow striped and olive mealworms behaved similarly to those of Schuler and Hesse; they pecked equally at both types of prey but picked up the striped prey less frequently. Yellow and bicolored prey were, if anything, preferred to olive, but the difference was slight. Black prey were strongly aversive and this aversion was manifest in all four measures of behavior; birds both pecked at and picked up black prey significantly less than olive prey. The second and third experiments

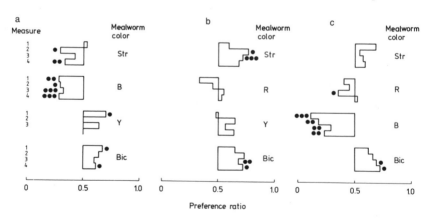

FIG. 3. Relative preference of chicks for striped (Str), plain-colored, or bicolored (Bic) prey painted in three different color combinations (yellow and black, red and yellow, red and black). The results are presented as a preference ratio, with plain olive mealworms as the control prey. Filled circles denote significance levels of .05, .01, and .001. 1, number of chicks first pecking experimental versus control mealworms; 2, number of chicks first picking up mealworms; 3, total number of pecks; 4, total number of pickups. B = black; Y = yellow; R = red. (From Roper and Cook, 1989.)

(Figs. 3b, c) replicated the strong aversion to black prey and showed a mild aversion to plain red prey and a mild preference for red-and-yellow striped, red-and-yellow bicolored, and red-and-black bicolored prey. Red-and-black striped prey were not treated differently from olive.

To summarize, Roper and Cook's experiments showed a clear aversion only to black-and-yellow striped and plain black prey, when the choice was between these and olive prey. Neither stripes nor bicolored patterns were generally aversive, nor was black aversive in combination with any other color (e.g., black-and-red striped and bicolored prey were not aversive, despite the fact that both black and red were aversive on their own). Because all the larvae were presented on a white background, differences in conspicuousness can be ruled out; and, because the chicks were unfed, mealworms of any color were novel. Thus, it was impossible to discern any general rule describing the chicks' relative preferences and aversions. Roper and Cook concluded that naive chicks possess specific aversions and preferences to certain specific colors and patterns.

In Roper and Cook's experiments the response to red was inconclusive; if anything, chicks preferred olive to red prey, but the difference was only significant for one measure of behavior in one experiment (Fig. 3c). Roper (1990) analyzed the response to red further by comparing chicks' responses to plain red versus plain brown mealworms. (The control prey were painted with a pigment chosen to match, as closely as possible, the natural color of mealworms.) He found that chicks consistently preferred brown to red, and this preference was manifest both in scores for pecking and in the number of mealworms actually eaten.

The results from these three sets of experiments (Schuler and Hesse, 1985; Roper and Cook, 1989; Roper, 1990) suggest two important conclusions and point to a third issue that needs further investigation. The first conclusion is that what we describe as an aversion to or preference for this or that prey type is only a relative aversion or preference; that is, its strength depends on the nature of the control prey used for purposes of comparison. Thus, chicks are more or less indifferent between red and olive prey (Roper and Cook, 1989), but red is aversive when compared with brown prey (Roper, 1990). Even with black-and-yellow striped or plain black prey the aversion was only quantitative; naive chicks did approach these prey, peck at them, and occasionally pick them up. Furthermore, with repeated exposure, a proportion of chicks overcame their aversion to black-and-yellow prey and consumed them at a high rate (Schuler and Hesse, 1985).

The second conclusion is that pecking at and eating prey do not constitute qualitatively different indexes of aversiveness. In naive chicks given black-and-yellow striped prey, eating is inhibited but pecking is not (Schuler and Hesse, 1985). However, with plain black prey there is inhibition of both pecking and eating (Roper and Cook, 1989).

The third issue (the one requiring further investigation) concerns the relative aversiveness of stripes. In many warningly colored insects, the color pattern consists of alternating transverse stripes or, in other cases, of blobs or spots of one color on a background of another color (e.g., Edmunds, 1974). Guilford (1990a) suggested that such patterns are especially effective as warning stimuli because they involve internal color-contrast boundaries that increase the prey's conspicuousness. Roper and Cook (1989) found that bicolored prey were always preferred to olive, implying that a single color boundary does not make prey even mildly aversive. Further, neither red-and-yellow striped nor red-and-black striped prey were aversive by comparison with olive prey (Figs. 3b, c). These findings argue against Guilford's hypothesis. On the other hand, if attention is restricted to the crucial comparison between striped and bicolored prey in Roper and Cook's results, then it does seem as if striped prey are usually less attractive. More experiments are clearly required comparing striped and bicolored prey over a wider range of color combinations.

   b. The Importance of Contrast. A question that has been debated by many workers in the field of warning coloration is: What features of a color pattern make it effective as a signal to predators? In other words, what stimulus properties contribute to "conspicuousness" in a prey item? One possible answer to this has been discussed in the previous section, namely, the idea that two-color patterns are conspicuous because they contain internal color-contrast boundaries (Guilford, 1990a). Another is that prey are conspicuous to the extent that they are novel (Coppinger, 1970; Turner, 1975; see Section II,A,1 for a discussion). Two further possibilities are that prey are conspicuous to the extent that they contrast with their background and that certain colors and patterns are inherently conspicuous, regardless of the context in which they are encountered.

   The idea that conspicuousness depends on contrast between a prey item and its background is an old one; it was firmly advocated by Cott (1940) and has subsequently been emphasized by many authorities (e.g., Edmunds, 1974; Gittleman and Harvey, 1980). Furthermore, there is good evidence that contrast between prey and background enhances the speed and effectiveness of avoidance learning when distasteful prey are encountered by a naive predator (see Section II,D,1). However, Harvey and Paxton (1981a) wrote that "if particular hues or intensities of colour are more easily recognized than others, contrast with the background may not be important in some cases of aposematic coloration." This statement seems to hint that certain colors or patterns in and of themselves might be inherently recognizable to a predator.

   To test the latter idea Sillén-Tullberg (1985a) gave zebra finches (*Taeniopygia guttata*) a choice between red and gray forms of distasteful *Lygaeus equestris* larvae, presented on red or gray backgrounds. She found no evidence of an effect of background color on attack rate; rather, red larvae were attacked less, regardless of the background on which they were presented. Thus, it seems that red coloration *per se* was the effective stimulus.

In Sillén-Tullberg's experiments, the insects used as prey were distasteful and the birds were allowed to make multiple attacks, so it is not clear to what extent the lower rate of attack on red prey represented faster avoidance learning as opposed to an unlearned aversion to red. Roper (1990) eliminated possible effects of learning by giving naive domestic chicks a single exposure to red or brown painted (palatable) mealworms on red, brown, or white backgrounds. The results were consistent with those of Sillén-Tullberg; brown mealworms were more often pecked at and eaten first, and more brown mealworms were eaten overall, on all three backgrounds (Fig. 4).

To conclude, as regards the unlearned responses of birds toward insect prey, there is evidence that the color of the prey *per se,* as opposed to the degree of contrast between prey and background, determines the strength of the bird's response. The same may well be true of pattern *per se,* but this remains to be tested.

B. UNLEARNED RESPONSES IN PHEASANTS

Although chicks are convenient as experimental animals, it may seem questionable to look for rather specialized adaptations, such as avoidance of warningly colored prey, in such a highly domesticated species. However, selection pressure to avoid warningly colored insects (e.g., wasps) would not be expected to have ceased totally during domestication because chickens kept outside will have continued to encounter such prey. Furthermore, even if a selection pressure vanishes entirely as a consequence of domestication, it does not necessarily

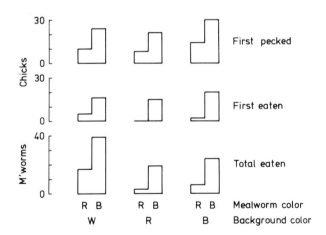

FIG. 4. Effect of background color on choice of red versus brown mealworms. *Upper:* Number of chicks whose first peck was directed toward a red (R) or a brown (B) mealworm. *Middle:* Number of chicks that first ate a red or brown mealworm. *Lower:* Total number of red or brown mealworms eaten. (From Roper, 1990.)

follow that the behavior pattern molded by it will disappear; the most frequent consequence of absence of selection is a quantitative diminution in the intensity of the feature in question plus an increase in its variability (Wilkens *et al.*, 1979).

Nevertheless, the idea that birds have an unlearned predisposition to avoid warningly colored prey requires corroboration from other species. Schuler (1982; see Section II,A,1) went some way toward providing comparative evidence by showing that starlings (*Sturnus vulgaris*) avoided black-and-yellow striped insect dummies. In this section, we review more detailed studies by Wrazidlo and Schuler using game pheasants (*Phasianus colchicus*) as subjects.

1. Response to Black-and-Yellow Prey in Young Pheasants

Wrazidlo (1986) offered a simultaneous choice of black-and-yellow striped and olive colored mealworms, in daily sessions, to pheasant chicks aged from 3 to 10 days. Her experiment was therefore a replication of Experiment 2 in Schuler and Hesse (1985), using pheasants instead of domestic chicks as subjects. The first larva pecked by the pheasant chicks was usually (in 11 out of 13 pairs of birds) an olive one and the first larva eaten was always olive colored. Furthermore, with continued testing, the pheasants persisted in almost totally rejecting black-and-yellow striped larvae while consuming more and more olive larvae. In a separate experiment, 9 out of 10 pairs of pheasants persisted in rejecting black-and-yellow striped mealworms even when no other prey was available, whereas in a control group, 7 out of 10 pairs accepted olive mealworms. This difference between groups was significant (Fisher test, $p < .01$).

These results suggest that by comparison with domestic chicks, pheasants have a stronger unlearned aversion toward warningly colored prey. First, whereas chicks pecked approximately equally at both colors of prey but failed to eat striped prey (Fig. 1b, Section II,A,1), pheasants neither pecked at nor ate striped prey. Second, whereas most chicks (6 out of 9 pairs) eventually came to accept striped larvae after repeated testing, only 1 out of 13 pairs of pheasants did so. Moreover, the range of values for the preference ratio (the proportion of black-and-yellow to all larvae eaten: cf. Roper and Cook, 1989) was smaller for pheasants (.0–.14) than had been found for chicks (.0–.45, calculated from the data of Schuler and Hesse, 1985; F test, $p < .001$). Thus, the results are consistent with the idea that increasing domestication has resulted in a quantitative reduction in the intensity of the response toward warningly colored prey.

2. Response to Black-and-Yellow Prey in Older Pheasant Chicks

Young chicks of any species are physically delicate, and this is especially true of pheasants; they are very vulnerable to low temperature, draughts and infections, and to feather-pecking by their companions. Older birds, by comparison, are conspicuously more robust. In addition, the effect of a noxious chemical on any species is usually related to body size; that is, a larger animal will be less affected by a poisonous dose of a given absolute magnitude. For both these reasons, we would expect the selection pressure that originates from warningly colored prey to be stronger in younger birds, because younger birds are more likely to be seriously injured by ingestion of defensive chemicals.

To test this prediction, Wrazidlo (1986, and unpublished data) gave pheasant chicks a simultaneous choice of black-and-yellow striped and olive mealworms from Days 14 to 21 under the same conditions as those tested from Days 3 to 10 (see Section II,B,1). One group of birds was reared on turkey starter crumbs, whereas a second group received chopped weeds plus a variety of wild-caught insects (not including black-and-yellow ones). The pheasants reared on turkey crumbs accepted (pecked at and ate) striped and olive mealworms roughly equally, whereas the birds reared on a mixed diet initially approached and pecked more at striped larvae but ate only olive larvae. In subsequent sessions, however, these latter birds gradually began to eat striped larvae and by the end of testing they were accepting both types of prey at the same rate. To summarize, the pheasants reared on a monotonous diet and aged 14 to 21 days showed no discrimination between striped and olive mealworms. Those reared on a varied diet showed a similar difference between pecking at and eating larvae of the two colors as did the young domestic chicks tested by Schuler and Hesse (1985).

These results are consistent with the prediction that the unlearned aversion to warningly colored prey should diminish with age, but they also show that the strength of the response varies with the animal's dietary history. Although it is unclear from Wrazidlo's experiment precisely what aspect of the diet of the second group of pheasants was responsible for their aversion to striped prey, it seems likely that the relevant factor was the inclusion of insects.

3.   The Signal Value of Colors and Stripes

The purpose of the experiments reported in this section was to compare the response of young pheasants (aged 3 to 10 days) toward prey of different colors and patterns to find out which features of the black-and-yellow striped pattern are responsible for the unlearned aversion (I. Wrazidlo, unpublished). In the first three experiments, the effect of plain colors was investigated. In each experiment, 12 pairs of pheasant chicks received in four daily sessions five mealworms painted with one of four colors. To exclude order effects, different colors of mealworm were presented in different sessions according to a Latin square design. In the first experiment, yellow, white, black, and olive larvae were presented; in the second experiment, olive and white were presented again, together with gray and brown; and in the third experiment, olive again, together with green, blue, and red. The data from the chicks receiving the four colors in different order were combined and in all three experiments, there was a significant effect of color on the total number of mealworms eaten (Friedman test, Experiments 1 and 2, $p < .005$; Experiment 3, $p < .001$). In the first experiment, white was preferred to olive (Wilcoxon test,

$p < .05$), yellow was taken at almost the same rate as olive, and black was eaten significantly less often ($p < .05$). In the second experiment, white was again preferred to olive, though in this case the difference was not significant ($p < .1$); brown and gray were accepted at the same rate as one another, but significantly less frequently than olive ($p < .05$ in both cases). In the third experiment, green was eaten less often than olive ($p < .05$) and blue and red at a much lower rate than green ($p < .05$ in both cases).

The scores for number of mealworms eaten were expressed as a preference ratio (PR) using olive as the standard, and results were combined over all three experiments because there was good agreement between the different experiments where the same color was presented more than once. This resulted in colors being ordered as follows: white (PR = .63), olive (PR = .5 by definition), yellow (PR = .46), green (PR = .38), gray (PR = .38), brown (PR = .30), black (PR = .16), blue (PR = .04), and red (PR = .00). Thus, black, blue, and red prey were all strongly aversive, with red prey being totally rejected by all the pheasants that were tested.

In the fourth experiment, the response to red prey was investigated in more detail by offering three groups of pheasant chicks, each consisting of six pairs, a choice between olive larvae and either plain red larvae or red larvae painted with one or three transverse black stripes. During the first four sessions, no red larvae, either plain or striped, were accepted, and olive control larvae were rejected as well. On the following 2 days, olive larvae alone were offered and were still rejected. Finally, white larvae were offered, and about half of these were accepted.

This experiment shows that red prey with or without stripes elicit an extreme avoidance response in pheasant chicks. Unlike avoidance of black-and-yellow prey, the aversion to red was sufficiently strong to generalize to olive prey when these were presented at the same time.

These results can be compared with those of Roper and Cook (1989), who used domestic chicks as subjects. Like Wrazidlo, they found little preference between yellow and olive mealworms and a strong aversion to black mealworms, but they reported only a very weak aversion to red and indifference toward red-and-black striped mealworms. The idea that domestication weakens the aversive response could explain why chicks respond less strongly than pheasants to red, but cannot explain why there is no similar diminution in chicks' response to black. An alternative possibility is that there are intrinsic species differences in the responses to different colors.

In two further experiments, I. Wrazidlo (unpublished) analyzed the effect of different patterns by offering pheasant chicks (six pairs per treatment) a simultaneous choice between olive and either black-and-yellow or black-and-white mealworms. In the experimental mealworms, the black pattern consisted either of three, two, or one transverse stripes, longitudinal stripes, or a pattern of dots. With a white background, there was no significant difference between the preference values for the four patterns (Kruskal Wallis H test). With a yellow background, however, the effect of type of black pattern was significant ($H = 13,46$; $p < .01$). One or two transverse stripes were equally effective (PR $= .08$ in both cases) and were both significantly more aversive than either longitudinal stripes (PR $= .22$; Mann-Whitney test, $p < .025$) or dots (PR $= .22$; $p < .05$).

Finally, the importance of contrast between stripes and background was investigated by presenting pheasant chicks (six pairs) with yellow mealworms painted with three transverse stripes of either black, gray, olive, or white. Black stripes were most effective (PR $= .00$), followed by olive (PR $= .05$), gray (PR $= .06$), and white (PR $= .27$). However, stripe color had no significant effect overall (Kruskal Wallis H test).

To summarize, the effectiveness of the black-and-yellow striped pattern in pheasants requires that at least one transverse stripe be present on a yellow background. The orientation of the stripes is important, but their number and color have relatively little significance as regards the strength of the bird's response. In addition, plain red, black, and blue are strongly aversive. The aversion of pheasants toward red prey is especially striking and deserves further study.

C.   Effects of Prior Experience on Unlearned Responses

Schuler and Hesse (1985) called the aversion of domestic chicks toward black-and-yellow striped mealworms "innate" on the grounds that it appeared in unfed birds. As Roper and Cook (1989) pointed out, however, Schuler and Hesse's chicks were acquired from a commercial hatchery so it is impossible to know what experience they had had prior to arrival at the laboratory. Furthermore, because the chicks were tested in the light during the course of several days in the presence of social companions, there was ample room for experiential factors to affect performance once testing had commenced. For example, chicks peck at one another's bills and feet, which are pink, eyes (black), plumage (yellow), and feces (brown or white), as well as at small spots or bits of debris on the walls or floor of the environment. Any of these experiences might affect their developing food preferences (cf. Wallman, 1979), as might the food that they were given in their home cages.

It is impossible, almost by definition, to remove from an animal's environment all possible experiential factors at one and the same time and, thus, create an animal that is in some absolute sense naive. However, one can manipulate, independently, the presence or intensity of particular factors that might be relevant. With this in mind, Roper and Cook (1989) kept chicks for 24 hours either in standard gray cages or in cages with alternating black and yellow walls. The birds were then given a choice between olive mealworms and either black-and-yellow striped, plain black, plain yellow, or black-and-yellow bicolored mealworms. (The latter were painted black on one half of the body and yellow on the other, see Section II,A,2,a.) The effect of prior exposure to black-and-yellow cages was to increase the response of the chicks toward mealworms that were either black or yellow, or both. Specifically, rearing in black-and-yellow cages reversed the chicks' normal aversion toward black-and-yellow striped prey, reduced their normally strong aversion toward black prey, increased their normally weak preference for yellow prey, and increased their normally moderate preference for black-and-yellow bicolored prey (Fig.5). The aversion toward striped prey was therefore changed by familiarity with relevant colors, despite the fact that the initial existence of this aversion cannot be explained in terms of novelty (see Section II,A,1).

The effect of previous experience was further investigated by Roper (1990), using red half-mealworms as experimental prey and brown half-mealworms as controls. As already noted, when chicks reared in gray cages are given a choice between red and brown half-mealworms, they peck at and eat more of the brown prey, and this relative aversion to red is shown regardless of the background color against which the prey are presented (Fig. 4, Section II,A,2,b). Roper (1990) showed that the aversion persisted in chicks that were prefed for 2 days on red food (chicks crumbs dyed with red food coloring), but was reversed by rearing chicks for the same amount of time in cages with red walls.

Taken together, the results of Roper and Cook (1989) and Roper (1990) suggest that the color of the environment in which chicks are reared can have a powerful effect on their subsequent choice of colored insect prey. However, this conclusion is undermined by a similar experiment by Wallner and Schuler (Wallner, 1986; Schuler, 1987). They reared chicks in either olive-colored cages or black-and-yellow striped cages (i.e., cages whose walls were painted with narrow vertical black stripes on a yellow background) and gave them a simultaneous choice between olive and black-and-yellow striped mealworms. Both groups of chicks were equally likely to direct their first peck toward a striped as opposed to an olive mealworm, but the first mealworm eaten in both groups was almost always an olive one. In addition, both groups, over the experiment as a whole, ate significantly more olive than black-and-yellow striped mealworms. Thus both groups, regardless of the cage color to which they were exposed, behaved like the subjects of Schuler and Hesse's (1985) original experiment. The only significant difference was that chicks reared in black-and-yellow striped cages ate fewer olive mealworms overall than did those reared in olive cages.

There is no obvious explanation as to why rearing chicks in cages with alternating black and yellow walls should dramatically affect their subsequent choice of prey, whereas rearing them in cages with striped walls should have virtually no effect. Given that environment color affects prey choice, one would expect the effect to be greater the greater the visual similarity between environment and prey. There are minor procedural differences between the experiment of Roper

Measure

Mealworm
color

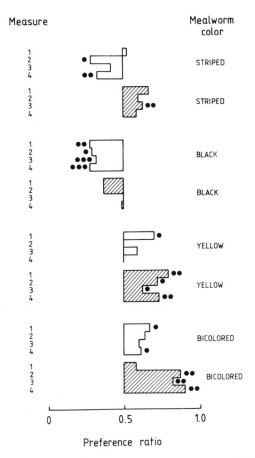

FIG. 5. Effect of cage color on chicks' choice of black, yellow, and black-and-yellow meal-worms. *Open bars:* chicks reared in gray cages. *Hatched bars:* chicks reared in cages with black and yellow walls and floor. Filled circles denote significance levels of .05, .01, and .001. 1, number of chicks first pecking experimental versus control mealworms; 2, number of chicks first picking up mealworms; 3, total number of pecks; 4, total number of pickups. Scores are presented as a preference ratio, with olive mealworms as control prey. (From Roper and Cook, 1989.)

and Cook and that of Wallner and Schuler, and these may account for the discrepancy. Clearly this is an area needing further investigation.

A final point that deserves comment is the fact that rearing chicks in red or brown cages affects their choice of red versus brown mealworms, whereas giving them red or brown chick crumbs to eat does not (Roper, 1990). This result seems paradoxical, because one might expect birds to generalize from one kind of food to another more readily than from cage walls to food. One possibility is that the total amount of exposure to the colors in question was greater when the walls were colored than when the food was dyed.

D. LEARNED AVOIDANCE OF WARNINGLY COLORED PREY

One of the earliest and most enduring hypotheses concerning the function of warning coloration is that it facilitates avoidance learning (see Section I,A). In other words, it is suggested that a predator learns to avoid noxious warningly colored prey more readily than equally noxious cryptic prey. This idea, originating from Wallace (1870) and Poulton (1890) and stated perhaps most strongly by Wickler (1968), has subsequently been widely assumed to be correct (e.g., Rettenmeyer, 1970; Turner, 1975; Matthews, 1977). Curiously, however, few attempts have been made to test it. In Section I,A, we reviewed some early studies that were relevant to the avoidance learning hypothesis in principle but were methodologically flawed in practice; here we review more recent evidence.

1. . The Effect of Contrast on Avoidance Learning

Gittleman and Harvey (1980) reasoned that if warningly colored prey are conspicuous to the extent that they contrast with their background (see Section II,A,2,b for a discussion), then a predator should learn to avoid contrasting noxious prey more readily than matching noxious prey. To test this idea they measured the intake rate of 3-day-old domestic chicks feeding on chick crumbs that were made noxious by the addition of a mixture of quinine sulphate and mustard. The crumbs were dyed either blue or green and were presented on either a green or a blue background. A separate group of chicks was assigned to each of the four test conditions, and the birds were tested over 13 hourly 2-min sessions. Initially, the chicks ingested contrasting crumbs at a higher rate than matching crumbs, suggesting that contrasting food is more attractive to or detectable by naive birds. With repeated exposure to the food, however, ingestion of contrasting crumbs rapidly tailed off, reaching a rate close to zero after four trials. Ingestion of matching crumbs, by contrast, continued at an almost undiminished rate over the whole series of 13 trials. The net result was that after 13 trials, more matching than contrasting crumbs had been eaten. The same result was obtained in a second experiment in which chicks were given a simultaneous choice of green and blue distasteful crumbs on either green or blue backgrounds (Gittleman et al., 1980).

These experiments confirm, at least for a laboratory environment, that noxious food items that contrast with their background "survive" better than items that match their background. This difference probably (though not necessarily: see Guilford, 1990a) results from a difference in the rate of avoidance learning. As Gittleman and Harvey (1980) note, however, a question remains as to how the learning effect was achieved. One possibility is that contrast per se facilitated avoidance learning, the other is that ingestion of conspicuous prey ceased more rapidly because these prey were initially eaten at a higher rate, thus providing more frequent punishment.

To show an effect of contrast *per se,* the confounding variable of differences in ingestion rate has to be removed. This has been done in two studies. In the first, Roper and Wistow (1986) essentially replicated the experiment of Gittleman and Harvey (1980), except that they terminated each test session when four chick crumbs had been ingested. Avoidance learning was measured in terms of within-trial ingestion rate. Like Gittleman and Harvey, Roper and Wistow found that ingestion rate was initially higher for contrasting than for matching crumbs, but subsequently fell at a faster rate for contrasting crumbs. Because overall ingestion rate was the same for both types of prey, the authors concluded that contrast *per se* was the factor responsible for the differences in rate of avoidance learning.

In the second study, Roper and Redston (1987) again equalized the rate at which chicks encountered noxious prey that either contrasted with or matched their background, but in this case they did so by using a one-trial learning paradigm. Chicks were allowed to peck once at a noxious colored bead that either matched or resembled its background. (The bead was made noxious by being painted with methyl anthranilate, which is highly distasteful to chicks.) The strength of avoidance learning following this single trial was subsequently tested by exposing the birds to nonnoxious beads of the same color for 4 min and measuring the number of pecks elicited. The results showed greater suppression of pecking when, in the training trial, the bead contrasted with its background. This study provides perhaps the most convincing evidence to date that contrast between prey and background, uncontaminated by any other variable, directly influences the effectiveness of avoidance learning.

In another experiment, Roper and Redston (1987) analyzed in more detail the memory of birds for a single aversive experience. Chicks were allowed to peck once at a noxious red or white bead on a white background and were then given test trials with a nonnoxious bead of the same color at different times after training. Different groups of chicks were used for each training-test interval. The results (Fig. 6) showed longer lasting memory for aversive red prey on a white background than for white prey on a white background. After experience involving a red bead, pecking remained suppressed for at least 72 hours, whereas after experience involving a white bead, pecking had recovered to its original level after 48 hours. Roper and Redston assume that contrast rather than bead color *per se* was responsible for the effect on memory, but, strictly speaking, a second group of birds, tested with red or white beads on a red background, is needed to confirm this.

To summarize, there is now good reason to suppose that birds learn more rapidly about noxious prey, and some reason to suppose that they retain the relevant learned information for longer, if those prey contrast with their

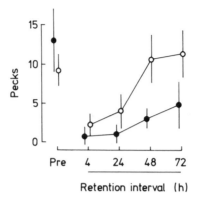

Retention interval (h)

FIG. 6. Memory of chicks for an aversive experience involving a bead that either contrasted with the background (filled circles) or matched the background (open circles). Scores are the mean and SD of the number of pecks per chick during a 4-minute pretraining (Pre) or test trial. (From Roper and Redston, 1987.)

background. Insofar as contrast is an element in warning coloration (see Section II,A,2,b), these experiments support the hypothesis that warning coloration facilitates avoidance learning.

2. The Effect of Novelty on Avoidance Learning

Several authors have suggested that warning coloration is effective because warningly colored prey look different from the cryptic prey that a predator more usually encounters. In other words, warning coloration is novel (e.g., Coppinger, 1970; Turner, 1975). The effect of novelty on avoidance learning has been investigated by Shettleworth (1972), who tested 10-day-old chicks with uncolored (familiar) or blue (novel) quinine-flavored water. Chicks learned more readily to discriminate between quinine-flavored water and unflavored water when the quinine-flavored water was blue and the unflavored water uncolored (Fig. 7).

Shettleworth's experiment is often cited as showing that avoidance learning proceeds more rapidly when the unconditioned stimulus is novel, but, in fact, avoidance learning proceeded equally rapidly regardless of whether the quinine-flavored solution was novel or familiar (compare lines "Novel/Unpal" and "Fam/Unpal" in Fig. 7). Rather, groups differed in their response to the *unflavored* water (compare lines "Fam/Pal" and "Novel/Pal"). The effect was that chicks discriminated between noxious and palatable solutions when the noxious solution was an unfamiliar color (Fig. 7a) but generalized when it was a familiar color (Fig. 7b).

More convincing evidence of the effect of novelty on visually mediated avoidance learning in birds was provided by Schuler (1980). He found that starlings

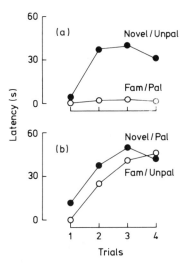

FIG. 7. Latency of chicks to contact water that was either novel or familiar in appearance and either unpalatable or palatable in taste. (a) Novel appearance paired with unpalatability. (b) Familiar appearance paired with unpalatability. (From Shettleworth, 1972.)

learned more rapidly to avoid a dark blue spotted quinine-treated mealworm pupa if it was novel than if it had previously been encountered in palatable form. Nevertheless, the relevance of novelty to learned avoidance of warningly colored prey deserves further attention.

3. Interactions between Unlearned and Learned Avoidance

None of the experiments described in the previous two sections examined the speed of avoidance learning using prey that initially elicited unlearned avoidance. If a naive predator is cautious about approaching a prey stimulus (as, for example, chicks are cautious when approaching black-and-yellow striped mealworms), does that stimulus support faster avoidance learning?

Roper and Cook (1989) attempted to answer this question by means of a one-trial avoidance learning procedure, using chicks as predator and black-and-yellow striped, black, yellow, or black-and-yellow bicolored mealworms as prey. The mealworms were made noxious by painting them with methyl anthranilate. Avoidance learning occurred with all four colors of mealworm, but none of four separate measures of behavior revealed a significant interaction between the strength of that learning and mealworm color. Because experiments had shown that black and black-and-yellow striped mealworms are aversive to naive chicks, whereas yellow and bicolored mealworms are attractive (Roper and Cook, 1989; see Section II,A,2,a), this experiment provided no evidence that unlearned preferences or aversions either facilitate or hinder avoidance learning.

A potential problem with Roper and Cook's experiment is that methyl anthranilate is so aversive to chicks that learning may have been too efficient to reveal an effect of prey color. In an elegant experiment using more naturalistic stimuli, Sillén-Tullberg (1985b) presented hand-reared great tits (*Parus major*) with distasteful larvae of *Lygaeus equestris*. One group of birds was given the normal red form of the larva while another was given a mutant gray form, and because both were presented on a gray background the red larvae were more conspicuous. On the first trial, significantly fewer birds attacked red than gray prey, suggesting an unlearned aversion toward red. In subsequent trials, moreover, some measures of behavior (including the total number of prey killed) showed significantly faster avoidance learning with red prey. This latter result could just be another example of avoidance learning being facilitated by contrast between prey and background (see Section II,D,1), but in a different experiment, Sillén-Tullberg (1985a) showed that unlearned avoidance of the red morph of *Lygaeus equestris* is elicited by the color of the larva, independent of background. In any case, Sillén-Tullberg's (1985b) results do suggest that a stimulus that birds are initially reluctant to attack does, when sampled, favor faster avoidance learning.

In a somewhat similar study, Codella and Lederhouse (1990) gave blue jays (*Cyanocitta cristata*) repeated trials with dead specimens of the naturally noxious pipevine swallowtail butterfly *Battus philenor*. (The jays had eaten butterflies before, but not noxious or warningly colored ones.) *Battus philenor* bears a striking orange and blue pattern on the ventral surface of its hindwings, and because it is normally preyed on while in a resting posture, this ventral wing pattern is assumed to be an instance of warning coloration. The dorsal surface of the wings, by contrast, is a uniform blue-green. Codella and Lederhouse presented butterflies in which either the ventral or the dorsal surface of the wings was exposed and scored the number of butterflies eaten. Jays given butterflies showing the ventral (patterned) wing surface attacked on average only 2.7 prey before consistently rejecting them, whereas those seeing the dorsal wing surface attacked an average of 6.3 prey, a difference that was just statistically significant. What we do not know, unfortunately, is whether naive jays or any other birds are more intimidated by the ventral wing pattern of *Battus philenor* than by the uniform blue-green dorsal wing color. Thus, although Codella and Lederhouse's experiment provides further confirmation that warning coloration facilitates avoidance learning, and does so with naturalistic stimuli, it does not demonstrate an interaction between unlearned and learned avoidance.

A fourth experiment relevant to this issue was conducted by Hesse and Schuler (Hesse, 1982; Schuler, 1987). Naive domestic chicks were given a simultaneous choice between black-and-yellow striped and green mealworms over a series of trials. For one group of chicks, the black-and-yellow striped mealworms were made noxious by adding quinine dihydrochloride and the green mealworms were uncontaminated, whereas in a second group, the green mealworms were made noxious and the black-and-yellow striped ones were palatable.

Mealworm color did not influence avoidance learning; distasteful larvae were attacked with equal frequency regardless of their color (means 7.6 and 6.8 attacks, respectively, over 10 sessions, $p > .05$). However, the response of the two groups to the palatable prey differed radically. Chicks given noxious black-and-yellow mealworms learned to eat palatable green ones, whereas chicks given noxious green mealworms also avoided eating palatable black-and-yellow striped ones. This result, which is reminiscent of the experiment by Shettleworth (1972; see Section II,D,2), is perhaps best described in terms of sensitization or generalization rather than avoidance learning *per se,* but in any case, the mechanism underlying it deserves further investigation. Functionally, it means that the predisposition to avoid black-and-yellow striped prey hinders discrimination between these and other prey when the former are harmless and the latter noxious. But because this is the opposite of the situation that generally obtains in the real world, the effect presumably has no adaptive significance.

4. Effect of Conspicuousness on an Experienced Predator

Guilford (1986, 1987) suggests that conspicuousness may influence prey choice in an experienced predator as well as during the process of avoidance learning. He argues that an experienced predator is less likely to attack by mistake a conspicuous unpalatable prey because its conspicuousness will enable the prey to be detected at a greater distance. Thus, the predator will have more time in which to decide whether or not to attack.

When he manipulated the distance between prey and predator, Guilford (1987) did not find an effect of conspicuousness on error (i.e., attack) rate. However, he found a significantly lower error rate when chicks were allowed to view a palatable and a colored unpalatable crumb for .23 sec before being allowed to peck at either (Guilford, 1986). This latter experiment is at best an indirect test of the "detection distance" hypothesis, because viewing time, rather than detection distance, was manipulated and the palatable and unpalatable prey were equally conspicuous.

To summarize this section, there is good evidence that certain features that contribute to a prey's visual distinctiveness (especially contrast between prey and background) enhance avoidance learning. The role of novelty, and of prey coloration independent of contrast, is less clear, as is the way (if any) in which unlearned predispositions to attack or avoid noxious warningly colored prey interact with subsequent avoidance learning. There is also some indirect evidence that conspicuousness lowers error rate in an experienced predator.

III. Discussion

For more than a century, biologists have theorized about the conditions leading to the evolution of warning coloration (see Section I,B), but in doing so they have considered predators as abstract entities whose only important characteristic is that they learn from experience. The possibility that the responses of predators have been altered by evolution continued to be ignored (e.g., Gilbert, 1983; Sillén-Tullberg and Bryant, 1983), even when convincing evidence of adaptive unlearned predator responses was available (Smith, 1975, 1977).

The fact is that different predators respond in different ways to warning coloration. We will argue that one can understand these differences most easily by considering warning coloration as a means of communication. We will then compare warning signals with other signals and discuss whether they have unique properties.

A. Warning Signals as a Means of Communication

By saying that warning coloration is a signal, we mean that it acts as a sign whereby prey animals indicate their unpalatability to potential predators. In the language of semiotics, such a process of animal communication generally involves a sender, which encodes a message into a signal, plus a receiver, which assigns a meaning to the signal and responds accordingly. In our case, the sender might be an insect that encodes the message "I possess defensive chemicals" into a visual warning signal, the signal is transmitted to a predator, and the predator assigns to it the meaning "This is unpalatable prey" and accordingly rejects the prey (see Fig. 8).

Generally, the meaning of a signal (which in the case of animals we have to infer from the elicited response) depends on the receiver. Consequently, the same message can have different meanings for different receivers (Slater, 1983). To illustrate this in the context of warning coloration, Table I compares the responses of different predators to black-and-yellow color patterns shown by prey that differ in the degree to which they are dangerous. Although the experiments cited are obviously not all directly comparable, Table I shows that the response to

SENDER → SIGNAL → RECEIVER → RESPONSE
(message)   (meaning)

PREY INSECT → WARNING → PREDATOR → REJECTION
(defensive   COLORATION   (unpalatable
chemicals)   prey)

Fig. 8. Schematic representation of a semiosis expressed in general terms (above) and applied to warning coloration as a means of communication between prey and predator (below).

TABLE I
RESPONSES OF NAIVE BIRDS TO BLACK-AND-YELLOW PREY

Birds	Test object	Level of danger[a]	Response	Reference
Herons, egrets	Sea snake	+++	Panicking flight	Caldwell and Rubinoff (1983)
Motmot, kiskadee	Coral snake dummy[b]	++	Excitement, alarm calls	Smith (1975, 1977)
Reed warbler	Wasp	+	Rejection	Davies and Green (1976)
Pheasant (3–10 days old)	Painted mealworm	+	Rejection	Wrazidlo (1986)
Chicken (1–5 days old)	Painted mealworm	+	Inhibited attack	Schuler and Hesse (1985)
Pheasant (14–21 days old)	Painted mealworm	(+)	Cautious attack	I. Wrazidlo (unpublished)
Starling	Insect dummy	(+)	Initial avoidance	Schuler (1982)
Bee-eater	Platelet	—	Preference	Koenig (1950)

[a]In cases of artificial prey, level of danger of their natural models.
[b]Pattern also contained red.

black-and-yellow depends on how dangerous the prey is. With lethally poisonous snakes, the response of the predator is a flight reaction. Warningly colored insects that are less dangerous are strongly avoided only by vulnerable species or age classes; in other cases, they are merely treated cautiously. If the predator is immune to the chemical defense of the prey, as bee-eaters are to the stings of wasps (Fry, 1984), black-and-yellow may elicit attack.

We argue that these differing responses are evolutionary adaptations for the following reasons. First, selection pressures must surely operate in the case of lethally poisonous snakes and also for noxious insects, where a young bird may be seriously harmed by the chemical defenses of the prey. Second, there is evidence that responses to colors and patterns can be altered in birds by artificial selection (Kovach, 1978, 1983). Third, whether or not different species of birds show unlearned avoidance of coral-snake patterns correlates with whether or not the species is exposed to coral snakes in its natural environment (Smith, 1980). Fourth, there is a close correlation between the type of coloration that elicits avoidance and the actual patterning of dangerous prey likely to be encountered in the natural environment of a particular predator species. For example, longitudinal black-and-yellow striping is aversive to potential predators of longitudinally striped sea snakes (i.e., to herons and egrets: Caldwell and Rubinoff, 1983), but not to predators of transversely striped coral snakes (i.e., motmots *Eumomota superciliosa:* Smith, 1975).

Of course, it is also true that unlearned responses to warning coloration are modified by experience during the lifetime of an individual predator. However, we would argue that adaptations also exist with respect to avoidance learning, because animals learn more readily to avoid conspicuous prey (see Section II,D). At present, however, the evidence of adaptiveness in learned responses is relatively weak and needs extending, for example, by comparing the avoidance learning capabilities of species that are more or less likely to encounter warningly colored prey in their natural environment.

One implication of our argument is that if responses to warning coloration are altered by natural selection, then an ontogenetically naive animal is not the same as an evolutionarily naive one (see Section II,A). It follows that in constructing scenarios for the evolution of warning coloration, we cannot simply use the former as a model for the latter. Rather, we need direct independent evidence of how animals responded when warning coloration first evolved.

B. THE DIVERSITY OF WARNING SIGNALS

Insects display many different types of warning coloration, but the most common are bright colors such as red, orange, and yellow, usually combined with black to form a contrasting pattern. The equivalent plain colors, such as red in fire beetles (*Pyrrochroa coccinea*), occur less frequently. There is agreement about what constitute typical cases of warning coloration, but for more marginal examples, opinions differ. For example, the cabbage white butterfly (*Pieris brassicae*) is considered warningly colored by Rothschild (1985) but was used as a novel non-warningly colored control in a test of birds' responses toward wasps (Davies and Green, 1976).

As naturalists have known since the time of Bates, warningly colored animals often have other characteristics that render them conspicuous, such as slow movement or gregariousness (Cott, 1940). The "warning coloration syndrome" encompasses all these features. Analyzing how the details of specific warning coloration syndromes are related to the properties of the natural environment of a particular species, as Süffert (1932) has done for cryptic coloration, might tell us more about what type of coloration is most useful under what circumstances.

Cott (1940) concluded that conspicuousness is a universal feature of all warning color patterns and that it is often produced by color contrast between the prey and its background. But he was well aware of the diversity of warning coloration, and stressed that one has to look at an animal in its natural environment to decide whether or not it is conspicuous. Subsequently, some authors adopted a reductionistic version of Cott's view, rigidly equating warning coloration with contrast between the prey and its background (Gittleman and Harvey, 1980; though see also Harvey and Paxton, 1981a). More recently Guilford (1990) added color contrast within a pattern as a possible additional source of conspicuousness.

We doubt whether a simple reductionistic view can really encompass the biological diversity of warning coloration; contrast is certainly an important aspect of warning coloration (Section II,D,1), but is not the only one. In addition, any view that relies on physical characteristics of the warning color or pattern fails to take account of the fact that the same physical signal may be used for opposing purposes. For example, plain red coloration is used both by the hawthorn tree (*Crataegus monogyna*) to advertise its fruit to birds and by the fire beetle to deter birds as potential predators.

A comparison with other signals may be more helpful in finding features common to all or most instances of warning coloration. Wiley (1983) points out that ritualized signals often involve redundancy, conspicuousness or contrast, small signal repertoire size, and alerting components. All of these features may also be found in warning coloration syndromes. Redundancy is often present in the form of repeating patterns of stripes or dots, conspicuousness or contrast are present almost by definition, small signal repertoires are shown by the simplicity of individual warning signals and also by the sharing of the same signal by different species in a Mullerian mimicry system, and alerting components may exist in the form of odors such as pyrazine (Rothschild *et al.*, 1984; Guilford *et al.*, 1987). Thus, warning coloration seems to have much in common with other ritualized signals.

According to semiotics and signal detection theory, the physical properties of a signal are determined by a combination of the sender, receiver, and transmission channel rather than by the message it carries. This means that the important characteristics of warning coloration cannot be found in the signal itself. Rather, warning coloration has to carry a certain message (i.e., unpalatability) from a specific sender to a specific receiver through a particular environment. Conspicuousness and other features of the warning coloration syndrome are necessary only to secure transmission of this message.

It follows from this analysis that both prey and predator must be taken into account in any consideration of warning coloration. In this article, we have emphasized the responses of predators to warning colors and patterns, but only because this is an aspect of warning signaling that has been relatively neglected in the past.

IV. Summary

Mimicry, warning coloration, and chemical defense in insects have been of interest to evolutionary biologists since the time of Darwin. Initially, debate centered around theoretical ideas and comparative evidence, with experimental tests of hypotheses lagging far behind. Recent scenarios for the evolution of warning coloration include individual, kin, and synergistic selection, the relative importance of which depends on the precise manner in which predators respond to novel warningly colored prey. Thus, further progress in understanding warning coloration requires detailed analysis of predatory behavior.

In domestic chicks (*Gallus gallus domesticus*), an unlearned aversion toward black-and-yellow striped prey has been demonstrated by testing prey-naive individuals with artificial, yet naturalistic, prey items. The aversion is specific to a black-and-yellow striped pattern; other patterns containing yellow, black and yellow, or stripes of other colors (including black) do not elicit a comparable response. However, plain black and plain red prey are also aversive.

By comparison with domestic chicks, young pheasants (*Phasianus colchicus*) show an even more pronounced aversion toward black-and-yellow striped and red prey. This suggests that aversive responses have been weakened by domestication in chicks. The aversion is also weaker in older pheasants, perhaps because they are more robust and are therefore less susceptible to selection pressure resulting from ingestion of chemically defended insects.

Rearing domestic chicks in boxes painted half black and half yellow reduced their aversion to black-and-yellow striped and black prey. However, rearing them in boxes with black-and-yellow striped walls or prefeeding them with colored food (chick crumbs) did not affect the aversion. The effects of previous experience on the aversive response deserve further study.

Warning coloration is a signal to potential predators. We interpret its signal value in terms of semiotics, according to which the meaning of a signal is not fixed but depends on who is the receiver. By comparing data from different species, we show that the intensity of the response of naive avian predators toward black-and-yellow warningly colored prey depends on how dangerous the prey is for the respective predator. We argue that these different unlearned responses are evolutionary adaptations, and suggest that adaptations also exist with respect to avoidance learning.

In nature, a rich diversity of warning colors and patterns can be found. We doubt whether this diversity can be reduced to a few simple principles, because properties such as contrast and novelty, which have been advocated as characteristics of warning coloration, are found also in other types of signal. Further analysis of the function of warning coloration requires investigation of the relationship between specific warning coloration syndromes (which comprise properties such as slow movement and gregariousness, in addition to coloration *per se*) and the natural environment in which they operate.

Acknowledgments

We thank Manfred Milinski and Peter Slater for inviting us to write this article and for their editorial help, Isolde Wrazidlo for permission to include unpublished results, Tim Guilford for many helpful comments on an earlier version of the manuscript, and Ellen Deusser-Schuler for hospitality during its preparation.

References

Alcock, A. S. (1896). An instance of the natural repellent effect of "warning colours." *J. Asiat. Soc. Bengal* **65**, Pt. 2, 539.

Bates, H. W. (1862). Contributions to an insect fauna of the Amazon valley. Lepidoptera: Heliconidae. *Trans. Linn. Soc. London* **23**, 495–566.

Brower, J. V. Z. (1958a). Experimental studies of mimicry in some North American butterflies. I. The monarch, *Danaus plexippus*, and viceroy, *Limenitis a. archippus. Evolution (Lawrence, Kans.)* **12**, 23–47.

Brower, J. V. Z. (1958b). Experimental studies of mimicry in some North American butterflies. II. *Battus philenor* and *Papilio troilus, P. polyxenes* and *P. glaucus. Evolution (Lawrence, Kans.)* **12**, 123–136.

Brower, J. V. Z. (1958c). Experimental studies of mimicry in some North American butterflies. III. *Danaus gilippus berenice* and *Limenitis archippus floridensis. Evolution (Lawrence, Kans.)* **12**, 273–285.

Brower, L. P. (1969). Ecological chemistry. *Sci. Am.* **220**(2), 22–29.

Brower, L. P., and Brower, J. V. Z. (1964). Birds, butterflies, and plant poisons: A study in ecological chemistry. *Zoologica (N. Y.)* **49**, 137–159.

Caldwell, G. S., and Rubinoff, R. W. (1983). Avoidance of venomous sea snakes by naive herons and egrets. *Auk* **100**, 195–198.

Clarke, C. A., and Sheppard, P. M. (1960). The evolution of mimicry in the butterfly *Papilio dardanus* Brown. *Heredity* **14**, 163–173.

Codella, S. G., Jr., and Lederhouse, R. C. (1990). The effect of wing orientation on aposematic signalling in the pipevine swallowtail butterfly *Battus philenor. Anim. Behav.* **40**, 404–406.

Coppinger, R. (1969). The effect of experience and novelty on avian feeding behavior with reference to the evolution of warning coloration in butterflies. Part I. Reaction of wild-caught adult Blue Jays to novel insects. *Behaviour* **35**, 45–60.

Coppinger, R. (1970). The effect of experience and novelty on avian feeding behavior with reference to the evolution of warning coloration in butterflies. II. Reactions of naive birds to novel insects. *Am. Nat.* **104**, 323–335.

Cott, H. B. (1940). "Adaptive Coloration in Animals." Methuen, London.

Curio, E. (1976). "The Ethology of Predation." Springer, Berlin.

Darwin, C. (1859). "On the Origin of Species." Murray, London.

Davies, N. B., and Green, R. E. (1976). The development and ecological significance of feeding techniques in the reed warbler (*Acrocephalus scirpaceus*). *Anim. Behav.* **24**, 213–229.

Dawkins, R. (1976). "The Selfish Gene." Oxford Univ. Press, Oxford.

Dawkins, R. (1989). "The Selfish Gene," 2nd ed. Oxford Univ. Press, Oxford.

Edmunds, M. (1974). "Defence in Animals." Longman, Harlow.

Eibl-Eibesfeldt, I. (1952). Nahrungserwerb und Beuteschema der Erdkröte (*Bufo bufo* L.). *Behaviour* **4**, 1–35.

Finn, F. (1895). Contributions to the theory of warning colours and mimicry. I. Experiments with a Babbler (*Crateropus canorus*). *J. Asiat. Soc. Bengal* **64**, 344–356.

Finn, F. (1896). Contributions to the theory of warning colours and mimicry. II. Experiments with a lizard (*Calotes versicolor*). *J. Asiat. Soc. Bengal* **65**, 42–48.

Fischer, G. L., Morris, G. L., and Ruhsam, J. P. (1975). Color pecking preferences in white leghorn chicks. *J. Comp. Physiol. Psychol.* **88**, 402–406.

Fisher, R. A. (1930). "The Genetical Theory of Natural Selection." Oxford Univ. Press (Clarendon), Oxford.

Fry, C. H. (1984). "The Bee-Eaters." Poyser, Calton, Staffordshire.

Gehlbach, F. R. (1972). Coral snake mimicry reconsidered: The strategy of self-mimicry. *Forma Funct.* **5**, 311–320.

Gilbert, L. E. (1983). Coevolution and mimicry. *In* "Coevolution" (D. J. Futuyma and M. Slatkin, eds.), pp. 263–281. Sinauer, Sunderland, Massachusetts.

Gittleman, J. L., and Harvey, P. H. (1980). Why are distasteful prey not cryptic? *Nature (London)* **286,** 149–150.

Gittleman, J. L., Harvey, P. H., and Greenwood, P. J. (1980). The evolution of conspicuous coloration: Some experiments in bad taste. *Anim. Behav.* **28,** 897–899.

Guilford, T. C. (1985). Is kin selection involved in the evolution of warning coloration? *Oikos* **45,** 31–36.

Guilford, T. C. (1986). How do warning colours work: Conspicuousness may reduce recognition errors in experienced predators. *Anim. Behav.* **34,** 286–288.

Guilford, T. C. (1987). Aposematism. Ph.D. Thesis. Oxford University, Oxford.

Guilford, T. C. (1990a). The evolution of aposematism. *In* "Insect Defenses" (D. L. Evans and J. O. Schmidt, eds.) pp. 23–61. State Univ. of New York Press, Albany.

Guilford, T. C. (1990b). Evolutionary pathways to aposematism. *Acta Oecol.* **11,** 835–841.

Guilford, T. C., Nicol, C. J., Rothschild, M., and Moore, B. P. (1987). The biological roles of pyrazines: Evidence for a warning odour function. *Biol. J. Linn. Soc.* **31,** 113–128.

Haase, E. (1892). "Untersuchungen über die Mimicry auf Grundlage eines natürlichen Systems der Papilioniden," Parts 1 and 2. Cassel, Germany.

Hamilton, W. D. (1964). The genetical theory of social behaviour. I. II. *J. Theor. Biol.* **7,** 1–52.

Harvey, P. H., and Paxton, R. J. (1981a). The evolution of aposematic coloration. *Oikos* **37,** 391–393.

Harvey, P. H., and Paxton, R. J. (1981b). On aposematic coloration: A rejoinder. *Oikos* **37,** 395–396.

Heikertinger, F. (1919). Zur Lösung des Trutzfärbungsproblems. Der Fall *Pyrrhocoris apterus* und das Prinzip der Ungewohntfärbung. *Wien. Entomol. Ztg.* **37,** 179–196.

Hesse, E. (1982). Untersuchungen zum Verhalten von Haushuhnküken (*Gallus domesticus*) gegenüber warnfarbiger Beute. Staatsexamensarbeit (Thesis), University of Göttingen.

Jeffords, M. R., Sternburg, J. G., and Waldbauer, G. P. (1979). Batesian mimicry: Field demonstration of the survival value of pipevine swallowtail and monarch color patterns. *Evolution (Lawrence, Kans.)* **33,** 275–286.

Koenig, L. (1950). Untersuchungen über Nahrungserwerb und Beuteschema des Bienenfressers. *Zool. Inf. (Biol. Stat. Wilhelminenberg)* **2.**

Kovach, J. K. (1978). Color preferences in quail chicks: Generalization of the effects of genetic selection. *Behaviour* **65,** 263–269.

Kovach, J. K. (1983). Perceptual imprinting: Genetically variable response tendencies, selective learning and the phenotypic expression of colour and pattern preference in quail chicks (*C. coturnix japonica*). *Behaviour* **86,** 72–88.

Krebs, J. R., and Davies, N. B. (1981). "An Introduction to Behavioural Ecology." Blackwell, Oxford.

Malcolm, S. B. (1990). Mimicry: Status of a classical evolutionary paradigm. *Trends Ecol. Evol.* **5,** 57–62.

Mallet, J. (1990). Is mimicry theory unpalatable? *Trends Ecol. Evol.* **5,** 344–345.

Mallet, J., and Singer, M. (1987). Individual selection, kin selection, and the shifting balance in the evolution of warning colours: The evidence from butterflies. *Biol. J. Linn. Soc.* **32,** 337–350.

Matthews, E. G. (1977). Signal-based frequency-dependent defense strategies and the evolution of mimicry. *Am. Nat.* **111,** 213–222.

Maynard Smith, J. (1964). Group selection and kin selection. *Nature (London)* **201,** 1145–1147.

Mayr, E. (1982). "The Growth of Biological Thought." Harvard Univ. Press, Cambridge, Massachusetts.

McAttee, W. L. (1932). Effectiveness in nature of the so-called protective adaptations in the animal kingdom, chiefly as illustrated by the food habits of Nearctic birds. *Smithson. Misc. Coll.* **85**(7), 1–201.

Morgan, C. L. (1896). "Habit and Instinct." Arnold, London.

Mostler, G. (1935). Beobachtungen zur Frage der Wespenmimikry. *Z. Morphol. Oekol. Tiere* **29**, 381–455.

Poulton, E. C. (1890). "The Colours of Animals." Kegan Paul, Trench, Trubner, London.

Reichstein, T., van Euw, J., Parsons, J. A., and Rothschild, M. (1968). Heart poisons in the monarch butterfly. *Science* **161**, 861–865.

Rettenmeyer, C. (1970). Insect mimicry. *Annu. Rev. Entomol.* **15**, 43–74.

Roper, T. J. (1990). Responses of domestic chicks to artificially coloured insect prey: Effects of previous experience and background colour. *Anim. Behav.* **39**, 466–473.

Roper, T. J., and Cook, S. (1989). Responses of chicks to brightly coloured insect prey. *Behaviour* **110**, 276–293.

Roper, T. J., and Redston, S. (1987). Conspicuousness of distasteful prey affects the strength and durability of one-trial avoidance learning. *Anim. Behav.* **35**, 739–747.

Roper, T. J., and Wistow, R. (1986). Aposematic coloration and avoidance learning in chicks. *Q. J. Exp. Psychol.* **38B**, 141–149.

Rothschild, M. (1985). British aposematic Lepidoptera. *In* "The Moths and Butterflies of Great Britain and Ireland" (J. Heath and A. Maitland Emmett, eds.), Vol. 2, pp. 9–62. Harley, Colchester, Essex.

Rothschild, M., Moore, B. P., and Brown, W. V. (1984). Pyrazines as warning odour components in the Monarch butterfly, *Danaus plexippus,* and in moths of the genera *Zygaena* and *Amata* (Lepidoptera). *Biol. J. Linn. Soc.* **23**, 375–380.

Rubinoff, I., and Kropach, C. (1970). Differential reactions of Atlantic and Pacific predators to sea snakes. *Nature (London)* **228**, 1288–1290.

Schuler, W. (1974). Die Schutzwirkung künstlicher Batesscher Mimikry abhängig von Modellähnlichkeit und Beuteangebot. *Z. Tierpsychol.* **36**, 71–127.

Schuler, W. (1980). Zum Meidenlernen ungenießbarer Beute bei Vögeln: Der Einfluß der Faktoren Umlernen, neue Alternativbeute und Ähnlichkeit der Alternativbeute. *Z. Tierpsychol.* **54**, 105–143.

Schuler, W. (1982). Zur Funktion von Warnfarben: Die Reaktion junger Stare auf wespenähnlich schwarz-gelbe Attrappen. *Z. Tierpsychol.* **58**, 66–78.

Schuler, W. (1987). Untersuchungen zur Bedeutung der unmittelbaren Erfahrung und des Lernens im Funktionskreis Nahrung beim Star. Habilitationsschrift (Thesis), University of Göttingen.

Schuler, W., and Hesse, E. (1985). On the function of warning coloration: A black and yellow pattern inhibits prey-attack by naive domestic chicks. *Behav. Ecol. Sociobiol.* **16**, 249–255.

Shettleworth, S. J. (1972). The role of novelty in learned avoidance of unpalatable 'prey' by domestic chicks (*Gallus gallus*). *Anim. Behav.* **20**, 29–35.

Sillén-Tullberg, B. (1985a). The significance of coloration per se, independent of background, for predator avoidance of aposematic prey. *Anim. Behav.* **33**, 1382–1384.

Sillén-Tullberg, B. (1985b). Higher survival of an aposematic than of a cryptic form of a distasteful bug. *Oecologia* **67**, 411–415.

Sillén-Tullberg, B., and Bryant, E. H. (1983). The evolution of aposematic coloration in distasteful prey. An individual selection model. *Evolution (Lawrence, Kans.)* **37**, 993–1000.

Slater, P. J. B. (1983). The study of communication. *In* "Animal Behaviour" (T. R. Halliday and P. J. B. Slater, eds.), Vol. 2, pp. 9–42. Blackwell, Oxford.

Smith, S. M. (1975). Innate recognition of coral snake pattern by a possible avian predator. *Science* **187**, 759–760.

Smith, S. M. (1977). Coral snake pattern recognition and stimulus generalization by naive great kiskadees (Aves: Tyrannidae). *Nature (London)* **265,** 535–536.

Smith, S. M. (1980). Responses of naive temperate birds to warning coloration. *Am. Midl. Nat.* **103,** 346–352.

Süffert, F. (1932). Phänomene visueller Anpassung. I–III. *Z. Morphol. Oekol. Tiere* **26,** 147–316.

Swynnerton, C. F. M. (1919). Experiments and observations bearing on the explanation of form and colouring, 1908–1913 in Africa. *J. Linn. Soc. London, Zool.* **23,** 203–285.

Trivers, (1985). "Social Evolution." Cummings, Menlo Park, California.

Turner, J. R. G. (1975). A tale of two butterflies. *Nat. Hist. N.Y.* **84,** 28–37.

Turner, J. R. G. (1977). Butterfly mimicry: The genetical evolution of an adaptation. *Evol. Biol.* **10,** 163–206.

Wallace, A. R. (1870). "Contributions to the Theory of Natural Selection." London.

Wallman, J. (1979). A minimal visual restriction experiment: Preventing chicks from seeing their feet affects later responses to mealworms. *Dev. Psychobiol.* **12,** 391–397.

Wallner, U. (1986). Untersuchungen zum Einfluß von Vorerfahrung, Hungerzustand und Geschlecht auf die Reaktion von Haushuhnküken (*Gallus domesticus*) gegenüber warnfarbener Beute. Diplomarbeit (Thesis), University of Göttingen.

Wickler, W. (1968). "Mimikry." Kindler, München.

Wiklund, C., and Järvi, T. (1982). Survival of distasteful insects after being attacked by naive birds: A reappraisal of the theory of aposematic coloration evolving through individual selection. *Evolution (Lawrence, Kans.)* **36,** 998–1002.

Wiley, R. H. (1983). The evolution of communication: Information and manipulation. *In* "Animal Behaviour" (T. R. Halliday and P. J. B. Slater, eds.), Vol. 2, pp. 156–189. Blackwell, Oxford.

Wilkens, H., Peters, N., and Schemmel, C. (1979). Gesetzmäßigkeiten der regressiven Evolution. *Verh. Dtsch. Zool. Ges.* **72,** 123–140.

Wilson, E. O. (1975). "Sociobiology." Harvard Univ. Press, Cambridge, Massachusetts.

Windecker, W. (1939). *Euchelia (Hypocrita) jacobaeae* L. und das Schutztrachtenproblem. *Z. Morphol. Oekol. Tiere* **35,** 84–138.

Wrazidlo, I. (1986). Untersuchungen zur Reaktion von Fasanen- und Wachtelküken auf warnfarbige Beute. Diplomarbeit (Thesis), University of Göttingen.

Analysis and Interpretation of Orb Spider Exploration and Web-building behavior

FRITZ VOLLRATH

DEPARTMENT OF ZOOLOGY
UNIVERSITY OF OXFORD
OXFORD, ENGLAND
AND ZOOLOGISCHES INSTITUT
BASEL, SWITZERLAND

I.   INTRODUCTION

The spider's web is a structure created by a highly specific behavior pattern. The structure is a trap and thus its construction is an aspect of foraging behavior. The web can be interpreted as a solidified foraging path because it is the record of a complex movement pattern that ultimately serves the purpose of catching prey. It is a movement pattern that may lead a spider of 1-cm length, like the garden cross spider *Araneus diadematus,* to cover an area of up to 1500 cm^2 after having traveled over 50 m, leaving 30-odd m of silken traplines in place (Witt *et al.,* 1968). Orb weavers like *Araneus* usually build their webs in one go, without interruption, and begin prey capture only after the structure has been completed. Thus, the web represents a search path that has been terminated long before any prey is caught, a phylogenetic rather than an immediate reaction to prey. Joining two threads, placing a connection, is an action that determines a section of path and a part of the web. It may well be that each of these actions is not a "free" decision at all but largely or fully predetermined by stimuli from the threads already in place. Certainly, not one of the actions associated with web construction is ever a *direct* reaction to prey encounter. Yet, its phylogeny and present function suggest that we may regard the web as a "frozen" search path. Historically, the web has evolved from a safety line trailed by a wandering spider actively searching for food. And even today, the success of a web (its rate of prey encounter) is determined as much by the spatial configuration of its threads (Eberhard, 1986) as by the place where it is built (Riechert and Gillespie, 1986).

When we compare a record of the spider's movement with a record of the web (Fig. 1), we discover an important fact: The web is not so much the embodiment of the spider's way-finding algorithm as of its thread-placement algorithm. There

147

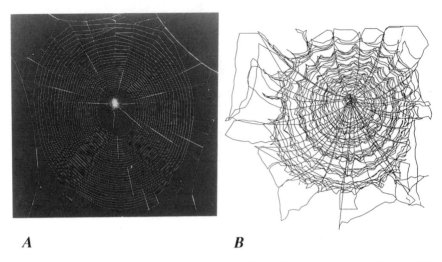

A   B

Fig. 1. Record of the movements and photograph of the orb web of *Araneus diadematus*. (A)
The photograph was obtained by placing a web against a dark background and lighting it from
behind. (B) The record of the spider's movement was obtained by tracking a backlighted spider using
an automatic image analysis system (time resolution .02 seconds). (Zschokke and Vollrath, 1992.)

exists a great discrepancy between body movement (the spider's fleeting path)
and web geometry (the more permanent placement of threads). The detailed
recording of a spider's locomotion provides a spatiotemporal pattern, a path,
whereas the web reveals the essence of the path, its rules. Although they are not
at all obvious, these rules can be deduced from the web's geometry. The signal-
to-noise ratio of information on these rules is many times better in the geometry
of the web than it is in the pattern of the spider's movement (Fig. 1). And
therefore, we have a fair chance of extracting these rules from the web but not
from the movement pattern, however accurately we might record or analyze it.
Of all the components of the spider's orb web, the path of the capture spiral is the
best indicator of these rules, as well as of the function they serve. The capture
spiral is the ideal paradigm of an idealized search path: ideal because of the
paradigm's clarity of expression and idealized because the path is free of "confusing" interactions with prey that would at each encounter affect its course.

The orb spider's set of web-construction rules has been fixed in its genome by
past selection; this is witnessed not least by the fact that it is often as easy to
distinguish spiders by features of their webs as by their morphology (Risch,
1977; Levi, 1978). Depriving spiders of web-building experience does not in any
way seem to affect their performance (Mayer, 1953; Reed *et al.*, 1970), which
indicates that learning plays little, if any, role in web construction. This notion is
supported by genetic studies of web parameters that seem to indicate that web-
building behavior is largely inherited (Rawlins and Witt, 1973). However, one

and the same spider can—within the general framework—build webs of many shapes (Fig. 2) using its inherited set of rules, the orb-algorithm (see Section III.C.).

The spider's web is the outcome of a long behavior sequence combining orientation in space and manipulation of silk. As the animal moves about busily connecting threads, a structure emerges: the web, a tangle of silken lines that, in principle, could be read like a track of footprints recorded in snow or sand. The web, like a track, has a handling component (an action executed at a particular location) and a locomotory component (a course between locations). The locomotory component can be analyzed as orientation behavior because most spiders are small in comparison with their webs. A feature of all orientation behavior is flexibility in response to changing environmental conditions; approaching the web as a product of orientation behavior has proved to be singularly successful in devising experiments to explore the inner workings of the web-building algorithm. But the handling component, the knitting together of two threads, also shows surprising flexibility under experimental conditions and therefore must not *a priori* be treated as a sequence or collection of fixed action patterns, as is sometimes done. One paragraph of this article will be devoted to a brief dissection of the two components of web building.

Unlike a track, the web is a structure assembled from a score of components, tangible as well as intangible. The materials that the builder has at its disposal are as important as the behavior. True, all material components are basically (biochemically) silks of one type or other, but the physical properties between them differ hugely, as befits their use (Tillinghast and Townley, 1987; Peters, 1987). I shall not here speculate on the chicken and egg question of which came first in evolution: the building material or the building behavior. It is, however, important to note that the materials, although providing the spider with opportunities, also impose constraints on its behavior. As analogy may serve the human architect who cannot neglect in the design of a bridge the available building material (e.g., wood, stone, concrete, or steel). Constraints also arise from the aerial existence of the structure and its exposure to the elements: wind, rain water, and solar radiation; we all know of the harm they can inflict on man-made structures. Construction needs time, and this is yet another constraint. However, time can be allocated in various ways and some spiders build their webs in minutes, others take hours or even spread the workload over days, daily adding bits and pieces (e.g., *Araneus diadematus* needs about 30 minutes, Witt *et al.,* 1968; *Uloborus conus* needs 3.5 hours, Lubin, 1986; *Cyrtophora citricola* usually takes 2 days, Wiehle, 1928). Many spiders that build webs costly in time are more likely to repair torn sections (like *Cyrtophora,* Lubin, 1973) rather than rebuild the entire structure as do those with less costly webs (e.g., *Araneus diadematus,* Breed *et al.,* 1964).

The web structure has a function: to support the spider and to catch the insect. This function is served in a variety of ways. Webs can be one, two, or three

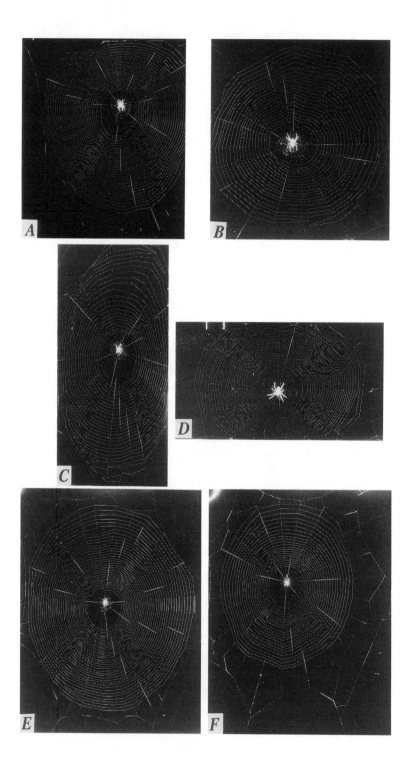

dimensional as well as sticky or nonsticky; single lines, sheets, orbs, or veritable tangles of threads are all *bona fide* webs. The most interesting of these structures is the orb web, not because it is the most highly evolved (it is not) or because it is the most elaborate (which is unlikely) but because it is fairly complex yet, at the same time, highly accessible for a detailed study. What is meant by a complex system? After all, the term "complexity" has a double meaning. It denotes "confusingly interrelated parts" (Webster, 1967) with such synonyms as "intricacy," "network," "web," and "tangle" (!). More often than not, it is a statement betraying a large measure of incomprehension of the underlying mechanisms, with synonyms like "confusingly," "complication," "problem," and "puzzle" (Longman, 1988). Take, for example, the wiring diagram of a car that may be "complex" to the average owner but is quite "simple" for a mechanic. Wehner (1987) elegantly demonstrated how an apparently "complex" behavior may in fact be a simple behavior pattern controlled by sensory filters that are matched to the task at hand. Biological complexity, then, is often a measure of our failure to understand rather than some inherently incomprehensible mechanism. The spider's web provides an ideal paradigm for studying behavioral complexity using the classic black box approach. The reduction of the behavior to the level of neuronal networks is impractical not least because the spider uses hemolymph pressure instead of muscles to stretch the legs. This discourages the neuroethological approach and leaves the field nearly entirely to the classical ethologist (but see Barth, 1985, or Seyfarth *et al.*, 1990).

The orb web represents complexity (i.e., tantalizing scientific questions) on three different levels: (1) building material and architecture—five or six different types of silk are used in orb-web construction, and we are only just beginning to understand the interplay of these silks (Peters, 1987; Tillinghast and Townley, 1987; Vollrath and Edmonds, 1989); (2) variability—orb-web geometry betrays an underlying order containing a startling measure of flexibility in terms of genetic (Rawlins and Witt, 1973) as well as phenotypic variability (Witt *et al.*, 1968), both as yet little explored, and (3) construction procedure—orb-web assembly follows four discernible and nearly inviolate stages: (i) radials and frame, (ii) auxiliary spiral, (iii) capture spiral, and (iv) hub (Peters, 1937a,b;

FIG. 2. Photographs of *Araneus diadematus* webs built under different conditions. (A) Typical web (conventionally, up is called "north" and down "south"). (B) Web tilted after construction of radials into the vertical and, subsequently, completed in the vertical (note untypical roundness and scarcity of spiral reverses). (C) Web built in a narrow upright frame (note the high number of reverses at the sides allowing the capture spiral to fill the frame yet maintain relative equidistance throughout). (D) Web built in narrow horizontal frame (again, note the reversals, this time leading to lateral filling out). (E) First web (at 0600 hrs) and (F) fourth web (at 2100 hrs) built by the same spider on the same day (web 2 built at 1500 hrs and web 3 built at 1800 hrs). Each subsequent web used successively less silk, incorporating fewer radials as well as spiral turns, and had a wider capture spiral mesh.

König, 1951). Each stage apparently has a different set of behavioral rules for orientation as well as manipulation. The degree of flexibility is surprisingly large, as is shown, for example, by the spider's ability to build a perfect orb with several legs missing (Szlep, 1952; Reed *et al.*, 1965) or with regenerated legs that at first are only half the length of their normal counterparts (Vollrath, 1987a). In this article, I shall be concerned mainly with the procedural aspect of web complexity, the other two aspects (material and structural) will be touched on only briefly and where it is necessary to explain the behavior.

This article is divided into four parts followed by a brief discussion. First, I shall explore the insights we can gain into the web-building behavior if we begin to study it specifically as orientation behavior. I shall also examine the spider's exploration behavior and choice of a web site and survey the literature on spider orientation, most of which deals with orientation during hunting rather than during web building. This survey will provide the basis for an evaluation of the orientation mechanisms that might be available to the web-building spider. I shall describe and discuss why web-building behavior is a special case of orientation behavior, special not least because of the tight constraints imposed by ergonomics and building materials. Second, I shall examine the actual process of knitting the threads together, the manipulative component of web construction. Here, I shall take up the case against it being a chain of not only stereotyped but also fixed behavior patterns, as is often assumed. Third, I shall discuss aspects of the evolution of the orb web. And, last but not least, I shall explore the notion of web construction and use as foraging behavior that is divisible into the stages of chosing a site, having a capture spiral search path, and operating the web from a central place.

The literature is full of descriptions of and experiments on various aspects of spider webs and web-building behavior (for reviews, see Tilquin, 1942; Witt *et al.*, 1968; Eberhard, 1982, 1990a; and specific chapters in Shear, 1986a). The interpretation of this wealth of information, however, is hindered by the absence of a unifying view of the web that might provide us with an interlinking network of testable hypotheses, both general and specific. I shall outline such a network and describe some specific hypotheses rather than give a comprehensive overview of the available store of facts. Limiting myself to referencing a small subset of the available literature (and often recent review articles, at that) does not limit my recognition of gratitude to the great many important and original works that remain uncited.

II. THE WEB SPIDER'S ORIENTATION SKILLS

The spider's web is, with few exceptions, larger than the spider, often by an order of magnitude. Clearly, the web functions as an extension of the spider's body. Because the web is large, building it as well as traversing it requires orientation, way-finding skills. In size, the garden spider on its orb is comparable to a man on a football field! Building the web, putting its threads in place, is pure orientation. But if web construction and operation require orientation skills, so too does the assessment of web sites.

A. *ARANEUS*, SPATIAL MAPS AND THE VALUE OF SITE CHOICE

The garden cross spider *Araneus diadematus* will serve as the main example throughout this article. It shows the longest history of detailed study and therefore the best set of the data, although data are far from comprehensive even for *Araneus*. This spider (like other orb weavers) has very poor vision (Homann, 1971; Land, 1985), and we can largely discount the use of visual cues in orientation not least because good webs are also built in total darkness or by blinded spiders (Witt *et al.*, 1968). This leaves *Araneus* with mainly haptic (tactile) information, and we may assume that the animal has knowledge only about places that it has already visited (or to which it is connected by threads). In its reliance on haptic cues, *Araneus* can be likened to a blind man who feels his way around, building up in memory a time series of tactile stimuli. The question is whether *Araneus*, like a blind human, also assembles tactile "snapshots" into a three-dimensional representation, a map, that stays with the animal when it moves about, and that allows the spider, like the human, to "envision" the spatial relationship of important points in its environment. This notion of a map in the spider's brain is not as unparsimonious as it might seem at first. After all, the highest abilities of orientation are found in animals; phylogenetically, these abilities precede human mental activities by hundreds of millions of years, and it is more likely than not that primate thinking has evolved from having to cope with intricate three-dimensional situations as well as intricate social interactions. In humans, the ability to use haptic cues or to orient in space is not (as far as I am aware) necessarily based on thinking (i.e., linguistic thought), or derived from it. Making good (fitness enhancing) use of spatial information, using spatial maps and making "intelligent" spatial connections, is not therefore *ipso facto* an anthropomorphism nor does it contravene Occam's razor. It may well be that the spatial "understanding" of animals is more highly developed than we are inclined to credit. The general feeling of scientists studying orientation and navigation in animals seems at the moment one of bewilderment, but by and large they seem inclined to abandon the behaviorist's simple "stimulus–response" attitude in favor of some sort of map (Ellen and Thinus-Blanc, 1987; Gould, 1986). This approach is not without controversy, especially where invertebrates are concerned (Wehner *et al.*, 1990). However this may be, the nonuse of visual information in *Araneus*' way-finding and web-building, combined with the spider's small size and considerable phylogenetic age, make it a model animal in which to tackle just these kinds of questions experimentally.

Let us, for the time being, leave aside the spider's handling of silk and begin our investigation with a study of the spider's orientation, in particular, its exploration of a potential web site. We note that the spider's spatial information is thought to be mainly haptic. Our knowledge of the sensory information and decision rules guiding *Araneus diadematus* through space is still very much in its infancy. Therefore, I shall examine the orientation of other spiders as well, in the hope that some of the abilities shown in other species might help clarify the position with respect to the orb spider.

Of special interest is the question of whether spiders, orb or otherwise, have the capability to orient by means other than sequential landmark recognition on a limited scale. Any efficient way of determining a site will have a high functional value as we can see immediately when we examine *Araneus'* foraging behavior: the structure of the web has a value as a trait. This value can be greatly enhanced or diminished by the positioning of the web, both in terms of *location,* like choice of habitat, height, or plant cover (Enders, 1973, 1974; Joqué, 1981; Toft, 1983; Hodge, 1987; Endo, 1988; Craig, 1988), and *orientation,* like position with respect to the prevailing winds or insolation (Carrell, 1978; Tolbert, 1979; Hieber, 1984, Craig *et al.,* 1985). Therefore, the first consideration of web construction is the selection of a site. Moreover, site choice affects the architecture of the final web (Ades, 1986), because long, narrow sites and wide, open sites impose different web shapes (see Fig. 2) with presumably different capture efficiencies (see following discussion). Site choice is functionally equivalent to the search for a food patch and subject to similar selection pressures: "In evolutionary terms, foraging strategies and navigational strategies are inextricably inter-twined" (Wehner *et al.,* 1983). The exploitation of the food patch is then left to the web (search path). In terms of life history parameters, too, site choice is a most important consideration: (1) *Araneus* moves between sites at night (Ramousse and Le Guelte, 1979); therefore, (2) *Araneus* only has 150 or so opportunities for a choice if its active life span is about 200 days and a web has to be up for at least 1 day before a new site can be visited. However, (3) a web spider on the move, searching for a site, is at much higher risk from predators than when it is sitting in its web (Rypstra, 1984; Vollrath, 1980). This is partly because the web may function as an early warning device (Finck *et al.,* 1975; Frings and Frings, 1966), partly because a spider motionless in its web or retreat is generally quite cryptic (Hingston, 1927), and partly because adaptations to life inside a web are not necessarily helpful when, webless, the spider is on the move.

Without knowledge one cannot chose. Consequently, choice of a web site requires that the spider has some information about that site, whether it is "indirect" information about factors like average wind or radiation direction (Hieber, 1984) and prey abundance (see Riechert and Gillespie, 1986) or whether it is direct spatial information about proximate factors like height above ground (Enders, 1974). The general understanding ("A spider can only react to environmental conditions, not predict them": Janetos, 1986) seems to indicate that a web site is chosen largely at random (Turnbull, 1964), unless data specifically indicate otherwise (Riechert and Luczak, 1982). This would imply that web-spider foraging is supposed to be based mostly on trial and error, which is not a very satisfying state of affairs when we consider the high costs of an error. These costs are not so much the immediate danger of starvation (Nakamura, 1987) as of a significant reduction in reproductive fitness (Wise, 1975; Vollrath, 1987b). The assessment of site quality may be important for decisions whether to settle or move on, either before or after sampling. The exploration of a site's structural diversity may be important for decisions about orientation of the web.

Is spatial information used? If so, how is it gained, what form does it take, and how detailed is it? How is it stored in the spider's memory? Could it be in the form of a spatial map? We do not yet know the answer to any of these questions, but we can outline the problem and a range of potential solutions. First, the evidence is strong that *Araneus* and other orb weavers do indeed use spatial information: not every site is accepted and in the lab one can to a certain extent predict (using only spatial correlates) which sites may and which may not be accepted (F. Vollrath, unpublished). Second, it seems that vital information on a potential site is gained during an inspection that precedes web construction. No web spider, when released in a cage or a three-dimensional maze immediately begins to spin a web; instead, it first explores, clambering about crisscrossing the available space, always trailing its silken safety line. Eventually, sometimes after hours of climbing about, the spider seems to "settle" for a particular area of the explored space (Chessell, 1986; Zschokke and Vollrath, 1992). Thereafter, things move quickly and the web is finished 30 or so minutes later (Fig. 3). Thus, in *Araneus,* site exploration may take much longer than web construction, a telling observation in favor of the assumption that it is also site assessment. If a site has proved itself profitable (because it feeds the spider in its web), a new web is built using part of the old framework without much further exploration of the surrounding vegetation.

B.   POSSIBLE PROCESSES OF SPIDER ORIENTATION

What exactly does the spider do when it explores? What kind of information is taken aboard? How is this information integrated? Before discussing spider exploration it may be helpful to briefly review some principles of orientation behavior. First of all, we must distinguish between pilotage (following landmarks) and navigation (approaching a goal not using landmarks). Landmarks can be used in something like a "road map" (that features in sequence a string of memory images) or a topological map (with three-dimensional representation of environmental features in correct relative position to one another). In a topological map, the animal "can compute its position relative to home when

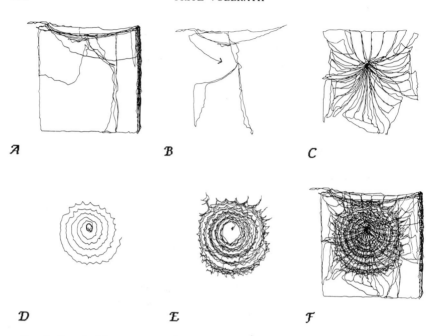

FIG. 3. Record of the movements of *Araneus diadematus* separated into six views. (A) Exploration incorporating long breaks; (B) determination of future hub and first radials; (C) radial and frame construction; (D) auxiliary spiral; (E) capture spiral; (F) all stages combined. The time span and distance traveled for each stage was: A: 848 min, 1007 cm; B: 3 min, 140 cm; C: 10 min, 652 cm; D: 3.5 min, 117 cm; E: 31 min, 859 cm; and finally F: the whole web, 44 min, 1628 cm, and exploration (see A) together. The spider was in third instar and 4 mm long, the web spanned 14 cm. A continuous record of the spider's movements (*x–y* coordinates) from the release in the environment (two vertical sticks 20 cm apart) until the end of web building was obtained by tracking the spider on a computer using image analysis (resolution, 0.2 sec) (after Zschokke and Vollrath, 1992).

transferred . . . . to any particular point of its spatial environment" (Wehner *et al.,* 1983), whereas in a roadmap, it can only follow known pathways. During navigation, the animal may use directional vectors pointing home (dead reckoning) or a vector map (with vectors pointing to features of the environment). Important information about a route may gathered by some sort of "inertial guidance system" and used for orientation by some form of "path integration" (Görner, 1972; Mittelstaedt and Mittelstaedt, 1973; Wehner, 1983) whereby, for example, all twists of a route taken are measured by proprioceptors and the vector pointing home is constantly recalculated (Mittelstaedt, 1978; Wehner and Wehner, 1986). Perception and action may be a kinesthetic or an idiothetic process: In the kinesthetic process, a sequence of actions is unrolled according to a learned program of motions, and in the idiothetic process, endogenous spatial cues from previous positions are used to calculate the next motion (Schöne,

1981). In the idiothetic process, cues provided by the different sensory inputs may be combined into a single "map." We can define such a spatial map as a representation in the animal's CNS of landmarks or vectors and their spatial arrangement to one another, often including also a global "compass" reference (like gravity, a light source, or magnetic North). To use the map, the animal needs to be aware of its own position on this map. We might therefore call such a map cognitive (Tolman, 1948); in other words, "it is this tentative map, indicating routes and paths and environmental relationships which finally determines what responses, if any, the animal will release" (Tolman, 1948, p. 192). A mental representation does not require a topological anatomical representation in the animal's CNS.

The questions that we face whenever we study orientation *per se* or activities that indicate directed movement in space, are the following. Does the animal know where it is, where to go, and how to get there? The answers to this set of questions would not only decide whether the animal in question navigates, possibly using a map, but also whether we might grant it cognition or at least certain cognitive abilities. With respect to the spider's exploration and site-choice behavior, the answer to these questions would also affect our interpretation of its web-building behavior proper. After all, exploration precedes web-building not only in each web's ontogeny but also in the spider's phylogeny. If the spider can memorize features of the environment and, possibly, can integrate them into a spatial map, it may also use these faculties during web construction. There is evidence that it might do so (see Section II,C). Therefore, it is important that we examine and discuss the spider's exploration behavior before studying its web-building behavior.

C. Exploration of a Web Site

Consider the problem that the spider faces in its exploration of a highly structured three-dimensional environment, such as a bush. The small spider must somehow determine anchor points that lie, more or less, in a plane. This often happens at night (Ramousse, 1980), in total darkness without the possibility of visual triangulation (Witt *et al.*, 1968). The spider can, however, sense the vector of gravity, although no sensory organ for this has yet been found (Vollrath, 1986). Light intensity can be used to time the start of web building (Homann, 1971), and a light (if present) can also provide directional information (Hieber, 1984; Crawford, 1984). No other senses have as yet been shown to be involved (but absence of evidence is only weak evidence of absence) and the spider may use wind direction, insolation, or a measure of height (Carrell, 1978; Enders, 1974).

How, then, is a site explored? In particular, how are those points, where the spider anchors the web's guy ropes, determined? After all, the anchor points determine both the position of the web in space and the degree of its planarity.

Three anchors can be put at random and still lie in a plane as they define a plane, but more than three (and *Araneus* commonly has eight or more) require some sort of mechanism to insure nonrandom placement. In nature and in the laboratory, the anchors seem to be placed nonrandomly to lie more or less in plane (F. Vollrath, unpublished). There are exceptions—sometimes a spider has anchors that deviate greatly from a plane and, consequently, the web is twisted (Searle, 1991). This is extremely rare, both in nature and laboratory (F. Vollrath, unpublished), and I suspect that such twisted webs are suboptimal in one way or another. The, as yet unanswered, question remains: How accurately must the spider estimate or calculate the placement of these points to insure planarity of the orb? Obviously, the length of the guylines also plays an important role: the longer they are, the smaller the effect of outlying anchor points. Moreover, each time a web is rebuilt, adjustments can be made, and thus older webs would presumably be better matched to a plane.

Unanswered is the important question concerning the mechanism that the spider uses to estimate or calculate the anchor points. A brief review of the options might provide some hypotheses. Obviously, the mechanisms used during building a new web and rebuilding an old one could be quite different. When the spider first encounters a potential site, it clambers about, as always trailing its safety line and occasionally attaching it to the support. A bridge thread (Peters, 1989) may be established by either of two methods: by tightening the safety thread after walking a detour or by floating a line in the wind and tightening it when the free end has caught somewhere. Thus, two crucial points are fixed. The third point must be placed somewhere below these two. With these three points forming some sort of **Y**, the plane of the web is more or less determined. The following anchors have to be matched to this plane, if the orientation of the plane is to be kept. To determine the latter points, the spider may or may not use a mental map (Fig. 4).

Araneus seems to determine anchors from the vantage of the existing network (see also Fig. 6); later anchors are attached after the **Y** and the future radial hub have been fixed. Our information on the construction of such anchors is sparse (Tilquin, 1942; Mayer, 1953; Eberhard, 1990a). It seems that the spider, connected to the hub or a radial thread by a line, clambers first to an existing anchor and then down along the vegetation. A detour from the vertical, if the vegetation requires it, can apparently be compensated for. Such detour compensation may be directed by sensory information from the web, to which the spider is always connected by a line. This line may transmit tensile information about deviations from the y or radial plane. Alternatively, a detour may be a case of more complex orientation. The spider may make use of path integration, calculating detour shape from body turns and detour distances from step number. Such route-referent orientation has been proposed as one mechanism underlying the homing of the spider *Agelena labyrinthica* on its horizontal sheet web (Mittelstaedt,

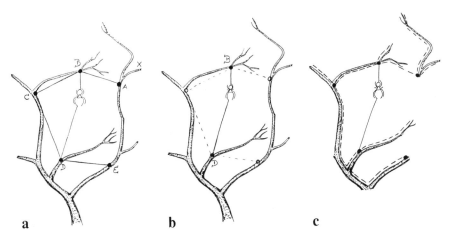

FIG. 4. How does the spider experience the physical environment? Most orb spiders build two-dimensional webs in a highly structured three-dimensional environment. How much information and what kind of information do they have about this environment? (a) The spider arrived at the branch at point X and built threads between A-B-C-D-E and B-D. (b) Does the animal only "know" the position of the attachment points B and D to which it is at the moment connected? (c) Does it remember the path (dotted line) on which it clambered along the branch, and what does it "know" about those points along the branch that it had visited? In addition, there exists the possibility that the spider might have a three-dimensional "cartesian" (allocentric) or a three-dimensional "polar" (egocentric) coordinate system that incorporates knowledge about the physical and structural environment encountered by the exploring spider.

1985). Indeed, a wide range of spiders seems to use path integration and vector navigation (see the following section), and we may assume that *Araneus*, too, has the ability to use these orientation mechanisms.

D. AN EXCURSION TO ORIENTATION IN OTHER SPIDERS

Because of this comparative argument, it is, at this point, necessary to briefly review the orientation mechanisms of some other spiders. This also illustrates the kinds of questions we can ask of spiders and the kinds of answers we may get. As two excellent reviews on spider orientation have been published quite recently (Görner and Class, 1985; Mittelstaedt, 1985), I shall limit myself to a brief and rather general examination of four exemplary case studies.

Agelena labyrinthica (Agelenidae): The web of the funnel spiders consists of a densely packed sheet of silk, often triangular with a silken tube retreat in one corner. Prey falls onto the sheet and is grabbed in a dash from the retreat by the spider running on top of the sheet. *Agelena labyrinthica* typically consumes its prey inside the tube. The return journey to the retreat is always a relatively straight line, even if the outward journey was circuitous. The spider finds the entrance of its retreat by using a variety of different mechanisms. Tensions and web elasticity are important (Baltzer, 1930), and so is the shape and positioning of the sheet (Holzapfel, 1933). The polarization pattern of the sky may be used (Görner, 1958), and a light source may provide a point of reference (Moller, 1970). Information about the outward path may be stored and made available for decisions concerning the return path by idiothetic memory (Görner, 1958; Dornfeld, 1975). Moreover, *Agelena,* like the related *Tegenaria,* may use some form of path integration on the outward journey to update this memory and facilitate homing (Mittelstaedt, 1978). Wherever the necessary information is collected, on site or en route, the behavior of both these funnel web spiders clearly shows that they navigate by a variety of cues and mechanisms (Görner, 1988).

Arctosa variana (Lycosidae): Many webless hunting spiders can be assumed to rely on their vision during their search for prey. Some of their eight eyes are for binocular, focal vision, others for peripheral vision (Land, 1985). Six of these eyes have a tapetum, indicating that they are used even in poor light conditions. The eyes are not only used to locate prey but also to orient in the vegetation. The wolf spider *Arctosa variana* lives at the edge of ponds and can run over water. To regain firm ground it may use visible landmarks or, if these are absent, astronomical cues, for example, the polarization pattern of the sky, seen by the principal eyes (Magni *et al.,* 1965), in conjunction with an internal clock (Papi and Syrjämäki, 1963). We note that hunting freely in a structured environment is phylogenetically older than operating a sheet, tangle, or orb web.

Cupiennius salei (Ctenizidae) and *Pardosa amentata* (Lycosidae): Some webless hunting spiders carry prey or an egg sac about. They might drop either when attacked and run away, but often attempt to return within minutes. If the hunting spider *Cupiennius salei* is chased away from a prey item, it can return in a more or less straight line, even if the outward journey was along a circuitous route. The spider's behavior indicates that it "knows" the direction as well as the distance of the shortcut (Seyfarth *et al.,* 1982). When anesthetized and robbed of her egg sac, the wolf spider *Pardosa amentata* will, after recovery, search the area of the mishap (Görner and Zeppenfeld, 1980). She will even return to that area if driven away without having made contact with her lost property. Because in both cases, *Cupiennius* and *Pardosa,* the relevant experiments were done under red light we may exclude the possibility that the spiders use only visual cues. It seems, instead, that the spiders do not use any external cues but an internal guidance system, the idiothetic memory (Mittelstaedt and Mittelstaedt, 1973). The cues necessary for such a system may be provided by the lyriform slit sense organs in the cuticula exoskeleton of particular legs: experiments have shown that their immobilization affects the spider's performance negatively (Seyfarth *et al.,* 1982).

Phidippus pulcherimus (Salticidae): Jumping spiders are highly visual, webless hunters. Some are quite territorial and may inhabit the same shrub for some time, during which they possibly acquire a good acquaintance with its architecture (Hill, 1979). The jumping spider's hunt consists of three stages: approach, stalk, and jump. Although the spider can spot prey a long distance away, it can jump only over relatively short distances. Therefore, a structured environment would often force the spider to approach a prey insect via a detour (Fig. 5). *Phidippus pulcherimus,* in a three-dimensional maze, turns away from a fly it has spotted at long distance, takes a detour during which it never sees the fly, and manages to approach it along the only possible route that allows stalking and jumping (Hill, 1979). It seems that an excellent sense of spatial orientation is coupled with a memory of the maze. Some knowledge of the surroundings is acquired visually. When tested on a single bar, *Phidippus pulcherimus* will approach a fly that it has briefly seen and orient correctly toward the fly's perch,

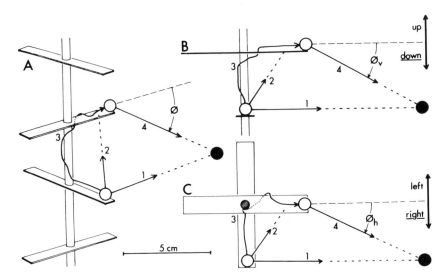

FIG. 5. Ability of the jumping spider *Phidippus pulcherimus* to orient in space. Hill (1979) studied the compensation for movement in three dimensions of the spider (white circle) sneaking up on prey (dark circle). (A) Perspective drawing of the experimental apparatus. After the initial orientation to face the prey in a horizontal plane, (1) the prey was immediately removed in each trial. Many spiders turned to face the secondary objective as shown in (2) and then moved to that objective (3) prior to reorientation (4). In this situation, a reorientation turn (magnitude Ø) that compensates for the movement should be both *down* and *to the right.* (B) Vertical plane projection of this problem. The component of reorientation in a vertical plane ($Ø_V$) should be directed distinctly downward to compensate for movement by the spider to a position above its prey. (C) Horizontal plane projection of the same pursuit. The horizontal component of reorientation ($Ø_h$) should be distinctly to the right, as shown, to compensate for movement. Eight *P. pulcherimus* performed in this experiment a total of 198 runs. In 158 trials they compensated both horizontal and vertical components, in 18 trials only the horizontal component, in 20 trials only the vertical component, and in 2 trials neither component (from Hill, 1979).

even if the lights are turned off and the fly is removed during the approach (Hill, 1979). It seems that during such "route-referent orientation," the spider calculates the fly's position relative to its own from a combination of visual and idiothetic memory. Hill's experiments (so far not independently repeated) strongly suggest that some jumping spiders possess a three-dimensional map of their immediate environment. We note that the latest, highly plausible theory on spider phylogeny claims that jumping spiders had web-building ancestors (Jackson, 1986).

Zygiella x-notata (Metinae-Tetragnathinae) and *Araneus diadematus* (Argiopidae): The orb spider *Zygiella x-notata* does not live on her web but inside a retreat hidden in the vegetation and connected to the capture web by a special radial thread free of spiral. After each prey capture, she returns to her lair along this signal thread. If the web is rotated 90° or 180° while she is on it, she will run along any radial leading in the direction where the retreat used to be, disregarding the sticky spiral that now hinders her path (Le Guelte, 1969). *Araneus diadematus* living on the hub of her web will also be misdirected if it is turned 180° during prey capture (Peters, 1932; Crawford, 1984). We can deduce that for both spiders, gravity is an important cue to define directions in their vertical webs. *Araneus* may use a light source to identify the two sides of the web, but she does not use it for orientation in the plane of the web (Crawford, 1984).

These studies demonstrate that some spiders can and do use their idiothetic memory for orientation. We may assume that the ancestors shared by the wolf spider, the jumping spider, and the funnel spider already possessed this trait; otherwise, it would have to have evolved independently in these three lineages, which is most unlikely. We may also assume that *Araneus* shares a common ancestor with these spiders and that, therefore, it is likely to share the ability to orient using these cues.

These spiders hunting on the ground, in the vegetation, or in their webs use a variety of cues to orient. In the case of web spiders, some of these cues, like thread layout, thread morphology, and tensions, derive directly from the web itself. These are cues that are difficult for us to measure or even imagine. Maybe a web spider "hears" its environment in the tensions and vibrations of its web (Barth, 1982, 1985) like a bat "hears" its environment in the reflections of its sonar pulses? The web certainly produces such cues in abundance (Liesenfeld, 1956; Vollrath, 1979; Masters and Markl, 1981; Masters *et al.*, 1986), and the orb spider has the sensory capability to register the smallest of tension differentials (Liesenfeld, 1961) and the finest of vibrations (Finck, 1972) down to nanometer values, it is claimed (Walcott, 1969).

E.   RETURN TO *ARANEUS* SITE EXPLORATION

During site exploration, tensile and vibratory cues derived from threads may be few and relatively insignificant in relation to tactile and haptic cues derived from the vegetation. After all, wherever it exists, exploration should serve to assess the spatial layout of a potential web site. All points along its route may be equally interesting as potential anchor points for web and guy lines to the spider when assessing a site. Moreover, the spatial structure of the site might provide the spider with important cues: for example, whether it is *structurally* a "good" site (e.g., a web exposed on the surface of a bush or a web built between a tree trunk and a grass blade may not function well on gusty days) and whether it is *functionally* a good site (a web on the surface of a bush might catch more prey, as well as attract predators, than a web deep inside the bush). We note that the spider exploring or assessing a potential web site initially has no "home." Such a central place or "home" is an important ingredient of many theories of orientation in which it is required to provide the animal with a point of reference (Wehner *et al.*, 1983; Görner, 1972).

First indications of this spider's spatial ability come from pilot studies (Chessell, 1986; Zschokke unpublished) where *Araneus* explored a stick maze before building its web in the only space large enough or a site that had previously provided prey. It appears that in a small maze of sticks, *Araneus* briefly walks about and then seems to fix on a particular spot, a "platform," to which it will afterwards return regularly and that thus forms the focal point of all further explorations, often rather protracted, of this particular site. This "platform" may well form a base from which to map. Eventually, after having settled on a site, the spider begins web construction proper.

III.   UNRAVELLING THE *ARANEUS* ORB

Web construction itself follows four principal stages: (1) radial and frame construction, (2) auxiliary and (3) capture spiral construction, and (4) hub rebuilding (see Fig. 3). Each stage has its substages (explained in more detail in the relevant section). The four principal stages are well-defined, and only under exceptional experimental conditions can a spider sometimes be "persuaded" to repeat or jump a stage (König, 1951; P. J. Peters, 1970). We do not yet know to what extent the various substages have their own stop-and-start rules and to what extent they are epiphenomena, the outcome of the interaction of one complex rule set with the nascent structure. The analysis of web ontogeny is not made easier by the fact that each action of the animal, by adding or taking away threads, forever changes the structure, which can be viewed as a network of "forces" that to a large extent guide each step. In this the "growing" web resembles embryonic development—on a behavioral rather than a morphological level.

Web building is a nested set of hierarchical behavior patterns or units. We can identify a set of goal "functions," which determine the geometry of the finished web. By goal, I do not here mean the ultimate goal of food acquisition but a sequence of proximate goals. The first of these is the manufacture of a frame and primary radials. Thus, the spider creates its own novel set of environmental features to be used as a working platform. This enables, facilitates, and guides the construction sequence of the next stages: that is, the secondary radials and the auxiliary spiral, which in turn provide scaffold and guide for the capture spiral. The final reworking of the hub is largely web tuning (Craig, 1987a). This may affect prey retention time and resistance to mechanical failure in wind or rain: that is, impair the web's effectiveness as a filter. It is also the spider's last action before the long wait for prey, allowing it to tighten or loosen the web to tune signal transmission.

A. RADIALS AND DETOURS

The laying down of radial and frame threads cannot be clearly separated. At the beginning of web construction, especially in a new site or after complete destruction of all frame and guy lines, the spider quickly establishes a protohub (a focal point in roughly the place where later the hub emerges) from where it lays lines to the surrounding vegetation. The determination of the points where these lines are anchored has been discussed earlier. Such lines are often cut and replaced or pulled into new positions (Fig. 6). Thus, during the early stages of web construction, the network continuously changes shape. Once the anchor points have all been fixed and the frame threads and primary radials connected into the working platform for the web, then the spider commences the construction of secondary radials. Even at this stage, occasionally, a new frame thread is added, for example, to span a corner. Clearly, radial and frame construction are not divisible, at least not early on, before a fair proportion of the radials have been placed (Peters, 1939; Tilquin, 1942; Mayer, 1953; Ades, 1986; Eberhard, 1990a). Sometimes radials are even added during auxiliary spiral construction: this is the rule in *Nephila,* common in *Zygiella,* and rare in *Araneus.*

Once the frame lines are anchored and the first radials linked in the future hub, the spider begins filling this framework with radials. Starting at the hub, she clambers along an existing radius, trailing a line, until she reaches a frame thread. Then she walks along the frame thread for a certain distance, pulls the trailing line taught, and attaches it to the frame. Now she returns to the hub along this new line, either replacing it with a new one in some cases (e.g., *Araneus diadematus*) or doubling it in the case of others (Eberhard, 1982). Again the hub is circled, with the spider holding onto the center with one set of legs and feeling for gaps in the radial wheel with legs one and two facing outward, as if measuring the angle between those legs. Whenever the gap (or angle ?) is too large for the spider's program, she places another radial. Radials are placed next to an existing radial, generally below it (Peters, 1937b). Subsequent radials are as a rule placed so as to oppose each other (McCook, 1889–1893), maybe to balance tensions (Eberhard, 1981), maybe not (Krieger, 1992).

Radial construction incorporates an interesting and telling feature (see Fig. 6). The lines are placed in such a way as to fix a particular angle at the hub, yet the attachment point whereby this angle is fixed is far away on the frame, reached by detour. If, in an experiment, a radial is cut, the spider soon replaces it with a new one. This is attached either on exactly the same spot or within a fraction of a millimeter of it (Reed, 1969). Such experimental destruction and subsequent rebuilding of a radial can be repeated up to 50 times, until the spider appears to run out of radial silk (König, 1951; Reed, 1969). The observation that a detour is involved led Peters (1937b) to hypothesize that *Araneus* uses path integration to "calculate" the attachment point of a radial on the frame. And indeed, if the detour is particularly large because the spider had to circumnavigate a corner in the frame, then the corresponding angle seems to deviate more from its neighboring angles (Mayer, 1953). However, so far we lack a detailed analysis of how the radial angle is determined, although this feature is a crucial piece in the puzzle of orb ontogeny. The early stages of web construction (frame and primary radials) are on the whole much less studied and understood than the subsequent events of spiral construction.

B.   SPIRALS AND PERTURBATION EXPERIMENTS

I earlier proposed the view that the spider's web is a record of complex spatial orientation. If this view is correct, then we should be able to interfere experimentally with the way-finding mechanism of the animal, comparable to interference with the orientation mechanisms of, say, a bee or a bird. And, indeed, such interference is possible, as I shall demonstrate for the case of gravity as a compass reference during spiral construction. The direction of gravity (down) is distinctly visible in the typical web of *Araneus* (see Fig. 2a). If, exceptionally, *Araneus* builds a horizontal web, the up/down asymmetry disappears (see Fig. 2b). The question arises whether the up/down asymmetry is the passive side effect of mechanical forces during web construction or whether it is the active outcome of the way in which gravity is used by the algorithm. A possible adaptive function of the up/down asymmetry is discussed later. First, after briefly introducing the two spirals of the *Araneus* web, I shall discuss some experiments that demonstrate the importance of gravity as a reference during web construction. In this section, I shall also present other experiments that allow us to test hypotheses about the algorithms that may be involved in the construction of these spirals.

1. The Two Spirals: Auxiliary and Capture

The auxiliary and capture spirals differ not only in their silk and their direction but also in their shape. The auxiliary or temporary spiral is nonsticky, begins at the hub, and reaches out to the periphery in geometric progression; that is, auxiliary spiral spacing continuously and specifically widens. The capture spiral

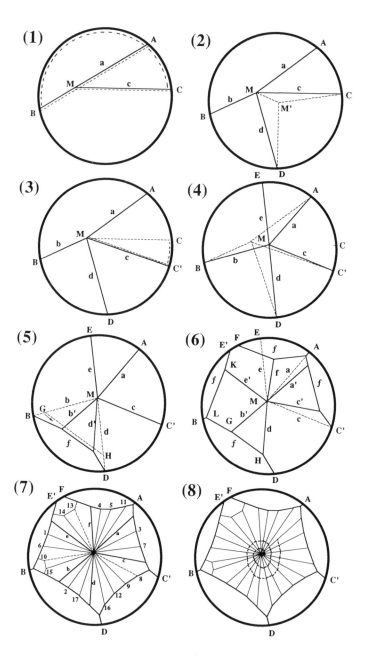

is sticky, begins at the periphery and circles inward in arithmetic progression; that is, capture spiral spacing is the same throughout much of the web. However, both statements (arithmetic vs geometric progression) are correct only for a part, albeit major part, of the spirals. Different rules seem to apply for the innermost and outermost spiral paths, both in the auxiliary (Gotts and Vollrath, 1992a) and the capture spirals (Peters, 1954; Vollrath and ApRhisiart, 1992). Moreover, the up/down asymmetry interferes in both spirals with the perfection of their geometry, a perfection and symmetry that orb webs built horizontally show is possible (Eberhard, 1987a; Meredith, 1987) (see Fig. 2b). Horizontal webs lack gravity as a compass reference in the plane of the web. However, during the construction of such webs, threads loaded by the weight of the building spider stretch outside the plane of the web. This fact makes it difficult to distinguish whether the typical asymmetry originates in the web algorithm or is the consequence of purely mechanical forces.

2. The Effect of Gravity

We can only tell whether the up/down asymmetry is a result of orientation rather than environment by obliterating gravitational cues, for example, by tilting

---

Fig. 6. Record of the construction of first radials and frame and guy threads by *Araneus diadematus*. The record is of the first web of a 3-week-old spiderling building in a wire frame of 12-cm diameter (redrawn after Mayer, 1953). Lines indicate existing threads, dotted lines indicate the path of the animal, dashed lines indicate threads that were removed by the animal. The diagram shows very well how threads are removed and how the hub is centered during the early phases of orb construction. (1) The spider goes from A to B where she tightens and fixes her safety (line), which thus becomes thread a; she returns along a, fixes the safety at M, goes back to A and along the frame to C, where she now tightens and fixes c, returns to M. (2) After some groping, she returns along c a short distance, cuts c (bridging the two ends of the thread with her body), extends c, and joins the two ends again in M'. She now drops down, finds the frame, attaches her safety at D, climbs up to M' along to M, and here tightens and attaches the safety, which thus becomes d. (3) She renews c by cutting it at M, bridges the line and walks toward C, walks along the frame to C' and attaches her safety, and returns to M where she tightens c'. (4) She replaces b by a new thread b, which is longer, thus readjusting (centering) M. Now at M she cuts, tightens, and reaffixes one after the other threads a, c', and d, thus creating a star of tight lines. She now goes to A and along the frame to E, fixes the safety, and returns to M where she fixes e. (5) Now she begins construction of fame threads. She renews b to b', fixes the safety at G, returns to M, goes along d to H, and attaches the safety. Now she doubles H-G and returns along f to G, halfway along she cuts both ends and rejoins them, thus tightening fBD. At G she cuts b, fixes the safety, and returns to M, renewing b' again. (6) She renews e to e', moves E along a little to the left to E', and lays a new frame thread fE'B by fixing the safety at K, going via M to L, and returning directly along fE'B to K, thus doubling it. She returns to M, replaces a by a', and constructs a frame thread fAC' as described for fE'B. From M she goes along e' to the wire, goes along the wire to F, fixes the safety f, and then proceeds to a', thus creating the frame thread fFA. (7) Although not all frame threads are in place, the spider now begins with the tertiary radials in the sequence 1–17, meanwhile (and where necessary) constructing more frame threads. (8) When the radial wheel is in place, then the spider circles the hub several times and builds the auxiliary spiral, widening outward.

the nascent web into the horizontal plane. This can be done separately for radial construction and for each spiral. The most convincing test would be to have spiders build webs in space. Such experiments, done by NASA during the 1963 spacelab mission (Witt *et al.*, 1977), demonstrated that *Araneus diadematus* can and will build webs even in the total absence of gravity. Analysis of videos of the spider building in space and of the finished web suggests that radial angles and capture mesh lack up/down asymmetry (Witt *et al.*, 1977). The absence of good photos prevents detailed analysis.

A less expensive experiment to study the effects of gravity involves tilting, swiveling, or rotating the building spider in an earthbound laboratory. In one such experiment (Vollrath, 1986), I held the vector of gravity constant while the spider was building its capture spiral by simulating a treadmill. This is done by slowly rotating the web around an (imaginary) axis through the center of the web, taking care to keep the spider quasistationary in one position in space. The resultant course of the spider showed that gravity is actively used as a compass reference (Fig. 7). Curiously, the deviation of the spiral path is only apparent when the spider is held in horizontal positions, that is, perpendicular to the vector of gravity. This suggests that the sensory perception of gravity occurs through a "lead and plummet" effect of the abdomen. Moreover, the increasingly rapid inward-turning spiral suggests that the spider has an "expectation" of its shifting positions in space under normal conditions. Under normal conditions, the spider circles the orb and with each step its body axis assumes a new angle to gravity in a predictable fashion. This is not so when the spider walks "treadmill fashion." Here, readjusting the body axis stepwise according to expectation, rather than merely following local landmarks, would result in a rapidly inward spiraling path ending at the hub, as indeed happens. That this path is not smooth indicates a conflict between local cues and global expectations.

Gravitational information can be perturbed in a more drastic way by using a klinostat (Mayer, 1953; Le Guelte, 1966). This works in a way similar to the treadmill, except that the web frame rotates constantly with a given speed on an imaginary axis through its center. Such an experiment (Vollrath, 1988a) has satisfyingly drastic results on web parameters (Fig. 8). At low speeds (< 1 rpm), the up/down asymmetry of the radials disappears but the spirals are hardly affected, except for small irregularities. At medium speeds (~ 10 rpm), radial asymmetry is lost and the capture spiral loses all form, although astonishingly the auxiliary spiral is hardly affected. At high speeds (> 100 rpm), the radials have no asymmetry, the auxiliary spiral is unchanged, and the capture spiral returns to normal. Thus at low rotational speeds, the slowly changing vector of gravity has no disruptive effect on the algorithm (or its variables) for either spiral; at medium speeds, the changes are highly disruptive for the capture spiral only; and at high speeds, the centripetal force of the spinning orb presumably overrides the stimulus from earth gravity and thus "fools" the algorithm.

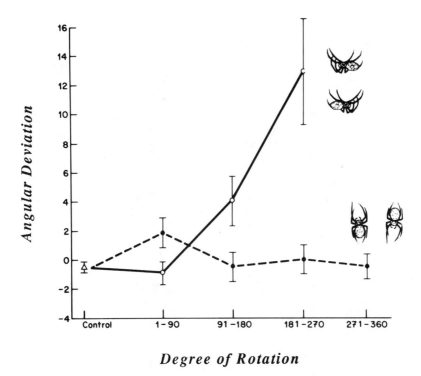

Degree of Rotation

Fɪɢ. 7. The position of *Araneus diadematus* in the treadmill affects the degree of deviation in the spiral path. Open circles represent nine webs in positions perpendicular to the vector of earth gravity (G perpendicular, *n* = 7 north, 2 south), solid circles represent six webs in positions parallel to gravity [with the spider moving up (*n* = 3) or down (*n* = 3)). Degree of rotation of the web and building spider is indicated on the *x* axis. Each point represents 50–100 measurements (6–12 per web), bars denote standard error. Angular deviation was calculated using the difference in radial-cut angle between the spiral path during rotation and the previous path on the same node before rotation (after Vollrath, 1986).

This experiment provides an unexpected result: although the vector of gravity is clearly used as a compass reference in the capture spiral, its influence on the auxiliary spiral is not at all obvious. Recent unpublished experiments showed me that auxiliary spiral construction, too, may use gravitational cues; for example, quickly standing the web on its head can result in reverses in the auxiliary spiral but this very much depends on the precise momentary action of the spider. However this may be, the klinostat experiments suggest that the perception of gravity has different effects on either spiral. It is possible that the two spirals may be built using different algorithms. Indeed, different algorithms are likely, given that the two spirals run in opposite directions and have different geometries (Vollrath and Mohren, 1985) and that during capture spiral construction the

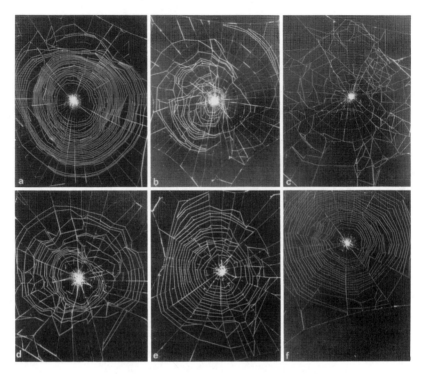

FIG. 8. Webs of *Araneus diadematus* highlighting the effect of vertical rotation on the capture, but not the auxiliary, spiral. The capture spiral shows up boldly, the auxiliary spiral much finer, when at all visible (e.g., in b and c). Often the course of the auxiliary must be deduced from its "remnants," visible as bright dots on the radii (c.f., Figs. 1 and 2). The webs were built in a klinostat rotating at different speeds: (a) 0.7 rpm; (b) 2.3 rpm; (c) 10 rpm; (d) 30 rpm; (e) 60 rpm; (f) 120 rpm (from Vollrath, 1988a).

auxiliary spiral seems to act as some sort of guiding line (S. Zschokke, personal communication).

Two additional experiments (originally done for different reasons) demonstrate the relative "stability" of the auxiliary spiral algorithm when the vector of gravity seems an unreliable signal. In the first experiment (unpublished), I altered the G-force acting on the building spider by rapidly spinning its frame, which was hanging from the blades of a ceiling fan, like a seat on its chains in a fairground merry-go-round. The spider continued to build its web in forces up to 15 G, which in itself is quite amazing (imagine running about with a load 14 times your weight on your back). Some webs showed increased perturbation of the capture spiraling with increasing G, but this perturbation seemed less pronounced in the auxiliary spiral. In the second experiment (also unpublished), I quickly stood the frame with the building spider on its head. If this was done when the spider was traversing the north or south threads during capture (but not auxiliary) spiral construction, the animal would move across the web to its former position in space (relative to the hub) and there resume its former path (Fig. 9). Thus, the hypothesis that the two spirals follow different rules appears to be confirmed. The construction algorithms for the two spirals may be totally different. Or they may be similar but incorporate different weightings (see Section III,G for gravitational information), for example, by averaging the G-vector over different time spans (Vollrath, 1988a).

3.   The Effect of Leg Length

A third, altogether different, experiment (Vollrath, 1987a) supports the finding that the two spirals may use different rules. Geometric spirals are equiangular, whereas arithmetic spirals are equidistant (Thompson, 1971). A working hypothesis, evoking parsimony of construction rules, might assume that the spider uses different rules for the two spirals: measuring angles in the auxiliary spiral and distances in the capture spiral. We can test this hypothesis because *Araneus* replaces lost legs with regenerates that are only about half the length of their normal counterparts (Fig. 10). Such legs are nevertheless used in web construc-

FIG. 9. Effect of gravity on the building *Araneus diadematus*. The path of a capture spiral-building spider that has been stood on its head when the animal was in the upper part of the web. Note that the spider (suddenly in the lower part of the web) subsequently crossed the web (arrows) to reach a new position in the web to corresponding to its "old" position in space. Here it resumed building (the photo was taken before the web was filled out by the capture spiral).

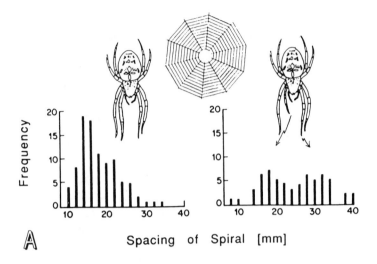

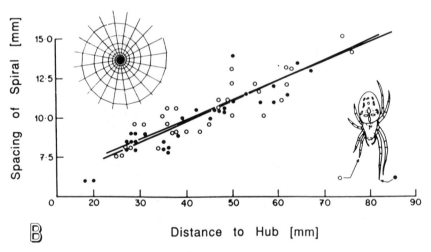

FIG. 10. Measurements in the spirals of *Araneus diadematus*. (A) Histogram reflecting the spacings (mesh size) of the capture spiral build by a spider with all legs normal (left) and another with a regenerated first leg (right). *Araneus* incorporates many U-turns in the capture spiral changing measuring legs at each U-turn. The length of the shorter, regenerated leg results in a bimodal rather than a normal distribution of mesh sizes in one and the same "spiral." (B) Scattergram reflecting the spacings of auxiliary spirals build by a lop-sided spider with all four legs on one side regenerated. These spirals do not reflect the length of a leg. The slopes of two spirals in two webs built in succession by the same spider are nearly identical, independent of whether they are build with the short legs facing inward (open circles) or outward (closed circles). Since auxiliary spirals have no U-turns a histogram would have been an inappropriate representation (after Vollrath, 1987a).

tion and we can examine their use as measuring sticks. It emerges that in *Araneus,* the first pair of legs are important for measuring certain distances, like the spacing of joints on a radial in the capture spiral. Moreover, it seems that the length of a "measuring" leg is important during the construction of the capture spiral, but not that of the auxiliary spiral (see Fig. 10).

This experiment (Vollrath, 1987a) shows that particular legs can be used to measure distances and, for example, influence the spacing of the capture spiral. However, another study (Vollrath and ApRhisiart, 1992) shows that the spacing of the capture spiral is not necessarily correlated to the length of the measuring leg and that a spider is able to vary this spacing. A particular individual of *Araneus diadematus* can maintain a particular mesh size through much of its life, although it grows tenfold in weight and quadruples its leg length. Yet at the same time, this individual can also alter its mesh size abruptly. For example, it may respond to a curtailed silk supply by increasing the mesh size and decreasing web diameter (see Fig. 2e,f). Apparently, the silk supply is taken into consideration when a web is begun (Eberhard, 1988a) and, when the supply is limited, a compromise is found between preferred mesh size and preferred web diameter.

C. COMPUTER SIMULATION OF AN ORB ALGORITHM

The three experiments outlined in Section III,B,1,2,3 seem to support the hypothesis that the two spirals are built according to different algorithms, although it is also possible that the same rule set is used but with different weightings. This hypothesis can be falsified (or supported) by drawing a spiral that uses the spider's algorithms—or what we believe to be the spider's algorithms. One early and pioneering attempt to simulate the construction of a capture spiral—in particular, the placing of reverses—was admittedly not very successful (Eberhard, 1969), mainly because of an insufficient algorithm. In the meantime, much has been learned (e.g., from further work by Eberhard and the present author) about the complexity of the spider's orb algorithm, and with modern programming techniques, the problem also seems more manageable. We are in the process of developing advanced computer programs to study the spiders's spiral algorithm (Gotts and Vollrath, 1991, 1992). One aim of our simulation models is the exploration and testing of detailed hypotheses about web-building algorithms. In a second objective, we hope to be able to study the evolution of web-building behavior by stepwise modifications of these algorithms.

Interesting results were obtained using artificial intelligence (AI) techniques and, in particular, a "production system" approach (Gotts and Vollrath, 1991). This procedure was chosen because one of the fundamental aspects of AI is the representation and manipulation of information, be it incoming "sensory" information or information stored in "memory" (Garnham, 1988). A production system represents knowledge procedurally (rather than declaratively) as sets of

Real webs with T-spiral   Model T-F-3A(3) T-spiral   Model T-F-4C(7) T-spiral

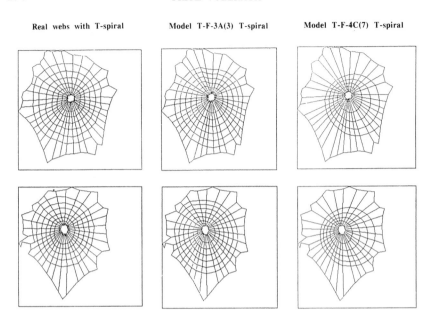

FIG. 11. Completion of *Araneus* webs by *Theseus*. The radial and frame representation of real *Araneus diadematus* webs was presented to our computer program (*Theseus*), which then had to provide the auxiliary spiral. Details of photographs of *Araneus* webs (A) built under laboratory conditions were entered into a computer database using a digitizing tablet, and were subsequently used to reconstruct the state of the web before and after the construction of the auxiliary or temporary "T"-spiral. Descriptions of these webs before the addition of the T-spiral were then given to a series of computational models called *Theseus*, written in the AI language Alpha-POP. The models had to construct a spiral, and the match of *Theseus* and *Araneus* spirals was later evaluated. (B) Model T-F-3A(3) produced perhaps the most realistic-looking spirals of any investigated so far. However, it is quite complex in terms of the number of independent numerical parameters used (Gotts and Vollrath, 1991). More recent models, although by no means perfect, show how apparently complex shapes can be generated by surprisingly simple rules. (C) These models (e.g., T-F-4C[7]) divide the T-spiral into just two parts, the first producing Phase 1 (a rapid widening), the second producing Phases 2 (consolidation), 3 (slow widening), and 4 (slow narrowing and stop).

rules, called productions, that can be applied whenever certain predetermined conditions are met. This attribute tempted us to apply this approach to the spider's web-building algorithm. Our most recent models for the auxiliary spiral (called *Theseus* after the mythical hero) are both simple and successful enough to warrant detailed testing against empirical findings (see Fig. 11).

1. General Description of Theseus *Models*

All *Theseus* models so far use a rule-based or production-system format (Davis and King, 1977). *Theseus* consists of an *interpreter* and a set of *rules*. Each rule consists of a *condition* and an *action*. A run of the model consists of a sequence of *rule-cycles:* the interpreter repeatedly tests the conditions of the rules, selects a rule with satisfied conditions, and performs the corresponding action. The spider represented by *Theseus* has just two properties: a *size* (relative to the particular web whose construction is being simulated) and a *position* in the web. The web is treated as a two-dimensional network of rigid one-dimensional "segments" meeting at zero-dimensional "attachment points" or "junctions." *Theseus* is treated as "jumping" from one attachment point to the next, and its web building therefore divides into a series of *attachment cycles*. During each attachment cycle, a new attachment point is added, together with a segment connecting it to its predecessor.

The models discussed embody versions of general working hypotheses about factors that influence *Araneus diadematus'* web-building behavior. They assume that local web geometry and global web orientation (relative to the vertical) are important factors for the placement of attachment points. They are supplemented only by a few simple items of information about nearby parts of the web: which web segments lead toward the hub from the spider's current position, the direction in which the spider is traveling around the hub, and the rate of change of the spider's relationship to the vertical.

Early models were constructed in an *ad hoc* fashion, using a variety of decision-making procedures to produce approximate matches to real T-spirals. After trying a number of approaches to determine positioning of spiral attachments, we settled on the use of *weighted averages* between two or more criteria. These were defined in terms of local web geometry combined with multiplication by variable *adjustment factors* calculated from the global position of the spider in the web (e.g., above or below the center, near or far from the periphery of the web). There is evidence (Hergenröder and Barth, 1983) that some spiders do carry out such simple additive and multiplicative operations on sensory information when deciding what movement to make.

2. *Specific Description of Some* Theseus *Models*

A broad class of models allowed for different weightings of criteria and different adjustment factors to be used in each of the four phases of T-spiral construction using three local criteria and two adjustment factors. Some results of the most successful of these four-phase models (e.g., T-F-3A[3]) are shown in Fig. 11. This model, like others of its class, uses five main measurements to determine where to place attachment points. Initially, a "raw" or "unadjusted" attachment point is calculated by weighing the outcomes of applying three local criteria against each other. The calculated "raw" attachment point is then subjected to two adjustments to reach a final attachment point. Local criteria are *spiral pitch* (the distance between successive turns of the spiral), *radial spacing* (the angle between the two radials that will be connected by the length of the spiral being added), and *parallelity* (of new and old segments between the same two radii). These three criteria generally suggest different attachment points; the exact formula used for calculating a compromise between them is determined by a set of three numerical parameters (weights), each specifying the importance to be assigned to one of the three. These weights may vary between models and between phases in a single model.

The first of the two adjustments applied to the "raw" attachment point position moves the attachment point further out from the hub (increasing p), if the spider is in the lower part of the web, and further in, if it is in the upper part. This reflects the important role that gravity plays in the construction procedure of *Araneus diadematus* (see Section III,B,2). The second adjustment reduces pitch as the spider approaches the web's periphery—as usually occurs in real T-spirals. The extent of these two adjustments is again determined by numerical parameters that can vary between models and phases.

Later models (e.g., T-F-4C[7]) divide the auxiliary spiral into just two parts, the first producing Phase 1 (a rapid widening), a second Phases 2 (consolidation), 3 (slow widening), and 4 (slow narrowing and stop). They work by taking a weighted average of the attachment points suggested by just two different criteria, one of which attempts to produce an arithmetic spiral maintaining a constant distance between adjacent spiral loops, whereas the other strives to produce a logarithmic spiral, maintaining a constant angle between the spiral and the radius that it crosses. A curious side effect, resistant to "tweaking," is shown by a lateral asymmetry of spiral looping (Fig. 11C). Nevertheless, the simplicity of the assumptions make these kinds of models particularly attractive to further development (after Gotts and Vollrath, 1991).

3. A Future for Theseus?

We are not entirely sure *why* some of our rule sets are much more successful than others, but the observation is encouraging that a small set of simple rules, with the right balance of weightings for each rule, *can* build a decent auxiliary spiral.

So far, we have neglected to incorporate into our programs structural, metrical, and material or physicochemical features of the web, whereas a fully developed simulation of the spider's construction skill clearly would require integration of these aspects (Gotts and Vollrath, 1992). For example, the building material may enter the web algorithm not only as a mechanical constraint but also as a limited resource because silk can have an effect through both quality (Zemlin, 1968) and quantity (Mayer, 1953; Eberhard, 1988a). Important for our simulations also is the possibility that the web-building spider may have a goal, that it may have not only knowledge about its present position but also a memory of former positions and an expectation about its next position. My experiments (see Section III,B), whereby the capture spiral-building *Araneus diadematus* traversed the web to regain a former position after perturbation, could be taken as

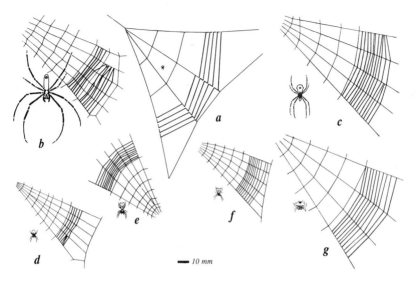

FIG. 12. Stereotypy in the orb web. (a) Entire web and (b–g) sections of webs built by a variety of orb weavers shown in outline drawings. (a) An entire web with its tiny owner in the middle, (b–f) sections of more or less complete orbs. (a) *Hyptiotes paradoxus,* (b) *Nephila clavipes,* (c) *Argyope argentata,* (d) *Cyclosa trifida,* (e) *Micrathena gracilis,* (f) *Micrathena duodecimspinosa,* (g) *Gasteracantha cancriformis* (after Peters, 1953).

indication of such a goal. Another indication comes from Eberhard (1988b), who burned sections away during the construction of auxiliary spiral and found that the spider, *Leucauge mariana,* adjusted its path gradually rather than abruptly. The spider behaves as if it uses a memory of distances and directions moved as well as an expectation for the position of each joint. How important memory and goal functions are in the web algorithm is at the moment being tested in a new generation of *Theseus* models that, *inter alia,* allow us to mimic experimental perturbations (like cutting threads or manipulating gravity).

The *Theseus* models will—hopefully and eventually—provide us with reasonable and testable hypotheses about the spider's spiral algorithms. It would be ideal if we could extend the models to include the actions of the various limbs (legs, fangs, and spinnerets) during spiral construction, but this is a distant prospect. The difficulties with this specific approach lie not least in the great variability of the behavior pattern where, for example, missing legs are always substituted and often regenerated. This variability interferes with modeling approaches. It also must preclude us from labeling the behavior as rigid or as a fixed action pattern *sensu* Lorenz (Tinbergen, 1951), as I shall explain in the following section.

IV. Manipulation of the Threads

Ultimately, success in modeling the spider's web-building behavior will depend on the correct assessment of flexibility and rigidity in the behavior pattern.
One way to begin is the dissection of the complex behavior pattern into its most
basic units, gripping and manipulation of silk. In the behavior pattern of measuring and manipulating threads, each leg has a specific task (Jacobi-Kleemann,
1953; Eberhard, 1982; Coddington, 1986; Weissmann, 1987). However, when
legs are lost, others take their place (Peters, 1937a; Jacobi-Kleemann, 1953;
Szlep, 1952; Reed *et al.*, 1965). The studies by Weissmann (1987) of leg use in
Araneus, Nephila, and *Zygiella* show that even quadruped spiders can build
species-specific webs. I have seen, in the field, an adult *Nephila clavipes* with
only three legs build and operate a functional, albeit far from perfect, web
(Vollrath, 1990). The reallocation of a specific task from one leg to another is a
sign of great flexibility and surprising central control.

A. The Importance of Sensory Feedback

Mechanical systems are controlled by one of two mechanisms: regulation or
steerage. Regulation uses feedback loops to attain the aspired value of a parameter, whereby a stream of information on the parameter's present value provides
the feedback necessary to constantly adjust the controlling mechanism. Steerage
has no feedback loop: the beginning and end of the process are connected by a
one-way causal relationship. Pure steerage is common in technology but rare in
biology, where it is found mainly in reflexes, that is, processes that are fast (and
must perforce be so?). An example combining both would be the strike of a
preying mantis at a fly: the strike is ballistic (steered) but its direction is aimed
(regulated) (Mittelstaedt, 1962).

The procedural aspect of spider web building can be separated into the animal's orientation and its manipulation of threads. Orientation (where to go next)
is clearly regulated by decisions based on information drawn from both the
spider's internal state and its external environment. Locomotion (climbing there)
is partly regulated by sensory feedback about the availability or nonavailability of
threads. Legs presumably encounter, grip, and join threads using a mix of feedback and reflex, but the feedback component is rather important. We have seen
that spiders with regenerated, shorter legs can build good webs. Shorter and
normal legs cooperate perfectly in handling threads and handing threads on from
one to the other, clearly showing the precedence of sensory feedback in this
activity. Because of their flexibility (Jacobi-Kleemann, 1953) the basic units of
web construction are best called modal action patterns (Barlow, 1968, 1977)
rather than fixed action patterns.

One candidate for important sensory input is the lyriform organs. These are highly regular aggregations of membrane-covered slits in strategic positions near leg joints (Vogel, 1923). They record the deformations of the hard exoskeleton, its strains and stresses, and are thought to thus infer the leg's position in space (Barth, 1972, 1985). These organs have also been implicated in providing information for path integration, as we have seen earlier. When particular lyriform organs on the legs of *Cupiennius salei* were cauterized, the spider still walked normally but largely lost its ability to run the typical path in search of a stolen prey (Seyfarth *et al.*, 1982). The lyriform organs on regenerated legs of *Araneus*, however, suggest that the role of these organs may not be fully understood. Regenerated legs bear particular lyriform organs that are often so malformed as to be nonfunctional, whereas others are not malformed but of atypical shape indicating an atypical signal (Vollrath, 1989). Of course, there are many other sources of sensory feedback, like proprioceptors (Barth, 1985). Sensory feedback clearly is important for coordinating and integrating leg movements during web construction.

B. LEG REGENERATION AND THE EVOLUTION
OF WEB ALGORITHMS

Regeneration of lost legs is an ancestral trait, present in the majority of spider families as well as related phyla (Vollrath, 1990). However, some spiders do not regenerate, and it is curious that all of them are web spinner and most are orb weavers. Moreover, the inability to regenerate is a derived trait and has evolved not by passive loss but by active suppression (Vollrath, 1990). When injured, most spiders shed entire legs at a specialized hip joint (Roth and Roth, 1984), presumably to prevent loss of hemolymph and a breakdown in the hydraulic pressure necessary for locomotion (Parry and Brown, 1959). Suppression of regeneration is localized at the hip joint (Randall, 1981). This suppression of regeneration can be inactivated experimentally by carefully amputating outer leg segments. The result is surprising: spiders that normally regenerate use the regenerated segments, whereas spiders that normally suppress do not use the regenerated segments (which in these spiders are of highly inferior morphology) (Vollrath, 1989, 1990).

Regeneration is ancestral and suppression is derived; moreover, suppression seems to have evolved only in web spiders. Therefore, it is tempting to speculate that it has evolved because their ancestors had difficulties in coping with the accurate integration of regenerated (and shorter) legs into the highly specific hand-shaking procedures necessary to weave a regular web. If this hypothesis were correct, then orb weavers that regenerate and those that do not might use different web-building algorithms (that either do or do not allow for variation in leg length). These hypothetical algorithms may have evolved independently or a common algorithm may have been adapted to either ignore or deal with abnormally short legs. This is a tantalizing question: Is the orb web a mono-phyletic behavior with an identical basic algorithm in all orb weavers or is it a polyphyletic or paraphyletic behavior with different algorithms? It is a question that can be tested experimentally, using well-established research animals like *Araneus* (which regenerates) and *Zygiella* (which suppresses) (Vollrath, 1990). First studies indicate that *Araneus* and *Zygiella* may use different legs to measure spacing of the capture spiral (Weissmann, 1987). A comparative study of formal rules that control a behavior (e.g., *Theseus*), rather than their outward ap-pearance, might be open to a more rigorous evolutionary analysis than could be provided by an examination of only the movement pattern (e.g., Eberhard, 1982; Coddington, 1986). Orb webs have evolved amazing shapes (Fig. 13). Each

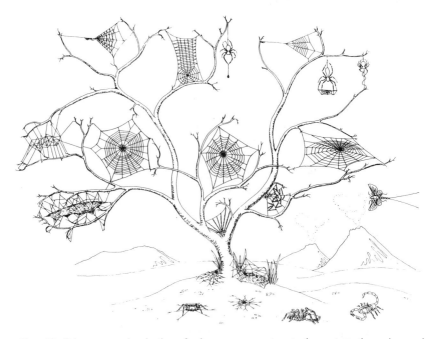

FIG. 13. Orb weavers. A selection of orb weavers on a tree to demonstrate the various web types—this is certainly not a phylogenetic tree. On the ground we see distant ancestors and relatives (scorpion, mygalomorph, trap door spider, and amaurobiid). Further ancestral relatives (eresid and agelenid) have built their webs on the base of the tree, a dictynid web spans the fork of the tree. The right-hand branch contains (in order from its base) the webs of *Stegodyphus*, *Uloborus*, *Hypotiotes*, *Deinopis*, and *Miagrammopes*. The center branch holds an orb web that might be by *Araneus*. The left-hand branch holds another orb web, which might be by *Meta* or *Tetragnatha*, this branch also supports (on the extreme left) three-dimensional webs by *Theridiion* (above) and *Linyphia* (below), as well as (upper left to right) orb webs by *Theridiosoma* and *Scoloderus*, and finally the *Mastophora* with its glue-drop web (from Vollrath, 1988b).

shape represents a behavior pattern that is controlled by one algorithm or other and that can be studied experimentally as well as modeled.

C. ORB WEAVER PHYLOGENY

Studies that unravel the spider's orb web-building behavior are urgently needed. For a classical textbook example of a complex behavior pattern, it is surprising how little we really know about it. And this is not only true for the web's ontogeny (as I have shown in previous sections) but for its phylogeny as well. A very large number of species (over a thousand) in a large number of families (up to 12 depending on the authority) build orbs or are descendants of orb-weaving ancestors (Coddington, 1986, 1989; Shear, 1986b). Yet, scientists are divided on the issue of the web's pedigree. We know that orb webs are very old, about as old as their insect prey and dating back at least to the Carboniferous period (Selden, 1989), although silk was already used more than 200 million years earlier by Devonian spiders (Shear *et al.*, 1989). We also know that the orb has experienced many independent changes to its basic pattern and even been given up several times (Coddington, 1986; Shear, 1986b; Stowe, 1986). About its origin we know next to nothing. It now seems that the orb pattern may be rather older than previously assumed, and that some spiders like the theridiid tangle-weavers are not ancestors, as formerly believed (Kaston, 1964; Kullmann, 1972), but descendants of orb weavers (Coddington, 1986, 1989). But this astonishing information still does not solve the vexed question of a singular or multiple origin of the orb-web algorithm.

1. Cribellate and Ecribellate Orbs

In the past, orb weavers were generally assigned to one of two distinct groups, classified by the basic type of capture silk (Foelix, 1982). The cribellate spiders use very fine silk of nanometer diameter that they comb, in hackled bands of several hundred threads at a time, onto support threads of micron diameter (Peters, 1987). The ecribellate spiders lack cribellum silk and, instead, coat their support thread with an aqueous solution that quickly forms droplets. Although the mechanism of cribellum silk stickiness is still a mystery (Eberhard, 1980), we now understand fairly well the mechanism of ecribellate capture silk. Here, coat and droplets are crucial for the function of the capture spiral. The high water content of the coat (80%) plasticizes the threads and renders them elastic (Gosline *et al.*, 1984; Work, 1985), the water is kept in the coat by hygroscopic chemicals (Vollrath *et al.*, 1990). The droplets, powered by surface tension, keep the threads tight by reeling them in when slackened and unraveling them again when stretched (Vollrath and Edmonds, 1989). The glue is concentrated in microscopic glycoprotein nodules that sit astride the core fibers beneath the droplets (Vollrath and Tillinghast, 1991). Although they use very different adhesive, cribellates and ecribellates both build very similar orb webs. Monophyly would require a transition from one glue to the other. The costs (e.g., silk, building behavior) of both types of webs are different (Kovoor, 1987; Lubin, 1986) and so are the benefits (e.g., stickiness, longevity) (Eberhard, 1972, 1980; Peters, 1987). On the whole (mainly because of the costs of the capture spiral), a cribellate orb web appears to be more expensive than the equivalent ecribellate web. Thus, the economic incentive for evolution away from cribellate into ecribellate mode is present.

2. *Do They Share One Orb Algorithm?*

Cribellate spiders are generally recognized as ancestral to ecribellate spiders (Foelix, 1982; Lehtinen, 1967; Coddington, 1986), which (as the name indicates) have lost the cribellum. It seems that ecribellates may have arisen several times independently from cribellate ancestors (Markl, 1986). One hypothesis about orb-weaver phylogeny (Thorell, 1886; Wiehle, 1928), recently revived and forcefully argued by Coddington (1986, 1989), claims that ecribellate orb weavers are a monophyletic group (the Araneoidea) with the cribellate Uloboridae as sister group. Under this hypothesis, all ecribellate orb weavers derive from one cribellate orb-weaving ancestor (emphasis on orb-weaving). The evidence for this theory is mainly circumstantial (Coddington, 1986, 1989) and the conclusions highly controversial (Shear, 1986b; Kovoor and Peters, 1988; Eberhard, 1987b, 1990b; Vollrath, 1990). However this may be, our null hypothesis, in my opinion falsifiable, might as well assume that all araneid orb weavers share a web-building algorithm inherited from one common uloborid ancestor. This hypothetical algorithm must then be a rule set that in its basic structure is identical for all orb weavers, although modifications may have evolved in the different taxa.

V.   Orb Webs as a Dynamic Filter

The puzzle of the web algorithm and its phylogenetic origin is only one of the big question marks against the orb web. Another concerns the ecological parameters responsible for the great variability of web shapes and types. Different orb spider species build webs that can be different in a great many ways. Some of these webs demonstrably catch specific prey (Stowe, 1986), whereas others are apparently nonspecific (Nentwig, 1983; Craig, 1987a). Clearly, the interspecific variance in web parameters is much higher than the intraspecific (Risch, 1977; Eberhard, 1986; Craig, 1987a,b), an observation that strongly suggests selection pressures for a species-specific web pattern. I consider it unlikely that web parameters are neutral or significantly affected by unrelated selection pressures (e.g., that a web pattern is significantly affected by sexual selection for longer legs). And therefore, I feel justified in considering the web an adapted structure, although this view is not generally accepted (Coddington, 1986, 1988). In this section, I shall outline a way that might allow us to formally test the view that the orb web is adapted to its builder, its environment, and its prey.

The finished web functions as a filter with an active ingredient. The spacing of the spiral loops (the mesh) determines to a fair degree what size prey might penetrate without hitting a sticky capture thread (Eberhard, 1986) and what size, weight, and speed of prey might be stopped by single or multiple threads. The web is a dynamic not a passive device: Its "mesh size" is not directly correlated with prey diameter; for ideal efficiency the mesh is slightly larger than the prey (Chacón and Eberhard, 1980). Moreover, parameters such as web tension and thread thickness have additive effects (Craig, 1987a). The dynamic properties of the different silks used in a web are therefore as important as the mesh size (Craig, 1987a). Thus, the web is a dynamic filter rather than a static sieve, but we cannot—as is sometimes done (Nentwig, 1983)—discount the mesh size as irrelevant and discard the web's function as a filter. Only if prey has been stopped, however briefly, can the spider assist its web. It is certainly not a coincidence that in many orb weavers, the mesh is kept relatively invariant throughout a large proportion of each web (c.f., Fig. 2).

Besides being traps, orb webs may have additional functions. All orb spiders make use of the web's transmittance and, possibly, amplification of vibrations (Masters and Markl, 1981; Masters *et al.,* 1986), vibrations that can indicate enemies as well as prey. For most web spiders, the web also functions as the male's dance floor, where he performs his song-and-dance routine of plucking threads and twitching his body to attract and stimulate the female (Robinson and Robinson, 1980).

A.   THE WEB AS A FUNCTIONAL UNIT

Despite its other roles, the main function of a web is as a trap. The web is an active trap incorporating a stationary yet dynamic filter: the spider pounces once an insect has ventured into the net. Perception of trapped prey is of paramount importance, as is information about its location in the web and its identity. Prey have evolved a variety of escape mechanisms and, if left untended, will get away. The radials of the orb are the spider's information lines and travel routes. As such, radials have a double function, belonging both to the "filter" and the "trap." The capture spiral, held in place by the radials, is the filter, and its only function is to retain prey for long enough to give the spider time for inspection. In fact, the capture threads are made of a material that, at the same time, appears to maximize capture effectiveness (energy absorption) and minimize interference with the information transfer of vibrations along the radials (Denny, 1976). I see the capture spiral as a foraging path and the frame, radials, auxiliary spiral, and hub as the spider's means of controlling this path.

B. AN OPTIMALITY APPROACH

Foraging behavior of animals can be analyzed using mathematical models (Pyke *et al.*, 1977). Parameters such as food intake, energy expenditure, and net energy gain can be calculated, or at least approximated, by the predictive theory of optimal foraging (Krebs, 1978). It is instructive to apply this theory to the orb spider's web. The spider's foraging behavior consists of three subunits: (1) choice of a site, (2) web construction, and (3) web operation. Each unit belongs to a different realm of foraging theory. (1) Selecting a site is patch choice (Pyke, 1983). At present we can only guess how the animal perceives the quality of a site (patch) and how much knowledge it has about a patch (Olive, 1982; Riechert and Gillespie, 1986; Gillespie and Caraco, 1987; Janetos, 1982a,b, 1986; Vollrath, 1985; Vollrath and Houston, 1986). (2) Constructing a web is comparable to walking a foraging path exploiting a patch. In the spider's web, this path is walked without direct interaction with the prey, the interaction comes later when the web is finished. We may assume that the windings of the path are the outcome of evolutionary interactions (Risch, 1977), a phylogenetic response (the "ghost of selection past") rather than a direct behavioral response to prey stimuli. Thus, knowledge about the patch is presumably indirect and incomplete. It is an interesting and open question whether the animal has any immediate response to prey (e.g., can adjust spiral spacing to the size of common prey insects). (3) Operating the web is central place foraging *sensu* Orians and Pearson (1979), with direct and full knowledge of the patch because the radials signal all relevant information (Robinson, 1975; Barth, 1982). In the following, I shall spin out the idea of the web as a foraging path and briefly discuss the economics of site choice, web construction, and web operation.

1. Criteria for Site Choice

Choice of a site incorporates two decisions: leaving a present site and accepting a new site. The decisions are generally linked; site desertion always precedes site selection, except for the cases of enforced eviction, accidental displacement, and the first web ever. The reasons for deserting a web site are a tantalizing aspect of spider foraging. Web spiders provide one of the best examples of sit-and-wait predators with a high investment, and understanding spider foraging tactics is important for any comprehensive foraging theory.

A number of studies have begun the task of elucidating this aspect of web spider behavior (e.g., Enders, 1976; Olive, 1982; Uetz *et al.*, 1978; Schoener and Spiller, 1987; Hodge, 1987; Christenson, 1990). Janetos (1982a,b), in a comparative study of a number of web-building spiders from two guilds ("ephemeral" orb webs and "lasting" space webs), found that orb weavers are more mobile than space web weavers. Janetos (1986) suggests that the degree of mobility may partly depend on the cost of a web and that the timing of site desertion may be random in space webs but not orb webs. This statement has to be modified in view of the results of an experimental study with caged spiders by Vollrath and Houston (1986), who found that the orb weaver *Nephila clavipes* is slow in responding to a complete lack of prey, and that, when it does, it abandons sites at random. *Nephila,* however, is one of those orb weavers with a high investment web, which might explain its functional response. Gillespie and Caraco (1987), in the orb weaver *Tetragnatha elongata* (which has a low invest-ment web), link mobility to the abundance of prey in the natural environment: in rich environments spiders move more than in poor environments. The authors inferred from this behavior that this spider's functional response is risk-sensitive rather than risk-prone (i.e., spiders move when the probability of finding other rich sites is high and stay put when this probability is low). Vollrath (1985), in an experimental study with artificially enriched and deprived seminatural environ-ments, observed the opposite behavior in *Nephila clavipes* (which has a high investment web). *Nephila* moves less in the rich environment. Moreover, *Nephila* overcompensates (moves more) the very moment that the rich environ-ment turns poor. This suggests that *Nephila* has an expectation of a given food input at a given site and thus indicates the possibility that this spider makes strategic decisions on site tenacity. Gillespie and Caraco (1987) consider such decisions unlikely in *Tetragnatha elongata.* However, there is a chance that their observations in the high density habitat may reflect not so much foraging deci-sions as web takeovers and other agonistic behavior (P. Smallwood, personal communication).

In all probability, web spiders use a whole range of functional responses to prey abundance at a given site, ranging from high-energy to low-energy, and from risk-prone to risk-averse, strategies. Weighing the costs of movement must also include considerations of (1) predation risk, which is different in the web and on the move (Vollrath, 1980; Rypstra, 1984) and which should influence not only the timing but also the distance of a move (Gillespie and Caraco, 1987), as well as costs associated with (2) the ability or inability to predict the quality of a future site (Riechert and Gillespie, 1986) and (3) the ability or inability to return to an old site (as I outlined before). About these costs of movement and site assessment, and their influence on spider site choice, we know next to nothing.

2. Criteria for the Spiral Path

Optimality considerations are never absolute. They are concerned with effi-ciency, and it is important to remember that effectiveness (quality) and efficiency (quality within constraints) are different things. The spider's web is built within constraints set by the building material silk. And the architecture requires a trade off between threads that have their specific requirements, like the capture spiral that must be sticky and soft (to adhere to prey and absorb energy) and the radials that must be nonsticky and stiff (for they are runways as well as sensors).

First approaches in the direction of using optimality criteria on spider-web geometry have been made by Lubin (1986), Eberhard (1986), and in my laboratory (Fig. 14). Lubin (1986) concerns herself mostly with the costs of silk and of time devoted to building. Eberhard (1986), whose approach is descriptive rather than normative, gives an inspired account also of biologically relevant constraints and trade offs. He concludes from his ingeniously simple simulations—

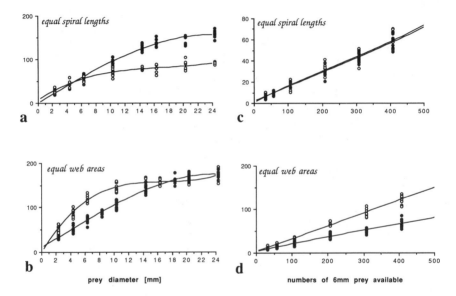

FIG. 14. Simulated "prey capture" by simulated orb webs. Plots of various diameter "prey" caught by two model "webs" with spacings of 10 mm (open circles) and 20 mm (filled circles). The ordinates represent the number of "prey" hitting a strand. Graphs a and b show the effect of differences in prey diameter, c and d the effect of differences in prey density of the "environment" on the "capture rate" of the two types of spacings when all prey have the same diameter (6 mm). Webs in a and c had equal spiral lengths, but different areas; in b and d, the areas were equal, but the finer meshed spiral was twice as long. Prey encounter rates were simulated in the computer by imposing disks onto line drawings representing stylized orb webs with 18 radials and evenly spaced capture spirals. Disks that hit a strand of web were counted once. Each "environment" contained 400 prey placed at random, and all simulations were repeated several times. The lines represent third order regressions. Webs with spirals of different spacings but equal lengths or equal areas catch different types and proportions of prey suggesting that the web *per se* is a filter. These graphs do not show the effects of: (1) hits that stick to several strands, (2) the costs of a spiral, and (3) the central place foraging aspect of a web, where distant hits are less likely to result in capture by the spider (based on ApRhisiart and Vollrath, 1992).

with paper "flies" thrown onto line drawings—that the same length of spiral drawn out into wider spaces between lines strikes more "prey" than if it forms a narrow mesh. However, this advantage appears to be counterbalanced by the comparatively greater costs of such webs. Based on an observation that radials can absorb 10 times more kinetic energy than sticky lines, Eberhard further concludes that webs with many radials may be better at stopping large and/or fast-moving prey than webs with few radials. Although the assumption is not always met, the conclusion appears to be generally right (Craig, 1987a), not least because many radii render webs stiff. Indeed, it appears that any model designed to include the absorption of a prey's kinetic energy will be far from simple, having to account for variables like radial number, tension, and strength (Craig, 1987a,b) as well as spiral spacing (Eberhard, 1986), elasticity (Denny, 1976), and adhesiveness (Nentwig, 1982).

However, even simple simulations can give interesting insights. Taking Eberhard's paper fly simulations a step further, I projected slides of real spider webs onto random plots of stars. The projections generated life-size webs on top of fruit fly-sized prey and, simply counting the "hits," gave an indication of the high efficiency of normal webs: about 87% of the prey that fell within the area covered by the capture spiral. The most interesting outcome of this, as yet unpublished, study was the effect that regular (normal) *Araneus'* webs "caught" significantly more "prey" than irregular webs of the same size and length of thread, which caught about 61%. Irregularity was generated by drugging spiders with caffeine (Witt *et al.*, 1968) or using the klinostat (see webs b,c,d in Fig. 9). But highly irregular webs not only catch fewer prey, they are also more difficult to operate, mainly because prey capture (but not prey localization) takes significantly longer (Fox, 1990).

3. Criteria of Web Operation and "Central Place Foraging"

The web is not a passive filter. Prey capture is a dynamic process, the spider is necessary not only for the manufacture of the trap but also for its operation. During operation, radials are used as signal lines and runways. Radials converge and project onto the hub, and the spider either rests on the hub or, if it rests in a hidden retreat, is connected to the hub by a signal line. In either case, the spider is a central place forager who always returns (with or without prey) to the hub. Indeed, the spider has great difficulties in locating prey from within the capture area of the web if spider and insect are separated by more than one radius (Klärner and Barth, 1982; Weissmann, 1987). The hub lies in the center of the food distribution, as befits a central place forager—or does it? Horizontal orbs are generally more or less round. Some vertical orbs are also quite round but most are asymmetric, as a rule, extending further down than up (Stowe, 1986). The most extreme are long and thin "ladder" webs like that of *Herennia ornatissima* (Robinson and Lubin, 1979). As an exception, the ladder web of

Scoloderus tubulifer extends upward, but this web is specialized to catch moths, which tumble down the long ladder, losing their scales on the way, into the fangs of the spider waiting below (Eberhard, 1975).

Why, if the spider is a central place forager, should the web be asymmetric? There is no obvious mechanical reason for the web to be that shape. One functional reason, however, is obvious: the spider can run down faster than up (Masters and Moffat, 1983) and, with few exceptions (e.g., *Cyclosa insulana*), it always rests on the hub facing downward (Wiehle, 1928). Prey retention times in the web can be notoriously short, and the spider's quick response in prey localization (with the front legs) and attack may be a bonus when prey is nimble and often well adapted to escaping, as it often is (Eisner *et al.*, 1964). At rest, the spider can only monitor one direction with its front legs and, consequently, must turn if prey arrive in any other direction. Turning and fine-tuning, necessary to localize the radius leading to the prey, takes time (Barth, 1982; Weissmann, 1987; Fox, 1990). Thus, the spider might as well face in the direction where prey are most likely to arrive (i.e., where the web has the largest area) assuming that prey arrive at random. It might be best to face downward because this is the direction in which, thanks to gravity, an attack can be executed the fastest.

VI. WEBS AND LIFE HISTORY

Viewing the spider's web as an exercise in foraging theory, invoking models of patch choice, foraging paths, and central place foraging may be unusual. However, I believe that adopting this view helps us in analyzing the function of a web. It implies using a formal approach that forces us to spell out our assumptions about *all* the costs of a web and our predictions about *all* its benefits. Only through formal models can we test assumptions and predictions and study their interaction. Such an approach also allows us to generalize our observations and ultimately integrate the web—after all, it provides the spider with most of its necessities—into the fabric of the spider's life history pattern.

One example of such an integrated approach comes from the interesting studies of Susan Riechert and her collaborators on the sheet weaver *Agelenopsis aperta* (Riechert and Gillespie, 1986). They viewed the web as the spider's territory and investigated the costs of web defense, examining short-term game-theoretical aspects (e.g., Riechert, 1978) as well as medium-term aspects of life history (e.g., Riechert, 1979) and even long-term aspects of genetics and population dynamics (Riechert, 1985; Riechert and Maynard Smith, 1989). Another example of an integrated approach is my own work on the decision faced by an immature web spider that must determine whether to move from a web site or adapt its growth to that site (Vollrath, 1985, 1988c) with all the repercussions if a wrong decision is taken and size at maturity becomes suboptimal (Vollrath, 1980, 1987b). Such decisions are a real dilemma for an animal that finds it hard to determine the marginal value of its habitat (because of the high cost of sampling). It is especially hard in the case of a mediocre site when averaging thresholds (that are inherited) cannot be used because such a site may be a good site in a bad season or a bad site in a good season. Obviously, information about the quality of the season (and thus about other sites in the vicinity) should influence the spider's decision. And such information can only be gathered at considerable cost. Observations (unpublished) that first webs at a new site are often smaller than later webs suggest that the spider might balance some of the costs of moving by adjusting parameters of its web algorithm.

VII. Conclusions

The orb web is a complex structure made of complex materials by an animal with a complex life history. To fully understand a web's value as a trap, it is insufficient to calculate only costs and benefits of the web itself. Additional factors can influence the success of a web, as shown for a fair number of orb-weaving genera belonging to different families (original studies by Uetz *et al.,* 1978; Olive, 1980, 1981; Rypstra, 1983, 1989; Toft, 1983; Lubin, 1986; Schoener and Spiller, 1987; Spiller and Schoener, 1989; Pasquet and Leborgne, 1990; Raynor and Uetz, 1990; and reviews by Bristowe, 1941; Turnbull, 1973; Denny, 1976; Nentwig and Wissel, 1986; Eberhard, 1986, 1990b; Stowe, 1986; Craig, 1987a,b; Uetz, 1988). It is time to begin to integrate the different studies into a single framework and, in new studies, to shift the emphasis from descriptions to formal models and hypothesis-testing experiments. This is as true for ecological studies of the web as for behavioral studies.

Singling out specific parameters of the web—for example, the capture spiral—and assessing their contribution to the spider's fitness may help us to understand the selection pressures acting on the web-building behavior as well as the set of rules that control this behavior. We must assume that the web algorithm has evolved in minute steps, as organisms typically evolve. It may be unusual, but is not wrong, to view the web and its construction like other aspects of the spider's phenotype (Dawkins, 1982). After all, the web is an extension of the spider's body. However, it is a part that is not only created out in the open, in full view so to speak, but it is also recreated daily anew. Thus, it is ideally suited for experimental interference. Analyzing the spiral as orientation behavior, guided by a set of rules that are inherited but greatly affected by the environment, may help us to envision, formulate, and test hypotheses about these minute steps. The success of this particular approach might well determine whether we can crack the spider's web-building code, and use it afterward to analyze and interpret the ecology and evolution of spiders and their webs.

VIII. SUMMARY

The spider's web is frozen behavior, a more or less permanent record of a fleeting activity. The tangle of threads, like a track in the snow, reveals the animal's path and most of its actions. The web, like a track, has a handling component (an action executed as a particular location) and a locomotory component (a direction of movement). This locomotory component can be analyzed as orientation behavior because most spiders are small in comparison with their webs. The web, rather than the observable behavior, allows us to access the underlying rules of orientation and silk manipulation.

Thus, the web allows us to study, in a relatively simple experimental set up, the cues that guide the spider and the rules that determine her decisions. The garden cross spider *Araneus diadematus* during web construction uses (a) local cues and (b) global cues, (c) she expects certain cues at certain stages of the construction process, and (d) she *might* even use some sort of mental map. For example: (a) the previous turn of the spiral is a local landmark used during construction of the sticky spiral; (b) gravity acts as a global reference throughout all phases of web construction; (c) during spiral construction, the spider aligns her body according to some inherent rule of "expected position," even sometimes overriding external cues; (d) during site exploration and radial construction she *might* use a spatial map.

Clearly, a spider's web is indeed an example of animal orientation (possibly even navigation) recorded by the animal itself in a sequence of modal action patterns and open to experiments and computer simulation. Webs have evolved and the evolution of the construction behavior may one day be traced, as may the constraints and selection pressures that have lead to a particular web geometry. This geometry can also be viewed from the vantage of optimal foraging theory, where (a) the choice of a web site, (b) the search path of the capture spiral, and (c) the considerations of a central place forager in the more or less orbicular web are all parameters that contribute to the selection process.

Acknowledgments

I thank Professors Bill Eberhard, Peter Görner, Manfred Milinski, Hans M. Peters, Peter Slater, and the anonymous Mike Land for their critical and helpful comments on the manuscript. As I sometimes resisted their suggestions, all faults with the article are mine. I thank Dr. Marian Dawkins, Dr. Alun ApRhisiart, and Dr. Nick Gotts for many stimulating discussions on the subject of spiders, Dr. Anne Magurran for editing, and Tamara Köhler for redrawing Fig. 6. My studies on spider webs have been supported by the DFG, SERC, Swiss NF, Smithsonian Institution, Christensen Foundation, Volkswagen-Stiftung, and last but not least, the kind patronage of Prof. Sir Richard Southwood.

References

Ades, C. (1986). A construçao de teia geométrica como programa comportamental. *Cienci. Cult. (Sao Paulo)* **38,** 760–775.

ApRhisiart, A., and Vollrath, F. (1992). Optimisation considerations in the spider's orb web. In preparation.

Baltzer, F. (1930). Über die Orientierung der Trichterspinne *Agelena labyrinthica* (Cl.) nach der Spannung des Netzes. *Rev. Suisse Zool.* **37,** 363–369.

Barlow, G. W. (1968). Ethological units of behavior. *In* "The Central Nervous System and Fish Behavior" (D. Ingle, ed.), pp. 217–232. Univ. of Chicago Press, Chicago, Illinois.

Barlow, G. W. (1977). Modal action patterns. *In* "How Animals Communicate" (T. A. Sebeok, ed.), pp. 98–134. Indiana Univ. Press, Bloomington.

Barth, F. G. (1972). Die Physiologie der Spaltsinnesorgane. I. Modellversuche zur Rolle des cuticularen Spaltes beim Reiztransport, *J. Comp. Physiol.* **78,** 315–336.

Barth, F. G. (1982). Spiders and vibratory signals: Sensory reception and behavioral significance. *In* "Spider Communication" (P. N. Witt, and J. S. Rovner, eds.), pp. 67–122. Princeton Univ. Press, Princeton, New Jersey.

Barth, F. G. (1985). Neuroethology of the spider vibration sense. *In* "Neurobiology of Arachnids" (F. G. Barth, ed.), pp. 203–230. Springer-Verlag, and Berlin New York.

Breed, A., Levine, V., Peakall, D. B., and Witt, P. N. (1964). The fate of the intact orb web of the spider *Araneus diadematus* Cl. *Behaviour* **23,** 43–60.

Bristowe, W. (1941). "The Comity of Spiders," Vol. II. Ray Society, London.

Carico, J. E. (1986). Web removal patterns in orb-weaving spiders. *In* "Spiders: Webs, Behavior and Evolution" (W. A. Shear, ed.), pp. 306–318. Stanford Univ. Press, Stanford, California.

Carrell, J. E. (1978). Behavioural thermoregulation during winter in an orb weaving spider. *Symp. Zool. Soc. London* **42,** 41–50.

Chacón, P., and Eberhard, W. G. (1980). Factors affecting numbers and kinds of prey caught in artificial spider webs, with considerations of how orb webs trap prey. *Bull. Br. Arachnol. Soc.* **5,** 29–38.

Chessell, D. L. M. (1986). The role of memory in the web-site selection behavior of *Argiope argentata* Cl. (Araneae: Araneidae). Honours Thesis, Oxford University, U. K. (unpublished).

Christenson, T. E. (1990). Natural selection and reproduction: A study of the golden orb-weaving spider. *In* "Contemporary Issues in Comparative Psychology" (D. A. Dewsbury, ed.), pp. 149–174. Sinauer Assoc., Sunderland, Massachusetts.

Coddington, J. (1986). The monophyletic origin of the orb web. *In* "Spiders: Webs, Behavior and Evolution" (W. A. Shear, ed.), pp. 319–363. Stanford Univ. Press, Stanford, California.

Coddington, J. (1988). Cladistic tests of adaptational hypotheses. *Cladistics* **4,** 3–22.

Coddington, J. (1989). Spinneret silk morphology: Evidence for the monophyly of orb-weaving spiders, Cyrtophorinae (Araneidae), and the group Theridiidae plus Nesticidae. *J. Arachnol.* **17,** 71–95.

Craig, C. L. (1987a). The ecological and evolutionary interdependence between web architecture and web silk spun by orb web-weaving spiders. *Biol. J. Linn. Soc.* **30,** 135–162.

Craig, C. L. (1987b). The significance of spider size to the diversification of spider-web architectures and spider reproductive modes. *Am. Nat.* **129,** 47–68.

Craig, C. L. (1988). Insect perception of spider orb webs in three light habitats. *Funct. Ecol.* **2**, 277–282.

Craig, C. L., Okubo, A., and Andreasen, V. (1985). Effect of spider orb-web and insect oscillations on prey interception. *J. Theor Biol.* **115**, 201–211.

Crawford, J. D. (1984). Orientation in a vertical plane: The use of light cues by an orb-weaving spider, *Araneus diadematus* Clerk. *Anim. Behav.* **32**, 162–171.

Davis, R., and King, J. (1977). An overview of production systems. *Mach. Intell.* **8**.

Dawkins, R. (1982). "The Extended Phenotype." Oxford Univ. Press, Oxford.

Denny, M. (1976). The physical properties of spider's silk and their role in the design of orb-webs. *J. Exp. Biol.* **65**, 483–506.

Dornfeld, K. (1975). Eine Elementaranalyse des Wirkungsgefüges des Heimfindevermögens der Trichterspinne *Agelena labyrinthica* (Cl.). *Z. Tierpsychol.* **38**, 267–293.

Eberhard, W. G. (1969). Computer simulation of orb-web construction. *Am. Zool.* **9**, 229–238.

Eberhard, W. G. (1972). The web of *Uloborus diversus* (Araneae: Uloboridae). *J. Zool.* **166**, 417–465.

Eberhard, W. G. (1975). The 'inverted ladder' orb web of *Scoloderus* sp. and the intermediate orb of *Eustala* (?) sp. (Araneae: Araneidae.). *J. Nat. Hist.* **9**, 93–106.

Eberhard, W. G. (1980). Persistant stickiness of cribellum silk. *J. Arachnol.* **8**, 283.

Eberhard, W. G. (1981). Construction behavior and the distribution of tensions in orb webs. *Bull. Br. Arachnol. Soc.* **5**, 189–204.

Eberhard, W. G. (1982). Behavioral characters for the higher classification of orb-weaving spiders. *Evolution (Lawrence, Kans.)* **36**, 1067–1095.

Eberhard, W. G. (1986). Effects of orb-web geometry on prey interception and retention. In "Spiders: Webs, Behavior and Evolution" (W. A. Shear, ed.), pp. 70–100. Stanford Univ. Press, Stanford, California.

Eberhard, W. G. (1987a). Effects of gravity on temporary spiral construction by *Leucauge mariana* (Araneae: Araneidae). *J. Ethol.* **5**, 29–36.

Eberhard, W. G. (1987b). Construction behavior of non-orb weaving cribellate spiders and the evolutionary origin of orb webs. *Bull. Br. Arachnol. Soc.* **7**, 175–178.

Eberhard, W. G. (1988a). Behavioral flexibility in orb web construction: Effects of supplies in different silk glands and spider size and weight. *J. Arachnol.* **16**, 295–302.

Eberhard, W. G. (1988b). Memory of distances and directions moved as cues during temporary spiral construction in the spider Leucauge mariana (Araneae: Araneidae). *J. Insect Behav.* **1**, 51–66.

Eberhard, W. G. (1990a). Early stages of orb construction by *Philoponella vicina, Leucauge mariana,* and *Nephila clavipes* (Araneidae, Uloboridae and Tetragnathidae) and their phylogenetic implications. *J. Arachnol.* **18**, 205–234.

Eberhard, W. G. (1990b). Function and phylogeny of spider webs. *Annu. Rev. Ecol. Syst.* **21**, 341–372.

Eisner, T., Alsop, R., and Ettershank, G. (1964). Adhesiveness of spider silk. *Science* **146**, 1058–1061.

Ellen, P., and Thinus-Blanc, C. (1987). "Cognitive Processes and Spatial Orientation in Animal and Man. Vol. I. Experimental Animal Psychology and Ethology." Martinus Nijhoff Publishers, Amsterdam.

Enders, F. (1973). Selection of habitat by the spider *Argiope aurantia* Lucas (Araneidae). *Am. Midl. Nat.* **90**, 47–55.

Enders, F. (1974). Vertical stratification in orb-web spiders (Araneidae, Araneae) and a consideration of other methods of co-existence. *Ecology* **55**, 317–328.

Enders, F. (1976). Effects on prey capture, web destruction and habitat physiognomy on web-site tenacity of *Argiope* spiders (Araneidae). *J. Arachnol.* **3**, 75–82.

Endo, T. (1988). Patterns of prey utilisation in a web of orb-weaving spider *Araneus pinguis* Karsch. *Res. Popul. Ecol. (Kyoto)* **30**, 107–122.

Finck, A. (1972). Vibration sensitivity in an orb-weaver. *Am. Zool.* **12**, 539–543.

Finck, A., Stewart, G., and Reed, C. F. (1975). The orb web as an acoustic detector. *J. Acoust. Soc. Am.* **57**, 753–754.

Foelix, R. (1982). "Biology of Spiders." Harvard Univ. Press (Belknap), Boston, Massachusetts.

Fox, R. (1990). Web geometry and prey capture behaviour in *Araneus diadematus,* an orb web spider. Honours' Thesis, Oxford University, U. K. (unpublished).

Frings, H., and Frings, M. (1966). Reactions of orb-weaving spiders (Argiopidae) to airborne sounds. *Ecology* **47**, 578–588.

Garnham, A. (1988). "Artificial Intelligence." Routledge & Kegan Paul, London.

Gillespie, R. G., and Caraco, T. (1987). Risk-sensitive foraging strategies of two spider populations. *Ecology* **68**, 887–899.

Görner, P. (1958). Die optische und kinesthetische Orientierung der Trichterspinne *Agelena labyrinthica. Z. Vergl. Physiol.* **41**, 111–153.

Görner, P. (1972). Resultant positioning between optical and kinesthetic orientation in the spider *Agelena labyrinthica* Clerk. *In* "Information Processing in the Visual Systems of Arthropods" (R. Wehner, ed.), pp. 73–95. Springer, Heidelberg.

Görner, P. (1988). Homing behavior of funnel web spiders (Agelenidae) by means of web related cues. *Naturwissenschaften* **75**, 209–211.

Görner, P., and Class, B. (1985). Homing behavior and orientation in the funnel-web spider, *Agelena labyrinthica.* Clerck. *In* "Neurobiology of Arachnids" (F. G. Barth, ed.) pp. 275–298. Springer-Verlag, Berlin and New York.

Görner, P. and Zeppenfeld, C. (1980). The runs of *Pardosa amentata* (Araneae, Lycosidae) after removing its cocoon. *Proc. Int. Congr. Arachnol., 8th* pp. 243–248.

Gosline, J., Denny, M., and DeMont, M. E. (1984). Spider silk as rubber. *Nature (London)* **309**, 551–552.

Gotts, N., and Vollrath, F. (1991). Artificial intelligence modelling of web-building in the garden cross spider. *J. Theor. Biol.* **152**, 485–511.

Gotts, N., and Vollrath, F. (1992). Physical and theoretical features in the simulation of animal behavior: The spider's web. *Cybernet. Syst.* (in press).

Gould, J. L. (1986). The locale map of Honey bees: Do insects have cognitive maps? *Science* **232**, 861–865.

Hergenröder, R., and Barth, F. G. (1983). Vibratory signals and spider behavior: How the sensory inputs from the eight legs interact in orientation. *J. Comp. Physiol., A.* **152**, 361–371.

Hieber, C. S. (1984). Orb-web orientation and modification by the spiders *Araneus diadematus* and *Araneus gemmoides* (Araneae: Araneidae) in response to wind and light. *Z. Tierpsychol.* **65**, 250–260.

Hill, D. (1979). Orientation by jumping spiders of the genus Phidippus (Araneae: Salticidae) during the pursuit of prey. *Behav. Ecol. Sociobiol.* **5**, 301–322.

Hingston, R. W. G. (1927). Protective devices in spiders' snares, with a description of seven new species of orb-weaving spiders. *Proc. Zool. Soc. London* **18**, 259–293.

Hodge, M. A. (1987). Factors influencing web site residence time of the orb weaving spider *Micrathena gracilis. Psyche* **94**, 363–372.

Holzapfel, M. (1933). Die nicht-optische Orientierung der Trichterspinne *Agelena labyrinthica* (Cl.) *Z. Vergl. Physiol.* **20**, 55–115.

Homann, H. (1971). Die Augen der Araneae. Anatomie, Ontogenie und Bedeutung für die Systematik. *Z. Morphol. Oekol. Tiere* **69**, 201–272.

Jackson, R. (1986). Web building, predatory versatility and the evolution of the Salticidae. *In*

"Spiders: Webs, Behavior, and Evolution" (W. A. Shear, ed.), pp. 232–268. Stanford Univ. Press, Stanford, California.

Jacobi-Kleemann, M. (1953). Über die Lokomotion der Kreuzspinne *Aranea diademata* beim Netzbau (nach Filmanalysen). *Z. Vergl. Physiol.* **34**, 606–654.

Janetos, A. C. (1982a). Active foragers vs sit-and-wait predators: A simple model. *J. Theor. Biol.* **95**, 381–385.

Janetos, A. C. (1982b). Foraging tactics of two guilds of web-spinning spiders. *Behav. Ecol. Sociobiol.* **10**, 19–27.

Janetos, A. (1986). Web site selection: Are we asking the right questions? *In* "Spiders: Webs, Behavior and Evolution" (W. Shear, ed.), pp. 9–22. Stanford Univ. Press, Stanford, California.

Jocqué, R. (1981). On reduced size in spiders from marginal habitats. *Oecologia* **49**, 404–408.

Kaston, B. J. (1964). The evolution of spider webs. *Am. Zool.* **4**, 191–207.

Klärner, D., and Barth, F. G. (1982). Vibratory signals and prey capture in orb-weaving spiders (*Zygiella x-notata, Nephila clavipes*; Araneidae). *J. Comp. Physiol.* **148**, 445–455.

König, M. (1951). Beiträge zur Kenntnis des Netzbaus orbiteler Spinnen. *Z. Tierpsychol.* **8**, 462–492.

Kovoor, J. (1987). Comparative structure and histochemistry of silk-producing organs in Arachnids. *In* "Ecophysiology of Spiders" (W. Nentwig, ed.), pp. 160–186. Springer-Verlag, Berlin and New York.

Kovoor, J., and Peters, H. M. (1988). The spinning apparatus of *Polenecia producta* (Araneae: Uloboridae): Structure and histochemistry. *Zoomorphology* **108**, 47–59.

Krebs, J. R. (1978). Optimal foraging decision rules for predators. *In* "Behavioral Ecology" (J. R. Krebs and N. B. Davies, eds.), pp. 23–63. Blackwell, Oxford.

Krieger, M. (1992). Radial construction in the orb web. Diplom Thesis, University of Basel, Switzerland.

Kullmann, E. (1972). The convergent development of orb-webs in cribellate and ecribellate spiders. *Am. Zool.* **12**, 395–405.

Land, M. F. (1985). The morphology and optics of spider eyes. *In* "Neurobiology of Arachnids" (F. G. Barth, ed.), pp. 53–78. Springer-Verlag, Berlin and New York.

Le Guelte, L. (1966). Structure de la toile de *Zygella-x-notata* Cl. et facteurs qui régissent le comportement de l'araignée pendant la construction de la toile. Ph.D. Thesis, University of Nancy, France.

Le Guelte, L. (1969). Learning in spiders. *Am. Zool.* **9**, 145–152.

Lehtinen, P. (1967). Classification of the cribellate spiders and some allied families, with notes on the evolution of the suborder Araneomorpha. *Ann. Zool. Fenn.* **4**, 199–468.

Levi, H. W. (1978). Orb-weaving spiders and their webs. *Am. Sci.* **66**, 734–742.

Liesenfeld, F. J. (1956). Untersuchungen am Netz und über den Erschütterungssinn von *Zygiella-x-notata* (Cl) (Araneidae). *Z. Vergl. Physiol.* **38**, 563–592.

Liesenfeld, F. J. (1961). Über Leistung und Sitz des Erschütterungssinnes von Netzspinnen. *Biol. Zentralbl.* **80**, 465–475.

Longman. (1988). "Synonyms." Longman, London.

Lubin, Y. D. (1973). Web structure and function: the non-adhesive orb-web of *Cyrtophora moluccensis* (Doleschall) (Araneae, Araneidae). *Forma Functio* **6**, 337–358.

Lubin, Y. (1986). Web building and prey capture in the Uloboridae. *In* "Spiders: Webs, Behavior, and Evolution" (W. A. Shear, ed.), pp. 132–171. Stanford Univ. Press, Stanford, California.

Magni, F., Papi, F., Savely, H. E., and Tongiorgi, P. (1965). Research on the structure and physiology of the eyes of a lycosid spider. III. Electroretinographic responses to polarized light. *Arch. Ital. Biol.* **103**, 136–158.

Markl, J. (1986). Evolution and function of structurally diverse subunits in the respiratory protein hemocyanin from anthropods. *Biol. Bull. (Woods Hole, Mass.)* **171**, 90–115.

Masters, W. M., and Markl, H. (1981). Vibration signal transmission in spider orb webs. *Science* **213**, 363–365.

Masters, W. M., and Moffat, A. (1983). A functional explanation of top-bottom asymmetry in vertical orb webs. *Anim. Behav.* **31**, 1043–1046.

Masters, W. M., Markl, H., and Moffat, A. (1986). Transmission of vibration in a spider's web. *In* "Spiders: Webs, Behavior and Evolution" (W. A. Shear, ed.), pp. 49–69. Stanford Univ. Press, Stanford, California.

Mayer, G. (1953). Untersuchengen über die Herstellung und Struktur des Radnetzes von *Aranea diadema* und *Zilla-x-notata* mit besonderer Berücksichtigung des Unterschiedes von Jugend- und Altersnetzen. *Z. Tierpsychol.* **9**, 337–362.

McCook, H. (1889–1893). "American Spiders and Their Spinning Work, Vols. I–III. McCook, Philadelphia, Pennsylvania.

Meredith, L. (1987). Web-building cues in the orb-weaving spider *Araneus diadematus* Clerck. Honours' Thesis, Oxford University, U. K. (unpublished).

Mittelstaedt, H. (1962). Control systems of orientation in insects. *Annu. Rev. Entomol.* **7**, 177–198.

Mittelstaedt, H. (1978). Kybernetische Analyse von Orientierungsleistungen. *Kybernetik* pp. 144–195.

Mittelstaedt, H. (1985). Analytical cybernetics of spider navigation. *In* "Neurobiology of Arachnids" (F. G. Barth, ed.), pp. 298–316. Springer-Verlag, Berlin and New York.

Mittelstaedt, H., and Mittelstaedt, M. (1973). Mechanismen der Orientierung ohne richtende Aussenreize. *Fortschr. Zool.* **21**, 46–58.

Moller, P. (1970). Die systematischen Abweichungen bei der optischen Richtungsorientierung der Trichterspinne *Agelena labyrinthica*. *Z. Vergl. Physiol.* **66**, 78–106.

Nakamura, K. (1987). Hunger and starvation. *In* "Ecophysiology of Spiders" (W. Nentwig, ed.), pp. 287–298. Springer-Verlag, Berlin and New York.

Nentwig, W. (1982). Why do only certain insects escape from a spider's web? *Oecologia* **53**, 412–417.

Nentwig, W. (1983). The non-filter function of orb webs in spiders. *Oecologia* **58**, 418–420.

Nentwig, W. (1985). Prey analysis of four species of tropical orb weaving spiders and a comparison with araneids of the temperature zone. *Oecologia* **66**, 580–594.

Nentwig, W., and Wissel, C. (1986). A comparison of prey lengths among spiders. *Oecologia* **68**, 595–600.

Olive, C. W. (1980). Foraging specialisations in orb-weaving spiders. *Ecology* **61**, 1133–1144.

Olive, C. W. (1981). Co-adapted foraging traits in a guild of orb-weaving spiders. *Oecologia* **49**, 88–91.

Olive, C. W. (1982). Behavioural response of a sit-and-wait predator to spatial variation in foraging gain. *Ecology* **63**, 912–920.

Orians, G. H., and Pearson, N. E. (1979). Central place foraging. *In* "Analysis of Ecological Systems" (D. J. Horn and G. R. Stairs, eds.), pp. 155–177. Ohio State Univ. Press, Columbia.

Papi, F., and Syrjämäki, J. (1963). The sun-orientation rhythm of wolf spiders at different latitudes. *Arch. Ital. Biol.* **101**, 59–77.

Parry, D. A., and Brown, R. H. J. (1959). The hydraulic mechanism of the spider leg. *J. Exp. Biol.* **36**, 23–433.

Pasquet, A., and Leborgne, R. (1990). Prey efficiency and prey selection from insects intercepted by trap in four orb-weaving spider species. *Acta Oecol.* **11**, 513–523.

Peters, H. M. (1932). Experimente über die Orientierung der Kreuzspinne *Epeira diademata* Cl. im Netz. *Zool Jahrb Abt. Allg. Zool. Physiol. Tiere* **51**, 239–288.

Peters, H. M. (1937a). Studien am Netz der Kreuzspinne (*Aranea diadema* L.). I. Die Grundstruktur des Netzes und Beziehungen zum Bauplan des Spinnenkörpers. *Z. Morphol. Oekol. Tiere* **32**, 613–649.

Peters, H. M. (1937b). Studien am Netz der Kreuzspinne (*Aranea diadema* L). II. Über die Herstellung des Rahmens, der Radialfäden und der Hilfsspirale. *Z. Morphol. Oekol. Tiere* **33**, 128–150.

Peters, H. M. (1939). Probleme des Kreuzspinnennetzes. *Z. Morphol. Oekol. Tiere* **36**, 179–266.

Peters, H. M. (1947). Zur Geometrie des Spinnenetzes. *Z. NaturforschB: Anorg. Chem., Org. Chem., Biochem., Biophys., Biol.* **2b**, 227–232.

Peters, H. M. (1953). Beiträge zur vergleichenden Ethologie und Ökologie tropischer Webspinnen. *Z. Morphol. Oekol. Tiere* **42**, 278–306.

Peters, H. M. (1954). Worauf beruht die Ordnung im Spinnen-Netz? *Umschau* **54**, 368–370.

Peters, H. M. (1987). Fine structure and function of capture threads. *In* "Ecophysiology of Spiders" (W. Nentwig, ed.), pp. 187–202. Springer-Verlag, Berlin and New York.

Peters, H. M. (1989). On the structure and glandular origin of bridging lines used by spiders for moving to distant places. *Acta Zool. Fenn.* **190**, 309–314.

Peters, P. J. (1970). Orb web construction: Interaction of spider *Araneus diadematus* (Cl.) and thread configuration. *Anim. Behav.* **18**, 478–484.

Pyke, G. H. (1983). Animal movements: An optimal foraging approach. *In* "The Ecology of Animal Movement" (I. R. Swingland and P. J. Greenwood, eds.), pp. 7–31. Oxford Univ. Press, Oxford.

Pyke, G. H., Pulliam, H. R., and Charnov, E. R., (1977). Optimal foraging: A selective review of theory and tests. *Q. Rev. Biol.* **52**, 137–154.

Ramousse, R. (1980). Temporal patterns of web-building in *Araneus diadematus* Clerck. *Proc. Int. Congr. Arachnol. 8th*, pp. 257–260.

Ramousse, R., and Le Guelte, L. (1979). Relations spatio-temporelles dans le comportement constructeur chez l'Epeire diadème. *Rev. Arachnol.* **2**, 183–192.

Randall, J. B. (1981). Regeneration and autotomy exhibited by the black widow spider, *Latrodectus variolus* Walckenaer. *Wilhelm Roux's, Arch. Dev. Biol.* **190**, 230–232.

Rawlins, J. O., and Witt, P. N. (1973). Appendix: Preliminary data on a possible genetic component in web-building. *In* "Behavioral Genetics: Simple Systems" (J. R. Wilson, ed.), pp. 128–133. Colorado Assoc. Univ. Press, Bolder.

Rayor, L. S., and Uetz, G. W. (1990). Trade-offs in foraging success and predation risk with spatial position in colonial spiders. *Behav. Ecol. Sociobiol.* **27**, 77–87.

Reed, C. (1969). Order of radius construction in the orb web. *Bull. Mus. Natl. Hist. Nat.* [2] **41**, 85–87.

Reed, C. F., Witt, P. N., and Jones, R. L. (1965). The measuring function of the first legs of *Araneus diadematus* Cl. *Behaviour* **25**, 98–119.

Reed, C. F., Witt, P. N., Scarboro, M. B., and Peakall, D. B. (1970). Experience and the orb web. *Dev. Psychobiol.* **3**, 251–265.

Riechert, S. E. (1978). Games spiders play: Behavioral variability in territorial disputes. *Behav. Ecol. Sociobiol.* **3**, 135–162.

Riechert, S. E. (1979). Games spiders play. II. Resource assessment strategies. *Behav. Ecol. Sociobiol.* **6**, 121–128.

Riechert, S. E. (1985). Decisions in multiple goal contexts: Habitat selection of the spider, *Agelenopsis aperta* (Gertsch). *Z. Tierpsychol.* **70**, 53–69.

Riechert, S. E., and Gillespie, R. (1986). Habitat choice and utilisation in web-building spiders. *In* "Spiders: Webs, Behavior, and Evolution" (W. A. Shear, ed.), pp. 23–49. Stanford Univ. Press, Stanford, California.

Riechert, S. E., and Luczak, J. (1982). Spider foraging: Behavioral responses to prey. *In* "Spider Communication" (P. N. Witt and J. Rovner, eds.), pp. 353–386. Princeton Univ. Press, Princeton, New Jersey.

Riechert, S. E., and Maynard Smith, J. (1989). Genetic analysis of two behavioral traits linked to individual fitness in the desert spider *Agelenopsis aperta*. *Anim. Behav.* **37**, 624–637.

Risch, P. (1977). Quantitative analysis of orb web-patterns in four species of spiders. *Behav. Genet.* **7**, 199–238.

Robinson, M. H. (1975). The evolution of predatory behaviour in araneid spiders. *In* "Function and Evolution in Behaviour" (G. Baerends, C. Beer, and A. Manning, eds.), pp. 292–312. Oxford Univ. Press (Clarendon), Oxford.

Robinson, M. H., and Lubin, Y. D. (1979). Specialists and generalists: The ecology and behavior of some web-building spiders from Papua New Guinea. I. *Herenia ornatissima, Argiope ocaloides* and *Arachnura melanura* (Araneae: Araneidae). *Pac. Insects* **21**, 97–132.

Robinson, M. H., and Robinson, B. (1980). Comparative studies of the courtship and mating behavior of tropical araneid spiders. *Pac. Insects Monogr.* **36**, 1–218.

Roth, V. D., and Roth, B. M. (1984). A review of appendotomy in spiders and other arachnids. *Bull. Br. Arachnol. Soc.* **6**, 137–146.

Rypstra, A. L. (1983). The importance of food and space in limiting web-spider densities: A test using field enclosures. *Oecologia* **59**, 312–316.

Rypstra, A. L. (1984). A relative measure of predation on web-spiders in temperate and tropical forests. *Oikos* **43**, 129–132.

Rypstra, A. L. (1989). Foraging success of solitary and aggregated spiders: insights into flock formation. *Anim. Behav.* **37**, 274–281.

Schoener, T. W., and Spiller, D. A. (1987). High population persistence in a system with high turnover. *Nature (London)* **330**, 474–477.

Schöne, H. (1981). Orientation. *In* "The Oxford Companion of Animal Behavior" (D. McFarland, ed.), pp. 429–438. Oxford Univ. Press, Oxford.

Searle, D. (1991). The anchorpoints of the *Araneus* orb web. Honours' Thesis, Oxford University, U. K. (unpublished).

Selden, P. A. (1989). Orb-web weaving spiders in the early Cretaceous. *Nature (London)* **340**, 711.

Seyfarth, E.-A., Hergenröder, R., Ebbes, H., and Barth, F. G. (1982). Idiothetic orientation of a wandering spider—Compensation of detours and etimate of goal distance. *Behav. Ecol. Sociobiol.* **11**, 139–148.

Seyfarth, E.-A., Gnatzy, W., and Hammer, K. (1990). Coxal hair plates in spiders: Physiology, fine structure, and specific central projections. *J. Comp. Physiol., A* **166**, 633–642.

Shear, W. A., ed. (1986a). "Spiders: Webs, Behavior, and Evolution." Stanford Univ. Press, Stanford, California.

Shear, W. A. (1986b). The evolution of web-building behavior in spiders: A third generation of hypotheses. *In* "Spiders: Webs, Behavior, and Evolution" (W. A. Shear, ed.), pp. 364–402. Stanford Univ. Press, Stanford, California.

Shear, W. A., Palmer, J. M., Coddington, J. A., and Bonamo, P. M. (1989). A Devonian spinneret: Early evidence of spiders and silk use. *Science* **246**, 479–481.

Spiller, D. A., and Schoener, T. W. (1989). Effect of a major predator on grouping of an orb-weaving spider. *J. Anim. Ecol.* **58**, 509–523.

Stowe, M. (1986). Prey specialisation in the araneidae *In* "Spiders: Webs, Behavior, and Evolution" (W. A. Shear), pp. 101–131. Stanford Univ. Press, Stanford, California.

Szlep, R. (1952). On the plasticity of instinct of a garden spider (*Aranea diadema*), construction of a cobweb. *Acta. Biol. Exp.* **16**, 5–22.

Szlep, R. (1966). Evolution of the web spinning activities: The web spinning in *Titanoeca albomaculata* Luc. (Araneae: Amaurobiidae). *Isr. J. Zool.* **15**, 83–88.

Thompson, D. W. (1971). "On Growth and Form" (abridged edition, J. T. Bonner, ed.). Cambridge Univ. Press, Cambridge, U. K.

Thorell, T. (1886). On Dr. Bertkau's classification of the order Araneae, or spiders. *Ann. Mag. Nat. Hist.* [5] **17**, 301–326.

Tillinghast, E. K., and Townley, M. (1987). Chemistry, physical properties, and synthesis of Araneidae orb webs. *In* "Ecophysiology of Spiders" (W. Nentwig, ed.), pp. 203–210. Spinger-Verlag, Berlin and New York.

Tilquin, A. (1942). "La toile géometrique des araignées." Presses Univ. Fr., Paris.

Tinbergen, N. (1951). "The Study of Instinct." Oxford Univ. Press, Oxford.

Tolbert, W. W. (1979). Thermal stress of the orb weaving spider *Argiope trifasciata* (Araneae). *Oikos* **32**, 386–392.

Tolman, E. C. (1948). Cognitive maps in rats and men. *Psychol. Rev.* **55**, 189–208.

Toft, S. (1983). Life cycles of *Meta segementata* and *Meta mengei* in Western Europe. *Verh. Naturwiss. Ver. Hamburg* **26**, 265–276.

Turnbull, A. L. (1964). The search for prey by a web-building spider *Achearanea tepidariorum* (Araneae, Theridiidae). *Can. Entomol.* **96**, 568–579.

Turnbull, A. L. (1973). Ecology of the true spiders (Araneomorpha). *Annu. Rev. Entomol.* **18**, 305–348.

Uetz, G. W. (1988). Risk sensitivity and foraging in colonial spiders. *In* "The Ecology of Social Behaviour" (C. N. Slobodchikoff, ed.), pp. 353–378. Academic Press, New York.

Uetz, G., Johnson, A., and Schemski, D. (1978). Web placement, structure, and prey capture in orb-weaving spiders. *Bull. Br. Arachnol. Soc.* **4**, 141–148.

Vogel, H. (1923). Über die Spaltsinnesorgane der Radnetzspinnen. *Jena. Z. Naturwiss.* **59**, 171–208.

Vollrath, F. (1979). Vibrations: Their signal function for a spider kleptoparasite. *Science* **205**, 1149–1151.

Vollrath, F. (1980). Male body size and fitness in the web-building spider Nephila clavipes. *Z. Tierpsychol.* **53**, 61–78.

Vollrath, F. (1985). Web spider's dilemma: A risky move or site dependent growth. *Oecologia* **68**, 69–72.

Vollrath, F. (1986). Gravity as orientation guide during web-construction in the orb spider Araneus diadematus. *J. Comp. Physiol. A* **159**, 275–280.

Vollrath, F. (1987a). Spiders with regenerated legs can build normal webs. *Nature (London)* **328**, 247–248.

Vollrath, F. (1987b). Foraging, growth and reproductive success. *In* "Ecophysiology of Spiders" (W. Nentwig, ed.), pp. 357–370. Springer-Verlag, Berlin and New York.

Vollrath, F. (1988a). Spiral orientation of *Araneus diadematus* orb webs built during vertical rotation. *J. Comp. Physiol.* **162**, 413–419.

Vollrath, F. (1988b). Untangling the spider's web. *Trends Ecol. Evol.* **3**, 331–335.

Vollrath, F. (1988c). Deducing habitat quality from spider growth. *Bull. Br. Arachnol. Soc.* **7**, 217–219.

Vollrath, F. (1989). Regenerating araneid lyriform organs: Morphology and function. *In* "Neural Mechanisms of Behavior" (R. M. J. Erber, H. J. Pflüger, and D. Todt, eds.), p. 34. Thieme, Stuttgart.

Vollrath, F. (1990). Leg regeneration in web spiders and its implications for orb weaver phylogeny. *Bull. Br. Arachnol. Soc.* **8**, 177–184.

Vollrath, F., and ApRhisiart, A. (1992). Analysis of *Araneus* orb web-geometry. In preparation.

Vollrath, F., and Edmonds, D. (1989). Modulation of normal spider silk by coating with water. *Nature (London)* **340**, 305–307.

Vollrath, F., and Houston, A. (1986). Previous experience and site tenacity in the orb spider *Nephila clavipes*. *Oecologia* **70**, 305–308.

Vollrath, F., and Mohren, W. (1985). Spiral geometry of the garden spider's orb web. *Naturwissenschaften* **72**, 666–667.

Vollrath, F., and Tillinghast, E. K. (1991). Glycoprotein glue inside a spider web's aqueous coat. *Naturwissenschaften* **78**, in press.

Vollrath, F., Fairbrother, W. J., Williams, R. J. P., Tillinghast, E. K., Bernstein, D. T., Gallagher, K. S., and Townley, M. A. (1990). Compounds in the droplets of the orb spider's viscid spiral. *Nature (London)* **345**, 526–528.

Walcott, C. (1969). A spiders vibration receptor: Its anatomy and physiology. *Am. Zool.* **9**, 133–144.

Webster, N. (1967). "Webster's 9th Collegiate Dictionary." G. & C. Merriam Company, Springfield, Massachusetts.

Wehner, R. (1983). Celestial and terrestrial navigation: Human strategies—Insect strategies. *In* "Neuroethology and Behavioral Physiology" (F. Huber and F. H. Markl, eds.), pp. 366–381. Springer-Verlag, Berlin and New York.

Wehner, R. (1987). Matched filters—Neural models of the external world. *J. Comp. Physiol. A* **161**, 511–531.

Whener, R., and Wehner, S. (1986). Path integration in desert ants. Approaching a long-standing puzzle in insect navigation. *Monit. Zool. Ital.* **20**, 309–331.

Wehner, R., Harkness, R. D., and Schmid-Hempel, P. (1983). "Foraging Strategies in Individually Searching Ants." Fischer, Stuttgart.

Wehner, R., Bleuler, S., Nievergelt, C., and Shah, D. (1990). Bees navigate by using vectors and routes rather than maps. *Naturwissenschaften* **77**, 479–482.

Weissmann, M. (1987). Web-building and prey capture in two orb weavers. MSc. Thesis, University of Oxford, U. K.

Wiehle, H. (1928). Beiträge zur Biologie der Araneen, insbesondere zur Kenntnis des Radnetzbaues. *Z. Morphol. Oekol. Tiere* **11**, 115–151.

Wise, D. H. (1975). Food limitation of the spider *Linyphia marginata* experimental field studies. *Ecology* **56**, 637–646.

Witt, P. N., Reed, C. F., and Peakall, D. B. (1968). "A Spider's Web: Problems in Regulatory Biology." Springer-Verlag, Berlin and New York.

Witt, P. N., Scarboro, M. P., Daniels, R., Peakall, D. B., and Gause, R. (1977). Spider web-building in outer space: Evaluation of records from the Skylab spider experiment. *Am. J. Arachnol.* **4**, 115–124.

Work, R. (1985). Viscoelastic behavior and wet super contraction of major ampullate silk fibres of certain orb web building spiders (Araneae). *J. Exp. Biol.* **118**, 379–404.

Zemlin, J. C. (1968). "A Study of the Mechanical Behavior of Spider Silks." Clothing and Organic Materials Laboratory, U. S. Army Natick Labs.

Zschokke, S., and Vollrath, F. (1992). Unfreezing spider behavior: Orb-geometry and orb-construction. In preparation.

Motor Aspects of Masculine Sexual Behavior in Rats and Rabbits

GABRIELA MORALÍ

DIVISIÓN DE NEUROCIENCIAS
UNIDAD DE INVESTIGACIÓN BIOMÉDICA DEL CMN
INSTITUTO MEXICANO DEL SEGURO SOCIAL
MÉXICO DF 03020, MEXICO

CARLOS BEYER

CENTRO DE INVESTIGACIÓN EN REPRODUCCIÓN ANIMAL
CINVESTAV-UAT
TLAXCALA 90000, MEXICO

I. Introduction

Copulation is a component of the sequence of events comprising sexual behavior. As Dewsbury (1979) has noted, a complete sequence of sexual behavior includes "courtship" or precopulatory behavior, copulation, termination, and sequelae to copulation. Of all the components of sexual behavior, copulation has been by far the most studied, not only from the behavioral side, but also as a convenient end point of the effect of hormones and neuroactive drugs on the brain (Larsson, 1979; Sachs and Meisel, 1988). We also have more information on the neural basis of copulation than on the other components of sexual behavior (see Larsson, 1979). However, in spite of the wealth of information on copulatory behavior, particularly in rodents, there have been few studies directed to establish the form or "morphology" of the various behavioral patterns involved in copulation. This type of study aims to describe the motor events involved in copulatory behaviors, including the patterning, strength, and duration of muscular contractions. This descriptive basis is a prerequisite for tackling other problems more directly related to the causation and function of behavior.

Male copulation involves the activation of three distinct, though interacting, components: (1) a motor component involving the contraction and relaxation of muscles involved in copulatory movements; (2) an external genital component

201

involving the penile responses participating in erection and penile insertion into the vagina; and (3) an internal genital component involving the pattern of contraction of the various organs participating in seminal emission and ejaculation. Ideally, a full understanding of copulation, and the functional significance of copulatory behavior, requires precise information on the interactions occurring among these three components.

The present article deals with the following topics: (1) the morphology of male copulatory behavior and its penile and visceral correlates in two representative species: the rat and the rabbit; (2) the morphology of pseudomale behavior, that is, malelike sexual behavior performed by females; (3) the neuromotor apparatus involved in the production of the male copulatory motor pattern; and (4) the effect of sex hormones in the differentiation and expression of the male and pseudomale copulatory motor patterns. Initially, we will describe some of the techniques used in our laboratories for the quantitative analysis of copulatory behavior.

II. Polygraphic Techniques for the Analysis of the Motor and Genital Components of the Male Copulatory Pattern

The morphological approach to the study of behavior requires accurate measurements of motor actions. However, in contrast to behavioral phenotypes such as sound, which can be precisely measured by sonagraphic analysis, motor patterns are difficult to analyze in a quantitative manner. Some advances have been made in the morphology of copulation by the use of high-speed cinematography (Bermant, 1965; Stone and Ferguson, 1940) and videotape recording (Sachs and Barfield, 1976) with subsequent analysis in slow motion. The use of these techniques, however, has been limited due to the fact that they are expensive or time consuming. Besides this, they do not provide quantitative information on the "size" of the motor action but only on its duration. An important advance in methods for the study of copulatory behavior was introduced by Rubin and Azrin (1967). These investigators designed an electric circuit that was closed when moist contact between the penis and the vagina of a copulating pair was established. The use of this device permitted the establishment of the precise duration of penile insertions during intromission and ejaculatory patterns in the rat (Peirce and Nuttall, 1961; Carlsson and Larsson, 1962) and similar details of the intromission associated with ejaculation in the rabbit (Rubin and Azrin, 1967). This technique, however, does not provide information about the copulatory motor activities themselves.

More recently, we (Contreras and Beyer, 1979; Beyer et al., 1981) introduced an "accelerometric" technique that permits the precise quantification of some motor aspects of copulation. With this technique, the accurate measurement of several parameters of the male copulatory motor pattern is achieved by placing an acceleration transducer on the male's back. The accelerometer is not sensitive to velocity; hence, if the object to which it is attached moves at a constant speed in the same direction, the transducer response is minimal. On the other hand, if, as is the case with repetitive pelvic thrusting, the object is alternately moving in one direction (forward) then in another (backward), the rapid changes in acceleration generate electrical signals that can be easily recorded following adequate amplification on a polygraph or on an oscilloscope (Fig. 1). The accelerometric technique allows the precise measurement of the following parameters: (1) duration of individual pelvic thrusts; (2) frequency of pelvic thrusting, that is, number of pelvic thrusts per sec; (3) acceleration of pelvic movements; (4) amplitude of pelvic thrusts; and (5) duration of mounting trains, that is, uninterrupted series of pelvic thrusts. When combined with power spectrum analysis, this technique also gives information on the rhythmicity of pelvic thrusting (Fig. 2). Figure 2 presents some images obtained when power spectrum analysis is added "on line" to the acceler-

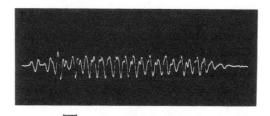

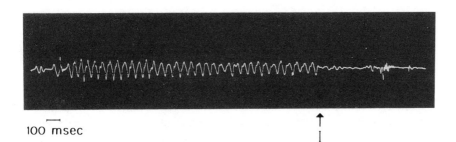

100 msec

FIG. 1. Typical oscilloscope records of signals generated by two successive mounting trains performed by an intact male rabbit carrying an accelerometer. Note the highly synchronic activity generated by pelvic thrusting and the small variation in the amplitude of the signals. Intromission (I) that occurred in the second mount (lower record) is marked by the vertical arrow. Pelvic thrusting is interrupted when intromission occurs. (From Beyer *et al.*, 1980. Reproduced with permission.)

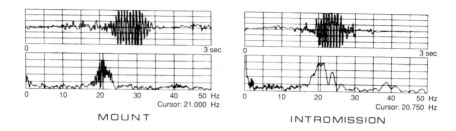

MOUNT   INTROMISSION

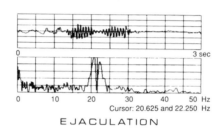

EJACULATION

FIG. 2. Power frequency spectrum analysis of the pelvic movements performed by an intact male rat during a typical mount, intromission, and a long ejaculation pattern. Upper graphs: record of the signals generated by the accelerometer during the behavioral responses. Lower graphs: frequency spectrum analysis (range: 0 to 50 Hz) of the signals generated during an 8-sec period within which individual responses were performed. The peak and dispersion of the spectrum give an estimation of the rhythmicity of the thrusting train. Note that the frequency analysis in both the mount and the intromission reveals a single component around the 18 to 22 Hz band, corresponding to the predominant frequency (F) of pelvic movements (cursor location at the peak indicates a value of 21.00 Hz for the mount and 20.75 Hz for the intromission pattern). The frequency analysis in the ejaculation pattern reveals two components (F = 20.625 and 22.250 Hz) associated with the two (extra and intravaginal) phases of pelvic thrusting.

ometric technique. As can be seen, for a selected range of frequencies (1 to 50 Hz), a spectrum is provided whose peak and dispersion give an estimation of the periodicity of the thrusting train.

To obtain information on some penile–vaginal interactions, the accelerometric technique is combined with the detection of genital contacts at copulation by using a modification of the electric circuit previously described by Rubin and Azrin (1967). As can be seen in Fig. 3, precise timing of penile insertion into the vagina, as well as durations of penile insertions during intromissions or ejaculations, can be obtained with the use of this technique.

In nearly all studies of sexual behavior, only the motor, nongenital aspects of copulation are analyzed. Therefore, there is scarce information about the com-

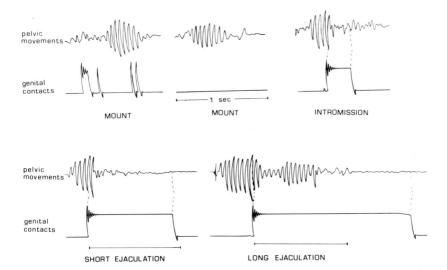

FIG. 3. Polygraphic recordings of both the signals generated by the accelerometer in relation to the pelvic movements of an intact male rat during typical mounts, intromission, and ejaculation patterns, and the genital contacts (as determined by using an intromission detection circuit) occurring during these behavioral responses. Note the fusiform organization of the mounting train. Only brief, occasional, or no genital contacts occur during mounts. Note the occurrence and duration of penile insertion during the intromission and the ejaculation thrusting trains. Two types of ejaculatory patterns can be recognized: short ejaculations, in which a brief period of intravaginal thrusting precedes ejaculation, and long ejaculations, showing different dynamic organization and in which a clear period of intravaginal thrusting (not previously demonstrated) is revealed by this combined methodology.

plex interactions between the copulatory movements, controlled by motor nerves, and the activity of the genital organs, controlled by autonomic nerves. Information about the activity of the internal genitalia, essential for a precise timing of the occurrence and duration of seminal emission and ejaculation, can be obtained by chronically implanting a catheter in the seminal vesicles. Changes in tone or contractions of this organ result in alterations in pressure that are continuously recorded with a polygraph linked to a pressure transducer (Fig. 4).

Therefore, through the use of the polygraphic methodology described above, and in combination with observational techniques, it is possible not only to quantitatively analyze the male copulatory motor pattern, but also to relate these events to penile–vaginal interactions and reflex responses of the male ejaculatory apparatus.

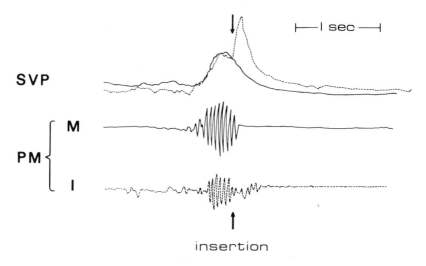

FIG. 4. Accelerometric records of pelvic movements (PM) of a copulating male rat during a mount (M) and an intromission pattern (I). In the upper tracing, the seminal vesicle pressure (SVP) change obtained during the intromission (dotted line) was drawn superimposed on the SVP record obtained during the performance of the mount. Note that the SVP response associated with mounting was similar in both behavioral patterns, and that penile insertion triggers a further sharp rise superimposed on the former one. (From Beyer *et al.*, 1982. Reproduced with permission.)

III. MORPHOLOGY OF THE MASCULINE COPULATORY MOTOR PATTERN IN THE RAT

A. HOMOTYPICAL BEHAVIOR

Stone and Ferguson (1940) recognized in the early 1940s that there are three stereotyped motor patterns in the masculine sexual behavior of the rat: mounts, intromission patterns, and ejaculation patterns (see also Bermant, 1965; Dewsbury, 1979; Larsson, 1956, 1979; Sachs and Barfield, 1976; Beyer, 1979). In all of them, climbing onto the female is accompanied by fast forepaw palpations of her flanks and the execution of even faster pelvic thrusting against the female's rump. Intromissive patterns apparently consist of a mount terminated by a deep pelvic thrust followed by a rapid dismount in which the male pushes vigorously away from the female and spreads his forepaws wide as he falls backward. Performance of several intromissions is normally required by male rats to ejaculate. Ejaculatory patterns are characterized by mounts terminated by a pelvic thrust prolonged for several seconds (2 or 3 sec) while repeated flexures of the hindquarters occur (Larsson, 1956; Young, 1961). During intromissive and ejaculatory patterns, insertion of the penis into the vagina is usually achieved. However, male rats may occasionally exhibit intromission patterns without the occurrence of intravaginal penile insertion. Furthermore, female rats may display intromissive and even ejaculatory patterns in the absence of the phallic development necessary to achieve penetration. Thus, the terms "intromissive pattern" and "ejaculation pattern" are used by most workers to refer solely to the expression of the corresponding motor patterns. In this context, the term "ejaculatory pattern" does not necessarily imply the expulsion of seminal material.

Several measures of copulatory behavior have been based on the identification of these three behavioral patterns and on the description of their temporal course. The description of the temporal pattern of copulatory behavior requires the determination of the mount latency, the number of mounts, the intromission latency, the number of intromissions, the ejaculation latency, and the postejaculatory interval (for a discussion of the use and value of these measures, see Sachs and Barfield, 1976). Derived measures such as the number of intromissions per minute or its inverse, the interintromission interval (Larsson, 1956), allow an estimate of the speed with which responses follow each other within a copulatory series, that is, within the sequence of mounts and intromissions culminating in ejaculation (Larsson, 1956). Another useful parameter is the rate of intromission in relation to the total number of mounts with and without intromission within a copulatory series. This measure, the so-called hit rate (Sachs and Barfield, 1976), gives information on the efficiency in the performance of copulation in the rat. Additionally, Sachs and Barfield (1970) have described the clustering of mounts and intromissions within a copulatory series in what they have called "mount bouts." These are composed of groups of one or more mounts or intromissions that are not interrupted by noncopulatory behaviors, except genital grooming or orientation movements of the male toward the female. These clusters are displayed independently of whether the male achieves intromissions or not. The intervals between these mount bouts, as well as their periodicity, have given valuable information (Lodder and Zeilmaker, 1976a; Pollak and Sachs, 1976; Sachs and Barfield, 1970). A thorough discussion of these measures, as well as their functional significance, is found in a review by Sachs and Meisel (1988).

The polygraphic analysis of the three behavioral copulatory patterns can reveal their form and fine organization. As can be seen from the accelerometric tracings in Fig. 3, mounts generate a series of synchronized signals of similar duration (mean $\pm$ SD: 54 ± 3 msec) but variable amplitude. The initial and last signals of a mounting train are usually of lower amplitude than the middle ones, giving the typical mount pattern a fusiform (spindle-shaped) appearance. Because the amplitude of the movement is related to the area under the curve generated by the pelvic thrust, for pelvic waves of similar duration, height is a good indicator of the pelvic displacement. Nearly all mounts were composed of 6 to 12 pelvic thrusts. Average duration of the mounts was 380 ± 80 msec (mean ± SD) (Beyer *et al.*, 1981). When using the intromission detection circuit, it can be seen that during a typical mount, none or only occasional, brief contacts occur between the penis of the male and the vagina of the receptive female (see Fig. 3) (Moralí *et al.*, 1983). Frequency spectrum analysis reveals that pelvic thrusting during mounting is periodic, usually with a frequency of thrusting clustering at between 18 to 22 Hz (see Fig. 2). When seminal vesicle pressure (SVP) recordings are also made (see Fig. 4), it can be seen that mounts may be associated with a slight increase in SVP, which appears in 52% of mounts as a single wave (Beyer *et al.*, 1982). This wave starts shortly before pelvic thrusting and peaks before termination of thrusting (see Fig. 4).

Pelvic thrusting trains at the intromission patterns are shorter in duration than at mounts (mean ± SD: 314 ± 70 msec) and are indistinguishable from them in their initial part, but differ in showing a final period of irregular broad signals coinciding with penile insertion and withdrawal (see Fig. 3). Usually, penile insertion is associated with a vigorous thrust, that is, a thrust of large amplitude, occurring after four to seven pelvic thrusts. Penile insertion into the vagina lasts an average of 410 ± 150 msec, mean ± SD (Moralí *et al.*, 1983), during which period no pelvic thrusting occurs. Figure 4 shows the typical change in SVP occurring during intromission patterns. As in the case of mounts, an increase in SVP occurs during pelvic thrusting, this rise being similar in shape and amplitude to that observed during the mount pattern. Yet, coinciding with penile insertion, a further sharp rise in SVP occurs. Thus, the increase in SVP during intromission consists of two components: a small, initial, relatively gradual rise, corresponding to thrusting, and a steeper rise, associated with intromission itself. The duration of the pressure rise is longer for intromissions than for mounts (Beyer *et al.*, 1982).

Pelvic thrusting trains at ejaculation last much longer than at either mounts or intromissions. The use of the accelerometric technique reveals two types of ejaculatory pattern in the male rat: long and short (Beyer *et al.*, 1982). These two patterns differ not only in their duration but also in their organization. As shown in Figs. 3 and 5, four successive phases are distinguished in long ejaculatory patterns (mean duration of the long ejaculatory thrusting train ± SD is 1041 ± 90 msec). During the first phase, preceding penile insertion, vigorous thrusting produces high amplitude signals; the second brief phase, corresponding to penile insertion, is characterized by low amplitude signals; during the third phase, repetitive intravaginal thrusting takes place and the signals (i.e., amplitude of thrusts) may increase in amplitude again (Fig. 5). The first three phases follow one another without interruption and culminate in the fourth phase, during which seminal emission and ejaculation occur. This last phase is characterized by irregular pelvic movements previous to penile withdrawal. The accelerometric recording combined with the use of the insertion detection circuit demonstrates

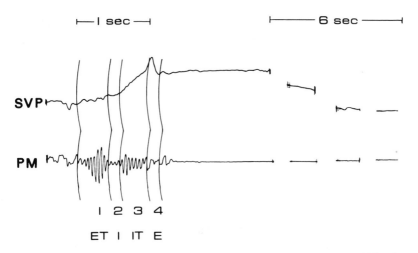

FIG. 5. Characteristics of pelvic movements (PM) and seminal vesicle pressure (SVP) changes during a long ejaculation pattern of a rat. Four different phases can be recognized in this motor pattern, accompanied by successive rises in SVP. Note the smooth gradual rise in SVP during the initiation of mounting and the sharp rises during penile insertion (I) and intravaginal thrusting (IT). ET, extravaginal thrusting; E, seminal emission. (From Beyer *et al.*, 1982. Reproduced with permission).

the existence of a period of intravaginal thrusting that had not been previously demonstrated by observational techniques (see Fig. 3). Power frequency spectrum analysis reveals in some cases that extravaginal thrusting in long ejaculations has a slightly higher frequency (around 1 to 2 Hz more) than intravaginal thrusting (see Fig. 2). In some other cases, it is possible that the two peaks of the frequency spectrum analysis merge in one broader wave, giving the impression that thrusting during the ejaculatory pattern would be slightly less rhythmic than during mounts or intromissions.

As shown in Fig. 3, short ejaculatory motor patterns (mean duration ± SD: 679 ± 160 msec) cannot be distinguished from an intromission on the basis of pelvic thrusting pattern. That is, a single thrusting phase of gradually increasing amplitude is seen, which culminates in a series of irregular pelvic movements associated with seminal emission. Thus, short ejaculations, in contrast to long ejaculations, do not show a clear differentiation between the extravaginal and the intravaginal thrusting phases. However, with the use of the intromission detection circuit, the occurrence and duration of penile insertion during short ejaculatory patterns are easily determined (see Fig. 3). The intravaginal thrusting phase of short ejaculation patterns usually involves only a few pelvic thrusts, in some cases only one or two (see Fig. 3). As in the case of mounting and intromission patterns, a smooth gradual rise in SVP occurs during the initiation of mounting in the ejaculatory trains, followed by a change in the slope of the curve associated with penile insertion (see Fig. 5). After a variable period of intravaginal thrusting, a further steep rise in SVP takes place and then declines just prior to the end of the ejaculatory pattern. This last phasic rise associated with seminal emission lasts approximately 100 msec. Thereafter, the SVP falls to its previous level, that is, to the maximum level that occurred during intravaginal thrusting (Fig. 5). After ejaculation, SVP remains above the baseline (pre-copulatory level) for variable periods, which are, however, longer than those observed in either mounts or intromissions.

B.   HETEROTYPICAL SEXUAL BEHAVIOR (PSEUDOMALE BEHAVIOR) IN THE RAT

The display of malelike sexual behavior is not exclusively shown by genetically male individuals. Thus, females of most mammalian species apparently possess the neuromotor apparatus required for the execution of male sexual behavior (Baum, 1979; Beach, 1968; Moralí and Beyer, 1979; Morris, 1955; Young, 1961). This conclusion is based on the observation that females of various species often show some or all the components of male copulation (for a review, see Beach, 1968). Morris (1955) suggested the term "pseudomale behavior" to describe those masculine patterns displayed by females. The term "pseudomale" implicitly considers the possibility that this behavior is not identical to that of the male. However, several investigators have concluded from pure observational techniques that male and pseudomale behavior are similar or even identical, at least in species such as the rat (Beach, 1942), dog (Beach et al., 1968), sheep (Fabre, 1977), rabbit (Yaschine et al., 1967), and guinea pig (Young, 1961).

Female rats display mount and intromission patterns superficially similar to those of males (Beach, 1942). Moreover, under particular experimental circumstances, like neonatal androgenization (see Baum, 1979; Gerall and Ward, 1966; Harris and Levine, 1965), long-term treatment with estrogen (Emery and Sachs, 1975), treatment with PCPA, a serotonin depletor (Emery and Sachs, 1976), or after painful stimulation (Barfield and Krieger, 1977), female rats can display the ejaculatory pattern. However, the morphology of pseudomale behavior has never been quantitatively compared with that of male sexual behavior in any species.

As seen in Fig. 6, a great similarity was found in the temporal organization and even in the vigor of the mounting and intromission motor patterns of female and male rats (Moralí et al., 1985). Power spectrum analysis of the frequency of the signals generated during mount and intromission patterns of intact female and male rats showed similar values (20 to 22 Hz) in both sexes, as well as similar rhythmicity and regularity (see Fig. 6). A longer duration of mounts in females was the only significant difference between the sexes.

The ejaculatory pattern was also compared between sexes by using neonatally

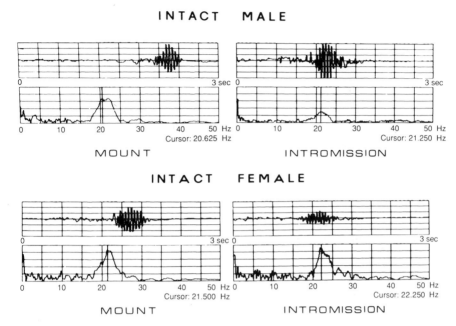

FIG. 6. Frequency analysis of the pelvic movements performed by intact male and female rats during typical mount and intromission patterns. Upper graphs: record of the signals generated by the accelerometer during the behavioral responses. Note the similar fusiform organization of male and female mounting patterns. Lower graphs: frequency spectrum analysis (range: 0 to 50 Hz) of the signals generated during an 8-sec period within which individual responses occurred. Note that the peak value corresponding to the predominant frequency (F) of pelvic thrusting, and the dispersion of the spectrum, as an indicator of rhythmicity, is similar between male and female responses. (From Moralí *et al.*, 1985. Reproduced with permission.)

androgenized females. Neonatally androgenized females displayed the ejaculatory pattern, in contrast to nontreated females who only showed mounts and intromissions. Although only two ejaculatory responses were displayed by our neonatally androgenized females, both were similar to the long ejaculatory pattern of male rats, with the only difference that the phase of low amplitude thrusts that normally coincides with penile insertion in males was not evident in females (Fig. 7).

C. Stereotypy and Sexual Isomorphism of the Male Copulatory Pattern in Rats

Analysis of the results obtained with the polygraphic technique confirms the belief that some aspects of male copulatory behavior in the rat are highly stereotyped or fixed. Thus, both the duration of individual pelvic thrusts and the

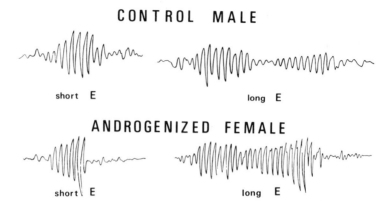

FIG. 7. Typical accelerometric records of the two types of ejaculatory patterns displayed by control male rats and by neonatally androgenized females. Note that the dynamic organization and temporal characteristics of the short ejaculatory patterns (short E) are similar in both sexes. The long ejaculatory patterns (long E) showed by neonatally androgenized females were similar to those of males, but lacked the phase of low amplitude movements that commonly coincides with penile insertion within the vagina. (From Moralí *et al.*, 1985. Reproduced with permission.)

frequency of thrusting showed coefficients of variation (CV) well below 10%. This relative invariance of pelvic thrust duration is surprising, considering that large variations in the amplitude of the thrusts were found within a thrusting train. For example, during the long ejaculatory motor pattern, the amplitude of the individual pelvic thrusts during the initial part of penile insertion can be one fifth of the amplitude of extravaginal thrusts while having the same duration (around 50 msec). It is known that several measures of copulatory behavior, such as mount latency, interintromission interval, and so forth, may vary considerably as a function of many situational factors. Thus, the stage of the female's cycle, the size of the testing arena, the illumination, and so forth, affect some of these parameters (see Sachs and Meisel, 1988). By contrast, the characteristics of the copulatory motor pattern were context-independent, because basically similar values were obtained under different experimental situations, such as different size of the testing arena and different illumination (J. L. Contreras, G. Morali, and C. Beyer, unpublished data). However, in spite of the stereotypy of the pelvic copulatory movement, some intraindividual and interindividual variability was determined. As could be expected, interindividual variability was greater than intraindividual variability. Thus, as shown in Fig. 8, some rats would consistently show a lower thrusting frequency (slow rats) than others (fast rats). Moreover, some rats apparently performed mounts with pelvic thrusts of lower amplitude (weak rats) than most normal rats. In this case, as noted in Fig. 9, the typical fusiform appearance of mounts and intromissions disappears. Because in

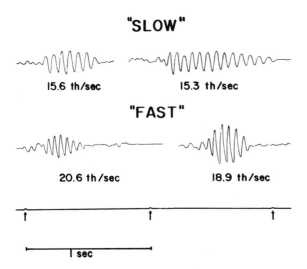

FIG. 8. Accelerometric records of mounts performed by rats that consistently showed lower thrusting frequency values (slow rats) than others (fast rats).

these studies highly estrous females were used as partners, it was not possible to determine if "weak" or "slow" mounts are less effective than normal mounts to facilitate lordosis. However, this possibility is supported by data obtained in the rabbit, to be discussed later (see Section IV,A).

A much larger variation exists in the duration of mounts, intromissions, or ejaculations, that is, in the number of pelvic thrusts comprising these motor

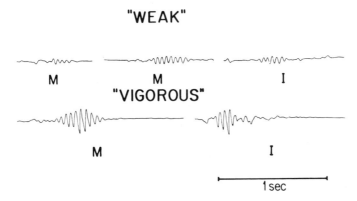

FIG. 9. Accelerometric records of mounts (M) and intromission patterns (I) in which differences (weak vs vigorous) in amplitude are seen. In low amplitude responses, the fusiform appearance of mounts and intromissions disappears.

patterns. This larger variation may be the result of variable interactions between the mounting male and the female rat, which is not a passive partner but actively provides signals throughout copulation to its sexual partner. Thus, the female rat not only needs to perform lordosis to permit insertion, but several data indicate that she moves her perineal region in the direction of the thrusting penis. Variations in these adjustive movements most likely influence duration of intromission or ejaculation. Similarly, duration of penile insertion, either during intromissions or ejaculations, are highly variable, penile insertions always carrying on beyond the period of rhythmic thrusting.

The fact that the temporal organization and even the vigor of pelvic thrusting in male and pseudomale copulatory behaviors were similar suggests that the neural substrate controlling the mounting, intromission, and even ejaculatory motor patterns are identical in both sexes. This sexual isomorphism of the male and pseudomale copulatory motor patterns in the rat strongly suggests that the organization of the neural substrate required for the expression of this behavior is genetically controlled, as was suggested by Whalen et al. (1969), for mounting. This idea is supported by the finding that variations in the neonatal concentration of androgen, owing to experimental manipulations such as the administration of androgen to newborn female rats or neonatal castration of males, did not affect the motor patterns involved in male sexual behavior (Moralí et al., 1985) (see Sections VI,A, and VI,B).

The isomorphism of male and female pelvic thrusting raises some interesting questions about the role of sensory information coming from the genitalia during copulation for the modulation of the copulatory motor pattern. The penis, the perineal skin, and male genital organs have a rich sensory innervation that is activated by the mechanical stimuli involved in copulation (Calaresu and Mitchell, 1969; McKenna and Nadelhaft, 1986; Purinton et al., 1973). Activation of these sensory receptors is involved in the autonomic reflexes related to penile erection and secretion and discharge of secretions from the sexual accessory organs (Bell, 1972; Larsson and Sodersten, 1973; Lodder and Zeilmaker, 1976a). Therefore, it would appear logical that sensory input from the penis and external genitalia would also play an important role in the fine tuning of the male copulatory motor pattern. However, from the morphological analysis of male and pseudomale behavior, one could conclude that the afferent information coming from the penis and the male genitalia during copulation has little or no effect on the motor and temporal aspects of copulation. Thus, the fact that females can display copulatory movements similar to those of males both in their vigor and temporal patterning (frequency of thrusting rhythm) indicates that the sensory information from the male genitalia (e.g., the penis) is not indispensable for the integration of the copulatory motor pattern. Moreover, the fact that the duration of the intromission pattern in females is similar to that of males rules out penile insertion as the normal stimulus for ending the intromission pattern. This could suggest that intromission duration is regulated by central, rather than by peripheral, factors. However, it is also possible that during mounting, sensory receptors in the genital and perigenital areas of the female, innervated, as is the male penis, by the pudendal nerve, would be activated to modulate intromission duration. This would explain the report that transection of the pudendal or the genitofemoral nerves in female rats abolishes the display of the intromission pattern (Lodder and Zeilmaker, 1976b).

IV. MORPHOLOGY OF THE MASCULINE COPULATORY MOTOR PATTERN IN THE RABBIT

A. HOMOTYPICAL BEHAVIOR

In contrast to the rat, copulation in the male rabbit involves only a single mount with a variable period of pelvic thrusting, depending on the readiness of the doe to show lordosis, and a single intromission during which ejaculation occurs. Following ejaculation, the male falls off the back of the doe, sometimes emitting a cry. Rubin and Azrin (1967), by passing monitored current through pairs of copulating rabbits, established some temporal characteristics of the copulatory behavior of American Dutch rabbits. Thus, they reported that these rabbits showed a rate of pelvic thrusting of 13 to 15 thrusts per sec. Figure 1 shows typical oscillographic records of the signals generated by male rabbits carrying an accelerometer during copulation (Beyer et al., 1980). Note that, after a few irregular pelvic thrusts at the beginning of mounting, the signals generated by pelvic thrusting become highly regular and periodic until penile insertion occurs, at which moment pelvic thrusting is interrupted. In some, but not all cases, the final thrusts preceding insertion are of lower amplitude and slightly longer duration. In spite of these slight changes in thrusting occurring during a mount, the duration of individual pelvic thrusts varies little (around 80 msec) both between individuals and in the same individual. On the other hand, the duration of mounting trains in males was variable. Effective mounts, that is, mounts terminating in intromission (and then in ejaculation), tended to be shorter (mean ± SD: 2.61 ± 1.50 sec) than ineffective ones (mean ± SD: 3.08 ± 2.16) (Contreras and Beyer, 1979).

Comparison of the frequencies of pelvic thrusting between effective and ineffective mounts also revealed some significant differences between them. Thus, frequency of pelvic thrusting was higher in effective than in ineffective mounts (13.5 vs 12.1 thrusts per sec). Similarly, frequency spectrum analysis revealed that ineffective mounts tended to be irregular, that is, less rhythmic than effective mounts. This suggests that the adequate stimulus to induce the lordosis posture in the female rabbit is a rhythmic "high" frequency pelvic thrusting. Interestingly, the copulatory motor pattern in the rabbit is not affected by previous sexual experience, as young rabbits isolated from females displayed normal male copulatory patterns the first time they copulated (Contreras and Beyer, 1979).

In contrast to the rat, in which pelvic thrusts follow each other in a continuous manner, in some rabbit mounts, gaps between individual thrusts may occur. Thus, changes in frequency of thrusting in the rabbit are mostly due to the intercalation of some of these short pauses in the mounting train.

Figure 10 illustrates the relationship between copulatory motor activity and the contraction of the seminal vesicles, indicative of ejaculation, in the rabbit (Contreras and Beyer, 1979). In contrast to the rat, initiation of mounting failed to alter the activity of the seminal vesicles. Shortly after intromission (mean ± SD: 230 ± 107 msec), a slow rise (mean time to peak ± SD: 260 ± 89 msec) in the pressure of the seminal vesicles was recorded (Fig. 10). Latencies to ejaculation varied somewhat among copulations and they were not related to the duration of the mount or to the order in which the copulation occurred in a copulatory series.

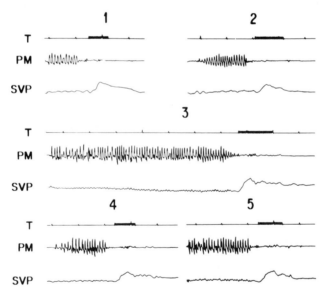

FIG. 10. Polygraphic record of five successive copulations of a male rabbit. Upper tracings: (T), time signal, and marks introduced by an observer when intromission occurred. Middle tracings: (PM), frequency and characteristics of pelvic movements recorded with an accelerometer. Note that each ejaculation was preceded by a variable period of mounting. Lower tracings: (SVP), seminal vesicle pressure. Note that pelvic thrusting is not associated with SVP changes, and that 100 to 300 msec after intromission, a gradual contraction of the seminal vesicles occurred. Note that the duration of the contraction of the seminal vesicles outlasts copulation. (From Contreras and Beyer, 1979. Reproduced with permission.)

The rise in pressure of the seminal vesicles outlasted copulation (mean ± SD: 1040 ± 369 msec). In nearly all cases, a single contraction was seen in the seminal vesicles.

B. MORPHOLOGY OF PSEUDOMALE BEHAVIOR
   ### IN THE FEMALE RABBIT

As in the case of the rat, a significant proportion of female rabbits, variable depending on the strain, display pseudomale behavior (Yaschine *et al.*, 1967). Yaschine *et al.* (1967), from an analysis of cinematographic recordings, suggested that mounts performed by female rabbits were similar to those of males. However, using the accelerometric technique, we (Soto *et al.*, 1984) found clear sexual differences in the vigor, frequency, and periodicity of pelvic thrusting displayed by mounting male and female rabbits (Fig. 11). As previously mentioned, signals generated by pelvic thrusting in male rabbits appeared in our polygraphic recordings as well-defined spikes lasting between 60 and 65 msec. Frequency spectrum analysis of these signals typically show a single peak around the 14 to 15 Hz band, indicating the rhythmical nature of thrusting in the male rabbit (Fig. 11). Display of mounting by females was variable and unpredictable. Duration of mounts was shorter in females (mean ± SD: 1.63 ± 0.41 sec) than in males. Characteristically, female mounting records were of low amplitude and were irregular, that is, weak, isolated pelvic movements of variable duration occurred during a mount (Fig. 11). As shown in Fig. 11, frequency spectrum analysis of female pelvic thrusting failed to reveal clear rhythmicity in female mounts. Only occasional pelvic thrusting records clustered around a well-defined frequency value, suggesting some rhythmicity in female mounting. However, in contrast to males, these "rhythmic" patterns were inconsistent not only among individuals but also among different mounts performed by the same individual.

C. STEREOTYPY OF THE MALE COPULATORY MOTOR PATTERN
   ### IN THE MALE RABBIT

Analysis of the various parameters of the male copulatory pattern in the rabbit shows that, as in the rat, duration of individual pelvic thrusts was highly consistent. Large variations in amplitude of individual pelvic thrusts were also observed. Thus, the pelvic thrusts preceding penile insertion were usually of lower amplitude than the previous ones, an adjustment probably related to the achievement of penile insertion. Thrusting frequency varied more both among rabbits and within the same male rabbit than in the rat. Variations in frequency were due to the appearance of pauses or intervals between individual thrusts, rather than to changes in the duration of the thrusts. The finding that low frequency mounts or nonrhythmic mounts rarely or never elicited lordosis even in highly estrous

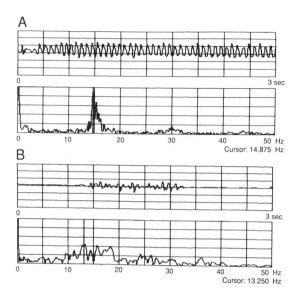

FIG. 11. Accelerometric record and frequency analysis of pelvic movements in typical mounts performed by intact male and female rabbits. Upper graphs: signals generated by the accelerometer. Lower graphs: frequency analysis (range: 0 to 50 Hz) of the signals generated during an 8-sec period in which mounting occurred. The frequency analysis of the male mount shows a single component with a peak frequency value of 14.875 Hz, as indicated by the cursor. In contrast, female mounting, besides being of low amplitude, does not show a dominant frequency but a series of ill-defined components. (From Soto *et al.*, 1984. Reproduced with permission.)

females supports the idea of Diamond (1970) that females have a "special vaginal code" that could act as a potential reproductive isolating mechanism. Moreover, the failure of female rabbits to display lordosis in response to weak, uncoordinated mounts could have an adaptive value by preventing fertilization by hypogonadal or sick individuals. Assuming that the optimal stimulus for eliciting lordosis is built up by sequences of periodic pelvic thrusts, alterations of this rhythm by pauses will decrease the effectiveness of mounting. Introduction of pauses in a variety of rhythmic structures has been shown to dramatically influence the perception of rhythmic stimulation (Fraisse, 1974).

D. SEXUAL DIMORPHISM OF THE MOUNTING MOTOR PATTERN IN THE RABBIT

The mounting motor pattern was clearly sexually dimorphic in the rabbit. Thus, in contrast to males, nearly all female mounts were weak and lacked rhythmicity. Therefore, they failed to stimulate lordosis in the receptive doe, though some investigators (Hammond, 1925) have occasionally reported ovulation in response to a female mount. The sexual dimorphism of mounting can be interpreted as an indication that female rabbits lack the neural circuitry involved in the production of rhythmic thrusting. Alternatively, females may possess this neural circuit but lack the adequate hormonal profile to activate this system. As will be discussed later (Section VI,D), this last condition appears to be responsible for the sexual differences in mounting behavior in the rabbit.

V. Central Mediation of the Male Copulatory Motor Pattern

Little is known about the neural mechanisms controlling the motor aspects of male copulation. Several data suggest that the cerebral cortex is not essential for the integration of the male copulatory pattern, as decorticated rats apparently perform normal mounts, intromissions, and ejaculations (Whishaw and Kolb, 1985). Moreover, the fact that pelvic thrusting has been observed following genital stimulation in spinal transected dogs (Hart, 1967a) and even in humans (Bors and Comarr, 1960; Comarr and Gunderson, 1975) suggests that this motor pattern is integrated at the spinal cord level. However, from these studies, it is not possible to ascertain if pelvic thrusting in spinal subjects had similar characteristics to those of normal subjects.

Some speculations can be made on the nature of the neural system controlling pelvic thrusting from data on other systems generating rhythmic, repetitive movements such as locomotion, swimming, flying, scratching, and some forms of tremor (Edgerton et al., 1976; Grillner and Kashin, 1976; von Holtz, 1954; Wilson and Waldson, 1968). Pelvic thrusting is characterized by fixed temporal and spatial relations between the discharge in different motor pathways, a kind of activity presumably reflecting the properties of a "neural pattern generator" (Kennedy and Davis, 1975). This type of system comprises the following elements: an oscillator, coordinating neurons, motoneurons, and command or triggering neurons. Most of these elements are located in the spinal cord, except for the command neurons, which are often located at supraspinal levels. Command neurons regulate the output of this neural system by triggering the motor pattern but do not contribute to its structure. Several studies strongly suggest that command neurons initiating the various motor and visceral acts involved in male copulation are located in the medial preoptic area (mPOA). Lesions in this area tend to suppress copulation in the rat and many other mammalian species (for reviews, see Larsson, 1979; Sachs and Meisel, 1988). Moreover, studies in rats (Malsbury, 1971; Van Dis and Larsson, 1970) and other mammals (opossum: Roberts et al., 1967; rhesus monkey: Perachio et al., 1979) also show that electrical stimulation of this area facilitates and often initiates male copulatory behavior. Interestingly, electrical stimulation of the mPOA also elicits seminal emission (Herberg, 1963; Van Dis and Larsson, 1970), a finding consistent with our observation that initiation of mounting in the male rat is associated with a rise in SVP (Beyer *et al.*, 1982). A particularly interesting study linking activity in mPOA to the initiation of male copulatory behavior was made by Oomura *et al.* (1983) who found that clear neural changes in the mPOA of the male rhesus monkey are related to the initiation of sexual behavior. According to these authors, preoptic neurons show their maximal level of activity at the beginning of mounting but abruptly decrease their firing rate during the development of copulation in the monkey. This suggests that medial preoptic neurons trigger, but do not drive, the activity of lower brain-stem and spinal reflex mechanisms involved in the motor aspect of copulation. Additional support for the role of the mPOA in the initiation of copulation comes from the observation that the excitability of preoptic-anterior hypothalamic neurons is modulated by androgen in the male rat, as shown by the electrophysiological findings of Kendrick (1983).

There is no doubt that the final common pathway of copulatory thrusting involves those motoneurons innervating the muscles of the pelvis and the back. Because copulation in most male mammals, including the rat and the rabbit, involves the performance of rhythmic pelvic thrusting against the female's rump, motoneurons must discharge rhythmically because of alternating periods of excitation and inhibition. Most models designed to explain rhythmic alternating motor patterns such as scratching, swimming, and walking include spinal inhibitory interneurons as the main modulators of these behaviors. Moreover, inhibitory spinal interneurons such as Renshaw cells have been observed to discharge in rhythmic patterns during alternating behaviors, (e.g., scratching). Analysis of the pelvic movements performed during copulation, that is, rhythmic alternation of contraction of flexor and extensor muscles during thrusting, suggests the participation of both Ia inhibitory interneurons and Renshaw cells in this motor pattern. These two inhibitory interneurons use glycine and GABA as neurotransmitters. Surprisingly, however, perispinal administration of strychnine, a glycine antagonist, or bicuculline, a GABA-A receptor antagonist, or a combination of both antagonists, failed to alter the organization of the copulatory motor pattern in male rats (Moralí *et al.*, 1989) (Fig. 12). This failure occurred in spite of the fact that administration of the antagonists, either alone or in combination, produced clear sensory and motor effects such as allodynia and even motor seizures, hence indicating an effective blockade of glycine and GABA-A receptors. This negative result could be interpreted as evidence that neither glycine nor GABA, the two main inhibitory neurotransmitters, participate in the control of pelvic thrusting during copulation. It is, however, possible that these amino acids do indeed control some of the characteristics of pelvic thrusting through activation of synapses that are insensitive to these antagonists. Thus, bicuculline antagonizes GABA effects only at GABA-A receptors but not at GABA-B sites (Andrews and Johnston, 1979). Therefore, GABA could theoretically still play a role

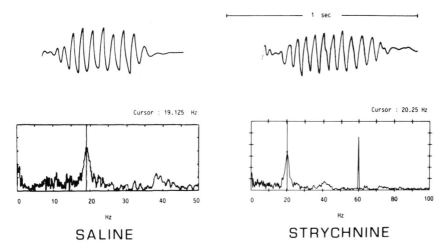

FIG. 12. Representative accelerometric (upper) and power frequency spectra (lower) tracings of a mount performed after saline administration and of a mount performed 3 min after the perispinal administration of 10 μg strychnine, when sensory effects already occurred. Note the similar duration, amplitude, and dynamic organization of both mounting trains. The frequency values (19.125 and 20.25 Hz) and the rhythmicity of both mounting trains, as indicated by the narrow dispersion of the frequency spectra, are also similar. The sharp peak resulting from an unfiltered 60-Hz electrical signal appears in the frequency spectrum of the mount performed under strychnine, for comparison purposes. (From Moralí *et al.*, 1989. Reproduced with permission).

in the pacing of pelvic thrusting by acting at the latter receptors. However, GABA transaminase inhibitors, at dosages that inhibit intromissions, failed to consistently modify the thrusting pattern in rats (Agmo and Contreras, 1990). More relevant to the failure of the amino acid antagonists to disrupt pelvic thrusting, is the observation that the pause in Renshaw cell discharge following their activation is resistant to both strychnine and bicuculline (Ryall *et al.*, 1972). This pause is due to enhanced inhibitory input from other glycinergic interneurons (mutual inhibition). Therefore, if the mutual inhibition of Renshaw cells is related to the patterning of motoneuron discharge during copulatory pelvic thrusting, this would explain our failure to disrupt pelvic thrusting with strychnine. It is of course also possible that brain-stem neurons, rather than spinal interneurons, regulate motoneuron discharge during pelvic thrusting. These neurons may impose a rhythmic firing pattern on the motoneurons involved in copulatory movements. Indeed, descending inhibitory influences capable of imposing rhythmic firing on motoneurons have been traced from noradrenergic locus coeruleus neurons (Nygren and Olson, 1977; Westlund *et al.*, 1983) as well as from raphe serotonergic neurons (Steinbusch, 1981; Lundberg, 1982). However, chemical lesion of these systems by perispinal administration of

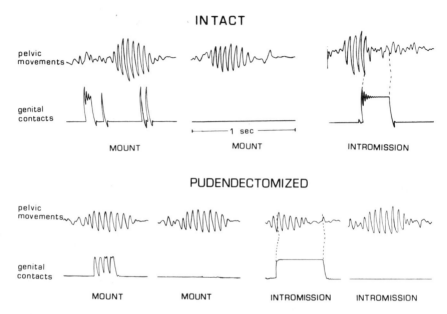

FIG. 13. Polygraphic recordings of the signals generated both by the accelerometer in relation to the copulatory pelvic movements of an intact and a pudendectomized rat and the genital contacts (as determined by using the intromission detection circuit) occurring during these behavioral responses. Note the similar duration of individual pelvic thrusts, of thrusting trains, and their similar organization in both intact and pudendectomized rats. Note, however, that in some intromission-like patterns of pudendectomized males, no penile insertion occurred or abnormally long periods of penile insertion were recorded.

6-hydroxydopamine (Hansen and Ross, 1983), though affecting some temporal parameters of copulation, did not alter the copulatory motor pattern in male rats. It is possible, however, that changes in pelvic thrusting organization may have been undetected by the purely visual observation used in this study.

There is agreement that most rhythmic motor patterns are largely controlled by a central oscillator in the CNS. However, sensory information from the effectors involved in the response or resulting from skin stimulation may modulate or alter the temporal characteristics of these motor patterns. Several studies indicate the importance of penile sensitivity in copulatory behavior. Thus, transection of the dorsal penile nerve (DPN) in the rat, a sensory branch of the pudendal nerve, which carries information from the skin of the penis, usually decreases the occurrence of intromissions and therefore of ejaculation (Larsson and Sodersten, 1973). On the other hand, from purely visual observation, mounts appear to be normal. Ventral viewing suggested that though erection was present in DPN-transected male rats, erections appeared to be smaller than in control rats. There-

INTACT

F = 14.0 /sec

PUDENDECTOMIZED

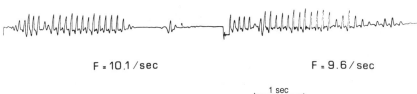

F = 10.1 /sec   F = 9.6 /sec

1 sec

FIG. 14. Accelerometric records of typical mounts displayed by a male rabbit before and after transection of the pudendal nerve. Note the decrease in thrusting frequency due to the appearance of pauses or intervals between individual thrusts.

fore, problems in penile insertion could explain the failure of DPN-transected rats to ejaculate. Polygraphic analysis of mounts and intromissions in pudendectomized rats (Moralí *et al.*, 1982) did not reveal striking alterations in either duration of individual pelvic thrusts, frequency of thrusting, or even duration of "mounts" or "intromissions" (Fig. 13). However, some abnormalities in the normal pattern of penile insertion were noted. Thus, in some intromission-like patterns, no penile insertion occurred. On the other hand, abnormally long periods of penile insertion were observed in other intromissions (Fig. 13). These results suggest that, though the motor thrusting pattern is not altered by penile deafferentation, an uncoupling between motor and genital (penile) events occurs. This conclusion is consistent with the observation that female rats show intromission and even ejaculatory patterns indistinguishable from those of the male.

In contrast to the rat, transection of the pudendal nerve in the rabbit produced clear alterations in the organization of the copulatory motor pattern (Moralí *et al.*, 1982). Figure 14 presents typical mounts displayed by a male rabbit before and after transection of the pudendal nerve. As can be seen from these tracings, the most striking effect of penile deafferentation was a marked decrease in thrusting frequency, owing to the appearance of pauses or intervals between individual thrusts. This effect was not due to an interference with the motor component of the pudendal nerve, because anesthetization of the penis by a local anesthetic tended to produce the same results (Moralí *et al.*, 1982).

VI. HORMONAL FACTORS IN THE REGULATION
OF THE MORPHOLOGY OF COPULATORY BEHAVIOR

It is well established that copulatory behavior in male mammals depends on
the secretion of testicular hormones. Thus, castration induces a decline, variable
in magnitude and temporal course among species, in copulatory behavior.

A. EFFECT OF HORMONAL MANIPULATIONS ON THE MALE
COPULATORY MOTOR PATTERN OF THE MALE RAT

In the case of the rat, a large proportion of castrated males stop displaying
copulatory behavior, but some animals continue to show sexual activity even for
several weeks after surgery. Analysis of 122 mounts, 82 intromissions, and 7
ejaculatory behavioral patterns performed by four castrated rats at different intervals, not less than 2 weeks after castration, showed that neither the thrusting
frequency nor the amplitude or duration of the individual pelvic thrusts was
significantly affected by castration (Fig. 15) (Beyer *et al.*, 1981). Moreover,
durations of intromissions and ejaculations were similar to those of intact rats.
Only the duration of mounts was somewhat longer in castrated rats (mean ± SD:
0.536 ± 0.020 sec vs 0.380 ± 0.080 sec in intact rats). These results could be
interpreted as an indication that sex steroids do not modulate the copulatory
motor pattern of the rat. However, it is also possible that rats stop copulating
before alterations in the copulatory motor pattern are detected. This would be the
case if motivation to copulate requires a higher concentration of sex steroids than
that needed for displaying a normal copulatory motor pattern. A similar observation has been previously made by Rosenblatt and Aronson (1958) in cats, who
found that some of the animals lost their motivation to copulate before they could
possibly have shown difficulties in the motor patterns of copulation. Mounts of
castrated rats could have been longer because of some failure either of penile
erection or in the orientation of the penis to the vaginal region as has also been
described in cats, along with a lengthening of mounts, after castration (Rosenblatt and Aronson, 1958).

Administration of androgen (5 mg of testosterone propionate (TP) for 6 weeks)
reestablishes full copulatory behavior in castrated rats. As shown in Fig. 15,
androgen-treated rats displayed copulatory patterns that were indistinguishable
from those displayed by intact normal rats (Beyer *et al.*, 1981). Moreover,
beginning with the first mounts performed by the castrated TP-treated rats, the
motor pattern was already completely normal.

Administration of estrogen (5 μg estradiol benzoate (EB) for 4 weeks and then
50 μg for 3 more weeks) to castrated males stimulated the performance of
mounts and intromission patterns, though these rats usually failed to ejaculate.

INTACT

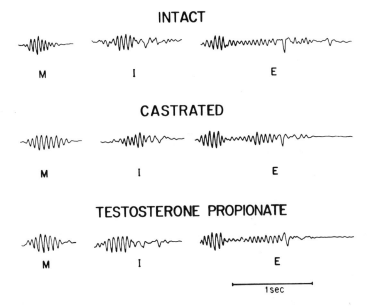

M   I   E

CASTRATED

M   I   E

TESTOSTERONE PROPIONATE

M   I   E

1 sec

FIG. 15. Accelerometric records of mounts (M), intromission patterns (I), and ejaculation patterns (E) in intact, castrated, and testosterone propionate treated male rats (From Beyer *et al.*, 1981. Reproduced with permission.)

The accelerometric analysis of intromissions performed by estrogen-treated rats showed thrusting frequencies significantly higher (mean $\pm$ SD: 22.15 $\pm$ 1.29 thrusts per sec) than those of intact rats (19.43 $\pm$ 1.57 thrusts per sec). The organization of pelvic thrusting was highly rhythmic, duration of individual pelvic thrusts being shorter than in normal or TP-treated rats. Only two ejaculatory patterns were observed in EB-treated rats. These patterns were of the short ejaculation type due both to their short duration and to the lack of differentiation between the extravaginal and intravaginal phases (Beyer *et al.*, 1981).

To investigate the possible role of perinatal androgen in the organization of the copulatory motor pattern, 3-day-old male rats were castrated and treated as adults with either TP (5 mg/day) or EB (50 μg/day) for 7 weeks (Moralí *et al.*, 1985). Such a long period of treatment allowed us to have a representative sample with enough copulatory responses. In half of the TP-treated rats, it was possible to restore full male copulatory behavior, including ejaculation, that showed identical motor characteristics to the copulatory motor pattern of control males (Fig. 16). Neonatally castrated rats, however, showed only short ejaculations. Neonatally castrated males receiving EB when adults never showed ejaculatory behavior.

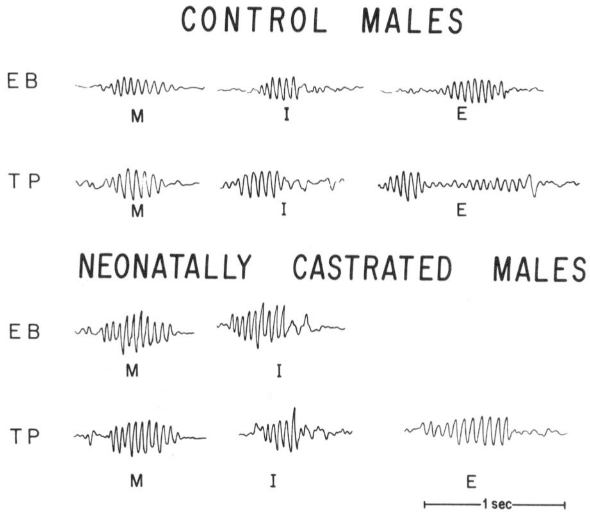

FIG. 16. Accelerometric records of mounts (M), intromission patterns (I), and ejaculation patterns (E) performed by control, postpuberally castrated male rats, and by neonatally castrated males when tested at adulthood under daily treatment with either estradiol benzoate (EB, 50 μg) or testosterone propionate (TP, 5 mg). Note the similarity in the organization of mount and intromission patterns displayed by both groups of males under either treatment. Neonatally castrated males did not ejaculate when treated with EB. Those receiving TP generally performed the short ejaculatory pattern, with similar characteristics to those of short ejaculations of control males. (From Moralí *et al.*, 1985. Reproduced with permission.)

B. EFFECT OF HORMONAL MANIPULATIONS ON THE PSEUDOMALE COPULATORY MOTOR PATTERN OF THE RAT

Treating ovariectomized rats with either TP (5 mg/day) or EB (50 μg/day) stimulated the expression of malelike sexual behavior both in neonatally androgenized and in control females; TP was more effective than EB in stimulating the display of pseudomale behavior. The copulatory motor patterns displayed by both neonatally androgenized and control females after ovariectomy and hormonal treatment were indistinguishable from those of normal male rats or from those of females before ovariectomy (Fig. 17) (Moralí *et al.*, 1985). Surprisingly, EB, which in castrated males significantly increased thrusting frequencies, lacked this action in ovariectomized rats.

C. EFFECT OF HORMONES ON MALE COPULATORY BEHAVIOR IN RABBITS

Castration of the male rabbit does not immediately abolish sexual activity, and mounting can continue for several months at a relatively high rate (Stone, 1932;

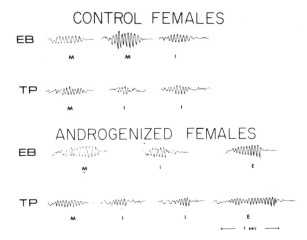

FIG. 17. Accelerometric records of mounts (M), intromission patterns (I), and ejaculation patterns (E) performed by control females and by neonatally androgenized females when tested at adulthood after ovariectomy and daily treatment with either estradiol benzoate (EB, 50 μg) or testosterone propionate (TP, 5 mg). Control females did not show ejaculatory behavior. Note the similarity in the organization of mount and intromission patterns displayed by both groups of females under either treatment. Neonatally androgenized females under EB treatment showed more often the short-type ejaculatory pattern, whereas those under TP treatment generally displayed the long ejaculatory pattern. (From Moralí *et al.*, 1985.)

Beyer *et al.*, 1980). Only a small proportion of the mounts performed by the castrated rabbits culminate in ejaculation, mainly because of a decrease in the effectiveness of the mount in stimulating lordosis in the female (Stone, 1932; Beyer *et al.*, 1980). In contrast to the rat, castration produced clear alterations in both the vigor and the temporal patterning of mounting in the male rabbit (Beyer *et al.*, 1980). Thus, a high proportion of the mounts performed by castrated rabbits showed periods of low amplitude movements and a decrease in thrusting frequency caused by the appearance of interthrust intervals (Fig. 18). Power spectrum analysis combined with interthrust interval analysis revealed that the decrease in thrusting frequency (number of distinct pelvic thrusts per sec) was not due to a slowing of pelvic movements, that is, a prolongation of individual pelvic thrusts, but to the appearance of pauses breaking the rhythm of thrusting. Pauses were caused by either irregular shallow pelvic movements or by the complete arrest of thrusting. At a later stage in the disorganization of the mounting pattern, pelvic thrusts disappeared and the mounts were characterized by tremorlike, weak pelvic movements. These mounts never stimulated lordosis even in highly receptive females. The changes in the copulatory motor pattern following castration occurred earlier than the decrease in the number of mounts per test, suggesting that these parameters (thrusting frequency and rhythm) are more sensitive to androgen deprivation than is sexual motivation. Androgen

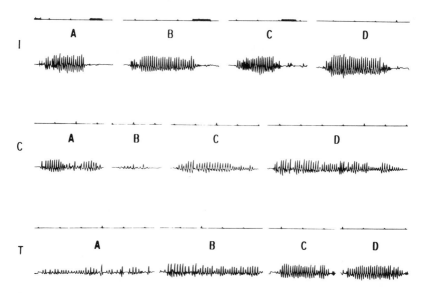

FIG. 18. Accelerometric records of the first four mounts performed by a New Zealand white rabbit when intact (I), 30 days after castration (C), and 15 days after the initiation of testosterone propionate administration (T). Upper traces in each record carry a time mark (1 sec) and a signal operated by the observer when detecting intromission. Note that castration results in a diminution of the amplitude of the thrusting movements and in the appearance of trains of small thrusts interspersed with periods of more vigorous activity. Note that T administration tended to restore the normal mounting pattern. (From Beyer *et al.*, 1980.)

administration (10 mg of TP daily for 15 days) to castrated rabbits gradually restored the incidence of mounting but not of intromission to the intact level. Androgen significantly increased thrusting frequency and strength of pelvic movements (Fig. 18) until the normal morphology of pelvic thrusting was restored.

D. HORMONAL REGULATION OF PSEUDOMALE BEHAVIOR IN THE FEMALE RABBIT

Surprisingly, as shown in Fig. 19, TP treatment (5 mg daily for 1 month) stimulated in ovariectomized rabbits copulatory mounting patterns that were similar to those displayed by male rabbits (Soto *et al.*, 1984). Thus, as shown in Fig. 19, androgen-treated females not only displayed vigorous pelvic thrusting in many cases but also clear rhythmicity with predominant frequencies similar to those of normal males. Most interestingly, estrogen treatment (EB, 10 μg for 1 month) induced hypersynchronic thrusting activity (Fig. 19), which had a significantly higher frequency than that of normal or TP-treated males.

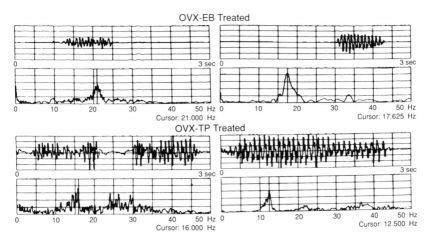

FIG. 19. Typical accelerometric records and frequency spectrum analysis of mounts performed by ovariectomized rabbits receiving estradiol benzoate (EB) or testosterone propionate (TP) treatments. Upper graphs: signals generated by the accelerometer during mounting. Lower graphs: frequency analysis (range: 0 to 50 Hz) of signals generated during an 8-sec period during which mounting occurred. Note sharp single components in the spectra of the EB-treated rabbits, showing also high thrusting frequencies (F = 21.000 and 17.625 Hz). Frequency analysis of TP-stimulated mounts reveals two characteristic mounting patterns: one with a well-defined component (F = 12.500) and the other showing both a dominant frequency (F = 16.000) and an ill-defined band of higher frequencies. (From Soto *et al.*, 1984. Reproduced with permission.)

E. SITE OF ACTION OF HORMONES FOR REGULATING THE MALE COPULATORY MOTOR PATTERN

The hormonal stimulation of the initiation of male sexual behavior in the rat seems to be exerted in the mPOA and anterior hypothalamic area. Thus, testosterone (T) or TP implants in this region restore male sexual behavior in castrated rats (Christensen and Clemens, 1974; Davidson, 1966; Johnston and Davidson, 1972; Lisk, 1967; for a review, see Sachs and Meisel, 1988). The copulatory activity stimulated by intracerebral implants of T seems complete to the extent that these castrated rats show mounting, intromission, and ejaculation behavioral patterns. However, Davidson (1966) noted that "analysis of the behavior of animals with hypothalamic-preoptic implants showed that the restored behavior was not completely normal in many cases." A plausible explanation for these differences, as compared with the normal copulatory pattern of the intact rats, is a lack of androgenic stimulation of the lower neural structures involved in male copulation. The possibility that sex steroids act at the spinal cord level to modulate some components of male copulation is suggested by several data. For

Intact Male

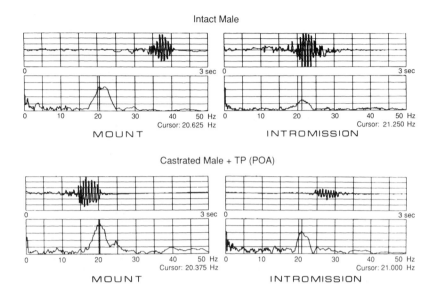

FIG. 20. Frequency spectrum analysis of the pelvic movements performed during mount and intromission patterns by male rats when intact and after being castrated and implanted with TP into the preoptic area (POA). Upper graphs: signals generated by the accelerometer during mounts and intromissions. Note the similar fusiform organization of mounts performed in the two experimental conditions. Lower graphs: frequency analysis (range: 0 to 50 Hz) of the signals generated during an 8-sec period within which individual responses occurred. Note that the spectral analysis of the responses in both conditions shows a peak around the 19 to 22 Hz band. Frequency (F) values (20.625 and 21.250 for the responses of the intact rat; 20.375 and 21.000 for those shown after castration and TP implantation) and dispersion of the spectra are similar under both experimental conditions. (From Moralí *et al.*, 1986. Reproduced with permission.)

example, androgen accumulates in neurons of the lumbosacral region of the spinal cord (Sar and Stumpf, 1977), including some sexually dimorphic nuclei (spinal nucleus of the bulbocavernosus and dorsolateral nucleus), which innervate muscles participating in penile reflexes (Breedlove and Arnold, 1980; Jordan *et al.*, 1982; Sachs, 1982). More direct evidence for the participation of sexual steroids in the regulation of spinal reflexes comes from the studies of Hart (1967b; 1978; Hart and Haugen, 1968) showing that the penile reflexes displayed by spinal transected rats are greatly enhanced by the local implantation of androgen in the lumbar region of the spinal cord. Therefore, it is possible that some temporal or dynamic characteristics of the copulatory thrusting pattern are under the control of androgen. To test this, in one study performed in our laboratory, the copulatory motor pattern of castrated rats whose sexual behavior was restored by local implants of TP in the mPOA was compared with that shown by the same individuals when intact (Moralí *et al.*, 1986). The vigor, frequency, and temporal organization of the copulatory pelvic thrusting shown by the castrated, TP-implanted rats were similar to those previously shown by the rats when intact (Fig. 20) or to normal intact rats. As judged by the atrophy of the sexual accessory organs, it appears likely that no important systemic diffusion of androgen from the intracerebral implantation site occurred, and therefore, that the spinal cord circuits involved in pelvic thrusting were also not exposed to significant amounts of circulating androgen. These data indicate that the spinal neurons related to the organization of pelvic thrusting during copulation in the male rat can function without direct androgenic stimulation.

VII. Concluding Remarks

Copulatory behavior in male mammals basically consists of a series of repetitive, cyclic pelvic movements during which penile insertion into the vagina takes place. Males from different species vary greatly in the number of pelvic thrusts (either extravaginal or intravaginal) required to achieve ejaculation. Some species, such as the sheep, require only one intravaginal thrust to ejaculate. Other species, like the rabbit, perform a variable number of extravaginal thrusts, but once penile insertion is achieved ejaculation ensues. Thus, in both the sheep and the rabbit, the stimulation associated with penile insertion is sufficient for triggering seminal emission and ejaculation. The use of the polygraphic technique allows us to recognize two different ejaculatory patterns in the rat: short and long. In the former one, ejaculation may occur as the result of only one or two pelvic thrusts (see Fig. 3). Therefore, depending on the type of ejaculation analyzed, the male rat can be classified either as a species performing intravaginal thrusting or not.

In both the rat and the rabbit, pelvic thrusting was characterized by being repetitive, pelvic cycles following one another and being highly rhythmic with a predominant thrusting frequency for each species. This situation (a single predominant frequency) is not typical of all mammalian species, because data on mice (McGill, 1962), male squirrel monkeys (Latta *et al.*, 1967), and marmosets (Dixson, 1988) have suggested differences in rate and vigor between extravaginal and intravaginal thrusting: extravaginal thrusting is usually faster than intravaginal thrusting whereas the latter is deeper. Indeed, preliminary results in mice (G. Moralí and B. D. Sachs, unpublished data) show that this species presents a very high frequency of extravaginal thrusting (about 25 Hz) followed by low frequency intravaginal thrusting (approximately 2 per sec) at penile insertion, which concludes with a high frequency rhythmic thrusting period (around 18 Hz) triggering ejaculation.

The basic motor unit of copulatory behavior is the pelvic thrust. Duration of pelvic thrusts is rather constant for each species, though their amplitude varies considerably within a mounting train, particularly in the rat. In this species, variations in amplitude follow a well-defined pattern in which successive pelvic thrusts gradually increase their amplitude until either penile insertion occurs or the amplitude gradually diminishes. This remarkably dynamic organization of pelvic thrusting gives mounts their typical spindle-shape appearance. The fact that penile insertion nearly always occurs during a large amplitude thrust and never during the "declining" phase of the thrusting train suggests that this dynamic pattern has an important signal value for the female, probably facilitating perineal adjustments toward the thrusting penis. In this model, the occurrence of a mount or an intromission would be dependent on the female's response to the male thrusting pattern. The female would determine if the thrusting train will be an intromission or a mount not only by allowing penile insertion but most likely by passing a signal to the mounting partner. This signal, most likely associated with perineal accommodation, should be detected not only through penile receptors but through sensory receptors perhaps located in the perigenital area. This would explain, additionally, why females display intromission patterns indistinguishable from those of males. Obviously, detailed analysis of the interactions between copulating pairs should be made to support this interpretation.

Frank Beach (1967), mainly based on his studies of the rat, proposed that male copulation depended on the activation of an arousal mechanism (AM) related to the initiation of copulation and of a consummatory mechanism (CM) controlling the copulatory movements themselves. He concluded that both mechanisms were largely independent in terms of the neural and hormonal factors controlling them. Thus, the AM, located in the telencephalon, was dependent on sexual hormones for its activation, whereas the CM functioned independently of hormonal factors. Our results in the rat support Beach's hypothesis. Thus, castration failed to alter the copulatory motor pattern (Beyer et al., 1981), and androgenic stimulation restricted to the mPOA in castrated rats restored copulatory behavior that was identical to that displayed by intact rats (Moralí et al., 1986). However, our results in the rabbit exemplify the difficulties in establishing valid generalizations in the area of the neuroendocrine regulation of sexual behavior. Thus, it was clear that lack of testicular hormones in the rabbit disrupted at least some parameters of its copulatory motor pattern, which could be restored to normality by hormonal administration (Beyer et al., 1980). Castrated rabbits still showed copulatory movements, indicating that signals from the AM were acting on the CM, but these movements were weaker and arrhythmical in comparison with those of normal rabbits.

There is practically no information about the neural circuitry involved in the patterning of cyclic discharge that occurs in those spinal motoneurons controlling the muscles involved in pelvic thrusting. However, from the temporal characteristics of thrusting (frequency and rhythmicity), it appears likely that this activity is generated, as are other rhythmic behaviors (walking, scratching, etc), by a central motor program (Kennedy and Davis, 1975) rather than by a chain reflex. In this model, proprioceptors or genital receptors (penile receptors) should not contribute information used by the central nervous system to generate the thrusting pattern. Again, this model appears to be partially supported in the rat in which penile or perigenital denervation, which can influence some genital aspects of copulation such as penile insertion, does not affect the motor thrusting pattern. On the other hand, some minor but clear effects in the organization of thrusting can be seen in the rabbit following transection of the pudendal nerve or local anesthetization of the penis. It is therefore possible that in the rabbit, sensory messages from the penis and perigenital area alter the characteristics of the neural oscillator involved in the generation of thrusting. This finding does not mean that pelvic thrusting in the rabbit should be viewed as a series of self-generated reflexes (pelvic thrusts), but rather that the characteristics of the neural oscillator, within a limited range, are influenced by sensory input, though most of the patterning is still produced by the center.

In contrast to the development of the neural circuits involved in sexual arousal, which are under the influence of perinatal sexual hormones, the thrusting pattern of the rat was not influenced by either neonatal castration of the male or neonatal administration of hormones to the female (Moralí et al., 1985). Moreover, the fact that both males and females in both rats (Moralí et al., 1985) and rabbits (Soto et al., 1984) display identical copulatory motor patterns under adequate hormonal conditions strongly suggests that the neural substrate for thrusting develops independently of hormones, therefore suggesting that it is under genetical control. On the other hand, sexual differences in responsiveness to gonadal hormones in the adult exist between male and female individuals, particularly in the rabbit. This difference, however, must be due to variations in the populations of steroid receptors owing to the difference in endocrine profiles existing between the sexes.

Although the motor component of copulation in the rat appears to be under the control of a central pattern generator, relatively little affected by sensory input from the genitalia, the penile and genital components of copulation are regulated by sensory messages from penile and perigenital receptors. The response of the seminal vesicles to copulation in the rat is a complex one. Three components can be differentiated in this response: (1) an initial weak contraction associated or coincident with the initiation of pelvic thrusting, probably produced through descending influences from the mPOA; (2) a secondary reflex response triggered by penile insertion; and (3) a final component usually elicited by repeated intravaginal thrusting. This final response is associated with emission and ejaculation. This complex response indicates a gradual recruitment of autonomic motor neurons by penile stimulation during copulation. On the other hand, seminal emission and ejaculation in the rabbit are triggered by penile insertion, the preparatory rise in SVP associated with mounting in the rat being absent in this species.

VIII. Summary

The present article describes the morphology (i.e., the temporal and dynamic characteristics) of the pelvic movements involved in copulation in the rat and the rabbit, as well as some of the penile and genital processes associated with copulation in these species. Using an accelerometric technique combined with the detection of penile intromission and with the chronic recording of the activity of the seminal vesicles, it was possible to measure accurately the duration and temporal organization of the sequence of pelvic thrusts and relate them to the penile and genital events comprising copulation. This methodological approach has permitted the identification of several features of copulation that were previously unrecognized, such as intravaginal thrusting in the rat. Similarly, the polygraphic analysis of the male copulatory motor pattern revealed the isomorphism (i.e., identical expression) of this behavior in male and female rats and its sexual dimorphism in the rabbit. Analysis of the male copulatory pattern in the rat under various experimental conditions showed that the thrusting pattern in this species is largely independent of sex steroids and sensory feedback from the genitalia. On the other hand, the copulatory motor pattern in the rabbit is affected by both a decline in testicular hormones or denervation of the genital area. Hormone dependency of the thrusting pattern explains the sexual dimorphism of this behavior in the rabbit, as androgen administration to ovariectomized females results in thrusting patterns undistinguishable from those displayed by males.

References

Agmo, A., and Contreras, J. L. (1990). Copulatory thrusting pattern in the male rat after acute treatment with GABA transaminase inhibitors. *Physiol. Behav.* **47,** 311–314.

Andrews, P. R., and Johnston, G. A. R. (1979). GABA agonists and antagonists. *Biochem. Pharmacol.* **28,** 2697–2702.

Barfield, R. J., and Krieger, M. S. (1977). Ejaculatory and postejaculatory behavior of male and female rats: Effect of sex hormones and electric shock. *Physiol. Behav.* **19,** 203–208.

Baum, M. J. (1979). Differentiation of coital behavior in mammals: A comparative analysis. *Neurosci. Biobehav. Rev.* **3,** 265–284.

Beach, F. A. (1942). Execution of the complete masculine copulatory pattern by sexually receptive female rats. *J. Genet. Psychol.* **60,** 137–142.

Beach, F. A. (1967). Cerebral and hormonal control of reflexive mechanisms involved in copulatory behavior. *Physiol. Rev.* **47,** 289–316.

Beach, F. A. (1968). Factors involved in the control of mounting behavior by female mammals. *In*

"Perspectives in Reproduction and Sexual Behavior" (M. Diamond, ed.), pp. 83–131. Indiana Univ. Press, Bloomington.

Beach, F. A., Rogers, C. M., and LeBoeuf, B. (1968). Coital behavior in dogs. II. Effects of estrogen on mounting by females. *J. Comp. Physiol. Psychol.* **66,** 296–307.

Bell, C. (1972). Autonomic nervous control of reproduction: Circulatory and other factors. *Pharmacol. Rev.* **24,** 657–736.

Bermant, G. (1965). Rat sexual behavior: Photographic analysis of the intromission response. *Psychon. Sci.* **2,** 65–66.

Beyer, C., ed. 1979. "Endocrine Control of Sexual Behavior." Raven Press, New York.

Beyer, C., Velázquez, J., Larsson, K., and Contreras, J. L. (1980). Androgen regulation of the motor copulatory pattern in the male New Zealand white rabbit. *Horm. Behav.* **14,** 179–190.

Beyer, C., Contreras, J. L., Moralí, G., and Larsson, K. (1981). Effects of castration and sex steroid treatment on the motor copulatory pattern of the rat. *Physiol. Behav.* **27,** 727–730.

Beyer, C., Contreras, J. L., Larsson, K., Olmedo, M., and Moralí, G. (1982). Patterns of motor and seminal vesicle activities during copulation in the male rat. *Physiol. Behav.* **29,** 495–500.

Bors, E., and Comarr, A. E. (1960). Neurological disturbances of sexual function with special reference to 529 patients with spinal cord injury. *Urol. Surv.* **10,** 191–222.

Breedlove, S. M., and Arnold, A. P. (1980). Hormone accumulation in a sexually dimorphic motor nucleus in the rat spinal cord. *Science* **210,** 564–566.

Calaresu, F. R., and Mitchell, R. (1969). Cutaneous mechanoreceptors in the glans penis of the rat. *Brain Res.* **15,** 295–297.

Carlsson, S., and Larsson, K. (1962). Intromission frequency and intromission duration in the male rat mating behavior. *Scand. J. Physiol.* **3,** 189–191.

Christensen, L. W., and Clemens, L. G. (1974). Intrahypothalamic implants of testosterone and estradiol and resumption of masculine sexual behavior in long-term castrated male rats. *Endocrinology (Baltimore)* **95,** 984–990.

Comarr, A. E., and Gunderson, B. B. (1975). Sexual function in traumatic paraplegia and quadriplegia. *Am. J. Nurs.* **75,** 250–255.

Contreras, J. L., and Beyer, C. (1979). A polygraphic analysis of mounting and ejaculation in the New Zealand white rabbit. *Physiol. Behav.* **23,** 939–943.

Davidson, J. M. (1966). Activation of the male rat's sexual behavior by intracerebral implantation of androgen. *Endocrinology (Baltimore)* **79,** 783–794.

Dewsbury, D. A. (1979). Description of sexual behavior in research on hormone behavior interactions. *In* "Endocrine Control of Sexual Behavior" (C. Beyer, ed.), pp. 1–32. Raven Press, New York.

Diamond, M. (1970). Intromission pattern and species vaginal code in relation to induction of pseudopregnancy. *Science* **169,** 995–997.

Dixson, A. F. (1988). Effects of dorsal penile nerve transection upon the sexual behaviour of the male marmoset (Callithrix jacchus). *Physiol. Behav.* **43,** 235–238.

Edgerton, V. R., Grillner, S., Sjöström, A., and Langger, P. (1976). Central generation of locomotion in vertebrates. *In* "Neural Control of Locomotion" (R. M. Herman, ed.), pp. 439–464. Plenum, New York.

Emery, D. E., and Sachs, B. D. (1975). Ejaculatory pattern in female rats without androgen treatment. *Science* **190,** 284–286.

Emery, D. E., and Sachs, B. D. (1976). Hormonal and monoaminergic influences on masculine copulatory behavior in the female rat. *Horm. Behav.* **7,** 341–352.

Fabre, C. (1977). Existence of an ejaculatory-like reaction in ewes ovariectomized and treated with androgens in adulthood. *Horm. Behav.* **9,** 150–155.

Fraisse, P. (1974). "Psychologie du rythme." Presses Univ. Fr. Paris.

Gerall, A. A., and Ward, I. L. (1966). Effects of prenatal endogenous androgen on the sexual behavior of the female albino rat. *J. Comp. Physiol. Psychol.* **62**, 370–375.

Grillner, S., and Kashin, S. (1976). On the generation and performance of swimming in fish. *In* "Neural Control of Locomotion" (R. M. Herman, ed.), pp. 181–202. Plenum, New York.

Hammond, J. (1925). "Reproduction in the Rabbit" Oliver & Boyd, Edinburgh.

Hansen, S., and Ross, S. B. (1983). Role of descending monoaminergic neurons in the control of sexual behavior: Effects of intrathecal infusions of 6-hydroxydopamine and 5,7-dihydroxytryptamine. *Brain Res.* **268**, 285–290.

Harris, G. W., and Levine, S. (1965). Sexual differentiation of the brain and its experimental control. *J. Physiol. (London)* **181**, 369–400.

Hart, B. L. (1967a). Sexual reflexes and mating behavior in the male dog. *J. Comp. Physiol. Psychol.* **64**, 388–399.

Hart, B. L. (1967b). Testosterone regulation of sexual reflexes in spinal male rats. *Science* **155**, 1282–1284.

Hart, B. L. (1978). Hormones, spinal reflexes and sexual behaviour. *In* "Biological Determinants of Sexual Behaviour" (J. B. Hutchison, ed.), pp. 319–347. Wiley, Chichester.

Hart, B. L., and Haugen, C. M. (1968). Activation of sexual reflexes in male rats by spinal implantation of testosterone. *Physiol. Behav.* **3**, 735–738.

Herberg, J. Z. (1963). Seminal ejaculation following positively reinforcing electrical stimulation of the rat hypothalamus. *J. Comp. Physiol. Psychol.* **56**, 679–685.

Johnston, P., and Davidson, J. M. (1972). Intracerebral androgen and sexual behavior in the male rat. *Horm. Behav.* **3**, 345–357.

Jordan, C. L., Breedlove, S. M., and Arnold, A. P. (1982). Sexual dimorphism and the influence of neonatal androgen in the dorsolateral motor nucleus of the rat lumbar spinal cord. *Brain Res.* **249**, 309–314.

Kendrick, K. M. (1983). Electrophysiological effects of testosterone on the medial preoptic-anterior hypothalamus of the rat. *J. Endocrinol.* **96**, 35–42.

Kennedy, D., and Davis, W. J. (1975). The organization of invertebrate motor systems. *In* "Handbook of Physiology" (D. W. Hamilton and R. O. Greep, eds.), Sect. 7, Vol. V, pp. 1023–1087. Am. Physiol. Soc., Washington, D. C.

Larsson, K. (1956). Conditioning and sexual behavior in the male albino rat. *Acta Psychol. Gothoburg.* **1**, 1–269.

Larsson, K. (1979). Features of the neuroendocrine regulation of masculine sexual behavior. *In* "Endocrine Control of Sexual Behavior" (C. Beyer, ed.), pp. 77–160. Raven Press, New York.

Larsson, K., and Sodersten, P. (1973). Mating in male rats after section of the dorsal penile nerve. *Physiol. Behav.* **10**, 567–571.

Latta, J., Hopf, S., and Ploog, D. (1967). Observation on mating behavior and sexual play in the squirrel monkey (*Saimiri sciureus*). *Primates* **8**, 229–246.

Lisk, R. D. (1967). Neural localization for androgen activation of copulatory behavior in the male rat. *Endocrinology (Baltimore)* **80**, 754–761.

Lodder, J., and Zeilmaker, G. H. (1976a). Effects of pelvic nerve and pudendal nerve transection on mating behavior in the male rat. *Physiol. Behav.* **16**, 745–751.

Lodder, J., and Zeilmaker, G. H. (1976b). Effects of genital deafferentation on mounting and intromission behavior in spayed female rats treated with estrogen. *Physiol. Behav.* **16**, 753–755.

Lundberg, A. (1982). Inhibitory control from the brain stem of transmission from primary afferents to motoneurons, primary afferent terminals and ascending pathways. *In* "Brain Stem Control of Spinal Mechanisms" (B. Sjolund and A. Bjorklund, eds.), pp. 179–224. Elsevier, Amsterdam.

Malsbury, C. W. (1971). Facilitation of male rat copulatory behavior by electrical stimulation of the medial preoptic area. *Physiol. Behav.* **7**, 797–805.

McGill, T. E. (1962). Sexual behavior in three inbred strains of mice. *Behaviour* **19**, 341–350.

McKenna, K. E., and Nadelhaft, I. (1986). The organization of the pudendal nerve in the male and female rat. *J. Comp. Neurol.* **248**, 532–549.

Moralí, G., and Beyer, C. (1979). Neuroendocrine regulation of estrous behavior in mammals. *In* "Endocrine Control of Sexual Behavior" (C. Beyer, ed.), pp. 33–75. Raven Press, New York.

Moralí, G., Contreras, J. L., and Beyer, C. (1982). Effects of penile denervation and genital anaesthetization on the motor copulatory pattern of the rat and the rabbit. *Conf. Reprod. Behav. 14th*, p. 77. East Lansing, Michigan.

Moralí, G., Carrillo, L., and Beyer, C. (1983). A method for assessing intravaginal thrusting during copulation in rats. *Conf. Reprod. Behav. 15th*, p. 54. Medford, Massachusetts.

Moralí, G., Carrillo, L., and Beyer, C. (1985). Neonatal androgen influences sexual motivation but not the masculine copulatory motor pattern in the rat. *Physiol. Behav.* **34**, 267–275.

Moralí, G., Hernández, G., and Beyer, C. (1986). Restoration of the copulatory pelvic thrusting pattern in castrated male rats by the intracerebral implantation of androgen. *Physiol. Behav.* **36**, 495–499.

Moralí, G., Komisaruk, B. R., and Beyer, C. (1989). Copulatory pelvic thrusting in the male rat is insensitive to the perispinal administration of glycine and GABA antagonists. *Pharmacol., Biochem. Behav.* **32**, 169–173.

Morris, D. (1955). The causation of pseudomale and pseudofemale behavior: A further comment. *Behaviour* **8**, 46–56.

Nygren, L.-G., and Olson, L. (1977). A new major projection from locus coeruleus: The main source of noradrenergic nerve terminals in the ventral and dorsal columns of the spinal cord. *Brain Res.* **132**, 85–93.

Oomura, Y., Yoshimatsu, H., and Aou, S. (1983). Medial preoptic and hypothalamic neuronal activity during sexual behavior of the monkey. *Brain Res.* **266**, 340–343.

Peirce, J. T., and Nuttall, R. L. (1961). Duration of sexual contacts in the rat. *J. Comp. Physiol. Psychol.* **5**, 585–587.

Perachio, A. A., Marr, L. D., and Alexander, M. (1979). Sexual behavior in male rhesus monkeys elicited by electrical stimulation of preoptic and hypothalamic areas. *Brain Res.* **177**, 127–144.

Pollak, E. I., and Sachs, B. D. (1976). Penile movements and the sensory control of copulation in the rat. *Behav. Biol.* **17**, 177–186.

Purinton, P. T., Fletcher, T. F., and Bradley, W. E. (1973). Gross and light microscopic features of the pelvic plexus in the rat. *Anat. Rec.* **175**, 697–706.

Roberts, W. W., Steinberg, M. L., and Means, L. W. (1967). Hypothalamic mechanisms for sexual, aggressive, and other motivational behaviors in the opossum *Didelphis virginiana. J. Comp. Physiol. Psychol.* **64**, 1–15.

Rosenblatt, J. S., and Aronson, L. R. (1958). The decline of sexual behavior in male cats after castration with special reference to the role of prior sexual experience. *Behaviour* **12**, 285–338.

Rubin, H. B., and Azrin, N. H. (1967). Temporal patterns of sexual behavior in rabbits as determined by an automatic recording technique. *J. Exp. Anal. Behav.* **10**, 219–231.

Ryall, R. W., Piercey, M. F., and Polosa, C. (1972). Strychnine resistant mutual inhibition of Renshaw cells. *Brain Res.* **41**, 119–129.

Sachs, B. D. (1982). Role of striated penile muscles in penile reflexes, copulation and induction of pregnancy in the rat. *J. Reprod. Fertil.* **66**, 433–443.

Sachs, B. D., and Barfield, R. J. (1970). Temporal patterning of sexual behavior in the male rat. *J. Comp. Physiol. Psychol.* **73**, 359–364.

Sachs, B. D., and Barfield, R. J. (1976). Functional analysis of masculine copulatory behavior in the rat. *In* "Advances in the Study of Behavior" (J. S. Rosenblatt, R. A. Hinde, E. Shaw, and C. Beer, eds.), Vol. 7, pp. 91–154. Academic Press, New York.

Sachs, B. D., and Meisel, R. L. (1988). The physiology of male sexual behavior. *In* "The Physiology of Reproduction" (E. Knobil and J. Neill, eds.), Vol. 2, pp. 1393–1485. Plenum, New York.

Sar, M., and Stumpf, W. E. (1977). Androgen concentration in motor neurons of cranial nerves and spinal cord. *Science* **197**, 77–79.

Soto, M. A., Reynoso, M. E., and Beyer, C. (1984). Sexual dimorphism in the motor mounting pattern of the New Zealand white rabbit: Steroid regulation of vigour and rhythmicity of pelvic thrusting. *Horm. Behav.* **18**, 225–234.

Steinbusch, H. W. M. (1981). Distribution of serotonin-immunoreactivity in the central nervous system of the rat-cell bodies and terminals. *Neuroscience* **6**, 557–618.

Stone, C. P. (1932). The retention of copulatory activity in male rabbits following castration. *J. Genet. Psychol.* **40**, 296–305.

Stone, C. P., and Ferguson, L. W. (1940). Temporal relationships in the copulatory acts of adult male rats. *J. Comp. Psychol.* **30**, 419–433.

Van Dis, H., and Larsson, K. (1970). Seminal discharge following intracranial electrical stimulation. *Brain Res.* **23**, 381–386.

von Holtz, E. (1954). Relations between the central nervous system and the peripheral organs. *Br. J. Anim. Behav.* **2**, 89–94.

Westlund, K. N., Bowker, R. M., Ziegler, M. G., and Coulter, J. D. (1983). Noradrenergic projections to the spinal cord of the rat. *Brain Res.* **263**, 15–31.

Whalen, R. E., Edwards, D. A., Lüttge, W. G., and Robertson, R. T. (1969). Early androgen treatment and male sexual behavior in female rats. *Physiol. Behav.* **4**, 33–39.

Whishaw, I. Q., and Kolb, B. (1985). The mating movements of male decorticate rats: Evidence for subcortically generated movements by the male but regulation of approaches by the female. *Behav. Brain Res.* **17**, 171–191.

Wilson, D. M., and Waldson, I. (1968). Models for the generation of the motor output pattern in flying locusts. *Proc. Inst. Electr. Eng.* **56**, 1058–1064.

Yaschine, T., Mena, F., and Beyer, C. (1967). Gonadal hormones and mounting behavior in the female rabbit. *Am. J. Physiol.* **213**, 867–872.

Young, W. C. (1961). The hormones and mating behavior. *In* "Sex and Internal Secretions" (W. C. Young, ed.), Vol. 2, pp. 1173–1239. Williams & Wilkins, Baltimore, Maryland.

On the Nature and Evolution of Imitation in the Animal Kingdom: Reappraisal of a Century of Research

A. Whiten and R. Ham*

SCOTTISH PRIMATE RESEARCH GROUP
PSYCHOLOGICAL LABORATORY
UNIVERSITY OF ST. ANDREWS
ST. ANDREWS, FIFE KY16 9JU
SCOTLAND

I. Introduction

Clearly important in transmissions of human culture such as language acquisition, yet apparently traceable in humbler forms in other parts of the animal kingdom, imitation was an obvious early target for study in the post-Darwinian beginnings of comparative psychology. Attempts to construct mental *scala naturae* for the whole animal kingdom, culminating in Romanes' *Mental Evolution in Animals* (1883), were based principally on casual or anecdotal observations of animal behavior. These soon incorporated a diverse collection of phenomena under the heading of "imitation." Several of these were due to Darwin himself, who had bequeathed to Romanes his unpublished manuscripts on psychological subjects. Darwin gave a delightful description of the behavior of honey bees, quick to "mimic" bumble bees who had been cutting open flowers to get at their nectar; and Romanes added this and other observations by Darwin to a long catalogue of apparently imitative phenomena, such as puppies adopting the washing pattern characteristic of their cat foster parents.

However, the nineteenth century was to see much more than these anecdotal beginnings. Important theoretical and experimental advances were also made. We shall begin our review by examining several of these in some detail, for they appear to have set the investigation of animal imitation onto certain pathways that, as the twentieth century progressed, became deeper ruts along which researchers traveled perhaps too unquestioningly. In recent years, however, the conclusions of a century of research have been disputed from a variety of concep-

*Present address: R. Ham, Scottish Primate Research Group, Department of Psychology, University of Stirling, Stirling, FK9 4LA Scotland.

tual and methodological perspectives, and it is this new ferment we review here, reappraising the earlier work in its light.

Our strategy is to begin at the beginning, first delineating the nineteenth-century origins of the fundamental issues to which we shall keep returning. Only then do we jump forward to summarize the thinking of today on the most basic of these issues: conceptualizing the nature of imitation, in comparison with the plethora of related psychological processes that may explain why one animal's behavior comes to resemble that of another. With this conceptual scheme in place, we step back again to review the methods and findings of research undertaken through the twentieth century up to the present day.

II. FOUR INFLUENTIAL LEGACIES OF NINETEENTH-CENTURY COMPARATIVE PSYCHOLOGY

Early work on imitation learning is not only of historical interest. The latter half of the 19th century saw the formulation of alternative approaches to the study of imitative phenomena that, even today, shape research in the area. The views of major figures in the behavioral biology and psychology of the last century provide an important foundation for understanding the origins of much contemporary disagreement and confusion as well as a benchmark from which to measure a century's progress in the study of imitative behavior (Galef, 1988, p. 4).

Accordingly, Galef (1988) quoted at some length, and set in context, the contributions of three major figures, in turn: Romanes, Thorndike, and Morgan. Rather than reiterate Galef's account, we pick out what seem to us the four influential legacies that the nineteenth century has bequeathed to our own: (1) the classification of imitative phenomena; (2) experimental paradigms; (3) the apparent imitative superiority of primates; and (4) the contrast in vocal versus nonvocal imitation, raised particularly in the case of bird behavior. These then provide a framework for the rest of this article.

A. DEFINING AND DISTINGUISHING IMITATIVE PHENOMENA

Romanes (1882, 1883) did not trouble to define imitation: to him the word was a perfectly ordinary, everyday expression. When Thorndike (1898) came to define imitation to test empirically for it, he used an expression that we are happy to adopt also as our basic definition of nonvocal imitation because it is concise and corresponds to everyday usage: imitation is "learning to do an act from seeing it done" (p. 50).

By the end of the century however, Baldwin (1895) and Morgan (1900) had appreciated that, whatever circumscribed definition one likes to apply to imitation, there are then many imitation-like processes with which we need to contrast it carefully in any sophisticated conception of animal behavior.

J. M. Baldwin's monumental attempt to achieve an integrated understanding of ontogenetic and evolutionary processes of behavioral change and their interactions (e.g., 1895, 1902) bequeathed the "Baldwin Effect" to evolutionary biology and laid the foundations for Piaget's (1951, 1967, 1974, 1976) equally far-reaching biological conceptions of the nature of psychological development, including imitation. In Baldwin's grand scheme, imitation played a central role. The 1895 volume devoted over one hundred pages to the subject of imitation, including one whole chapter devoted to "organic imitation," which was contrasted with "conscious (i.e., mental) imitation." What Baldwin argued was that there is an essentially imitative quality in *all* adaptation by processes of selection, because this involves a certain *replication* of previous states: thus, "we may say that all organic adaptation in a changing environment is a phenomenon of *biological* or *organic imitation*" (p. 278). Although the breadth of this conception of imitation was soon challenged by Morgan (1900, pp. 179–183), imitation could never again be seen as an inherently narrow and easily circumscribed phenomenon!

Morgan (1890, 1896, 1900) developed his own three-way dissection of the phenomenon of imitation, although, like Baldwin, he applied his analysis to both ontogeny and evolution—a common enough endeavor of the period, given the ascendancy of the idea that "ontogeny recapitulates phylogeny" (Gould, 1978). Thus, according to Morgan:

> In the case of the human child we may see three stages in the development of imitation. First, the instinctive stage, where the sound which falls upon the ear is a stimulus to the motor-mechanism of sound production. Secondly, the intelligent stage . . . if we assume that the resemblance of the sounds he utters to the sounds he hears is itself a source of pleasurable satisfaction (and this certainly seems to be the case), intelligence, with the aid of any higher faculty, will secure accommodation and render imitation more and more perfect. And this appears to be the state reached by the mocking-bird or the parrot. But the child soon goes further. He reflects upon the results he has reached; he at first dimly, and then more clearly realizes that they are imitative; and his later efforts at imitation are no longer subject to the chance occurrence of happy results, but are based on a scheme of behavior which is taking place in his mind, are deliberate and intentional, and are directed to a special end more or less clearly perceived as such. He no longer imitates like a parrot; he begins to imitate like a man (Morgan, 1990, pp. 192–193).

This third stage Morgan called "reflective imitation." His analysis of progress from simple to complex levels of imitation was the forerunner of more elaborate schemes of developmental and evolutionary stages that have followed in this century, including those of Piaget (1951) and, most recently, Mitchell (1989).

In the context of such distinctions between simple and complex, "clever" imitation, it is instructive to recall that Romanes (1883), while neglecting any explicit definition of imitation, clearly implied that for him (as for Darwin before him), imitation was a process of only relatively mindless and unintelligent stamp. He noted that human infants imitate very early, but in later life the imitative tendency "may be said to stand in an inverse relation to originality or the higher powers of the mind. Therefore among idiots of a higher grade (though of course not too low) it is usually very strong and retains its supremacy through life . . . the same thing is conspicuously observable in the case of many savages" (p. 225). The everyday expression "to ape" still seems to carry this particular connotation of imitation as simple-minded, rote copying, a situation contrasting ironically with the advanced cognitive abilities that, as we shall detail later on, have recently been suggested to underlie certain forms of imitation special to highly encephalized species.

B.   EXPERIMENTAL PARADIGMS

The approach of Darwin and Romanes (1883) to using anecdotal evidence did not have to wait for twentieth-century behaviorism to be dismissed as uncritical. Of their new animal psychology, Wundt, for example, remarked that "its implicit principle . . . is precisely the opposite of the approved maxim of the exact natural sciences that we should always have recourse to the simplest explanation possible" (1894, p. 345).

The answer of Thorndike (1898) was to experiment. His essential paradigm represented an important advance in rigor and imagination—although we suggest that this was not often matched by the way it was copied by others, with only minor modifications, for much of the experimental work that followed in the present century! The technique was first to allow one animal to learn the behavior required to escape from a "puzzle box" (a cat might have to pull a particular string with its paw, for example); observer cats were then allowed to watch an animal who had become competent in this way and were later compared with naive cats, who had not observed, in their success at escaping when put in the puzzle box themselves. Two types of measure were available: similarity of action pattern and speed of escape. Thorndike emphasized that, while judgments were somewhat subjective as to whether the acts of the observer were copies of the other animal, "we have in the impersonal time records sufficient proofs of [in the case of the cats' latency to escape] the absence of imitation." It is only in the very recent work we describe in the following section that experiments have overcome the difficulty inherent in the distinction Thorndike made: that while speed of learning can be easily and objectively measured, it is insufficient to discriminate imitative copying from alternative types of social learning. To achieve this in the Thorndike paradigm, the experimenter is still thrown back on subjective judgments of similarity in behavioral patterns of the "demonstrator" and putative imitator.

C. Monkey See, Monkey Do

Despite the early optimism, the nineteenth century closed with a negative verdict on the ability of animals truly to imitate, according to the only experiments conducted so far—those of Thorndike. The failures included chicks, cats, and dogs. However, Morgan noted that it was still the case that:

> Professor Thorndike is of the opinion that monkeys are probably imitative in ways beyond the capacity of dogs and cats; but, at the time of writing, he had not substantiated his opinion, by analogous experiments. If so, it will perhaps prove that they are rational beings in the narrower sense defined in a previous chapter of this work. For it appears that the kind of imitation which Mr. Thorndike's experiments go far to disprove, is what we may term reflective imitation . . . the cat had not in any sense grasped the nature of the problem before it, had no notion of just where the difficulty lay, had not the wit to see that the performance of the other cat supplied the missing links (1900, pp. 185–186).

Perhaps monkeys *would* have the wit?

Visalberghi and Fragaszy (1990) noted that in many different languages the words for imitation and monkey (or ape) have common roots. In English, we have the expression "to ape" and the saying "monkey see, monkey do." We do not know how far back such assumptions go, but they are vivid in the earlier treatises we have considered: "Allied, perhaps to the emotions, is what Mr. Darwin calls 'the principle of imitation.' It is proverbial that monkeys carry this principle to ludicrous lengths, and they are the only animals who imitate for the mere sake of imitating" (Romanes, 1882, p. 477). "as the faculty of imitation depends on observation, it is found in greatest force, as we should expect, among the higher or more intelligent animals—reaching its maximum in the monkeys" (Romanes, 1883, p. 225).

"As we should expect" (Romanes' words), the twentieth century did produce experimental results in support of the superiority of primates in imitation, to which were added ethological observations of protocultural behaviors in wild populations presumed to be transmitted by imitation (see Nishida, 1987, for a review). Animal behavior textbooks have tended to present a story of primate imitativeness prefigured in the observations of Romanes (e.g., Manning, 1979; McFarland, 1985).

Recently, however, the superiority of both monkeys and apes has been challenged (Whiten, 1989) and we shall need to discuss the evidence in some detail. Most of the research on imitation this century has, in fact, concerned primates rather than other taxa, excepting the case of vocal imitation in birds.

D. The Special Case of Vocal Imitation in Birds

"The psychology of imitation is difficult of analysis, but it is remarkable as well as suggestive that it should be confined in its manifestations to monkeys and certain birds among animals" (Romanes, 1882, p. 477).

However, there is an obvious difference between these two apparently gifted taxa: almost without exception, research has focused on *vocal* imitation in the case of birds and on *visual* imitation (performance of actions previously watched) in the case of primates and other mammals. Thorndike was eventually to conclude that the two were not deeply connected and that birds' facility, although a "mystery" deserving further study, was a specialization rather than a reflection of a general (and thus "true") imitative ability:

> though the imitation of sounds is so habitual, there does not appear to be any marked general tendency in these birds. There is no proof that parrots do muscular acts from having seen other parrots do them . . . we cannot, it seems to me, connect these phenomena with anything found in the mammals or use them in advantage in a discussion of animal imitation as the forerunner of human (Thorndike, 1911, p. 77).

"In what follows they will be left out of account," Thorndike continues. In this we shall follow him, omitting studies of vocal imitation, a huge research industry in its own right (for reviews, see Kroodsma and Miller, 1982; Slater, 1986). However, it *is* very relevant for us to assess (1) recent explanations offered for *why* the bird-vocal/primate-visual dichotomy might exist, and (2) recent studies that *have* examined the imitation of "muscular acts" in birds, as Thorndike advocated.

III. DEFINING AND DISTINGUISHING IMITATIVE PHENOMENA TODAY

We now revisit each of the four fundamental issues previously discussed. In the case of the first two—the conceptual and the methodological issues—we concentrate on the position today. With this in mind, we shall then examine the empirical evidence gathered through this century for imitation, respectively, in mammals (principally primates) and in birds, where a smaller and more recent literature has emerged.

The classification of mimetic phenomena has been reviewed and revised recently. Galef (1988) analyzed the many terms used to distinguish imitation and imitation-like behavior, and Mitchell (1989), in the spirit of Morgan as described before, distinguished a number of levels of complexity in imitation. The following owes much to these thoughtful and comprehensive essays, although we have to disagree with Galef and with Mitchell on some fundamental points. The array of terms and concepts generated by a century of writing still remains potentially bewildering (Table I). In the next section, our intention is thus to classify all the major concepts in one coherent scheme.

TABLE I
SOME VARIATIONS IN TERMINOLOGY FOR MIMETIC PROCESSES[a]

Preferred terms	Related terms
Mimicry (Wickler, 1968)	First-level imitation (Mitchell, 1989)
Social mimetic processes (implicit in Fig. 1)	Observational learning (Hall, 1963) Imitation (Morgan, 1900) Social learning (Box, 1984)
Social influence (Fig. 1)	Social enhancement (Galef, 1988)
Contagion (Fig. 1: Thorpe, 1963)	Instinctive imitation (Morgan, 1900) Imitation (Humphrey, 1921) Imitative suggestion (Guillaume, 1926) Mimesis, allelominesis (Armstrong, 1951) Pseudi-vicarious instigation (Berger, 1962) Social facilitation (Thorpe, 1963) Coaction (Zajonc, 1965) Stages 2 and 3 imitation (Piaget, 1951) Second-level imitation (Mitchell, 1989)
Social support (Fig. 1)	Social facilitation (Zajonc, 1965)
Stimulus enhancement (Fig. 1: Spence, 1937)	Local enhancement (Thorpe, 1963)
Imitation (Fig. 1) a. Third-level imitation (Mitchell, 1989)	Intelligent imitation (Morgan, 1900) Persistent imitation (Baldwin, 1902) Trial-and-error imitation (Guillaume, 1926) Stage 4–5 imitation (Piaget, 1951)
b. Fourth-level imitation (Mitchell, 1989)	Reflective imitation (Morgan, 1900) Internal persistent imitation (Baldwin, 1902) Symbolic imitation (Guillaume, 1926) Stage 6 imitation (Piaget, 1951) Pretence (Mitchell, 1989)
Goal emulation	Emulation (Tomasello et al., 1987) Fourth-level imitation (Mitchell, 1989)

[a]This is not an exhaustive list but illustrates the proliferation of expressions. Note that by calling terms "related" we mean just that: they are not necessarily synonymous, but rather have significant (and potentially confusing) overlap of meaning.

A. CLASSIFYING SOCIAL MIMICRY: DESCRIPTION AND EXPLANATION

Galef (1988) advocated distinguishing what he calls *descriptive* terms from a number of other terms that refer to possible *explanations* for the behavioral changes so described. The three descriptive terms (see Table I for alternative terms used by others) are *social learning, social enhancement,* and *social transmission.* We agree with Galef that, having merely described a behavioral change such as the emergence and spread of a novel act in a population, the question remains open of just what type of transmission process is responsible.

However, we would dispute that his "descriptive" terms are really only descriptive. The term *social learning,* for example, surely invokes a certain explanatory mechanism: that is, that an animal has acquired a behavior through processes involving both learning and social influence. We suggest that all three of Galef's "descriptive" terms are better regarded as *generic* explanatory terms for why animals have come to act as they do. Within each generic term, more *specific* explanatory distinctions can be made, these including processes that Galef himself is happy to consider "explanatory." Thus, all the (22!) terms that Galef reviews can, in principle, be rearranged into a hierarchically organized explanatory classification along the lines of (although not identical to) our own taxonomy set out in Fig. 1. We still need a supergeneric term for the apex of this taxonomy, and here we use *Mimetic Processes.* By this we mean *all processes whereby some aspect of the behavior of one animal, B, comes to be like that of another, A,* and "mimetic" here implies no more than this. *Mimicry* in the sense of B's behavior being in some sense *copied from* A's is just one specific case among such processes generating behavioral conformity between A and B.

B. A TAXONOMY OF MIMETIC PROCESSES

Figure 1 provides a map of our scheme, which the reader is advised to use in conjunction with the rationale that follows.

1. *Nonsocial Mimetic Processes*

We shall deal with these relatively briefly. They are not of central interest in this article, but it is obviously important to distinguish them. They are defined by exclusion: they do not involve social interaction between A and B.

At the most general level, we must acknowledge the possibilities of *convergence,* where natural selection has caused B to resemble A in its behavior through the exploitation of similar ecological niches and the facing of similar selective pressures, and *common descent,* where B resembles A because of evolutionary descent from a common ancestor. Flying in birds and bats would be an example of the former, and flying in different taxa of birds an example of the latter.

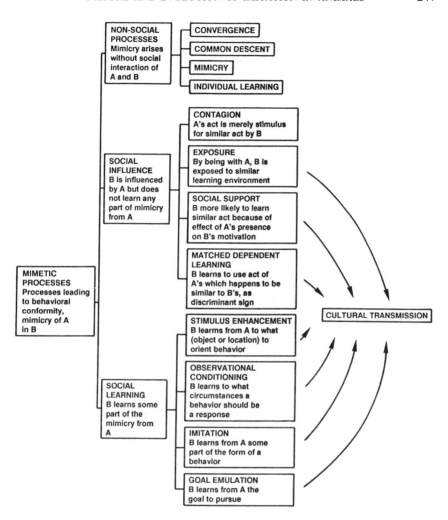

FIG. 1. A taxonomy of mimetic processes. Three layers of categorization are shown. Logically, a category of "Social Processes" should be included, creating four layers. This has been omitted here for simplicity. Seven subcategories have the capacity to produce cultural transmission of behavior (in which behavioral conformity spreads nongenetically through a population and/or across generations), as indicated on the right.

A more specific category is *mimicry,* where natural selection has led members of one population to resemble, and through this means exploit, the behavioral strategy of another. One species may in this way mimic another, as when female fireflies of the genus *Photuris* replicate the female courtship signals of other firefly species, so capturing males of those species for food (Lloyd, 1965).

Alternatively, one sex may mimic the other within a single species: male scorpion flies, for example, mimic females' behavior and then steal food from other males so attracted (Thornhill, 1979). Unlike similarity of behavior achieved through convergence or common descent, mimicry of A by B is maintained and refined by natural selection *because* of the resemblance. In this sense, B can be said to be a copy or imitation of A, and so Mitchell (1989) calls this *level 1 imitation,* the only one of the nonsocial processes we list here to be included in his scheme of imitative phenomena. Although imitation as a learning mechanism (see Fig. 1) is commonly distinguished from mimicry by the criterion that B's imitation of A is derived from B's *observation of* A, Mitchell notes that the existence of a mimic B also depends on observation of A; however, in this case, the observation is not *by* B, but by other individuals whose mistaking of B for A is the basis of the shaping process of natural selection.

Finally, turning to nonsocial processes operating within a single individual's lifetime, we have *individual learning,* where each of two or more individuals independently acquire the same behavior through encountering and being shaped by similar learning environments. This is the ontogenetic analogue of phylogenetic convergence described earlier. Such individual learning can, of course, be further subdivided into many different processes (e.g., trial-and-error, insight, and so forth: Thorpe, 1963), but these need not detain us further here.

2. Social Mimetic Processes: Social Influence and Social Learning

Social processes (see Fig. 1) in which the mimicry of A by B is dependent on social effects of A on B is subdivided, in turn, into *social influence* versus *social learning.* The difference between social learning and social influence is that in the former, B *learns* some aspect of the behavioral similarity *from* A, whereas in *social influence* B does not learn the similarity from A, but is nevertheless subject to one or other sort of social influence from A that, in concert with nonsocial processes such as trial-and-error learning, brings about a similarity in the behavior of A and B. *Social influence* includes what Galef labels *social enhancement* ("a generic to refer to all social influences on performance of established responses" 1988, p. 13), but we avoid his expression to avoid confusion with *local* or *stimulus enhancement,* one of the accepted subcategories of social learning (see Fig. 1 and the following).

We can subdivide processes of *social influence* in terms of the *type of influence* that occurs between A and B, giving us four categories: *contagion, exposure, social support,* and *matched dependent learning.* We subdivide social *learning* using the same principle, but here the social effects can be expressed specifically in terms of *what B learns from A;* this gives us *imitation* and three other categories.

Before we describe these categories of social learning and social influence, we wish to make explicit two of our attitudes to classification and definition. These attitudes are those we take to all of scientists' technical analyses of phenomena like "intelligence," "play," and "imitation," which are already covered, less precisely, by everyday language (see also Whiten and Byrne, 1988b).

First, we believe it is futile to argue about what imitation "really" or "truly" is: the question of what scientists or other people usually mean by "imitation" is a legitimate and empirical one, but the business at hand, instead, is to make certain important *conceptual distinctions* between categories, to the clear definition of which we then need to attach convenient labels, one of which happens to be the everyday word "imitation."

Second, it does not follow that anybody can set themselves up to "legislate" on what, henceforth, the formal distinctions and definitions shall be. Distinctions are likely to be adopted and maintained in the discipline just so long as they do a useful job. There is no *absolute* meaning of "imitation" that we might waste time debating. Each investigator will be well advised to define such terms at the time of each new application of them.

3.   Types of Social Learning

Earlier in this paper we adopted Thorndike's simple definition of imitation: "learning to do an act from seeing it done." But we must be careful to discriminate a number of ways through which B may have learned from A the basis of a subsequent similarity between their actions.

a.   Stimulus Enhancement (Local Enhancement). This is the category perhaps most often confused with imitation in practice. Its nature is nicely illustrated by the example of milk-bottle opening by tits (*Parus caeruleus*: Fisher and Hinde, 1949; Hinde and Fisher, 1951), the cultural spread of which seemed difficult to explain by anything other than a process corresponding to Thorndike's definition. However, following Krebs *et al.* (1972), Sherry and Galef (1984) showed that the transmission of such behavior could be explained by an observer bird simply having its attention drawn to open bottle tops: trial-and-error learning could achieve the rest.

Thus, if we make a distinction between the actions involved in opening a milk-bottle top and orientation to milk bottles, it is only the latter that B learns from A in the case of local enhancement. A subdivision may be helpful in some contexts, between *local enhancement,* as defined by drawing attention to a particular locale in the environment, and *stimulus enhancement,* where attention is drawn to an object or part of an object, irrespective of its location.

The term imitation would thus be reserved for cases where B learns something about the *form* of the act: about *how* to open milk bottles, for example, as opposed to a mere concentration of attention on the bottle tops themselves. We shall see that the imitation/local enhancement distinction is a crucial one when we come to survey evidence across the animal kingdom. However, we should also emphasize that in practice it may be difficult or impossible, in a case of local enhancement, to distinguish whether animal B is indeed *only* having its attention drawn to some environmental features (learning nothing about behavior *per se*) or is, in fact, learning to *orient its behavior* to those environmental features. We could think of the latter as a form of imitative copying restricted just to the specific behavioral feature of *orientation* with respect to the environment. Thus, when we normally use the term imitation, we imply more than this: we imply that B has learned something of the intrinsic form of an action from A, apart from any extrinsic aspects of orientation to features of the environment.

b. Observational Conditioning. Mineka *et al.* (1984) found that juvenile monkeys (*Macaca mulatta*) who initially showed no fear of snakes, did so when observing their wild-born parents acting fearfully in the presence of snakes, and continued to react fearfully themselves when later exposed to snakes without the parent present. The juveniles' actions were mimetic of their parents' on a number of measures, including avoidance and facial expression. Mineka *et al.* called this "observational conditioning": a form of classical conditioning in which an un- conditioned response (in this case, fearful behavior as a response to fearful behavior in others) becomes associatively conditioned to a new stimulus (in this case, the snake). Later work has indicated constraints on the flexibility of such learning: fear is not so readily conditioned to biologically irrelevant objects like flowers (Cook *et al.,* 1987; Mineka and Cook, 1988).

Observational conditioning is similar to the process of stimulus enhancement insofar as B learns from A *to what* it should direct actions already in its reper- toire; it is just that stimulus enhancement typically refers to appetitive actions and observational conditioning, as studied by Mineka *et al.,* to avoidance reactions. This is a trivial difference and if it were the only one, the two categories should be collapsed together. However, in observational conditioning, the animal learns more than just an *orientation* element: the monkeys in the snake experiment appeared to have learned something more general about the *significance* of the stimulus that led to other aspects of behavioral conformity, such as fearful facial expressions and bodily postures. More importantly, it is necessary for observa- tional conditioning that B initially shows an unconditioned mimetic response contingent on A's reaction to the stimulus, whereas this appears not to be the case in stimulus enhancement, where B may merely watch A and then much later express its "latent learning" (Thorpe, 1963).

c. Imitation. We can distinguish from these processes the one in which B learns some aspect(s) of the intrinsic *form* of an act from A, and this is what we mean by imitation. This seems to be fully consistent with everyday usage as well as with Thorndike's definition, previously mentioned. Of course, no imitation of A by B will be perfect, and "some aspect(s)" in our definition is intended to acknowledge that imitative copying of the form of another individual's act may vary between the faithful and the poor and encompass only a subset of the elements potentially copyable.

A further question is what is to be meant by "learning" in our (and in Thorndike's) definition. In the everyday sense, a person can imitate another doing some everyday act like waving, yet the imitator is not "learning to wave" insofar as some sort of waving is already in their behavioral repertoire. The sense in which this *is* learning is that of *being shaped through information transfer:* the form of the imitator's act is derived from the information gained in observing the other's waving. To be reasonably consistent with everyday usage it is this relatively broad notion of learning that we must prefer, noting as we do so that in the animal literature, the emphasis is often on learning in the more restricted sense of acquiring behaviors novel to the individual's repertoire. But imitation of acts that can be said to be already in B's repertoire must also be distinguished from the mere social influence involved in contagion (see the following).

d. Goal Emulation. One particular element whose copying deserves a special category is that which is the culmination of a goal-directed sequence. Tomasello *et al.* (1987) found that juvenile chimpanzees (*Pan troglodytes*) who had watched another chimpanzee use a stick to rake in out-of-reach food were then themselves quicker to do the same than control animals who had not watched; however, the youngsters invented their own ways of using the stick, rather than copying the particular form of the behavior they had previously observed. Tomasello *et al.* suggested that the chimpanzees were not attempting to reproduce the model's *behavior* so much as the *results* they achieved. Following a distinction made by the child psychologist David Wood, (1988) Tomasello *et al.* (1990) call the first of these "impersonation" (equivalent to imitation as we have defined it) and the second "emulation."

Two comments on this distinction must be made. First, we would argue that a distinction between copying *behavior* versus its *results* is not clear-cut in practice. Any "result" of an action sequence will have to be achieved by a final act in that sequence that, however variable the acts that precede it, will inevitably have some consistency of form. In the example under discussion, that might be described as "raking the food in." Put more generally, what we are saying is that any imitation is unlikely to be perfect and thus always to be partial; and partial imitative copies might include just the final act, or the final act and a subset of elements preceding it, or several of these elements without the final act. Thus, emulation as described by Tomasello could be redescribed as just *imitation* of the final act in a goal-directed sequence. It is for this reason, coupled with the fact that dictionaries tend to equate emulation with imitation, that we add "goal" to the label "emulation" to distinguish it from (other) imitation.

Indeed, our second comment is that imitation of only the "goal act" in a sequence *is* of sufficient interest to justify maintaining a special category called emulation. Emulation may in some cases require sufficient intelligence to recognize a goal achieved by others (e.g., "getting the food raked in") *as* a goal—and a goal potentially achievable by one's own novel problem-solving attempts. This leads to an expectation different from the traditional one that imitation should be shown by particularly intelligent taxa of animals: if emulation is the mark of intelligence, thorough imitative copying of the form of others' acts may often be *avoided* by intelligent species—even if it is within their capability.

4. Types of Social Influence

We must briefly distinguish from the processes discussed in the last section a number in which mimicry depends on some social influence of A on B, without B actually acquiring from A the information underlying the resemblance. We shall need to return to these distinctions later on when we discuss social facilitation.

a. Contagion. Thorpe (1963) defined contagion as the "unconditioned release of an instinctive behavior in one animal by the performance of the same behavior in another animal." *Social facilitation* is a common synonym. An example would be the chicken who is allowed to eat until satiated, but on being introduced to others that are feeding, resumes eating (McFarland, 1985). Actions subject to contagion are likely to be shared by populations (or subpopulations such as one sex). This distinguishes contagion from imitation based on acts already in the repertoire, which may occur between just two individuals (see the example of Fifi and Gilka on page 265).

b. Exposure. By simply being with (or following) A, B may be exposed to a similar learning environment and thus acquire similar behavior. As Galef (1988) says of one of Thorndike's (1911) own examples, "it seems unlikely that birds lose their fear of trains as a result of socially induced enhanced attention to them. Socially induced increased exposure to trains and consequent habituation to the threatening stimuli that trains emit seem a likely explanation of the observed social transmission of behavior."

c. Social Support. B may also be more likely to learn behavior like A's in the mere presence of A and its learning environment, because A affects B's motivational state. For example, the presence of conspecifics can reduce fear (Stamm, 1961). Zajonc (1969) suggested that the presence of companions may "energize" others, but this has proved difficult to distinguish from fear reduction (Galef, 1988).

d. Matched Dependent Learning. Miller and Dollard (1941) showed that a rat could learn through reinforcement to use the actions of another as a discriminative stimulus to guide its own behavior. Where the experimenter arranges that the two actions are similar (e.g., B learns that if A turns right in a maze, it should do the same to gain reinforcement), behavioral conformity is the result. The essential learning process is operant conditioning—B could just as well be trained to act in this way (turning right) using rat A performing a different act (e.g., turning left) or even replacing rat A with a flashing light as the discriminative stimulus. However, this does not mean the process is an oddity produced only in the experimentalist's laboratory; indeed, Skinner (1953) showed that the requirements for learning matched dependent behavior are likely to be common in nature. It is often the case that an animal is reinforced when it uses an act (e.g., a foraging technique) like the one it has just observed a conspecific perform. However, no part of the similarity in the form of A's and B's behavior is based on B copying what it has observed A do: the similarity is entirely due to piggyback reinforcement contingencies.

IV.   NEW METHODOLOGIES

A.   VARIATIONS ON THORNDIKE'S PROCEDURE

The essential contribution of Thorndike in distinguishing among mimetic processes was the experimental design in which a "demonstrator" animal performed a task in front of a naive observer, the test then being whether the observer required a smaller number of trials to achieve some criterion of success on the task when compared with an animal who had not been allowed to observe the demonstrator. The eager acceptance of this method by comparative psychologists during the present century gave rise to several variations that, following Thorndike's negative results with nonprimates and optimism about primates' abilities, have almost exclusively been applied to monkeys and apes. However, none of these methods can satisfactorily distinguish imitation from all the alternative processes now arrayed before us (see Fig. 1).

In the Kline single-cage method (e.g., Haggarty, 1909), the naive individual is housed with the demonstrator so it can manipulate the task apparatus between episodes of demonstration. This is, perhaps, a more natural situation than the original Thorndike design where the observer watches from a separate compartment and is only later allowed access to the manipulandum itself. However, both designs suffer from an inability to distinguish imitation from local or stimulus enhancement. As in the case of tits and milk bottles, the observer may solve the problem more quickly than nonobservers because its actions are directed more often to the relevant area or object, thereby facilitating learning by trial-and-error.

Apparently circumventing this criticism, Warden and Jackson (1935) introduced a duplicate-cage approach in which the observer was provided with an identical task to that being performed at the time by the demonstrator in an adjacent cage—in this case, pulling a chain to expose food in a recess. But, as Galef (1988) has recently emphasized, although this may rule out local or stimulus enhancement (in the precise sense referring to the unique object manipulated by the demonstrator), it does not do so in the more general sense where stimulus enhancement is taken to refer to the entire *class of objects* sharing the stimulus characteristics of the object manipulated by the demonstrator (the sense in which Spence (1937) actually defined stimulus enhancement). If an observer monkey's attention was directed in this fashion toward its duplicate chain apparatus, as seems plausible, the faster acquisition of chain-pulling that Warden and Jackson recorded still does not count as evidence for imitation as opposed to stimulus enhancement.

B.   THE DAWSON AND FOSS "TWO-ACTION" TEST

It was not until 1965 that a design was offered by Dawson and Foss that explicitly distinguishes imitation from local enhancement. Dawson and Foss's experiment was also interesting in that it appears to be the first after Thorndike's to test for (nonvocal) imitation in birds. In their experiment, observer budgerigars (*Melopsittacus undulatus*) watched one of three trained demonstrators working with the same task of removing the lid from a dish of food; however, one did this with its foot, another by grasping with its beak, and the third by nudging with its beak. If observers tended to use a technique more similar to the one they had seen, rather than one they had not seen, this appears to be explicable only by imitation. Local enhancement is ruled out by use of the same manipulandum for each of the different types of action. Dawson and Foss did, in fact, find that their subjects used the techniques each had observed, although, with only five subjects, the authors interpreted their results as preliminary. A replication has been attempted that we shall discuss later.

C.   HAYES AND HAYES' "DO-AS-I-DO" TEST

The important principle of the Dawson and Foss procedure is that alternative actions are performed with the same manipulandum. Two alternatives, as opposed to the three they used, would suffice for the logic of the design. However, as the number of alternatives is increased, the probability of chance concordance between demonstrator and observer techniques falls, and it should then be possible to demonstrate any imitative ability that exists with a relatively small number of subjects. An approach used by Hayes and Hayes (1952) with a single chimpanzee can perhaps be seen as an extreme extension of this logic. The Hayes' *trained* their home-reared chimpanzee, Viki, to imitate so that on the command "Do this!" she would usually attempt to copy the action the human performed next, such as clapping or pulling the mouth wide open. It took about 12 rewarded acts for Viki to grasp the general rule, after which imitation could be tested by recording only spontaneous, nonrewarded imitations. This continued through 70 different types of action, 55 of which were judged to be responded to with a correspondingly similar act. The probability of such concordance occurring by chance is vanishingly small. This study is, therefore, often taken to be the most convincing demonstration of the fact that chimpanzees can imitate. Presumably, one cannot "train" an animal to imitate in this way unless it has some inherent imitative capacity. Unfortunately, like Dawson and Foss, Hayes and Hayes did not mention many details of procedure that (quite apart from the sample size!) means that the method, which appears powerful in principle, begs replication.

D. SYSTEMATIC FIELD OBSERVATION

The twentieth century has seen the emergence of systematic and quantitative field studies that have taken the study of cultural transmission and observational learning far beyond the naturalistic anecdotes of the preceding century (Nishida, 1987). Thus, for example, it has been possible to classify different subcultures of chimpanzees (*P. troglodytes*) that show variations in the use of certain tools and food types not explicable by the local availability of the raw materials (McGrew, et al., 1979; McGrew, 1992). Cross-fostering showed that oyster catcher (*Haematopus ostralegus*) chicks adopt the particular technique of the local cultural group to which their parents belong—those that stab or those that hammer to open the shells of the mussels they eat (Norton-Griffiths, 1969). Perhaps most famous of all, the diffusion of new feeding techniques in groups of Japanese macaques (*Macaca fuscata*) has been documented in some detail (Kawai, 1965; Itani and Nishimura, 1973). The literature has become enormously rich with such observational evidence; in a nonexhaustive survey of foraging behavior alone, Lefebvre and Palameta (1988; Table 7.1) list 73 studies claiming social transmission in fish, reptiles, birds, and mammals.

The role of imitation or other mechanisms through which transmission occurs is much less well specified. However, with an increasingly refined understanding of the discriminations that must be made in the field between the alternative mimetic processes that may underlie the spontaneous behavior observed (see Section III), some fieldworkers have recently attempted the critical observations. Thus, in a group of vervet monkeys (*Cercopithecus aethiops*) previously observed for many years, Hauser (1988) was able to document the emergence and spread of the use of acacia pods to extract exudate from a hole in an acacia tree. The whole process was quite rapid, with four individuals adopting the technique within 9 days and another two within 22 days. Given continuity of observation, details of the first incorporation of the act into each animal's repertoire provided evidence that different individuals acquired the technique by different routes. One appeared to deduce what to do from observing the end product (the model finally eating dipped pods), whereas another watched the model prepare and consume pods "and then performed the whole behavior."

The latter observation is still not a watertight demonstration of imitation because it must remain possible that some parts of the developing actions escaped observation and these might have been subject to other processes like trial-and-error learning; unless such a case study is seamlessly continuous, convincing field evidence for imitation may remain elusive. What such detailed case studies can achieve is to specify more clearly than before the scope for imitation and how it might interact with other mimetic processes—an important advance in field studies.

V. The Distribution of Imitation in the Animal Kingdom

We have already noted that the preliminary conclusion of the nineteenth century has become the common "textbook" wisdom of the twentieth: primates, almost alone among animal taxa, have been seen as having a special aptitude for imitation. No experimental work appears to have even been attempted on invertebrates or on vertebrates other than birds and mammals. Even then, following early negative results, little work has been carried out with nonprimate species. Passingham's (1982) review mentioned just a little evidence for imitation in cetaceans, in addition to that for primates.

In the past few years, however, the presumed special ability of primates to imitate has come under strong attack. At the same time, fresh attempts to investigate imitation in birds and in other mammals have offered positive results. Century-old received wisdoms suddenly appear questionable.

A. Monkey See, Monkey Do?

1. Observational Studies of Imitation by Monkeys

"Probably the single most impressive case of imitation on record concerns the changes in food technology of the Japanese macaques on Koshima Island" (Premack, 1984, p. 17). The novel potato-washing of a juvenile female, Imo (Kawai, 1965), "soon was imitated by other monkeys" (McFarland, 1985, p. 514); and the habit "was copied . . . subsequently by nearly all the younger members of her troop" (Manning, 1979, p. 199).

This flagship case of imitative cultural transmission in monkeys has recently been questioned from several directions. First, Green (1975) noticed that potatoes were selectively given by the provisioner only to those animals that washed potatoes, suggesting reinforcement as the potential shaper of the behavior. The proximity of particular age groups and matrilines to the provisioner might even explain the social pattern through which the behavior spread. Second, Galef (1990) scrutinized the time course over which the novel act spread and noted that both mean and median times for acquisition of potato washing after Imo showed the behavior were about 2 years. A second habit called placer mining, in which wheat grains were separated from sand by releasing them into the water, spread even more slowly. This is hardly consistent with acquisition by imitation, which, when investigated under experimental conditions, is assumed to require only moments for implementation (e.g., Warden and Jackson, 1935; Hayes and Hayes, 1952; Meltzoff, 1988). In short, although the behavior *may* have been transmitted by imitation, this remains unproved. Stimulus enhancement—in which the behavior of potato washers drew the attention of others to the potatoes, the water, and their conjunction—coupled with trial-and-error learning, possibly enhanced by caretakers, would appear sufficient to explain the phenomenon.

We have already noted that, even with careful attention to such distinctions in the case of a much more rapidly transmitted act—pod-dipping in vervet monkeys—Hauser (1988) had to concede that clear evidence for imitation was not forthcoming. Indeed, in another study where researchers were alert for signs of imitation, its absence was striking, given the use to which it could apparently have been put. Boinski and Fragaszy (1989) found that, although infant squirrel monkeys (*Saimiri oerstedii*) had ample time to observe adults using the technique of rubbing noxious spines off caterpillars using their tail tips, the infants did not themselves attempt this when starting to handle caterpillars. Instead, they appeared to have to learn through trial and error, involving direct experience of the noxious spines.

Despite monkeys' reputation, other studies in wild populations have actually generated rather few additional claims of imitative transmission (Table II). None provide stronger evidence for imitation than those we have just reviewed. Taken together with other studies on food selectivity, they do suggest that observational learning at the level of stimulus enhancement often plays an important role in the development of food selection and foraging behavior (Whitehead, 1986; Whiten, 1989). However, even at this level there is evidence that species-specific foraging patterns may develop without opportunity to learn by observation of elders (Milton, in press).

2. Experimental Studies of Imitation by Monkeys

Tables III and IV list experimental studies of monkeys' social learning, which have, respectively, claimed positive and negative evidence for imitation. The two lists are about equal in size and, given different reasons for doubting the basis for both kinds of results, do not hold promise of a clear verdict.

In the case of the positive results, the most common problem is, yet again, a failure to distinguish imitation from local or stimulus enhancement. Recall that even the duplicate cage method of Warden and Jackson (1935) does not avoid this problem, because it exactly duplicates the stimulus characteristics for the potential imitator.

This does not disprove imitation but, as in the case of the observational

TABLE II
NATURAL OBSERVATIONS CLAIMED TO BE REPORTS OF IMITATION IN MONKEYS

Reference	Genus	Observation	Possible explanation[a]
Carpenter (1887)	Macaca	Learning to open oysters with stones	SE
Tinklepaugh and Hartman (1930)	Macaca	Young induced to eat afterbirth after observing mother	SE
Imanishi (1957)	Macaca	Potato washing, rice throwing, caramel eating	T&E, SE
Carner (1955)	Macaca	Trained by imitation to aid experimenter in his botanical collections	SE
Hall (1963)	Papio	Dug in the same place after observing another	SE
Marais (1969)	Papio	Cracking the fruit of the baobab tree by pounding it with stones	T&E
Hamilton and Tilson (1985)	Papio	Catching fish	T&E, SE
Hauser (1988)	Cercopithecus	Dipping pods into exudate from a tree	T&E, SE

[a]SE, Stimulus enhancement; T&E, trial and error.

studies, it means that imitation is not yet proved. What is required is application of the methods used either by Dawson and Foss or Hayes and Hayes, reviewed earlier. Strangely, neither of these approaches has been applied to the most studied group, the monkeys, until recently.

In using a Dawson and Foss "two-action" approach, Ham (1990) also aimed to avoid a criticism that can be made of most of the *negative* results in Table IV: that they require tool use such as using a stick to obtain food. By contrast with chimpanzees (to be discussed later), macaques and, indeed, most monkeys are not naturally extensive tool users. Ham therefore used a task designed to be an analogue of routine manipulation in food processing. Observer monkeys (*Macaca arctoides*) watched one of two types of model working at exactly the same manipulandum, essentially a T-bar that could be grasped with both hands like the handlebars of a bicycle. One model twisted this and the other pulled it forward and, in each case, the T-bar disgorged a peanut. Observers were then given access to the apparatus, and the effect of having watched either pulling or twisting was gauged through various measures of the effort put into pulling versus twisting.

This test for imitation by the observers was conducted without any reinforcement being available, reflecting a further criticism of many of the earlier experiments where testing for "imitation" was continued, even after a successful performance gained a food reward. Warden and Jackson (1935), for example, quoted the results of six trials for each action; but if a reward is gained in the first trial, the other five are not independent tests of imitation because they are contaminated with the effects of reinforcement (not necessarily in an effective way, however: in only 3 of 11 cases was a successful first "imitation" of chain-pulling followed by "imitation" in the next trial!). In Ham's experiment, with no reward, whether the observer had watched pulling or twisting had no significant effect on the ratio of its own subsequent pulling versus twisting, either in the first few attempts or over the whole of the 3-min manipulation period.

Although further experiments of this type are now needed, combining the rigor of an unreinforced two-action test with a user-friendly food-processing analogue, the current verdict on monkey imitation must be "not proved." Note also, however, that nearly all the work (see, especially, Table III) has been restricted to the genus *Macaca*—the white rat of the laboratory primatologist. Other taxa may yet turn out to be (better) imitators.

B. APING

1. Observational Studies of Imitation by Apes

Nearly all the evidence for imitation in apes comes from common chimpanzees (*P. troglodytes*). Chimpanzee tool culture often follows Japanese monkey potato-washing in the classic textbook accounts of primate imitation. Thus, for example, we hear of "the use of simple tools which is certainly learnt afresh when each new generation of young chimpanzees copies from its parents" (Manning, 1979, p. 199), and "the technique of fishing for termites is learned by imitation and is passed through the population by cultural tradition" (McFarland, 1985, p. 513). However, the basis for this conclusion is essentially that juveniles closely observe mature tool users and later come to adopt the behavior in a gradual step-wise manner (McGrew, 1977). This, however, is a process that takes many years, and it seems impossible to disprove that it results from trial-and-error learning directed by the actions of others toward certain stimulus arrays (termite mounds, sticks, and possibly their conjunction): in other words, by stimulus enhancement.

In addition, captive chimpanzees reared without access to models to imitate may show tendencies to poke sticks into holes (Lancaster, 1975). Social facilitation of this maturing tendency is thus another process that may be operative. This is a further general problem in identifying imitation in the wild. Consider the following (is it a case of imitation or local enhancement combined with social facilitation of a maturing tendency?):

TABLE III

CLAIMED POSITIVE LABORATORY EVIDENCE FOR IMITATION IN MONKEYS

Reference	Genus	Task	Method[a]	Possible explanation[b]
Hobhouse (1901)	Various	Manipulative	B	SE, SF
Kinnaman (1902)	Macaca	Pulling a plug	B	SE, SF
		Pressing a lever		
		Opening a box		
Haggarty (1909)	Various	Manipulative, involving a rope, screen, plug, and button	A	SE, SF
Aronowitsch and Chotin (1929)	Macaca	Learned by observation to respond opposite to training	A	OC
Warden and Jackson (1935)	Macaca	Pulling a chain to expose a raisin in hole	C	SE, SF
Warden et al. (1940)	Various	Manipulative	C	SE, SF
Presley and Riopelle (1959)	Macaca	Avoiding an electric shock by jumping over a barrier	B	OC
Miller et al. (1959)	Macaca	Fear response	A	OC

Reference	Genus	Behavior	Method[a]	Mechanism[b]
Myers (1970)	Macaca	Learned to respond on a multiple reinforcement schedule	B	OC
Beck (1976)	Macaca	Throwing action of tool at inaccessible food	A	T&E
Cook et al. (1985)	Macaca	Fear of snakes	B	OC
Anderson (1985)	Macaca	Manipulating metal rods to reach otherwise inaccessible food	B	SE, SF
Chevalier-Skolnikoff (1989)	Ateles	Putting things in mouth, ringing bells, examining objects, interactions with a bucket (Piagetian Stages 3 and 4)	A	SE
	Cebus	Banging two objects together, putting tub in a moat, draping a cloth on a branch (Piagetian stages 5 and 6)	A	SE, T&E

[a]A, Kline Single Cage Method; B, Thorndike Observation Cage Method; C, Warden Duplicate Cage Method.
[b]SE, stimulus enhancement; SF, social facilitation; OC, observational conditioning; T&E, trail-and-error.

TABLE IV
CLAIMED NEGATIVE LABORATORY EVIDENCE FOR IMITATION IN MONKEYS

Reference	Genus	Task	Method[a]
Thorndike (1898, 1901)	Cebus	Opening a box	B
Watson (1908, 1914)	Cebus Macaca Papio	Manipulative	B
Beck (1972, 1973a,b)	Papio	Use a tool to reach inaccessible food	A
Beck (1974)	Macaca	Reaching pan with stick	A
Antinucci and Visalberghi (1986)	Cebus	Cracking nuts	A
Visalberghi (1987)	Cebus	Cracking nuts	A
Westergaard and Fragaszy (1987)	Cebus	Probing for syrup	A
Adams-Curtis (1987)	Cebus	Mechanistic puzzle	A
Visalberghi and Trinca (1987)	Cebus	Displacing reward in a horizontal tube	A
Fragaszy and Visalberghi (1989)	Cebus	Cracking nuts using tools, displacing reward in tube using stick	A
Fragaszy and Visalberghi (1990)	Cebus		A

[a]A, Kline Single Cage Method; B, Thorndike Observation Cage Method.

"A three-year-old male (Atlas), for example, ran to the security of his mother as an adult male gave pant-hoots preceding a charging display, then watched as a male ran, slapping the ground with his hands, stamping with his feet, ending his display by jumping up and drumming with his hands on a treetrunk. When the adult male had moved away, the infant left his mother, ran a short distance with much stamping of feet, then paused near the drumming tree. He gazed at it, approached, and—very cautiously and gently—hit it twice with his knuckles" (Goodall, 1986, p. 336).

Such ambiguities mean that much of the more convincing evidence of spontaneous imitation comes from studies of captive animals, whose adoption of human patterns of behavior cannot be explained away as the interaction of enhancement and maturation of species-specific tendencies. Such evidence is anecdotal by its very nature, yet it must be said that, taken as a whole, it goes significantly beyond anything described for any species of monkey, both in scale (numbers of records by different observers on different individuals: Table V) and

TABLE V
OBSERVATIONAL REPORTS OF IMITATION IN CHIMPANZEES

Reference	Observation	Possible explanation[a]
Rothman and Teuber (1915)	Learned to open doors, insert keys into locks, use a lever to regulate water supply, scrub floor, sweep with a broom	SE, I
Shepherd (1915)	Opening a watch	SE
Furness (1916)	Learned to dig with a spade, screw with a screw, scrub, and sweep	I
Sheak (1923)	Learned to wipe nose with a handkerchief, drive nails with a hammer, and to sew	I
Kellogg and Kellogg (1933)	Learned to brush hair, open cupboards	I, SE
Kohler (1925)	Learned to use a paintbrush, to stack boxes to reach a banana	T&E
Yerkes (1943)	Learned to spit, to imitate facial expressions	I
Kearton (1925)	Learned to wash clothes	I
Hayes (1951)	Learned to brush hair, to apply lipstick, brush teeth, sharpen pencils	I
Hayes and Hayes (1951)	Imitated on command	I
Hayes and Hayes (1952)	Stick and tunnel, stick and string problems, ball throwing	SE
Hayes and Hayes (1953)	Imitation set series—patting head, clapping hands, protruding tongue	I
Gardner and Gardner (1969)	Soaping and drying a doll in imitation	I
Menzel et al. (1972), Menzel (1973)	Creation of ladders	SE
Tomasello et al. (1989)	Throwing chips as a way of initiating play	I, SE
Locale-specific behaviors		
van Lawick-Goodall (1973)	Termite fishing	T&E, SE
Sugiyama and Koman (1979)	Cracking nuts with stones, using various techniques to reach lower branches of a tree	T&E, SE

(*continued*)

TABLE V
(*continued*)

Reference	Observation	Possible explanation[a]
de Waal (1982)	Limping gait	I, OC
Sumita *et al.* (1985)	Cracking walnuts with stones	SE, T&E
Nishida and Hiraiwa (1982)	Differences in population in preferred ant species	T&E
Fouts *et al.* (1989)	Acquisition of sign language	I

[a]SE, Stimulus enhancement; OC, observational conditioning; T&E, trial and error; I, imitation.

apparent accuracy and complexity of copying. Space permits support of the latter assertion with just a small selection of examples.

In one case, Hayes and Hayes (1952) described how the home-reared chimpanzee Viki "appropriated a lipstick, stood on the washbasin, looked in the mirror, and applied the cosmetic—not at random, but to her mouth. She then pressed her lips together and smoothed the color with her finger, just as she had seen the act performed" (p. 451) and "when she saw an experimenter sharpen some pencils, she could not imitate immediately; but within a minute she got a pencil from the next room, returned with it, put it in the sharpener, and turned the crank."

Goodall (1986) cites an incident "in which Maurice Temerlin was ill. After having been violently sick, he staggered to his bed, followed by a concerned Lucy. A few minutes later she went back to the bathroom, stood upright, leaned over the toilet (as he had done), opened her mouth wide, and made gagging sounds as if trying to imitate his vomiting (Temerlin, 1975)."

A common feature of such episodes as listed in Table V is that they have no obvious reward beyond performing the act itself. This is in contrast to the monkey records in Table 2, where all the imitation claimed is for cases in which obtaining food was the end, so that trial-and-error coupled with stimulus enhancement can be invoked as an alternative explanation. This is not the case for the chimpanzee records in which there is no extrinsic goal at stake. Perhaps it was really just chimpanzees that Romanes (1882) had in mind when he talked of "the only animals who imitate for the mere sake of imitating." Of course, if these records are taken for evidence of imitation, then it becomes likely that imitation does play an important part in the life of wild chimpanzees also, as suggested in other records cited in Table V; although "imitation for imitation's sake" can be quite persuasive evidence of the *ability* to imitate, we must presume that the functional significance of imitation in the wild is *generally* to imitate behavior that *does* achieve useful ends. Unfortunately, it is exactly in such natural cases that it will be difficult or impossible for the scientist to discriminate imitation from other mechanisms.

This does not mean that an animal with the capacity to imitate in the wild will not adopt particular cultural "fashions" so long as they confer no selective *disadvantage*. Possible examples include the "grooming handclasp" (McGrew and Tutin, 1978), a special posture adopted in grooming, and the "leaf-clipping display" (Nishida, 1980), in which a courting male rapidly bites a large leaf: each pattern has been observed in some chimpanzee populations but not in others that have been studied for years. Goodall (1986) described a case that appeared to show the beginnings of such cultural transmission, through imitation: "At Gombe a juvenile, Fifi, suddenly showed *wrist-shaking* . . . Fifi used it when threatening an older female. A younger individual, Gilka, was with Fifi at the time. The following week not only was Fifi seen to wrist-shake again (in a similar context), but Gilka too used the gesture. Subsequently Gilka wrist-shook frequently and in a variety of contexts" (p. 145).

Claims for imitation based on observation of other apes (Table VI) are fewer, which may in part reflect the smaller number of studies on them. They also appear to lack the quality of those quoted above for chimpanzees, particularly the copying of arbitrary actions, with just one exception, digging by an orangutan (Furness, 1916). Yerkes remarked on the contrasts with chimpanzees in orangutans' failure to imitate stacking of boxes to reach bananas (1916) and gorillas'

TABLE VI
OBSERVATIONAL REPORTS OF IMITATION IN OTHER APES

Reference	Genus	Observation	Possible explanation[a]
Vosmaer (1778)	Pongo	Spitting in imitation of man	T&E,*
Abel (1818)	Pongo	Imitation of a kiss	T&E,*
Furness (1916)	Pongo	Digging with a spade	
Yerkes and Yerkes (1927)	Pongo	Learned by observation to lift the lid of a sewage tank	SE
Carpenter (1937)	Gorilla	Synchrony of moods and play behavior	C, T&E, OC
Harrison (1960)	Pongo	Nest building and feeding habits	T&E, SE
Wright (1972)	Pongo	Flaking stone tools	SE, T&E
Galdikas (1982)	Pongo	Tool use	SE, T&E

[a]SE, Stimulus enhancement, SF, social facilitation; OC, observational conditioning; T&E, trial-and-error; C, contagion; *, history of animal unknown.

failures to imitate the solving of lock and key problems (Yerkes and Yerkes, 1927), although these may reflect only a lack of chimpanzees' tool-using pro-clivities in these other apes. It would be premature to conclude that the chim-panzee is the only ape to imitate (Russon and Galdikas, 1991), although that is an intriguing hypothesis.

One final observation consistent with this is the recent reporting of intentional teaching in chimpanzees (Boesch, 1991) in which a mother was described as performing nut-cracking in a slower and more deliberate way following a display of incompetence by her infant. Boesch interprets this as *demonstration,* which has not been shown for any other nonhuman species. There would, of course, be no functional role for demonstration in a species that did not also have an imitative capacity.

2. *Experimental Studies of Imitation by Apes*

We should not have to agonize over whether the observational evidence ade-quately demonstrates imitation in chimpanzees (or other apes): if such ability is so apparent, it should be demonstrable experimentally. Yet the extraordinary fact is that, until recently, the only thorough experimental study was the unique "do-as-I-do" sequence, already described in our discussion of methodology (Hayes and Hayes, 1952). Moreover, Tomasello *et al.* (1987) pointed out that no experi-mental test of imitation of *conspecifics* had been attempted. Their effort to remedy this is important for a number of reasons. First, although we naturally assume that if a chimpanzee can imitate a human, the capacity has evolved to permit conspecific imitation, the nature of transmission may be different in the two cases (e.g., humans are likely to be better intentional demonstrators) and so conspecific imitation requires investigation in its own right. Second, to make fair comparisons with evidence for imitation in other species, we must standardize on conspecific imitation: the morphological similarity between human and chim-panzee clearly favors interspecific imitation in ways beyond the reach of more distantly related species. Third, as the natural function of imitation is (we as-sume, mostly) intraspecific, this is really what we should be focusing on.

The experiment of Tomasello *et al.* largely followed the conventions of monkey studies already described. Observers watched a model using a stick to rake in food, and were then compared with nonobservers in the way they re-sponded to the problem of being presented with out-of-reach food. Observers clearly benefitted from observing and were quicker to use the rake and apply it successfully to rake in the food. However, Tomasello *et al.* emphasized that the manner in which they did so should not be called imitative in the sense of copying the form of the models' act; instead, observers appeared to develop their own techniques, and did not copy the two-part hooking approach of the model that appeared quite distinctive to the human observers.

The authors conclude that the observers did not attempt to copy the model's behavior so much as attempt to recreate the *results* of their efforts, a process they call *emulation*. Presumably, the "results" in this case would be "food getting raked in," because the evidence for emulation was essentially that the observers spent more time than nonobservers directing the rake to the goal of pulling in the food. However, it is not so clear that local enhancement (of the food) coupled with stimulus enhancement (of the sticks) would not suffice to explain the actions of the observers. Further alternatives would seem to be either that what was enhanced was the *conjunction* of rake and food or that imitation was indeed taking place, but with respect to the form of the behavior described at a relatively general level (along the lines of "rake in food"), with the details of the technique provided by the individual.

Whatever the merits of these alternative explanations, what these chimpanzees acquired seems not dissimilar to what was gained by cebus monkey observers in an experiment by Visalberghi and Trinca (1987). Here the task was to use a stick to poke a reward out of a tube. Animals that had observed conspecifics demonstrate this did not imitate in the sense of then succeeding in the task, but they did make more contacts with both stick and tube than nonobservers.

In short, the only experimental tests of conspecific imitation in chimpanzees have not upheld the reputation of the species based on observational and experimental studies of human-to-chimpanzee imitation. No similar experiments are known for other apes.

C.   IMITATION IN OTHER MAMMALS

We are aware that, as primatologists, we may appear chauvinistic in lumping "the rest" under this one heading. However, the reason is simple. As Passingham (1982) notes, "well-authenticated accounts of imitation in mammals are hard to find": indeed, "the only reported case where we can be certain that true imitation occurred is in the dolphin (*Tursiops aduncus*) in captivity." This was reported by Tayler and Saayman (1973), who described the responses of a dolphin when it came to share a pool with a seal. One example is in the pattern of swimming. The dolphin normally uses its flukes to provide propulsion, only using its flippers to steer, whereas it is the flippers that the seal uses in propulsion. Yet, when the seal had been with the dolphin for a few months, the latter "was frequently seen moving forward very slowly on the surface, holding her flukes motionless and propelling herself with seal-like strokes of the flippers" (p. 288). Similar accounts are given of the dolphin apparently copying in some detail the comfort movements and sleeping style of the seal, as well as the swimming movements of a skate. The authors noted that "the clumsiness with which the dolphin executed these movements emphasised their unnaturalness" (p. 289). Another dolphin, "after repeatedly observing a diver removing algae growth from the glass underwater viewing port, was seen cleaning the window with a seagull feather while emitting sounds almost identical to that of the diver's air-demand valve and releasing a stream of bubbles from the blowhole in a manner similar to that of exhaust air escaping from the diving apparatus" (p. 290).

It may be no accident that the quality of these apparent imitations—their arbitrary nature and complexity—seem alone to match those produced by the other highly encephalized species we discussed earlier—the chimpanzee. We shall consider the cognitive demands of such imitation in Section VI.

Unfortunately, there appears to have been no experimental investigation of cetacean imitation. Recently, however, experiments have been performed with other mammals—mice and rats. These are of great interest, not only because they use the "two-action" method we have already advocated in the case of primates, but because their theoretical framework of animal learning theory offers a different perspective on the distinctions at stake. Indeed, the bibliographies of these studies barely overlap with those of the other recent work we have reviewed, which have their roots more often in ethology, and it would now seem fruitful to attempt to bring the different approaches together (see Zentall and Galef, 1988, for an important step in this direction).

In Heyes and Dawson's (1990) experiment using rats, observers faced toward and watched one of two conspecific models. One model pushed a lever to the left for food reward, the other pushed it to the right. Observers were then tested in a number of phases, in all of which they had access to the lever themselves from the direction in which the model had operated it, which was thus the reverse of the direction they had viewed the modeling from earlier. In the first test, pushes to both left and right were rewarded until a set number had been achieved in the direction the model had pushed the lever. The proportion of left pushes was significantly higher for those who had watched left pushes (0.86) than for those who had watched right pushes (0.29). Similar evidence for an imitative effect was obtained in further tests in which reversal learning (pushing in the opposite direction) was speeded by intervening observation of a model pushing in the new direction, and extinction of a response was inhibited by watching a model perform the act. Collins (1988) performed a similar experiment with mice, finding that they pushed a pendulum door to the left more often after observing a model push it to the left, then after watching one pushing to the right. In this experiment, the observer mouse viewed the manipulandum from the same side as it later operated it.

Were these rats and mice imitating? The main concern of Heyes and Dawson is whether they have provided evidence for the observational learning of a response-reinforcer (R-S*) relationship (e.g., push lever to left to obtain reward: what we would call imitation) or only of a stimulus-reinforcer (S-S*) relationship (lever moving to left signals reward and may thus itself acquire reinforcing properties). An animal that has learned only the latter may then generate behavior appropriate to achieving that end (getting the lever to move to the left), but here an imitative behavior would not actually be necessary. The rat could, in principle at least, push the lever with its nose or its paw, irrespective of the technique it had watched the model use (although natural constraints might well lead to the same action being used by both model and observer, giving a false impression of imitative copying). The plausibility of this second, S-S* alternative is demonstrated in an experiment by Denny *et al.* (1983) in which there were two actions that *could* have been done by models, but in fact were not: rats observed either one or the other of two distinctive levers moved *automatically* to signal delivery of food. When given access to the levers the rats pushed the one whose movements had previously signaled food reward. Of course, if the levers had originally been pushed by "demonstrator" rats, the subsequent actions of the observers would likely have been similar and the results would probably have been interpreted as demonstrating observational learning—but at the level of stimulus enhancement, rather than the imitation of particular acts on the same single object that Heyes and Dawson (1990) claim to have demonstrated. In any case, these authors argue against the learning of only a S-S* link in their experiment because the observers saw the lever originally from the opposite point of view to that from which they later operated it, and the cues to be seen in the two cases were rather different. This may be true, but there is a good deal of evidence that rats are actually rather good at defining absolute directions relative to the gross structure of their environment, even when they see the latter from various different points of view (Olton, 1979). As Heyes and Dawson admit, the matter can only be finally resolved by an experiment in which the lever is moved automatically.

Heyes and Dawson and Denny *et al.* (1983, 1988) thus raised a general criticism of the "two action" test. Where the two actions are done with the same part of the body on the same object, stimulus enhancement is nicely ruled out, but R-S* and S-S* learning are not discriminated. Until this is done with "disembodied" or automatic movement, imitative copying of the form of the action used has not been unequivocally demonstrated. Where, on the other hand, the two actions are done on the same object but with different parts of the body (as in the original study by Dawson and Foss, 1965), it could be said that here imitation is a rather special case anyway; that is, it involves copying *only* of *the part of body used* rather than the *form* of the act done with any particular body part.

These distinctions are discussed further in Section VI. To summarize the conclusions of the work reviewed so far, we have some surprising contrasts. As we have just seen, rats and mice have been shown apparently to "do an act from seeing it done" in a two-action test, which allows us to rule out stimulus enhancement. By contrast, the monkeys tested by Ham in a similar fashion did not do what they had seen done. Chimpanzees have not yet been tested properly in this way, but the one experiment using conspecific observation was interpreted by its authors (Tomasello *et al.*, 1987) as providing no evidence of imitation in any case. Visalberghi and Fragaszy (1990) reviewing recent primate research, could conclude only that "apes probably do ape each other, at least in behaviors not involving tools. This is still nearly a statement of faith, however." It would seem that a century's assumptions about the supremacy of primate imitation have still to be experimentally confirmed.

VI. Explaining the Distribution of Imitation: Computational Requirements of Imitating the Seen versus the Heard

A. Computations Involved in Imitating Seen Acts

The gloomy conclusion we have just reached about experimental evidence does, of course, ignore all the observations of spontaneous imitation, as well as Hayes and Hayes' human →ape "do-as-I-do" results, which suggest a very sophisticated imitative ability in chimpanzees, and perhaps dolphins also, although the latter evidence is based on a single report. Indeed, the achievement of the rats, just reviewed, in learning through observation to perform the simple act of pushing a lever to one side rather than the other (which in any case may be S-S* rather than R-S* learning) pales in comparison to the accurate reproduction of many complex and arbitrary acts by chimpanzees such as those described earlier. Thus, our working hypotheses are that (1) chimpanzees can indeed imitate, and do so well—a hypothesis admittedly requiring further experimental testing, particularly in the conspecific case; (2) dolphins may be able to imitate in a similar way, although we can be even less sure of this; (3) imitation is either absent in monkeys and other taxa or it is a much more fragile phenomenon, compared with that in chimpanzees, than has hitherto been recognized. The status of apes other than chimpanzees in this picture is currently unknown.

A similar judgement about the relative capacity of monkeys and chimpanzees to imitate appears in the context of Cheney and Seyfarth's (1990a) recent and independent review of primate social intelligence. What, then, is so special about chimpanzees' cognition? Whiten (1988) and Whiten and Byrne (1991) suggested that imitation is part of a larger pattern of cognitive differences, the background to which requires a slight digression.

1. Mental Representation and Metarepresentation

Leslie (1987) reviewed the findings of much recent work on children's development of a natural "theory of mind" (referred to by ethologists as "natural psychology" [Humphrey, 1980] or "mindreading" [Krebs and Dawkins, 1984; Whiten, 1991]). By the age of 5, children are usually capable of attributing beliefs different from their own to other people. The origins of this tendency to mentally represent another's mentality (representation of representations, or metarepresentation) can be traced back to earlier years—even 2-year-olds attribute wants to others, for example (Wellman, 1991). Leslie suggests that the earliest manifestation of metarepresentation is seen in pretend play. Evidence for this in children includes the sequence of emergence of pretense and theory of mind in normal development and, perhaps more impressively, a dual deficit in theory of mind and pretend play in children afflicted with the social difficulties of autism.

This ontogenetic pattern finds a parallel in the phylogenetic contrast of chimpanzees with monkeys (Whiten and Byrne, 1991). Chimpanzees provide the only evidence of both true pretend play and mindreading. Records of spontaneous play with imaginary objects have been reported for chimpanzees by Hayes (1951) and Savage-Rumbaugh and McDonald (1988). The claim in the case of mindreading is that chimpanzees attribute intentional states to others, a claim supported both experimentally (Premack and Woodruff, 1978; Premack, 1988; Povinelli *et al.*, 1990) and by observational data on deception and counterdeception (Whiten and Byrne, 1988a, 1991; Byrne and Whiten, 1991). These latter studies do not suggest a similar ability in monkeys, and recent experiments with vervet and macaque monkeys are consistent with this monkey/ape difference (Cheney and Seyfarth, 1990a,b).

2. Imitation as Mindreading

Chimpanzees thus appear to have some facility in metarepresentation that monkeys do not, and Whiten and Byrne (1991) further suggested that this may be linked to the difference in imitative ability between the taxa. To imitate in the visual mode involves B copying an action pattern of A's that was originally organized from A's point of view (Bruner, 1972). It is necessarily a different pattern from B's point of view, yet it has then to be re-represented in its original organizational form so as to be performed from B's point of view. The expression "re-represented" seems unavoidable and is used advisedly: it translates as second-order representation or metarepresentation (Leslie, 1987; see also Dennett, 1988). To put the idea more graphically, we might say that B has to get the program for the behavior out of A's head: in other words, to engage in a type of mindreading. The hypothesis predicts that, as acts to be imitated become more complex, so it will be difficult to achieve imitation when the viewpoints of model and imitator differ, as opposed to B watching over A's shoulder.

B. NEW DATA FOR BIRDS: IMITATING THE SEEN VERSUS THE HEARD

The preceding interpretation presents imitation of observed actions as a rather high-level cognitive achievement. This is consistent with a distribution restricted to only highly encephalized species. It thus fits with the apparent lack of imitation in the visual modality in birds, despite the widespread capacity for imitation in the auditory modality, which it will be recalled, Thorndike (1911) wished to set aside as a "special case." As Palameta (1989) notes, "in order to copy a novel movement, a bird cannot rely, as in song learning, on comparing its own product with the perceived act in the same sensory modality." More specifically, in song learning, the bird does not have to represent what is in effect the model's representation of the act as it does in the case of visual imitation; instead, it need only adjust its own output until the sound of this matches what it originally heard (one level of representation). This may be an extra dimension in visual imitation that makes it more demanding than vocal imitation in its computational requirements.

The demonstration of visual imitation in birds would challenge this interpretation, insofar as relatively small-brained animals might lack the required computational power. As we have seen, Thorndike noted a lack of evidence for this type of imitation in birds. Rowley and Chapman (1986) have reported that galahs (*Cocatua roseicapilla*) raised by Mitchell's cockatoo (*C. leadbeateri*) foster parents "mimicked" the wing-beat motions of these foster parents; however, the report suggests the similarity resulted from learning to fly slower than normal so as to stay in the foster flock. This would appear to be an interesting version of "exposure" (see Fig. 1), in this case to slow travel times.

We earlier cited the work of Dawson and Foss on budgerigars, which did offer some support for what Thorndike called "doing muscular acts from seeing them done." In view of the tentative nature of Dawson and Foss's results, Galef *et al.* (1986) attempted to replicate it more thoroughly and with adequate numbers of subjects. They found a tendency for observer budgerigars to use the part of the body they had seen the model use, but this achieved significance only on the second of five trials (in all of which, we should note, reinforcement was given for success, so introducing a confounding factor of conditioning); overall, the 60% concordance between model and observer acts was not significant. Galef *et al.* generously concluded that this "relative fragility" of the Dawson and Foss finding "renders it unsuitable as a model system for exploring the phenomenon of imitation learning" (p. 191).

Palameta (1989) similarly found no signs of imitation in budgerigars performing acts like those used by Dawson and Foss, but had more success with pigeons. In an attempt to avoid the stimulus enhancement explanation for results of a previous study (Palameta and Lefebvre, 1985), an apparatus was designed in which not only did animals work at the same object, but even contacting it with the beak was held constant; what differed was what the beak did next, so this is an analogous procedure to Ham's in which monkeys pulled or twisted a bar. In one experiment, observer birds were pretrained to lift a stopper out of a depression to reveal a food reward. They then watched either a model who demonstrated a grasping and lifting action or another who, instead, grasped the stopper and pulled down, rotating the disk into which the stopper was set and so revealing a second hole with a food reward in it. Both groups were then given an opportunity to perform under the second condition, where the stopper could not be removed but, instead, had to be pulled down to reveal the second hole. The group that had observed models performing the rotating action required a shorter time to solve this task and used fewer pecks, both differences being significant. This, together with the similarly positive results of a test with naive observers, Palameta interpreted as evidence, finally, for imitation in the visual mode in birds.

However, the design of the experiment is essentially similar to that of Heyes and Dawson in which rats pushed a lever to right or left, and in which we were forced to consider the possibility that what the observer had learned was an S-S* rather than an R-S* relationship. In the case of Palameta's experiment, the S-S* link would be something like "disc rotating signals appearance of food," and the pecking actions of the birds that had been able to observe this would be interpreted as behavior directed toward getting the disk to rotate in this way, as distinct from the less purposeful efforts of the observationally naive controls. One way to exclude this possibility would appear to be to run the experiment without models, rotating the disk automatically as a demonstration.

Until this is done, the claim stands that imitation as evidenced in chimpanzees is not proved in other mammals (including monkeys and rats) or in birds.

C. EMULATION: INFERRING OTHERS' GOALS OR NOTICING THEIR RESULTS?

Hogan (1988) gives a name to the S-S* process referred to by Heyes and Dawson: "valence transformation." We have already noted that this involves more than stimulus enhancement, and also, of course, we have distinguished it from imitation (R-S* learning in Heyes and Dawson's terms). We might then ask where it fits into the scheme illustrated in Fig. 1.

Our answer is that it is not yet obvious just how it differs significantly from "emulation" as defined by Tomasello et al. (1987). In both cases, it is suggested that what the animal learns is not the form of an act, but the nature of some desirable *result* of the model's act, which the observer later tries to recreate. It is just that in the case of Tomasello's chimpanzees, the animals came up with a variety of ways to do this, so imitation was not apparent, whereas in the case of the rat and pigeon experiments, such emulation could have led to similar behavior to that of the model because the tasks were sufficiently circumscribed that there was only one best way for the species to achieve them.

However, perhaps because "emulation" has been generated by human and chimpanzee workers and "valence transformation" by rat/learning theory workers, different assumptions will be made about their significance, and it is important to make these explicit. Thus, on the one hand, valence transformation is interpreted as being a social phenomenon in a relatively trivial sense; indeed, the test suggested for it involves removing the model and having the manipulanda go through their movements automatically. At the other extreme, if emulation is seen as attempting to replicate the *goals* rather than the form of the models actions, then we are considering a rather sophisticated social interpretation in its own right—that the observer is perceiving the *aims* of the model. Cheney and Seyfarth (1990a), in a parallel argument to that of Whiten and Byrne (1991) previously described, suggest that "chimpanzees and other apes seem more adept than monkeys at learning to use tools through observation, possibly because they are more adept at imputing purposes to others" (p. 228).

Such distinctions raise a host of alternative hypotheses about what is occurring in episodes like those studied by Tomasello *et al*. Were observers learning nothing about how to behave (imitate), as such, but only about what movements the *objects* needed to make (that the rake had to catch the food in a certain way and then shift toward the cage)? Alternatively, were they imitating the form of the demonstrator's act, but only at a very crude level of resolution ("raking"), supplying idiosyncratic details of how to do this themselves? Or were they attempting to replicate the goal of the demonstrator ("trying to get food raked in")? Or to recreate a result of the demonstrator's actions they themselves found attractive ("food getting raked in")? Or perhaps some combination of these?

Such possibilities lead to a number of experimental refinements. We need to compare the effects of, for example: (1) a model that is seen (e.g., on videotape?) attempting to reach food (with no stick in view) and then wielding a stick (with no food in view), a display presumably sufficient for a "double" (food plus stick) stimulus enhancement effect; (2) a model wielding a stick near (or even touching) the food but not raking, thus providing local and stimulus enhancement, but presumably no basis for emulation; (3) the rake lined up with the food, or somehow automatically raking with no chimpanzee model in view (or with a chimpanzee in view but not doing the raking), which should be sufficient to elicit valence transformation; or (4) a model who is observed attempting to rake in food but not yet succeeding, presumably sufficient for an observer to infer the model's *goal*, yet not revealing the ultimate *result* of its actions.

D.   SIMPLE VERSUS COMPLEX IMITATION

There is another way of looking at valence transformation. This is to argue that to limit the concept of "behavior" to bodily movements is arbitrary. When an animal acts, it moves its limbs, but it may also move tools or affect the environment in various ways. In the case of tool use like raking, we can regard the movements of the rake as just an extension or indeed part of, *the behavior of raking* [cf., Dawkins' (1982) concept of the extended phenotype]. It follows that copying even the movements of the rake could be said to be "imitation of (part of) the form of the action." Similarly, pigeons copying the rotating of the disk itself and rats copying the movement of the lever in the experiments described would then count as imitation.

Whether imitation in monkeys, rats, or pigeons is confirmed either by accepting this semantic argument or by experimentally ruling out valence transformation, we would still appear to be left with a difference in the complexity of imitation demonstrated by chimpanzees when compared with other taxa. Of course there are inherent anatomical limits on complexity in each species—some have hands and others do not, for example. Nevertheless, it is the case that the rat and pigeon candidates for imitation, which we have been considering, involve movements whose simplicity can be characterized as almost two dimensional, by contrast with the many degrees of freedom involved in, say, Viki's lipstick episode. So far, much of the debate about phylogenetic differences in imitation has been of an all-or-none character, scrutinizing evidence for imitation as distinct from other mimetic processes, but it begins to look as if some formal way of comparing relative complexity will provide important insights into species differences and the mechanisms proposed to explain them; the computational demands of metarepresentation as discussed by Whiten and Byrne, for example, might become limiting only as the complexity of the action to be imitated places more demands on its mental representation.

VII. Conclusion

What then, are the advances generated by a century of research? On the one hand, the verdict must be "very few." When we survey the scene with hindsight, we must admit how little is firmly empirically established about which species can and do imitate and through what mechanisms.

But the reason for this dull conclusion is an exciting revolution that has mainly taken place in the past decade in all of the four matters that have concerned us in this article as we traced their fortunes from the nineteenth century through the present one. With respect to our conceptualization of imitation in relation to a host of other mimetic processes, we have become much more sophisticated, and there are grounds for optimism that the major distinctions that need to be tackled empirically are recognized and laid out in some detail. In addition, we have seen that methods are now at hand to make progress on making these distinctions in practice, by contrast with the extensive series of studies we have reviewed from earlier times. Long-standing assumptions about the superiority of certain taxa have taken such a pounding that we can now proceed to judge the evidence in a less prejudiced fashion. And finally, those phylogenetic differences that we have taken as our "working hypothesis," together with differences in imitating the seen versus the heard, have now provoked initial attempts to understand the cognitive mechanisms that underlie the process of imitation.

VIII. SUMMARY

Systematic research on imitation has been pursued for over a century, but methods and conclusions generated in this time have come under strong attack in recent years. Among the most influential ideas have been several that date back to the beginnings of the field in the nineteenth century. In the present article, four of these are distinguished and their consequences and reappraisal in the present century are examined. First, despite early recognition of varieties of imitation, distinctions now made between a greater number of processes by which one animal can come to act like another mean that many conclusions drawn in the first half of this century require revision. Second (and closely related to these theoretical distinctions), experimental paradigms developed in the nineteenth century have been adhered to for much of the present one; only relatively recently have techniques been invented that can adequately distinguish imitation from a range of imitative-like processes. This is important because the latter have important social and cognitive implications in their own right. Third, early assumptions about phylogenetic differences in imitative ability—particularly the superiority of primates—have been reinforced by both observational and experimental studies for much of the present century. Results obtained in recent studies have combined with reappraisal of earlier ones to question these phylogenetic differences. We argue that imitation is as yet unproved in monkeys, whereas chimpanzees (and possibly other apes) share with humans an imitative capacity consistent with other aspects of social cognition examined in recent research. Fourth, it was early argued that auditory-vocal imitation (characteristic of many birds) is distinct from visual imitation (shown by mammals). We use recent research findings to suggest why visual imitation may exert greater computational demands, but also review new studies suggesting that a dichotomy between the vocal imitation of birds and the visual imitation of encephalized mammals is too simplistic to accommodate all the phenomena.

Acknowledgments

For most helpful comments on the manuscript, we are grateful to the editors and to Kim Bard, Freddy Chen, Deborah Custance, Cecilia Heyes, David Perrett, Anne Russon, and Mike Tomasello. We also particularly thank Richard Byrne, Dorothy Fragaszy, and Elisabetta Visalberghi for penetrating discussion of some of the issues addressed here.

References

Abel, C. (1818). "Narrative of a Journey in the Interior of China." London.

Adams-Curtis, L. E. (1987). Social context of manipulative behavior in *Cebus apella*. *Am. J. Primatol.* **12**, 325.

Anderson, J. R. (1985). Development of tool use to obtain food in a captive group of *Macaca tonkeana*. *J. Hum. Evol.* **14**, 637–645.

Antinucci, F., and Visalberghi, E. (1986). Tool-use in *Cebus apella:* A case study. *Int. J. Primatol.* **7**, 349–361.

Armstrong, E. A. (1951). The nature and function of animal mimesis. *Bull. Anim. Behav.* **9**, 46–48.

Aronowitsch, G., and Chotin, B. (1929). Uber die Nachanmung bei den Affen (*Macaca rhesus*). *Z. Morphol. Oekol. Tiere* **16**, 1–25.

Baldwin, J. M. (1895). "Mental Development in the Child and the Race." Macmillan, New York.

Baldwin, J. M. (1902). "Development and Evolution." Macmillan, New York.

Beck, B. B. (1972). Tool use in captive hamadryas baboons. *Primates* **13**, 277–296.

Beck, B. B. (1973a). Observation learning of tool use by captive Guinea baboons (*Papio papio*). *Am. J. Phys. Anthropol.* **38**, 579–582.

Beck, B. B. (1973b). Cooperative tool use by captive hamadryas baboons. *Science* **182**, 594–597.

Beck, B. B. (1974). Baboons, chimpanzees and tools. *J. Hum. Evol.* **3**, 509–516.

Beck, B. B. (1976). Tool use by captive pigtailed monkeys. *Primates* **17**, 301–310.

Berger, S. M. (1962). Conditioning through vicarious instigation. *Psychol. Rev.* **69**, 450–466.

Boesch, C. (1991). Teaching among wild chimpanzees. *Anim. Behav.* **41**, 530–532.

Boinski, S., and Fragaszy, D. M. (1989). The ontogeny of foraging in Squirrel monkeys (*Saimiri oerstedi*). *Anim. Behav.* **37**, 415–428.

Box, H. O. (1984). "Primate Behaviour and Social Ecology." Chapman & Hall, London.

Bruner, J. S. (1972). Nature and uses of immaturity. *Am. Psychol.* **27**, 687–708.

Byrne, R. W., and Whiten, A. (1991). Computation and mindreading in primate tactical deception. *In* "Natural Theories of Mind: Evolution, Development and Simulation of Everyday Mindreading" (A Whiten, ed.), pp. 127–141. Basil Blackwell, Oxford.

Carner, R. (1955). Botanical collecting with monkeys. *Proc. R. Inst. G. B.* **36**(162), 1–16.

Carpenter, A. (1887). Monkeys opening oysters. *Nature (London)* **36**, 53.

Carpenter, C. R. (1937). An observational study of two captive mountain gorillas. *Hum. Biol.* **9**, 175–196.

Cheney, D. L., and Seyfarth, R. M. (1990a). "How Monkeys See the World." Univ. of Chicago Press, Chicago, Illinois.

Cheney, D. L., and Seyfarth, R. M. (1990b). Attending to behaviour versus attending to knowledge: Examining monkey's attribution of mental states. *Anim. Behav.* **40**, 742.

Chevalier-Skolnikoff, S. (1977). A Piagetian Model for Describing and Comparing Socialization in Monkey, Ape and Human Infants. *In* Primate Bio-social development: Biological, Social and Ecological Determinants" (S. Chevalier-Skolnikoff and F. E. Poirier, ed.), pp. 159–187. Garland, New York.

Chevalier-Skolnikoff, S. (1989). Spontaneous tool use and sensorimotor intelligence in Cebus compared with other monkeys and apes. *Behav. Brain Sci.* **12**, 561–627.

Collins, R. L. (1988). Observational learning of a left-right behavioural asymmetry in mice (*Mus musculus*). *J. Comp. Psychol.* **102**, 222–224.

Cook, M., Mineka, S., Wolkenstein, B., and Laitsch, K. (1985). Observational conditioning of snake fear in unrelated rhesus monkeys. *J. Abnorm. Psychol.* **94**, 591–610.

Cook, M., Mineka, S., and Ekman, J. (1987). Observational conditioning of fear to fear-relevant versus fear-irrelevant stimuli in rhesus monkeys. Cited by Mineka and Cook (1988).

Dawkins, R. (1982). "The Extended Phenotype." Freeman, Oxford.

Dawson, B. V., and Foss, B. M. (1965). Observational learning in budgerigars. *Anim. Behav.* **13,** 470–474.

Dennett, D. C. (1988). The intentional stance in theory and practice. *In* "Machiavellian Intelligence: Social Expertise and the Evolution of Intellect in Monkeys, Apes and Humans" (R. W. Byrne and A. Whiten, eds.), pp. 180–202. Oxford Univ. Press (Clarendon), Oxford.

Denny, M. R., Bell, R. C., and Clos, C. F. (1983). Two-choice observational learning and reversal in the rat: S-S versus S-R effects. *Anim. Learn. Behav.* **11,** 223–228.

Denny, M. R., Clos, C. F., and Bell, R. C. (1988). Learning in the rat of a choice response by observation of S-S contingencies. *In* "Social Learning: Psychological and Biological Perspectives" (T. R. Zentall and B. G. Galef, eds.), pp. 207–223. Erlbaum, Hillsdale, New Jersey.

de Waal, F. (1982). "Chimpanzee Politics." Jonathan Cape, London.

Fisher, J., and Hinde, R. A. (1949). The opening of milk bottles by birds. *Br. Birds* **42,** 347–357.

Fouts, R. S., Fouts, D. H., and Van Cantfort, T. E. (1989). The infant Loulis learns signs from cross-fostered chimpanzees. *In* "Teaching Sign Language to Chimpanzees" (R. A. Gardner, B. T. Gardner, and T. E. Van Cantfort, eds.), pp. 280–292. State University of New York Press, New York.

Fragaszy, D. M., and Visalberghi, E. (1989). Social influences on the acquisition and use of tools in tufted capuchin monkeys (*Cebus apella*). *J. Comp. Psychol.* **103,** 159–70.

Fragaszy, D. M., and Visalberghi, E. (1990). Social processes affecting the appearance of innovative behaviors in capuchin monkeys. *Folia Primatol.* **54,** 155–65.

Furness, W. H. (1916). Observations on the mentality of chimpanzees and orang-utans. *Proc. Am. Philos. Soc.* **55,** 201–290.

Galef, B. G., Jr. (1988). Imitation in animals: History, definitions, and interpretation of data from the psychological laboratory. *In* "Social Learning: Psychological and Biological Perspectives" (T. Zentall and B. Galef, eds.), pp. 3–28. Erlbaum, Hillsdale, New Jersey.

Galef, B. G., Jr. (1990). Tradition in animals: Field observations and laboratory analyses. *In* "Interpretations and Explanations in the Study of Behaviour: Comparative Perspectives" (M. Bekoff and D. Jamieson, eds.), pp. 74–95. Westview Press, Boulder, Colorado.

Galef, B. G., Jr., Manzig, L. A., and Field, R. M. (1986). Imitation learning in budgerigars: Dawson and Foss 1965 revisited. *Behav. Processes* **13,** 191–202.

Galdikas, B. M. F. (1982). Orang-utan tool use at Tanjung Puting Reserve, Central Indonesian Borneo (Kalimantan Tengah). *J. Hum. Evol.* **10,** 19–33.

Gardner, R. A., and Gardner, B. T. (1969). Teaching sign language to a chimpanzee. *Science* **165,** 664–672.

Goodall, J. (1986). "The Chimpanzees of Gombe." Harvard Univ. Press, Cambridge, Massachusetts.

Gould, S. J. (1978). "Ontogeny and Phylogeny." Belknap, Boston, Massachusetts.

Green, S. (1975). Dialects in Japanese monkeys. *Z. Tierpsychol.* **38,** 305–314.

Guillaume, P. (1926). "Imitation in Children." Univ. of Chicago Press, Chicago, Illinois.

Haggarty, M. E. (1909). Imitation in monkeys. *J. Comp. Neurol.* **19,** 337–455.

Hall, K. R. L. (1963). Observational learning in monkeys and apes. *Br. J. Psychol.* **54,** 201–226.

Ham, R. (1990). Do monkeys see monkeys do? M.Sc. Thesis, University of St. Andrews, Scotland.

Hamilton, W. J., and Tilson, R. L. (1985). Fishing baboons at desert waterholes. *Am. J. Primatol.* **8,** 255–257.

Harrison, B. (1960). Orang-utan behaviour in semi-wild state. *Sarawak Mus. J.* **9,** 422–447.

Hauser, M. D. (1988). Invention and social transmission: New data from wild vervet monkeys. *In* "Machiavellian Intelligence: Social Expertise and the Evolution of Intellect in Monkeys, Apes and Humans" (R. W. Byrne and A. Whiten, eds.), pp. 327–343. Oxford Univ. Press (Clarendon), Oxford.

Hayes, C. (1951). "The Ape in Our House." Harper, New York.

Hayes, K. J., and Hayes, C. (1951). The intellectual development of a home-raised chimpanzee. *Proc. Am. Philos. Soc.* **95**, 105–109.

Hayes, K. J., and Hayes, C. (1952). Imitation in a home-raised chimpanzee. *J. Comp. Physiol. Psychol.* **45**, 450–459.

Hayes, K. J., and Hayes, C. (1953). Picture perception in a home-raised chimpanzee. *J. Comp. Physiol. Psychol.* **46**, 470–474.

Heyes, C. M., and Dawson, G. R. (1990). A demonstration of observational learning in rats using a bidirectional control. *Q. J. Exp. Psychol.* **42B**, 59–71.

Hinde, R. A., and Fisher, J. (1951). Further observations on the opening of milk bottles by birds. *Br. Birds* **34**, 393–396.

Hobhouse, L. T. (1901). "Mind in Evolution." Macmillan, London.

Hogan, D. E. (1988). Learned imitation by pigeons. *In* "Social Learning: Psychological and Biological Perspectives" (T. R. Zentall and B. G. Galef, eds.), pp. 225–238. Erlbaum, Hillsdale, New Jersey.

Humphrey, G. (1921). Imitation and the conditioned reflex. *Pedagog. Semin.* **28**, 1–21.

Humphrey, N. K. (1980). Nature's psychologists. *In* "Consciousness and the Physical World" (B. Josephson and V. Ramachandran, eds.), pp. 57–80. Pergamon, Oxford.

Imanishi, K. (1957). Identification: A process of enculturation in the subhuman society of *Macaca fuscata*. *Primates* **1**, 1–29.

Itani, J., and Nishimura, A. (1973). The study of infrahuman culture in Japan. A. Review. *In* "Precultural Behavior" (E. W. Menzel, Jr., ed.), pp. 26–50. Karger, Basel.

Kawai, M. (1965). Newly-acquired pre-cultural behavior of the natural troop of Japanese monkeys on Koshima Islet. *Primates* **6**, 1–30.

Kearton, C. (1925). "My Friend Toto: The Adventures of a Chimpanzee and The Story of his Journey from Congo to London." London.

Kellogg, W. N., and Kellogg, L. A. (1933). "The Ape and the Child." McGraw-Hill, New York.

Kinnaman, A. J. (1902). Mental life of two (*Macacus rhesus*) monkeys in captivity. *Am. J. Psychol.* **13**, 98–148.

Kitahara-Frisch, J., and Norikoshi, K. (1982). Spontaneous sponge making in captive chimpanzees. *J. Hum. Evol.* **11**, 41–47.

Kohler, W. (1925). "The Mentality of Apes." Routledge & Kegan Paul, London.

Krebs, J. R., MacRoberts, M., and Cullen, J. M. (1972). Flocking and feeding in great tit *Parus major*—An experimental study. *Ibis* **114**, 507–30.

Krebs, J. R., and Dawkins, R. (1984). Animal signals: Mind reading and manipulation. *In* "Behavioural Ecology: An Evolutionary Approach" (J. R. Krebs and N. B. Davies, eds.), pp. 380–401. Blackwell, Oxford.

Kroodsma, D. E., and Miller, G. E., eds. (1982). "Acoustic Communication in Birds, Vol. 2." Academic Press, New York.

Lancaster, J. (1975). "Primate Behaviour and the Emergence of Human Culture." Holt, Rinehart & Winston, New York.

Lefebvre, L., and Palameta, B. (1988). Mechanisms, ecology, and population diffusion of socially learned, food-finding behavior in feral pigeons. *In* "Social Learning: Psychological and Biological Perspectives" (T. Zentall and B. Galef, eds.), pp. 141–164. Erlbaum, Hillsdale, New Jersey.

Leslie, A. M. (1987). Pretense and Representation in infancy: The origins of "theory of mind." *Psychol. Rev.* **94**, 84–106.

Lloyd, J. E. (1965). Aggressive mimicry in *Photuris:* Firefly femmes fatales. *Science* **149,** 653–654.

Manning, A. (1979). "An Introduction to Animal Behaviour." 3rd ed. Edward Arnold, London.

Marais, E. (1969). "The Soul of the Ape." Atheneum, New York.

McFarland, D. (1985). "Animal Behaviour." Pitman, London.

McGrew, W. C. (1977). Socialization and object manipulation by wild chimpanzees. *In* "Primate Biosocial Development" (S. Chevalier-Skolnikoff and F. E. Poirier, eds.), pp. 261–288. Garland Press, New York.

McGrew, W. C. (1992). "Chimpanzee Material Culture: Implications for Human Evolution." Cambridge Univ. Press, Cambridge, U. K. (in press).

McGrew, W. C., and Tutin, C. E. G. (1978). Evidence for a social custom in wild chimpanzees. *Man* **13,** 234–251.

McGrew, W. C., Tutin, C. E. G., and Baldwin, P. J. (1979). Chimpanzees, tools, and termites: Cross-cultural comparison of Senegal, Tanzania, and Rio Muni. *Man* **14,** 185–214.

Meltzoff, A. N. (1988). The human infant as Homo Imitans. *In* "Social Learning: Psychological and Biological Perspectives" (T. Zentall and B. Galef, eds.), pp. 319–341. Erlbaum, Hillsdale, New Jersey.

Menzel, E. W. (1973). Further observations of the use of ladders in a group of young chimpanzees. *Folia Primatol.* **19,** 450–457.

Menzel, E. W., Davenport, R. K., and Rodgers, S. C. M. (1972). Protocultural aspects of chimpanzee responsiveness to novel objects. *Folia Primatol.* **17,** 161–170.

Miller, N. E., and Dollard, J. (1941). "Social Learning and Imitation." Yale Univ. Press, New Haven, Connecticut.

Miller, R. E., Murphy, J. V., and Mirsky, L. A. (1959). Nonverbal communication of affect. *J. Clin. Psychol.* **15,** 155–158.

Milton, K. (1992). Diet and social organization of a free-ranging spider monkey population in Panama: The development of species typical behavior in the absence of adults. *In* "Juvenile Primates: Life History, Development and Behaviour" (M. E. Periera and L. A. Fairbanks, eds.). Oxford University Press, Oxford.

Mineka, S., and Cook, M. (1988). Social learning and the acquisition of snake fear in monkeys. *In* "Social Learning: Psychological and Biological Perspectives" (T. Zentall and B. Galef, eds.), pp. 51–73. Erlbaum, Hillsdale, New Jersey.

Mineka, S., Davidson, M., Cook, M., and Keir, R. (1984). Fear of snakes in wild and lab-reared rhesus monkeys. *J. Abnorm. Psychol.* **93,** 355–372.

Mitchell, R. W. (1989). A comparative developmental approach to understanding imitation. *Perspect. Ethol.* **7,** 183–215.

Morgan, C. L. (1890). "Animal Life and Intelligence." Edward Arnold, London.

Morgan, C. L. (1896). "Habit and Instinct." Edward Arnold, London.

Morgan, C. L. (1900). "Animal Behaviour." Edward Arnold, London.

Myers, W. A. (1970). Observational learning in monkeys. *J. Exp. Anal. Behav.* **14,** 225–235.

Nishida, T. (1980). The leaf-clipping display: A newly discovered expressive gesture in wild chimpanzees. *J. Hum. Evol.* **9,** 117–128.

Nishida, T. (1987). Local traditions and cultural transmission. *In* "Primate Societies" (B. B. Smuts, D. L. Cheney, R. M. Seyfarth, R. W. Wrangham, and T. T. Struhsaker, eds.), pp. 462–474. Univ. of Chicago Press, Chicago, Illinois and London.

Nishida, T., and Hiraiwa, S. (1982). Chimpanzees, tools and termites: Another example from Tanzania. *Curr. Anthropol.* **21,** 671–672.

Norton-Griffiths, M. N. (1969). The organization, control and development of parental feeding in the oystercatcher (*Haematopus ostralegus*). *Behaviour* **34,** 55–114.

Olton, D. S. (1979). Mazes, maps and memory. *Am. Psychol.* **34,** 583–596.

Palameta, B. (1989). The importance of socially transmitted information in the acquisition of novel feeding foraging skills by pigeons and canaries. Ph.D. Thesis, Cambridge University, Cambridge, U. K.

Palameta, B., and Lefebvre, L. (1985). The social transmission of a food finding technique in pigeons: What is learned? *Anim. Behav.* **33**, 892–896.

Passingham, R. (1982). "The Human Primate." Freeman, New York.

Piaget, J. (1951). "Play, Dreams, and Imitation in Childhood." Norton, New York (transl. 1962).

Piaget, J. (1967). "Biology and Knowledge." Edinburgh Univ. Press, Edinburgh (transl. 1971).

Piaget, J. (1974). "Adaptation and Intelligence: Organic Selection and Phenocopy." Univ. of Chicago Press, London (transl. 1980).

Piaget, J. (1976). "Behaviour and Evolution." Routledge & Kegan Paul, London (transl. 1979).

Povinelli, D. J., Nelson, K. E., and Boysen, S. T. (1990). Inferences about guessing and knowing by chimpanzees (*Pan troglodytes*). *J. Comp. Psychol.* **104**, 203–210.

Premack, D. (1984). Pedagogy and aesthetics as sources of culture. *In* "Handbook of Cognitive Neuroscience" (M. S. Gazzaniga, ed.), pp. 15–35. Plenum, New York and London.

Premack, D. (1988). "Does the chimpanzee have a theory of mind?" revisited. *In* "Machiavellian Intelligence: Social Expertise and the Evolution of Intellect in Monkeys, Apes and Humans" (R. W. Byrne and A. Whiten, eds.), pp. 160–179. Oxford Univ. Press (Clarendon), Oxford.

Premack, D., and Woodruff, G. (1978). Does the chimpanzee have a theory of mind? *Behav. Brain Sci.* **1**, 515–526.

Presley, W. J., and Riopelle, A. J. (1959). Observational learning of an avoidance response. *J. Genet. Psychol.* **95**, 251–254.

Romanes, G. J. (1882). "Animal Intelligence." Kegan Paul Trench & Co., London.

Romanes, G. J. (1883). "Mental Evolution in Animals." Kegan Paul Trench & Co., London.

Rothman, M., and Teuber, E. (1915). "Einzelausgabe aus der Anthropoidenstaton auf Teneriffa. Ziele und Aufgaben der Station sowie rste Beobachtungen an den auf ihr gehaltenen Schimpansen." *Abh. Preuss. Akad. Wiss., Math.-Naturwiss. Kl.* pp. 1–20.

Rowley, I., and Chapman, G. (1986). Cross-fostering, imprinting and learning in two sympatric species of cockatoo. *Behaviour* **96**, 1–16.

Russon, A. E., and Galdikas, B. M. F. (1991). Imitation in ex-captive orang-utans (*Pongo pygmaeus*). Unpublished manuscript, York University, Toronto.

Savage-Rumbaugh, S., and McDonald, K. (1988). Deception and social manipulation in symbol-using apes. *In* "Machiavellian Intelligence: Social Expertise and the evolution of Intellect in Monkeys, Apes and Humans" (R. W. Byrne and A. Whiten, eds.), pp. 224–237. Oxford Univ. Press (Clarendon), Oxford.

Sheak, W. H. (1923). Anthropoid apes I have known. *Nat. Hist. N. Y.* **23**, 45–55.

Shepherd, W. T. (1915). Some observations on intelligence of the chimpanzee. *J. Anim. Behav.* **5**, 391–396.

Sherry, D. F., and Galef, B. G. (1984). Cultural transmission without imitation: Milk bottle opening by birds. *Anim. Behav.* **32**, 937–938.

Skinner, B. F. (1953). "Science and Human Behaviour." Macmillan, New York.

Slater, P. J. B. (1986). The cultural transmission of bird song. *Trends Ecol. Evol.* **1**, 94–97.

Spence, K. W. (1937). Experimental studies of learning and higher mental processes in infra-human primates. *Psychol. Bull.* **34**, 806–850.

Stamm, J. S. (1961). Social facilitation in monkeys. *Psychol. Rep.* **8**, 479–484.

Sugiyama, Y., and Koman, J. (1979). Tool-use and making behaviour in wild chimpanzees at Bossou Guinea. *Primates* **20**, 513–524.

Sumita, K., Kitahara-Frisch, J., and Norikoshi, K. (1985). The acquisition of stone-tool use in captive chimpanzees. *Primates* **26**, 168–181.

Tayler, C. K., and Saayman, G. S. (1973). Imitative behaviour by Indian Ocean bottlenose dolphins (*Tursiops aduncus*) in captivity. *Behaviour* **44**, 286–298.

Temerlin, M. K. (1975). "Lucy: Growing Up Human." Science & Behaviour Books, Palo Alto, California.

Thorndike, E. L. (1898). Animal Intelligence: An experimental study of the associative process in animals. *Psychol. Rev. Monogr.* **2**(8), 551–553.

Thorndike, E. L. (1901). Mental life of monkeys. *Psychol. Rev. Monogr. Suppl.* **15**, 442–444.

Thorndike, E. L. (1911). "Animal Intelligence." Macmillan, New York.

Thornhill, R. (1979). Adaptive female-mimicking behaviour in a scorpion-fly. *Science* **205**, 412–414.

Thorpe, W. H. (1963). "Learning and Instinct in Animals." Methuen, London.

Tinklepaugh, O. L., and Hartman, C. G. (1930). Behavioural aspects of parturition in the monkey, *Macaca rhesus. J. Comp. Psychol.* **1**, 63–98.

Tomasello, M. (1990). Cultural transmission in the tool use and communicatory signalling of chimpanzees? *In* "'Language' and Intelligence in Monkeys and Apes: Comparative Developmental Perspectives" (S. Parker and K. Gibson, eds.), pp. 274–311. Cambridge University Press, Cambridge.

Tomasello, M., Davis-Dasilva, M., Camak, L., and Bard, K. (1987). Observational learning of tool-use by young chimpanzees. *Hum. Evol.* **2**, 175–183.

Tomasello, M., Gust, D., and Forst, T. (1989). A longitudinal investigation of gestural communication in young chimpanzees. *Primates* **30**, 35–50.

van Lawick-Goodall, J. (1973). Cultural elements in a chimpanzee community. *In* "Precultural Primate Behaviour" (E. W. Manzel, ed.), pp. 144–184. Karger, Basel.

Visalberghi, E. (1987). Acquisition of nut-cracking behavior by 2 capuchin monkeys (Cebus apella). *Folia Primatol.* **49**, 168–181.

Visalberghi, E., and Fragaszy, D. (1990). Do monkeys ape? *In* "'Language' and Intelligence in Monkeys and Apes: Comparative Developmental Perspectives" (S. Parker and K. Gibson, eds.), pp. 247–273. Cambridge Univ. Press, Cambridge, U. K.

Visalberghi, E., and Trinca, L. (1987). Tool use in capuchin monkeys, or distinguishing between performing and understanding. *Primates* **30**, 511–521.

Warden, C., and Jackson, T. (1935). Imitative behavior in the rhesus monkey. *J. Gen. Psychol.* **46**, 103–125.

Warden, C. J., Field, H. A., and Koch, A. M. (1940). Imitative behaviour in Cebus and Rhesus monkeys. *J. Genet. Psychol.* **56**, 311–322.

Watson, J. B. (1908). Imitation in monkeys. *Psychol. Bull.* **5**, 169–178.

Watson, J. B. (1914). "Behaviour: An Introduction to Comparative Psychology." Holt, New York.

Wellman, H. M. (1991). From desires to beliefs: Acquisition of a theory of mind., *In* "Natural Theories of Mind: Evolution, Development and Simulation of Everyday Mindreading" (A. Whiten, ed.), pp. 19–38. Basil Blackwell, Oxford.

Westergaard, G. C., and Fragaszy, D. (1987). The manufacture and use of tools by capuchin monkeys (*Cebus apella*). *J. Comp. Psychol.* **101**, 159–168.

Whitehead, J. M. (1986). Development of feeding selectivity in mantled howling monkeys (*Alloutta palliata*). *In* "Primate Ontogeny, Cognition and Social Behaviour" (J. Else and P. C. Lee, eds.), pp. 105–117. Cambridge Univ. Press, Cambridge, U. K.

Whiten, A. (1988). From literal to non-literal social knowledge in human ontogeny and primate phylogeny. *Primate Eye* **37**, 11 (abstr.).

Whiten, A. (1989). Transmission mechanisms in primate cultural evolution. *Trends Ecol. Evol.* **4**, 61–62.

Whiten, A., ed. (1991). "Natural Theories of Mind: Evolution, Development and Simulation of Everyday Mindreading." Basil Blackwell, Oxford.

Whiten, A., and Byrne, R. W. (1988a). Tactical deception in primates. *Behav. Brain Sci.* **11**(2), 233–273.

Whiten, A., and Byrne, R. W. (1988b). Taking Machiavellian intelligence apart. *In* "Machiavellian Intelligence: Social Expertise and the Evolution of Intellect in Monkeys, Apes and Humans" (R. W. Byrne and A. Whiten, eds.), pp. 50–65. Oxford Univ. Press (Clarendon), Oxford.

Whiten, A., and Byrne, R. W. (1991). The Emergence of Metarepresentation in Human Ontogeny and Primate Phylogeny. *In* "Natural Theories of Mind: Evolution, Development and Simulation of Everyday Mindreading" (A. Whiten, ed.), pp. 267–281. Basil Blackwell, Oxford.

Wickler, W. (1968). "Mimicry in Plants and Animals." McGraw-Hill, New York.

Wood, D. (1988). "How Children Think and Learn." Basil Blackwell, London.

Wright, R. V. S. (1972). Imitative learning of a flaked-tool technology—The case of an orang-utan. *Mankind* **8**, 296–306.

Wundt, W. (1894). *Lectures on human and animal psychology*. Transl. by J. E. Creighton and E. B. Titchener. London.

Yerkes, R. M. (1916). The mental life of monkeys and apes: A study of ideation behaviour. *Behav. Monogr. (Baltimore)* **3**, 1–145.

Yerkes, R. M. (1943). "Chimpanzees." Yale Univ. Press, New Haven, Connecticut.

Yerkes, R. M., and Yerkes, A. W. (1927). The mind of a gorilla. *Genet. Psychol. Monogr.* pp. 281–293.

Zajonc, R. B. (1965). Social facilitation. *Science* **149**, 269–274.

Zajonc, R. B. (1969). Coaction. *In* "Animal Social Psychology" (R. B. Zajonc, ed.), pp. 9–12. Wiley, New York.

Zentall, T. R., and Galef, B. G., eds. (1988). "Social Learning." Erlbaum, Hillsdale, New Jersey.

Index

A

Aboutness, cognitive ethology and, 93–94
Accelerometric technique, masculine sexual behavior and
  hormonal factors, 225
  polygraphic analysis, 202–204
  rabbit, 215, 217
  rat, 208
Acoustic signals, parasites, role in sexual selection and, 44, 47, 58, 62
Actions
  cognitive ethology and, 75, 89–93, 103
  imitation in animals and, 252, 275
  spider web-building behavior and, 156, 174, 178
Adaptation
  cognitive ethology and, 103
  imitation in animals and, 241
  parasites, role in sexual selection and, 42
  primate social relationships and, 9
  spider web-building behavior and, 154, 183, 188
  warning coloration and, 112, 140
Adjustment factors, spider web-building behavior and, 175–176
Affiliation, primate social relationships and, 15, 19, 29, 31
Agelena labyrinthica, web-building behavior and, 158–160
Agelenopsis aperta, web-building behavior and, 188
Aggression
  cognitive ethology and, 95
  primate social relationships and, 4, 30–31
    sexual behavior in males, 7
    social rank in males, 7–11
    stress hormones, 11, 13–16, 25

Algorithms, spider web-building behavior and, 149, 189
Araneus orb, 171, 173–177
  manipulation of threads, 179–182
Altruism
  cognitive ethology and, 91
  warning coloration and, 117
Amino acids, masculine sexual behavior and, 220–221
Amphibians, parasites, role in sexual selection and, 58
Amygdala, primate social relationships and, 22, 27–28, 31
Androgens
  masculine sexual behavior and, 224–231, 234
    central mediation, 220
    rat, 210–211, 214
  primate social relationships and, 3
Animals, imitation in, *see* Imitation in animals
Anxiety, primate social relationships and, 19
Apes
  imitation in, 270, 276
  primate social relationships and, 2
Aping, imitation in animals and, 242–243, 259, 262–267
Aposematic coloration, 113, 124
Araneus, web-building behavior and, 147, 163–164
  computer simulation, 173–177
  dynamic filter function, 187
  manipulation of threads, 178–180
  orientation, 158–159, 162–163
  radials, 164–165
  spirals, 165–173
Araneus diadematus, web-building behavior and, 147, 149, 190
  computer simulation, 175–176
  orientation, 153–156, 162

radials, 164
spirals, 168, 172–173
Arctosa variana, web-building behavior and, 160
Arousal mechanism, masculine sexual behavior and, 232
Artificial intelligence
  cognitive ethology and, 74, 102
  spider web-building behavior and, 173
Artificial selection, warning coloration and, 139
Asymmetry, spider web-building behavior and, 165, 167–168, 176, 187–188
Attachment cycles, spider web-building behavior and, 175
Attachment points, spider web-building behavior and, 176
Auditory imitation in animals, 272, 276
Automatic movement, imitation in animals and, 269, 274
Automatism, cognitive ethology and, 71, 73
Autonomic nerves, masculine sexual behavior and, 205, 233
Autonomic responses, primate social relationships and, 22–24, 27–28, 31
Auxiliary spiral, spider web-building behavior and, 151
  Araneus orb, 164–170, 173–174, 176–177
  dynamic filter function, 184
Avian predators, responses to warning coloration in, 111–115, 141–142
  communication, 138–140
  learned avoidance, 132–137
  signal diversity, 140–141
  theories, 115–118
  unlearned responses
    domestic chicks, 118–125
    pheasants, 125–129
    prior experience, 129–132
Avoidance
  imitation in animals and, 250
  primate social relationships and, 30
  warning coloration and, 114–117, 142
    communication, 139–140
    learned avoidance, 132–137
    unlearned responses, 121, 124–126, 128
Awareness, cognitive ethology and, 70, 74–75, 77, 104–105
  consciousness, 78–80, 83
  language, 85–89

B

Back propagation, cognitive ethology and, 101
Bats
  cognitive ethology and, 80–81
  imitation in animals and, 246
Beetles, parasites, role in sexual selection and, 49
Behaviorism
  cognitive ethology and, 77, 81, 97
    actions, 90–93
    awareness and language, 88
  imitation in animals and, 242
  spider web-building behavior and, 153
Birds
  imitation in animals and, 276
    comparative psychology, 240, 243–244
    current phenomena, 244, 246
    distribution, 271–273
    new methodology, 254
  parasites, role in sexual selection and, 49, 53, 59
    interspecific tests, 42–48
  warning coloration and, *see* Avian predators
Blindsight, cognitive ethology and, 82–83
Blue jays, warning coloration and, 115, 119, 136
Bonding, primate social relationships and, 23–25, 31
Brain, cognitive ethology and, 100–102
Bridgewater Treatises, cognitive ethology and, 72
Brightness, parasites, role in sexual selection and, 42–44, 47–48, 52, 56
Budgerigars, imitation in, 254, 272
Butterfly, warning coloration and, 112–116, 119, 136, 140

C

Capture spiral, spider web-building behavior and, 148, 151, 189
  Araneus orb, 163–165, 167–170, 173
  dynamic filter function, 183–184, 186
  manipulation of threads, 180–181
Cardiovascular responses, primate social relationships and, 22
Carotenoids, parasites, role in sexual selection and, 39, 52–54, 60, 62
  pigmentation, 52–54, 62

Carpodacus mexicanus, parasites, role in sexual selection and, 52
Castration
    masculine sexual behavior and, 224–225, 227, 229–230, 232–233
    parasites, role in sexual selection and, 55
    primate social relationships and, 5
Caterpillars, warning coloration and, 114, 116
Central nervous system
    masculine sexual behavior and, 222, 233
    primate social relationships and, 19
    spider web-building behavior and, 157
Central place foraging, spider web-building behavior and, 187–188
Cercopithecus aethiops, imitation in, 255
Cerebrospinal fluid, primate social relationships and, 4, 10, 19, 29–30
Chemical defense, warning coloration and, 111, 117, 141–142
Chemical signals, warning coloration and, 113
Chickens, parasites, role in sexual selection and, 53
Chicks, domestic, *see* Domestic chicks
Chimpanzees
    imitation in animals and, 276
        current phenomena, 251
        distribution, 258–259, 263, 266–271, 273–275
        new methodology, 254–255
    primate social relationships and, 2
Circadian rhythm, primate social relationships and, 5, 10, 30
Class of objects, imitation in animals and, 254
Coadaptation, parasites, role in sexual selection and, 43, 62
Cocatua, imitation in, 272
Coccidia, parasites, role in sexual selection and, 53
Coefficient of variation, masculine sexual behavior and, 212
Cognition, primate social relationships and, 27–28, 30
Cognitive ethology, 104–105
    awareness and language, 85–89
    computers, 100–104
    consciousness
        awareness, 75–79
        coherence, 83–85
        privacy of experience, 80–82
        sensory receptiveness, 82–83

contra folk psychology, 97–100
    history, 69–75
    intention, 89–93
    intentionality, 93–95
    language of thought, 95–97
Cognitive maps, spider web-building behavior and, 157
Cognitive skills, imitation in animals and, 242, 268, 270–271, 276
Coloration
    parasites, role in sexual selection and, 46–47, 52–53
    warning responses to, in avian predators, *see* Avian predators
Combinatorial explosion, cognitive ethology and, 100
Common descent, imitation in animals and, 246
Communication, warning coloration and, 138–140
Competition
    parasites, role in sexual selection and, 39, 55, 58
    primate social relationships and, 4, 13, 15
Complex behavior, spider web-building behavior and, 151
Complex imitation in animals, 241, 274–275
Computations, imitation in animals and, 270–272, 275–276
Computer simulation, spider web-building behavior and, 173–177
Computers, cognitive ethology and, 100–104
Comte, cognitive ethology and, 76
Conation, cognitive ethology and, 70, 104
Conceptual distinctions, imitation in animals and, 249
Condition, spider web-building behavior and, 174
Conditioning, imitation in animals and, 250, 252, 272
Conformity, imitation in animals and, 252
Conjunction, imitation in animals and, 267
Connectionism, cognitive ethology and, 100–102
Connotation, cognitive ethology and, 93
Consciousness, cognitive ethology and, 70–71, 75–77, 104
    awareness, 78–79, 86, 89
    coherence, 83–85
    sensory receptiveness, 82–83

Conspecifics
  imitation in animals and, 266
  primate social relationships and, 3
Conspicuousness, warning coloration and,
    112–115, 117
  communication, 140
  domestic chicks, 123–124
  learned avoidance, 137
  signal diversity, 140–141
Constraints, spider web-building behavior and,
    149, 152, 185, 190
Consummatory mechanism, masculine sexual
    behavior and, 232
Contagion, imitation in animals and, 248, 252
Contra folk psychology, cognitive ethology
    and, 97–100
Contrast, warning coloration and, 124–125,
    132–134, 140–141
Convergence, imitation in animals and, 246
Copernicus, cognitive ethology and, 104
Copulation, see Masculine sexual behavior,
    motor aspects of
Cortex, primate social relationships and, 28,
    31
Cortisol, primate social relationships and, 4,
    30
  aggression in males, 9–11
  stress hormones, 11, 14, 16, 19–20
Cribellate orbs, spider web-building behavior
    and, 181–182
Crickets, parasites, role in sexual selection
    and, 58–59
Cues
  parasites, role in sexual selection and, 44
  primate social relationships and, 2
  spider web-building behavior and, 190
    Araneus orb, 167–169
    orientation, 156–157, 160, 162–163
Cupiennius salei, web-building behavior and,
    160, 179
Cyclic disruption, primate social relationships
    and, 16–17
Cyrtophora citricola, spider web-building be-
    havior and, 149

D

Darwin
  cognitive ethology and, 72–73, 87, 92, 105

imitation in animals and, 239, 242–243
warning coloration and, 113
Deception
  cognitive ethology and, 90–91
  imitation in animals and, 271
Decision-making, cognitive ethology and, 91–
    92
Decision rules, spider web-building behavior
    and, 154
Demonstrators, imitation in animals and, 242,
    253–254, 266, 269, 274
Dennett, cognitive ethology and, 103–104
Denotation, cognitive ethology and, 93
Depression, primate social relationships and,
    24, 30
Descartes, cognitive ethology and, 71, 73–75,
    85–87, 105
Descriptions, cognitive ethology and, 88
Descriptive terms, imitation in animals and,
    246
Detection distance, warning coloration and,
    137
Dimorphism
  masculine sexual behavior and, 218–219,
    230, 234
  parasites, role in sexual selection and, 55
Discrimination
  cognitive ethology and, 70, 80
  warning coloration and, 137
Disease resistance, parasites, role in sexual se-
    lection and, 40–41, 49, 56
Displacement, primate social relationships and,
    15
Dissonance, cognitive ethology and, 99
Do-as-I do test, imitation in animals and, 254–
    255, 266, 270
Dolphin, imitation in, 267–268, 270
Domestic chicks, warning coloration and, 114,
    142
  learned avoidance, 132
  unlearned responses, 118–126
Domestication, warning coloration and, 125–
    126, 128, 142
Dominance
  parasites, role in sexual selection and, 50
  primate social relationships and, 4–5, 29–
    31
    aggression in males, 8–9
    inhibition, 19–20, 22
    stress hormones, 11, 13–15

Dopamine, primate social relationships and, 23, 25, 30

Dorsal penile nerve, masculine sexual behavior and, 222–223

Drosophila, parasites, role in sexual selection and, 48, 59

Drug dosage, primate social relationships and, 21, 24

Dynamic filter function, spider web-building behavior and, 182–188

E

Ecribellate orbs, spider web-building behavior and, 181–182

Effectiveness, spider web-building behavior and, 185

Efficiency, spider web-building behavior and, 185

Ejaculation, masculine sexual behavior and, 202, 231, 234
  central mediation, 219, 222–223
  hormonal factors, 224–225, 227, 229
  polygraphic analysis, 202, 205
  rabbit, 215–216
  rat, 206–214

Emotion, primate social relationships and, 27–28, 30

Emulation, imitation in animals and, 251–252, 267, 273–274

Endocrine mehanisms, primate social relationships and, 1–3, 29–31
  aggression in males, 9
  stress hormones, 21–22, 27–28

β-Endorphin, primate social relationships and, 19–20, 22–31

Energy
  parasites, role in sexual selection and, 40, 47, 56
  spider web-building behavior and, 185, 187

Enhancement, imitation in animals and, *see* Local enhancement; Social enhancement; Stimulus enhancement

Environment
  imitation in animals and, 250, 269
  parasites, role in sexual selection and, 41
  primate social relationships and, 28–29
  spider web-building behavior and, 149, 178, 185

Araneus orb, 164, 167
  orientation, 154–157, 162
  warning coloration and, 130, 140, 142

Estradiol benzoate, masculine sexual behavior and, 224–226

Estrogen
  masculine sexual behavior and, 210, 224–225, 228
  primate social relationships and, 4, 16

Estrus, primate social relationships and, 1–2, 23, 28

Ethology, cognitive, *see* Cognitive ethology

Evolution
  cognitive ethology and, 72, 74, 83, 90
  computers, 103–104
  contra folk psychology, 99
  language of thought, 96
  imitation in animals and, 241, 246
  parasites, role in sexual selection and, 39, 41–42, 48, 50, 62
  spider web-building behavior and, 152, 179–182, 184, 190
  warning coloration and, 111–112, 116, 118, 138–142

Evolutionary continuity, cognitive ethology and, 87

Existential generalization, cognitive ethology and, 94

Expectations, spider web-building behavior and, 168, 185

Experience, privacy of, cognitive ethology and, 80–83

Explanations, imitation in animals and, 246

Exploration, spider web-building behavior and, 152, 155, 157–159

Exposure, imitation in animals and, 248, 252, 272

Extension, cognitive ethology and, 93

F

Facilitation, warning coloration and, 114, 135–136

Feedback
  masculine sexual behavior and, 234
  primate social relationships and, 16
  spider web-building behavior and, 178–179

Field observation, imitation in animals and, 255–256

Finches, parasites, role in sexual selection and, 52

Finitary predicament, cognitive ethology and, 100

Firefly, imitation in animals and, 247

Fish, parasites, role in sexual selection and, 44, 59

Fitness
  cognitive ethology and, 91
  parasites, role in sexual selection and, 40–41, 50
    intraspecific tests, 59
    ornament production, 52, 56–57
  spider web-building behavior and, 155, 189

Flexibility, spider web-building behavior and, 152, 178

Fodor, cognitive ethology and, 96, 101–102

Folk psychology, cognitive ethology and, 75, 97–105

Foraging
  imitation in animals and, 255, 257
  parasites, role in sexual selection and, 49, 53–54, 62
  spider web-building behavior and, 147, 188, 190
    dynamic filter function, 184–185, 187–188
    orientation, 154–155

Foundationalism, cognitive ethology and, 88–89

Frame construction, spider web-building behavior and, 151, 163–165, 168, 170, 184

Frequency spectrum analysis, masculine sexual behavior and, 208–209, 215, 217

Function, spider web-building behavior and, 163, 178, 182–188

Functionalism, cognitive ethology and, 97, 102–103

G

GABA, masculine sexual behavior and, 220–221

Galah, imitation in animals and, 272

Gallus Gallus domesticus, warning coloration and, 114, 142
  learned avoidance, 132
  unlearned responses, 118–126

Generalization, warning coloration and, 128, 131, 137

Generic explanatory terms, imitation in animals and, 246

Genetics
  masculine sexual behavior and, 214, 233
  parasites, role in sexual selection and, 40–41, 57, 62
    interactions, 51–52
    interspecific tests, 45
    ornament production, 52, 56–57
  spider web-building behavior and, 148, 151, 188
  warning coloration and, 114, 117, 121

Glycine, masculine sexual behavior and, 220–221

Goal-directed behavior, cognitive ethology and, 90

Goal emulation, imitation in animals and, 251–252, 273–274

Goals, spider web-building behavior and, 163–164

Gonadal hormones, primate social relationships and, 1–2, 29–31
  sexual behavior in males, 4–5, 7
  stress hormones, 19

Good genes models, parasites, role in sexual selection and, 45, 53

Gravity, spider web-building behavior and, 165, 167–171, 176, 188, 190

Group cohesion, primate social relationships and, 3

Grouping, primate social relationships and, 24, 27, 30

Gryllus, parasites, role in sexual selection and, 58–59

H

Habituation, imitation in animals and, 252

Haematopus ostralegus, imitation in, 255

Hamilton–Zuk hypothesis, parasites, role in sexual selection and, 41–42, 48, 61–62
  interspecific tests, 44–45, 47
  intraspecific tests, 57–58
  ornament production, 57

Handling
  spider web-building behavior and, 149, 153, 178, 190
  warning coloration and, 119, 121

Haptic cues, spider web-building behavior and, 153, 162

Hematozoa, parasites, role in sexual selection and, 59, 61–62

Herennia ornatissima, web-building behavior and, 187

Heterosexual condition, primate social relationships and, 1, 4, 30
  aggression in males, 10
  sexual behavior in males, 5
  stress hormones, 15–16

Heterotypical masculine sexual behavior, rat, 210–211

Hierarchy, primate social relationships and, 30
  aggression in males, 8–10
  sexual behavior in males, 4, 7
  stress hormones, 13, 15

Homotypical masculine sexual behavior
  rabbit, 215–217
  rat, 206–210

Hormones
  masculine sexual behavior and, 201–202, 232–234
    rabbit, 219, 226–229
    rat, 224–227
    site of action, 229–231
  parasites, role in sexual selection and, 54–58, 62
  primate social relationships and, 1–2, 29–31
    aggression in males, 9
    β-endorphin, 24–28
    females, 13–18
    inhibition, 19–22
    opiates, 22–24
    sexual behavior in males, 4
    stress hormones, 11–13

Hub, spider web-building behavior and, 151, 163–165, 188

Hume, cognitive ethology and, 75

Huxley, cognitive ethology and, 73

Hypothalamus
  masculine sexual behavior and, 220, 229
  primate social relationships and, 19, 22

I

Idealized search path, spider web-building behavior and, 148

Identity, cognitive ethology and, 97

Idiothetic processes, spider web-building behavior and, 156–157, 160, 162

Imagery, cognitive ethology and, 75, 82

Imitation, warning coloration and, 111

Imitation in animals, 239–240, 275–276
  comparative psychology, 240
    birds, 243–244
    definitions, 240–242
    experimental paradigms, 242
    monkeys, 243
  current phenomena, 244–245
    classification, 246
    taxonomy of processes, 246–253
  distribution, 256, 267–270
    aping, 259, 262–267
    birds, 271–273
    computations, 270–271
    emulation, 273–274
    monkeys, 256–262
    valence transformation, 274–275
  new methodology, 253–256

Immune system, parasites, role in sexual selection and, 54–57, 62

Impersonation, imitation in animals and, 251

Individual learning, imitation in animals and, 248

Individual selection, warning coloration and, 116–117, 142

Influence, imitation in animals and, 248–249

Information processing
  cognitive ethology and, 100
  primate social relationships and, 31

Information transfer, imitation in animals and, 251

Inheritance
  spider web-building behavior and, 148, 182, 189
  warning coloration and, 114

Inhibition
  imitation in animals and, 268
  masculine sexual behavior and, 220–221
  primate social relationships and, 19–22
  warning coloration and, 121, 123

Insects
  parasites, role in sexual selection and, 50
  warning coloration and, 111, 113, 115, 117, 141–142
    communication, 139
    signal diversity, 140
    unlearned responses, 124–127, 130

Intelligence
  cognitive ethology and, 87
  imitation in animals and, 249, 252, 270
Intension, cognitive ethology and, 93
Intention, cognitive ethology and, 75, 89–93, 96, 104
Intentional states, imitation in animals and, 271
Intentionality, cognitive ethology and, 75, 93–95, 103–105
Interactionism, cognitive ethology and, 71
Interneurons, masculine sexual behavior and, 220–221
Interpreter, spider web-building behavior and, 174
Interspecific tests, parasites, role in sexual selection and, 42–48, 62
Intraspecific tests, parasites, role in sexual selection and, 47–48, 57–61
Intromission, masculine sexual behavior and, 232, 234
  central mediation, 219, 221–223
  hormonal factors, 224–225, 228–229
  polygraphic analysis, 202, 204
  rabbit, 215–216
  rat, 206–215
Introspection, cognitive ethology and, 76, 78–79
Isolation, primate social relationships and, 20, 24
Isomorphism, masculine sexual behavior and, 211–215, 234
Isosexual condition, primate social relationships and, 4–5, 14–15
Ithomiids, warning coloration and, 112

J

James, cognitive ethology and, 76

K

Ketamine, primate social relationships and, 4–5
Kin selection
  cognitive ethology and, 92
  warning coloration and, 111, 115–118, 142
Kinetic energy, spider web-building behavior and, 187

L

Language, cognitive ethology and, 75, 85–89, 91–92, 104
Language of thought, cognitive ethology and, 95–97, 101
Latent learning, imitation in animals and, 250
Learned avoidance, warning coloration and, 132–137, 140, 142
Learning
  imitation in animals and, 248–252, 273
  observational learning, 257–258, 266–269, 271–273
  warning coloration and, 114–115, 125
Leg length, spider web-building behavior and, 171–173
Leg regeneration, spider web-building behavior and, 179–181
Leucauge mariana, web-building behavior and, 177
Level I imitation in animals, 248
Ligands, primate social relationships and, 23, 25
Limbic brain, primate social relationships and, 23, 27–28, 30
Linguistics, cognitive ethology and, 86–87
Local enhancement, imitation in animals and
  current phenomena, 248–250
  distribution, 257, 259, 267, 274
  new methodology, 253–254
Locke, cognitive ethology and, 71–72, 75
Locomotion
  masculine sexual behavior and, 219
  spider web-building behavior and, 148–149, 178–179, 190
Logical rules, cognitive ethology and, 94
Lordosis
  hormonal factors, 227
  rabbit, 215, 217–218
  rat, 213–214
Luteinizing hormone, primate social relationships and, 4, 20

M

Macaca, imitation in, 259–262
Macaca arctoides, imitation in, 258
Macaca fuscata, imitation in, 255
Macaca mulatta, imitation in, 250

Manipulation, spider web-building behavior and, 152, 178–182, 190
Maps
  cognitive ethology and, 96
  spider web-building behavior and, 153–156, 158, 162, 190
Masculine sexual behavior, motor aspects of, 201–202, 231–234
  central mediation, 219–223
  hormonal factors, 224
    rabbit, 226–229
    rat, 224–227
    site of action, 229–231
  polygraphic analysis, 202–206
  rabbit
    dimorphism, 218–219
    homotypical behavior, 215–217
    pseudomale behavior, 217
    stereotypy, 217–218
  rat
    heterotypical behavior, 210–211
    homotypical behavior, 206–210
    isomorphism, 211–215
Matched dependent learning, imitation in animals and, 248, 252–253
Mate choice, parasites, role in sexual selection and, 39–40, 51, 62
  interspecific tests, 44, 46, 48
  ornament production, 52–54
Materialism, cognitive ethology and, 73, 89
Maternal behavior, primate social relationships and, 23, 25, 28–29
Mating patterns, parasites, role in sexual selection and, 39, 55, 58
Medial preoptic area, masculine sexual behavior and, 219–220, 229–230, 232–233
Melopsittacus undulatus, imitation in, 254
Memory
  cognitive ethology and, 70, 72
  parasites, role in sexual selection and, 46
  primate social relationships and, 29
  spider web-building behavior and, 155, 160–162, 173, 176–177
  warning coloration and, 133
Mental representation
  cognitive ethology and, 95, 101
  imitation in animals and, 270–271, 275
Mental states, cognitive ethology and, 81–82, 94, 98, 104–105

Mentality, cognitive ethology and, 74, 94, 103–104
Metarepresentation
  cognitive ethology and, 79
  imitation in animals and, 270–271, 275
Mice, imitation in, 268
Mimicry
  imitation in animals and, 275
  current phenomena, 244–245, 247–248, 252
  new methodology, 253, 256
  warning coloration and, 111–114, 141
Mind–body problem, cognitive ethology and, 71, 80
Mind–brain identity theory, cognitive ethology and, 97
Mindreading, imitation in animals and, 270–271
Minimalist theory, cognitive ethology and, 79
Miopithecus talapoin, primate social relationships and, 3
Monkeys
  cognitive ethology and, 91
  imitation in animals and, 243, 250, 276
    distribution, 256–262, 267, 269–272, 274
    new methodology, 253, 255
  masculine sexual behavior and, 231
  primate social relationships and, 1–4, 29
    aggression in males, 8
    inhibition, 19, 22
    stress hormones, 11, 14–15, 17, 24, 27
Morgan, imitation in animals and, 240–241, 243
Morphine, primate social relationships and, 22–23, 25, 29
Morphology
  imitation in animals and, 265
  masculine sexual behavior and, 201–202, 234
    hormonal factors, 224–231
    rabbit, 215–219
    rat, 206–215
  parasites, role in sexual selection and, 39, 46–47, 52, 55
  spider web-building behavior and, 148, 163
  warning coloration and, 111
Mother–infant relationship in primates, 24, 29, 31
Motivation
  cognitive ethology and, 93

imitation in animals and, 252
primate social relationships and, 23, 27–29, 31
Motor aspects of masculine sexual behavior, *see* Masculine sexual behavior, motor aspects of
Motor nerves, masculine sexual behavior and, 205
Mounting, masculine sexual behavior and, 231–232
    bouts, 207
    central mediation, 219–220, 222–223
    hormonal factors, 224, 226–227, 229
    rabbit, 215–219
    rat, 206–208, 211–215
Mutation, warning coloration and, 111, 116–118, 136
Mutual inhibition, masculine sexual behavior and, 221

N

Nagel, cognitive ethology and, 80
Naloxone, primate social relationships and, 20, 22–23, 29
Naltrexone, primate social relationships and, 20, 22, 25
Natural selection
    cognitive ethology and, 92
    imitation in animals and, 246–248
    warning coloration and, 111–112, 116, 140
Necessity, cognitive ethology and, 90
Nematodes, parasites, role in sexual selection and, 53, 55, 59, 61
Neonatal androgenization, 226
    rat, 210–211, 214
Nephila, web-building behavior and, 164, 178, 185
Nephila clavipes, web-building behavior and, 178, 185
NETtalk, cognitive ethology and, 101–102
Neural circuitry, masculine sexual behavior and, 219–220, 232–233
Neural mechanisms, primate social relationships and, 2–3, 29–31
    stress hormones, 19, 25, 27
Neuroendocrine mechanisms, primate social relationships and, 1, 3, 19–24

Neuromotor apparatus, masculine sexual behavior and, 202, 210
Neurons, masculine sexual behavior and, 201, 219–221, 229–233
Neuroscience, cognitive ethology and, 79, 97, 100–102
Neurotransmitters, masculine sexual behavior and, 220
Nonsocial mimetic processes in animals, 246–248

O

Observation, field, imitation in animals and, 255–256
Observational conditioning, imitation in animals and, 250
Observational learning, imitation in animals and, 257–258, 266–269, 271–273
Odors, primate social relationships and, 29
Olfaction, primate social relationships and, 27–28
Operant conditioning, imitation in animals and, 252
Operationalism, cognitive ethology and, 88
Opiates, primate social relationships and, 19–24
Opiods, primate social relationships and, 23–24
Optimality
    cognitive ethology and, 92
    spider web-building behavior and, 184–188
Orb spider, *see* Spider web-building behavior
Organic imitation in animals, 241
Orientation
    imitation in animals and, 250
    spider web-building behavior and, 149, 152, 189–190
    Araneus orb, 165, 167
    skills, 152–163
Ornaments, parasites, role in sexual selection and, 39–41, 47, 49
    genetic interactions, 51–52
    intraspecific tests, 57–58, 61
    production, 52–57
Oscilloscope, masculine sexual behavior and, 203, 215
Ovarian hormones, primate social relationships and, 2–3

Ovariectomy
  masculine sexual behavior and, 226, 228,
    234
  primate social relationships and, 3–4, 16
Ovaries, primate social relationships and, 17

P

Pan troglodytes, imitation in animals and, 251,
    255, 259
Parallelity, spider web-building behavior and,
    175
Parasites, role in sexual selection and, 39–41,
    48–51, 61–62
  genetic interactions, 51–52
  Hamilton–Zuk hypothesis, 41–42
  interspecific tests, 42
    acoustic signals, 44
    future, 44–48
    plumage brightness, 42–44
    sexual dichromatism, 44
  intraspecific tests, 57–61
  ornament production, 52–57
Pardosa amentata, web-building behavior and,
    160
Parturition, primate social relationships and,
    23, 25, 28
Patch, spider web-building behavior and, 184,
    188
Path integration, spider web-building behavior
    and, 156, 159–160
Pathogenesis, parasites, role in sexual selection
    and, 50, 62
  interspecific tests, 45–46
  intraspecific tests, 57, 61
  ornament production, 53, 56–57
Pelvic thrusting, masculine sexual behavior
    and, 231–234
  central mediation, 219–222
  hormonal factors, 224–225, 227–228, 230
  polygraphic analysis, 203
  rabbit, 215–218
  rat, 206–209, 211–214
Peptidergic systems, primate social relation-
    ships and, 19, 29
Peptides, primate social relationships and, 22–
    23
Perception, cognitive ethology and, 79–80,
    82, 105

Perceptrons, cognitive ethology and, 100
Pheasants, warning coloration and, 125–129,
    142
Phenotype
  masculine sexual behavior and, 202
  parasites, role in sexual selection and, 51
  spider web-building behavior and, 151, 189
  warning coloration and, 117
Phidippus pulcherimus, web-building behavior
    and, 160–161
Philosophical behavior, cognitive ethology
    and, 81, 97
Philosophy, *see* Cognitive ethology
Photuris, imitation in, 247
Phylogeny
  cognitive ethology and, 85
  imitation in animals and, 241, 275–276
  parasites, role in sexual selection and, 44,
    48
  primate social relationships and, 25
  spider web-building behavior and, 147
    dynamic filter function, 182, 184
    manipulation of threads, 181–182
    orientation, 153, 157, 160, 162
Piaget, imitation in animals and, 241
Pigeons, imitation in, 272, 275
Pigmentation, parasites, role in sexual selec-
    tion and, 52–54, 62
Pilotage, spider web-building behavior and,
    155
Play, imitation in animals and, 249, 271
Plumage brightness, parasites, role in sexual
    selection and, 42–44, 47, 52, 56
Polygraphic analysis, masculine sexual be-
    havior and, 202–206, 231, 234
  central mediation, 223
  rabbit, 217
  rat, 207, 211
Positivism, cognitive ethology and, 89
Predators
  cognitive ethology and, 91
  parasites, role in sexual selection and, 39–
    40, 49, 51
  primate social relationships and, 3, 13, 24
  responses to warning coloration, *see* Avian
    predators, responses to warning colora-
    tion
  spider web-building behavior and, 154
Preference ratio, warning coloration and, 128
Pregnancy, primate social relationships and, 28

Premack, cognitive ethology and, 69, 87–88
Primate social relationships, 1–4, 28–31
  aggression in males, 7–11
  imitation, 244, 253, 256, 259, 270
  sexual behavior in males, 4–7
  stress hormones, 11–13
    β-endorphin, 24–28
    female behavior, 13–18
    inhibition, 19–22
    opiates, 22–24
Prior experience, warning coloration and, 129–132
Privacy of experience, cognitive ethology and, 80–83
Prolactin, primate social relationships and, 4, 30
  aggression in males, 10
  stress hormones, 11, 16, 19–20, 22
Proprioceptors
  masculine sexual behavior and, 233
  spider web-building behavior and, 156, 179
Pseudomale behavior, 202
  hormonal factors, 226, 228
  rabbit, 217
  rat, 210
Pudendal nerve, masculine sexual behavior and, 215, 222–223, 233

Q

Qualia, cognitive ethology and, 80–81, 83–84, 89
Quantitative dimunition, warning coloration and, 126
Quantitative field studies, imitation in animals and, 255
Quantum mechanisms, cognitive ethology and, 103
Quine, cognitive ethology and, 88–89

R

Rabbit, masculine sexual behavior and, 231, 233–234
  central mediation, 223
  dimorphism, 218–219
  homotypical behavior, 215–217
  hormonal factors, 226–229

  pseudomale behavior, 217
  stereotypy, 217–218
Radial thread, spider web-building behavior and, 162
Radials, spider web-building behavior and, 190
  Araneus orb, 163–165, 168, 173, 176
  dynamic filter function, 183–184, 186–188
Radiation direction, spider web-building behavior and, 154
Rank
  parasites, role in sexual selection and, 44, 46
  primate social relationships and, 31
    aggression in males, 7–11
    sexual behavior in males, 4–7
    stress hormones, 11–28
Rat
  imitation in, 259, 268–270, 273, 275
  masculine sexual behavior and, 231–232, 234
    central mediation, 222–223
    heterotypical behavior, 210–211
    homotypical behavior, 206–210
    hormonal factors, 224–227, 230–231
    isomorphism, 211–215
Receptivity
  cognitive ethology and, 80
  primate social relationships and, 2–3
Reductionism, warning coloration and, 140–141
Referential opacity, cognitive ethology and, 93–95
Reflection, cognitive ethology and, 79, 83
Reflective imitation in animals, 241
Regeneration, spider web-building behavior and, 179–181
Reindeer, parasites, role in sexual selection and, 55
Reinforcement
  imitation in animals and, 252–253, 256–259, 268–269, 272
  primate social relationships and, 30
Relativity theory, cognitive ethology and, 103
Renshaw cells, masculine sexual behavior and, 220–221
Representation, cognitive ethology and, 103
Reproduction
  parasites, role in sexual selection and, 41, 49–51

primate social relationships and, 1–2, 4, 30–31
  stress hormones, 13, 16–17, 19–20
  spider web-building behavior and, 155
Resistance, parasites, role in sexual selection and, 41, 52–54, 56–57, 59
Response-reinforcer (R-S*), imitation in animals and, 268–270, 273
Retrospection, cognitive ethology and, 76
Reversal learning, imitation in animals and, 268
Reward network, primate social relationships and, 22–24, 28
Rhythmic patterns, masculine sexual behavior and, 231, 233
  central mediation, 219–222
  hormonal factors, 225, 227–228
  rabbit, 217–218
Risk, spider web-building behavior and, 185
Romanes
  cognitive ethology and, 70
  imitation in animals and, 239–243
Rules, spider web-building behavior and, 174–175

S

Saimiri oerstedii, imitation in animals and, 257
Saturation, cognitive ethology and, 101
Scoloderus tubulifer, web-building behavior and, 188
Secondary radials, spider web-building behavior and, 164
Secondary sexual characters, parasites, role in sexual selection and, 39–41, 48, 61–62
  intraspecific tests, 58–61
  ornament production, 56
Selection
  imitation in animals and, 241, 246–248
  sexual, role of parasites in, *see* Parasites, role in sexual selection and
  spider web-building behavior and, 148, 182, 190
  warning coloration and, 111–112, 115–118, 140, 142
Selection pressure
  imitation in animals and, 246

spider web-building behavior and, 154, 182, 189–190
warning coloration and, 125, 127, 142
Selective disadvantage, imitation in animals and, 265
Selfishness, cognitive ethology and, 91
Semantics, cognitive ethology and, 97
Seminal vesicle pressure, masculine sexual behavior and, 208–210, 220, 234
Seminal vesicles, masculine sexual behavior and, 207, 216–217, 233–234
Sensations, cognitive ethology and, 70, 75, 79–81
Sensory awareness, cognitive ethology and, 83
Sensory feedback
  masculine sexual behavior and, 234
  spider web-building behavior and, 178–179
Sensory receptiveness, cognitive ethology and, 82–83
Sexual behavior
  masculine, motor aspects of, *see* Masculine sexual behavior, motor aspects of
  primate social relationships and, 1–4, 30–31
    males, 4–7
    stress hormones, 11, 13–14, 16, 19–22, 28
Sexual dichromatism, parasites, role in sexual selection and, 44
Sexual dimorphism
  masculine sexual behavior and, 218–219, 230, 234
  parasites, role in sexual selection and, 55
Sexual selection
  role of parasites in, *see* Parasites, role in sexual selection and
  spider web-building behavior and, 182
  warning coloration and, 113
Showiness, parasites, role in sexual selection and, 42–47, 56, 62
Signals
  masculine sexual behavior and, 207–208, 215, 232
  warning coloration and, 111
    communication, 138–140
    diversity, 140–141
    pheasants, 127–129
Simple behavior, spider web-building behavior and, 151
Simple imitation in animals, 241, 274–275

Site selection, spider web-building behavior and, 190
  dynamic filter function, 184–185
  orientation, 154–155, 157, 163
Skin swelling, primate social relationships and, 17, 29
Snakes
  imitation in animals and, 250
  warning coloration and, 115, 139–140
Social enhancement, imitation in animals and, 246, 248, 262
Social facilitation, imitation in animals and, 252, 259
Social learning, imitation in animals and, 246, 248–252
Social relationships, primate, see Primate social relationships
Social support, imitation in animals and, 248, 252–253
Social transmission, imitation in animals and, 246
Spatial maps, spider web-building behavior and, 153–157, 190
Species specificity
  imitation in animals and, 262
  spider web-building behavior and, 178, 182
Specific explanatory terms, imitation in animals and, 246
Spencer, cognitive ethology and, 72–73
Spider web-building behavior, 147–152, 189–190
  Araneus orb, 163–164
    computer simulation, 173–177
    radials, 164–165
    spirals, 165–173
  dynamic filter function, 182–184
    optimality, 184–188
  life history, 188–189
  manipulation of threads, 178
    leg regeneration, 179–181
    phylogeny, 181–182
    sensory feedback, 178–179
  orientation, 152–153, 159–162
    processes, 155–157
    site exploration, 157–159, 162–163
    spatial maps, 153–155
Spinal cord
  masculine sexual behavior and, 229–231
  primate social relationships and, 22

Spiral path, spider web-building behavior and, 185–187
Spiral pitch, spider web-building behavior and, 175–176
Spirals, see also Auxiliary spiral; Capture spirals spider web-building behavior and, 165–177, 187, 190
Starlings, warning coloration and, 115, 119, 126, 134
Status, primate social relationships and, 13, 19, 21, 30
Stereotypy, masculine sexual behavior and, 206, 211–215, 217–218
Steroids
  masculine sexual behavior and, 224, 230, 233–234
  primate social relationships and, 3
Stimuli
  masculine sexual behavior and, 214, 218
  spider web-building behavior and, 147, 184
  warning coloration and, 124, 134–136
Stimulus, imitation in animals and, 250, 252–253
Stimulus enhancement, imitation in animals and
  current phenomena, 248–250
  distribution, 257, 259, 264, 269
  hormonal factors, 272–274
  new methodology, 253–254
Stimulus meaning, cognitive ethology and, 88
Stimulus-reinforcer (S-S*), imitation in animals and, 268–270, 273
Stimulus–response
  cognitive ethology and, 100
  spider web-building behavior and, 153
Stream of consciousness, cognitive ethology and, 76
Stress hormones, primate social relationships and, 9, 11–28
Striate cortex, cognitive ethology and, 82–83
Stripes, warning coloration and, 141–142
  domestic chicks, 119, 121–124
  learned avoidance, 135–137
  pheasants, 126–129
Sturnus vulgaris, warning coloration and, 119
Subordinates, primate social relationships and, 30
  aggression in males, 8–9
  sexual behavior in males, 5, 7
  stress hormones, 11, 13–15, 19–20

Suppression
primate social relationships and, 15–17, 20, 31
spider web-building behavior and, 179
Susceptibility, parasites, role in sexual selection and, 55–57
Symbolic logic, cognitive ethology and, 100
Symbols, cognitive ethology and, 100–101
Synergistic selection, warning coloration and, 117–118, 142
Syntax, cognitive ethology and, 87–88, 96, 98, 101–102

T

T-spirals, spider web-building behavior and, 175–176
Tactile cues, spider web-building behavior and, 162
Talapoins, primate social relationships and, 3, 29
aggression in males, 10
sexual behavior in males, 4
stress hormones, 11, 14, 17, 19
Taxonomy
imitation in animals and, 246–255
parasites, role in sexual selection and, 43, 47–48
Tegenaria, web-building behavior and, 160
Tenebrio molitor, warning coloration and, 119
Testosterone
masculine sexual behavior and, 229
parasites, role in sexual selection and, 46, 54–58, 60, 62
primate social relationships and, 1, 4, 29–30
sexual behavior in males, 4–5, 7
stress hormones, 11, 19–21
Testosterone propionate, masculine sexual behavior and, 224–226, 228–230
Tetragnatha elongata, web-building behavior and, 185
Theseus, web-building behavior and, 174–177
Thorndike, imitation in animals and
comparative psychology, 240, 243–244
current phenomena, 250, 252
hormonal factors, 272
new methodology, 253–254
Time, spider web-building behavior and, 149

Titchener, cognitive ethology and, 75–76
Tokens, cognitive ethology and, 97–98
Trial-and-error learning, imitation in animals and, 259, 264
Tribolium, parasites, role in sexual selection and, 49
Tursiops aduncus, imitation in, 267–268
Two-action test, imitation in animals and, 254, 258, 269

U

Uloborus conus, web-building behavior and, 149
Unlearned avoidance, warning coloration and, 115, 132–137, 139
Unlearned responses, warning coloration and, 142
avoidance, 135–137
communication, 139–140
domestic chicks, 118–125
pheasants, 125–129
prior experience, 129–132
Unpalatibility, warning coloration and, 112–114, 116–118, 137

V

Valence transformation, imitation in animals and, 273–275
Vector maps, spider web-building behavior and, 156–157, 159
Verificationism, cognitive ethology and, 88–89
Vesicles, seminal, masculine sexual behavior and, 207–210, 216–217, 220, 233–234
Vigor, parasites, role in sexual selection and, 40–41, 47, 49
Vision, spider web-building behavior and, 160, 162
Visual cortex, cognitive ethology and, 82
Visual imitation in animals, 244, 276
Visual mode, imitation in animals and, 271–273
Visual monitoring, primate social relationships and, 7–8
Visual signals, parasites, role in sexual selection and, 47
Vocal imitation in animals, 243–244, 272, 276

W

Warning coloration, responses to, in avian predators, *see* Avian predators

Web-building behavior, *see* Spider web-building behavior

Web geometry, spider web-building behavior and, 147–148, 175, 186, 190

Weighted averages, spider web-building behavior and, 175–176

Withdrawal, primate social relationships and, 15, 24, 30

Wittgenstein, cognitive ethology and, 81, 88–89

Wundt
cognitive ethology and, 75–76
imitation in animals and, 242

Z

Zygiella, web-building behavior and, 162, 164, 178, 180

Contents of Previous Volumes

Volume 11

Interrelationships among Ecological, Behavioral, and Neuroendocrine Processes in the Reproductive Cycle of *Anolis carolinensis* and Other Reptiles
DAVID CREWS

Endocrine and Sensory Regulation of Maternal Behavior in the Ewe
PASCAL POINDRON and PIERRE LE NEINDRE

The Sociobiology of Pinnipeds
PIERRE JOUVENTIN and ANDRÉ CORNET

Repertoires and Geographical Variation in Bird Song
JOHN R. KREBS and DONALD E. KROODSMA

Development of Sound Communication in Mammals
GÜNTER EHRET

Ontogeny and Phylogeny of Paradoxical Reward Effects
ABRAM AMSEL and MARK STANTON

Ingestional Aversion Learning: Unique and General Processes
MICHAEL DOMJAN

The Functional Organization of Phases of Memory Consolidation
R. J. ANDREW

Volume 12

Pavlovian Conditioning of Signal-Centered Action Patterns and Autonomic Behavior: A Biological Analysis of Function
KAREN L. HOLLIS

Selective Costs and Benefits in the Evolution of Learning
TIMOTHY D. JOHNSTON

Visceral–Somatic Integration in Behavior, Cognition, and "Psychosomatic" Disease
BARRY R. KOMISARUK

Language in the Great Apes: A Critical Review
CAROLYN A. RISTAU and DONALD ROBBINS

Volume 13

Cooperation—A Biologist's Dilemma
JERRAM L. BROWN

Determinants of Infant Perception
GERALD TERKEWITZ, DAVID J. LEWKOWICZ, and JUDITH M. GARDNER

Observations on the Evolution and Behavioral Significance of "Sexual Skin" in Female Primates
A. F. DIXSON

Techniques for the Analysis of Social Structure in Animal Societies
MARY CORLISS PEARL and STEVEN ROBERT SCHULMAN

Thermal Constraints and Influences on Communication
DELBERT D. THIESSEN

Genes and Behavior: An Evolutionary Perspective
ALBERTO OLIVERIO

Suckling Isn't Feeding, or Is It? A Search for Developmental Continuities
W. G. HALL and CHRISTINA L. WILLIAMS

Volume 14

Group Mating in the Domestic Rat as a Context for Sexual Selection: Consequences for

the Analysis of Sexual Behavior and Neuroendocrine Responses
MARTHA K. MCCLINTOCK

Plasticity and Adaptive Radiation of Dermap-
teran Parental Behavior: Results and
Perspectives
MICHEL VANCASSEL

Social Organization of Raiding and Emigra-
tions in Army Ants
HOWARD TOPOFF

Learning and Cognition in the Everyday Life
of Human Infants
HANUŠ PAPOUŠEK and MECHTHILD
PAPOUŠEK

Ethology and Ecology of Sleep in Monkeys
and Apes
JAMES R. ANDERSON

Volume 15

Sex Differences in Social Play: The Socialization of Sex Roles
MICHAEL J. MEANEY, JANE STEWART,
and WILLIAM W. BEATTY

On the Functions of Play and Its Role in
Behavioral Development
PAUL MARTIN and T. M. CARO

Sensory Factors in the Behavioral Ontogeny of
Altricial Birds
S. N. KHAYUTIN

Food Storage by Birds and Mammals
DAVID F. SHERRY

Vocal Affect Signaling: A Comparative
Approach
KLAUS R. SCHERER

A Response-Competition Model Designed to
Account for the Aversion to Feed on Con-
specific Flesh
W. J. CARR and DARLENE F. KENNEDY

Volume 16

Sensory Organization of Alimentary Behavior
in the Kitten
K. V. SHULEIKINA-TURPAEVA

Individual Odors among Mammals: Origins
and Functions
ZULEYMA TANG HALPIN

The Physiology and Ecology of Puberty Modu-
lation by Primer Pheromones
JOHN G. VANDENBERGH and DAVID M.
COPPOLA

Relationships between Social Organization and
Behavioral Endocrinology in a Monogamous
Mammal
C. SUE CARTER, LOWELL L. GETZ, and
MARTHA COHEN-PARSONS

Lateralization of Learning in Chicks
L. J. ROGERS

Circannual Rhythms in the Control of Avian
Migrations
EBERHARD GWINNER

The Economics of Fleeing from Predators
R. C. YDENBERG and L. M. DILL

Social Ecology and Behavior of Coyotes
MARC BEKOFF and MICHAEL C. WELLS

Volume 17

Receptive Competencies of Language-Trained
Animals
LOUIS M. HERMAN

Self-Generated Experience and the Development of Lateralized Neurobehavioral Organization in Infants
GEORGE F. MICHEL

Behavioral Ecology: Theory into Practice
NEIL B. METCALFE and PAT MONAGHAN

The Dwarf Mongoose: A Study of Behavior
and Social Structure in Relation to Ecology
in a Small, Social Carnivore
O. ANNE E. RASA

Ontogenetic Development of Behavior: The
Cricket Visual World
RAYMOND CAMPAN, GUY BEUGNON,
and MICHEL LAMBIN

Volume 18

Song Learning in Zebra Finches (*Taeniopygia
guttata*): Progress and Prospects

PETER J. B. SLATER, LUCY A. EALES, and N. S. CLAYTON

Behavioral Aspects of Sperm Competition in Birds
T. R. BIRKHEAD

Neural Mechanisms of Perception and Motor Control in a Weakly Electric Fish
WALTER HEILIGENBERG

Behavioral Adaptations of Aquatic Life in Insects: An Example
ANN CLOAREC

The Circadian Organization of Behavior: Timekeeping in the Tsetse Fly, A Model System
JOHN BRADY

Volume 19

Polyterritorial Polygyny in the Pied Flycatcher
P. V. ALATALO and A. LUNDBERG

Kin Recognition: Problems, Prospects, and the Evolution of Discrimination Systems
C. J. BARNARD

Maternal Responsiveness in Humans: Emotional, Cognitive, and Biological Factors
CARL M. CORTER and ALISON S. FLEMING

The Evolution of Courtship Behavior in Newts and Salamanders
T. R. HALLIDAY

Ethopharmacology: A Biological Approach to the Study of Drug-Induced Changes in Behavior
A. K. DIXON, H. U. FISCH, and K. H. MCALLISTER

Additive and Interactive Effects of Genotype and Maternal Environment
PIERRE L. ROUBERTOUX, MARIKA NOSTEN-BERTRAND, and MICHELE CARLIER

Mode Selection and Mode Switching in Foraging Animals
GENE S. HELFMAN

Cricket Neuroethology: Neuronal Basis of Intraspecific Acoustic Communication
FRANZ HUBER

Some Cognitive Capacities of an African Grey Parrot (Psittacus erithacus)
IRENE MAXINE PEPPERBERG

Volume 20

Social Behavior and Organization in the Macropodoidea
PETER J. JARMAN

The t Complex: A Story of Genes, Behavior, and Populations
SARAH LENINGTON

The Ergonomics of Worker Behavior in Social Hymenoptera
PAUL SCHMID-HEMPEL

"Microsmatic Humans" Revisited: The Generation and Perception of Chemical Signals
BENOIST SCHAAL and RICHARD H. PORTER

Lekking in Birds and Mammals: Behavioral and Evolutionary Issues
R. HAVEN WILEY